More Amazing, Incredible Birds

Revised Enlarged Edition

By
Dr. Kenneth J. Johnson

Good birding
Ken Johnson

This book is dedicated to my wife,
Adele G. Johnson,
loving helpmate, always ready to go birding.

TABLE OF CONTENTS

WHY THIS BOOK WAS WRITTEN

This book was written to fill a void in the realm of books on birds.

That empty spot is a book, not yet in existence, that selects each familiar bird and tells the reader about the unique characteristics about that species that is not common knowledge.

There are now four types of bird books:

1. The field guide. This is a taxonomically arranged list of species, with pictures, range map, and brief description of identifying features. It is pocket sized. It is fine for somebody seeing a bird, that then wants to know exactly what he is looking at.

2. The coffee table picture book. It is large sized, with pretty pictures of flamboyantly colored birds, with a brief text on each. It is fine for somebody at leisure wanting to be entertained, curious enough about birds as to browse through this volume.

3. A technical treatise in a specialty journal, appealing to scientists and serious readers with a special interest in birds.

4. A book investigating the amazing incredible phenomena exhibited only by a certain species or small group of birds. I have found only one book that achieves this, and that book takes up one topic at a time, mentioning rare birds throughout the world that are examples of that characteristic. This present new type of book, which you are now holding, on the other hand, concentrates mostly on familiar American birds, one species at a time. It reveals amazing incredible things about that particular bird, previously unknown to the average bird-watching reader. Now to illustrate what we mean by specific examples of specific birds, read down the long list below of amazing incredible birds, all if which are found in this book, and see if you can name each bird.

The bird that lays its egg on a roof top.

It picks bugs out of the ears of calves.

The only bird with two toes.
Its nest is people's gourmet food.
Religious bird sings, "Ho-say, Maria."
It has a magnet on its upper bill.
Seven ways to place a bird in a hypnotic trance.
This bird survives because it has a runny nose.
This one never lands on the ground.
Nomads use its hollowed egg as a canteen.
This one climbs down tree trunks head first without
    falling off.
Forest fires prevent this warbler from becoming extinct.
Bird that vomits on its enemies.
This female mates with the male that sings the most
    songs.
One that can fly backwards.
One that likes to fly upside down.
This bird sings with its tail.
Land bird that smells its food from far away.
Water bird that smells its food from far away.
Female that uses its own breast feathers to feather its nest.
Bird that shows men where wild bees store their honey.
This one feeds its nestlings only once every two weeks.
When this bird feeds its young it remains behind them.
How birds may lose their ability to migrate.
Why is a high-powered rifle needed for banding birds?
Wild bird that has chosen unwilling man to sustain it.
Bird that will adopt an orphan from another species' nest.
A certain dove that is sacrificed to God.
The most abundant bird on the face of the earth.
The only bird that roosts lengthwise on a branch, not
    perpendicular to it, like other birds do.
You must wade through deep snow to find this perching
    bird's nest.
This bird is named after its favorite food.
Water bird that cannot walk on land.
The bird that cools off by urinating on its legs.
It never lands on the ground except to have sex.

A bird identified by the length of its middle toe.

This bird gets its food by swimming around in circles.

This bird is so oily people have lit it and used it as a lamp.

With a windpipe six feet long, it can be heard three miles away.

It can see behind without turning its head.

Has to turn its head sideways to pick up something.

Combs its mustache bristles with a comb on its middle toe.

Its migrants are segregated by sex and age.

Both birds, side by side, set upon the nest.

The oldest living fossil.

Extra wing feathers prevent turbulence in flying.

Male has penis 18 inches long.

All these birds are waiting for you to find them, in the following pages.

INTRODUCTION BY WAY OF AVIAN FOLK SAYINGS

Do you realize how much birds have been a part of our culture? Consider all these folk sayings which reveal how true this is. Finding them certainly was no wild goose chase.

Even from up in the crow's nest of an old sailing ship, it is clear that this is no cock-and-bull story. A little bird told me this will be as easy as duck soup. I am no coward so you can't call me chicken, so I intend to get to the point, straight like the crow flies yet quit cold turkey even if you stick your head in the sand like an ostrich.

If there is any secret, I will sing like a canary, even if I look like the cat that swallowed the canary. I am a wise old owl and I don't give a hoot since I am happy as a lark and proud as a peacock, since I have my nest egg, and I'm shaking my tail feathers.

I am an old crow but no bird brain, even though I am pigeon-toed and waddle like a duck and am skinny as a rail. I eat like a bird since what's sauce for the goose is sauce for the gander. If you think I'm cuckoo, or crazy as a loon, that's water off a duck's back, since yours truly never killed the goose that lays the golden eggs. I never run around like a chicken with its head cut off.

Now don't put all your eggs in one basket, and don't count your chickens before they hatch, for birds of a feather flock together, and chickens come home to roost. Remember, a bird in the hand is worth two in the bush. When you come to me and hover like vultures, remember that if you aim to kill a mockingbird, our Lord knows if a sparrow falls (Matthew 10:29), and you will be like a lame duck in Congress, and if you waddle like a duck and eat like a duck you must be a duck. I have all my ducks in a row.

Though I might act like a mother hen, I will never appoint a fox to guard the henhouse. You might think I am a hen-picked husband, but such an opinion weighs on me as light as a feather. Have you seen us bill and coo like love birds?

You might have if you had an eagle eye, for I am still as young as a spring chicken. When I set myself up this way I am as vulnerable as a sitting duck, and condemned to get an albatross hung around my neck, a fate that is strictly for the birds.

This may stick in your craw, but from here I have a bird's eye view, so I hope I don't lay an egg with this, for someone who can explain the birds and the bees is as rare as hen's teeth, or even as dead as a dodo. If you can, that's a feather in your cap.

When I was a young cock acting like a bantam rooster and romancing around with chicks, I was as naïve as the little chick that hadn't scratched yet. When I was a gangly adolescent they called me a long-legged shitepoke, but now I am just an old coot with crow's feet around my eyes that no longer can rise up on wings like an eagle or act like the bluebird of happiness. People will think I am Chicken Little warning that the sky is falling, so I will imitate the Little Red Hen and "do it myself." You can kill two birds with one stone if you're too big to be called pewee without being pigeon-holed.

When you stay up late at night like a night owl it's hard to be the early bird that gets the worm. This may ruffle your feathers, but you are as free as a bird to fly off on a tangent.

So it is no surprise that mankind's continued attention to birds has become manifested into today's interest in birders and bird watching; these two fit together like a dovetail joint. This text is meant to abet people as they enjoy, appreciate and get insight into our feathered friends. These pages sometimes mention Bismarck and North Dakota, which is tourism's new discovery, but mostly this little text covers the birding hobby all over America and beyond.

I. PARLOR GUIDE TO WATER BIRDS AND GAME BIRDS

Why The Ostrich Is Named The Camel Bird

Sally Rand, that well-known fan dancer burlesque star of the 1930s, performed on stage using ostrich plumes to cover what I politely call her center of gravity. When the Pope is carried in his processional chair, two chamberlains on either side of him each carry a long pole which carries a great fan of ostrich plumes, tipped with peacock feathers (A. Parmelee, *All the Birds of the Bible*). In the case of the Pope the ostrich feathers suggest power, and the peacock feathers indicate immortality. In the case of Sally Rand the ostrich plumage suggests coquetry and imply intrigue. In explaining why the Pope uses ostrich plumes, they suggested power in ancient times because it required extreme bravery to obtain feathers from the tail of a creature as dangerous as an ostrich.

An ostrich is dangerous. As one ostrich and I were facing each other on opposite sides of a chain link fence, I noticed its muscular thighs, sturdy legs, and huge feet consisting of two huge toes, each with a wide fleshy padded sole. The bird was eight feet tall, weighing 350 pounds. The Texas rancher, owner of the exotic animals, said one blow from the ostrich's foot could kill a man. I believed him.

The Arabian camel also has feet that are two-toed with thick padded soles to travel on that same desert sand.

The ostrich's scientific name is *Struthio camelus*. The genus name is from the Greek word "struthion" for ostrich. The species name *camelus* takes note of the similarity of the feet and habitat of the ostrich and camel. The ostrich is the only bird, and the camel is

CAMEL   OSTRICH

ONLY CAMEL AND OSTRICH
FEET HAVE TWO TOES

the only mammal, except for the two-toed sloth, with a foot with only two toes (not rigid cloven hooves). Doesn't that justify the ostrich's scientific specific name to be *camelus*? The ostrich of the *Bible* belonged to the subspecies *S. camelus syriacus*, which lived in the Arabian and Syrian Deserts securely until 1914. It was able to run 40 miles per hour, but with the appearance of the automobile and firearms in Arabia after World War I it was doomed. This subspecies was extinct by 1941.

The *Bible* mentions the ostrich several times. Parmelee says the Bible's most accurate description of this largest living bird is in Job 39:13-18. This description is acclaimed by modern ornithologists as being very correct.

In verse 13 the Lord asks Job if the ostrich's plumage indicates that it has love for its offspring. No, he implies it does not, and verse 14 is given as proof.

Verse 14 observes that the ostrich lays its eggs on the ground, to be incubated by the sun's warmth. True, but the female does lay on them much of the time. Its eggs can stand the desert sun if exposed.

Verse 15 worries that the eggs may be stepped on and crushed. Unlikely, for an ostrich egg shell is glazed and ten times as strong and six times as thick as a hen's egg. The emptied shell has even been used as a durable water bottle by desert nomads.

Verse 16 feels that the mother ostrich ignores her young. Ground nesting species of bird's eggs hatch out precocial young, who are able to run around and fend for themselves upon hatching. Ostriches do tend to their young and they do protect them, however.

Verse 17 claims ostriches have no wisdom. They are very primitive birds, living on instinct. Incidentally, the saying, "to stick your head in the sand," meaning ignoring an obvious danger, is a misinterpretation of the ostrich's actions. When feeding in grass its head is lost from our view by the grass, not stuck in the sand. When hiding it crouches down and flattens its long neck and head against the ground, but never buries it.

Verse 18 notes that this bird can easily outrun a horse. True.

Now go fast-forward to today. The ostrich of the Bible is extinct, but the ostrich lives wild in Africa, mainly in east Africa and also in South Africa. This is the subspecies *S. camelus australis.* The subspecies name is from the Latin "auster," meaning south. It is grown in captivity on ostrich farms in many countries including the United States, where the birds are raised for an amazing variety of products.

One ostrich egg will make a giant omelet of a size that would require two dozen hen's eggs! A blown egg can be made into an art object by painting or engraving, or it can be placed unchanged on a stand as an ornament. It has been used as a water bottle.

Ostrich feathers leave no dust and have been used as feather dusters. They eliminate static electricity and are used as electrostatic cleaners in electronics and in automobile manufacture. The ostrich plume has no hooks on its barbules, so the so-called semiplume is fluffy, allowing air to flow through the feather because the fine soft strands don't lock together. So the plume has been used for centuries, in a Roman soldier's helmet, in an African Masai warrior's headdress, in royalty's fans, in Victorian ladies' hats, in scarves, showgirls' head pieces, and as centerpieces for home, office, parties and weddings.

Ostrich meat is low in fat, calories, cholesterol and sodium, but high in protein and iron.

Ostrich leather is tough yet pliable. It resists drying or cracking, due to its oily content. Popular uses are in purses, wallets, brief cases, and hand bags.

In the days before ball-point pens or metal pen points with nibs, some quill pens used ostrich feathers.

Some cosmetics have used ostriches for oil and soap.

So ostrich farms have gone almost as far as the slaughterhouse that said it uses every part of the pig except the squeal!

This Bird Is Off-balance But Not Loony

We were canoeing on a small glacial lake in Northern Minnesota and decided to explore a cove. There among the reeds we saw a low pile of reeds, on top of which was a loon on its nest. We paddled closer, and closer, and drifted without a sound or a movement, as the loon crouched down perfectly still. When our canoe got so close I could have whacked the loon with my paddle if I had been that loony, it finally slipped into the water to disappear beneath the surface. It did so without a sound or a ripple to disturb the flat smooth surface. No other bird or mammal can dive or slip into the water that smoothly or quietly. The shape of its body is a factor in that ability.

Common loon. Photograph by Erlend Haarberg.

The shape of its body has been likened to that of a torpedo. When this bird swims, it is not like a turtle or a penguin or a rowboat with an oar-like appendage on each side. The loon is more like a sculler, or one who propels a boat by maneuvering an oar over the stern of the boat, since the loon's two feet are used far posteriorly and closely together, although not in contact with each other.

Another name for this bird is the Great Northern Diver, for it can dive deep – 250 feet below the surface – and stay under for long times – 30 or 40 minutes. That depth has been proven by finding loons entangled in fish nets that were set at that depth, and by timing loons with a second-hand watch. Instead of resting after such a dive, they were able to take a series of such marathon dives with just a few seconds for a gulp of air between each dive. To dive that deep for that long the loon must be a powerful swimmer, but how can it hold its breath that long? A human does well to hold his breath one tenth that long.

This loon may be the most powerful and efficient catcher of fish. It can outmaneuver a merganser for any fish, and no fish, even a trout, can escape the loon, once the loon selects it as its next meal.

To achieve this degree of expertise it loses any skill in walking. It seems Nature decrees that as one talent is developed another is lost to compensate. To be so gifted as a swimmer, with its legs set so far back on its body, its center of balance is displaced forward. So when attempting to walk its body drags on the ground ahead of its legs, and is not balanced over the legs, as in birds that walk or hop.

We were doing a breeding bird census in Saskatchewan. The route was on a road parallel to Tobin Lake, but far enough away from the water to allow a new field, recently tilled, to lie between the road and the lake. On the field lay a loon, flat on its belly, pushing with its legs and beating its wings on the freshly plowed dirt. A pair of magpies soon saw its plight, and landed and began harassing it. But as it pushed up to a slight rise in the ground, it finally in desperation managed to take off and escape. Chandler Robbins, the professional ornithologist and field guide author, told me that in a newly opened farming frontier, a plowed field never before seen is mistaken from the air as a body of water.

The loon can float high in the water with its sides showing, or low in the water with only its back in view, or submerged with only its head above the water. When it sinks lower in the water it squeezes air out from between its feathers and exhales. When it rises higher in the water it inhales to become more buoyant.

In winter we have seen them from the beach at the Great Bend of Texas. The Gulf of Mexico with its sea water has water not as clear as in the glacial lakes of Northern Minnesota and the Boreal Region of Canada, so the loon cannot see as clearly to dive as deeply as in summer. But it doesn't need to, for the relatively shallow water off shore has enough fish for this bird in its drab winter plumage.

W. Earl Godfrey in his book, *The Birds of Canada*, credits this loon with three loud and resonant calls. One is a maniacal, bloodcurdling laughing tremolo. This is the voice credited for the expression, "Crazy as a loon." But this bird isn't loony, it just sounds like it is.

The second is called a weird yodel. Does any other bird yodel?

The third is a wolf-like wail. This one makes a tenderfoot woodland camper's hair stand on end.

When television commercials wish to convey a sensation of being out in the wilderness, they place a loon's call on their sound track.

Linnaeus has been betrayed. That 1700s Swede who devised the binomial system of Latin or Greek names for each living creature intended them to be immutable and permanent. But look at what happened to the common loon. It was *Urinator imber* then *Colymbus torquatus*, then *Gavia immer*. Did I miss any?

In today's scientific name of the common loon the genus name *Gavia* is from the Latin *gavia* meaning a bird. The species name *immer* seems to be a variation of the original species name *imber*, which is from the Danish *imber*, meaning an ember-goose, meaning a loon.

In the early days men with firearms would shoot loons because hunters thought they had a monopoly on fish and loons were stealing the fish from humans, or they shot the loons just because they were a moving target. Today men have a more sensible attitude, and loons are protected by federal law. A lake harboring a pair of nesting loons is off-limits to boats, since boats or gunfire scares the loons away from nesting.

Squealing Tires

The Big City dweller was enjoying the quiet serenity of the wilds of western Canada. Resting by the shore of this reedy lake set in the aspen-spruce forest, he was listening to the gentle soothing sounds of the wilderness.

Then suddenly very close by he was jarred by the sound of squealing tires – a hot-rodder pushing gas pedal to the floor to make the tires spin and smoke on pavement. Or if not burning rubber, a speeding driver slamming on his brakes for a sudden stop trying to prevent a multiple car crash in traffic.

"What wild animal was that?" he asked as he trembled. "That was just a bird, a red-necked grebe, hidden in those reeds," his guide reassured him. "Tell me more," the neophyte asked. "That is truly an amazing incredible bird; let me elaborate," his guide replied. So he proceeded.

"It is easy to see and identify on its migration route, but in its summer home it is extremely shy. When you get near, it has already noted you, and is under water with only its eyes and bill above water, watching your every move. This grebe can float in the water at all levels by adjusting the amount of air between the feathers and in the lungs.

Its young are capable of running around as soon as they are hatched, but they like to climb up on their mother's back and ride along. If danger approaches and she dives head first, they continue to cling and stay on her back as she swims below the surface.

When this red-necked grebe swims it extends its legs out laterally and paddles alternately, putting its legs together beneath it only for occasional bursts of speed.

Its foot has three forward-facing toes provided with a wide flange on both sides of each toe, which provides a powerful thrust with each stroke in swimming. A most unique feature on these

Sketch from page 15 of
The Birds of Canada,
by W. Earl Godfrey.

three toes is the nail, not shaped like a bird's claw, but wide and flat like a human toe nail. That would increase the surface of the paddle, to make each stroke more powerful.

Its legs are set far back on the body, for superb swimming, but the bird is very awkward on land. If it lands on ice it is helpless, able to move only a few inches, so it starves or is killed by a predator then.

Its tail is so tiny it isn't called a tail but a vestigial tail.

Before we mentioned its plumage, it has a narrow bald forehead. This patch of bare skin is of unknown practical value.

Its plumage is striking, in that the crown is deep black, the cheek and throat are bright white, and the neck is a rich ruddy red. But what is amazing and incredible is that the ruddy duck, a much smaller bird, has exactly the same colored plumage! And the breeding ranges of the two species partly overlap.

Convergent evolution: black crown, white cheek, red neck. Red-necked grebe on left, ruddy duck on right.

So in Alberta, for example, there is a big water bird and a little water bird swimming around in the same lake or marsh that have the same colors in the same places.

Strangely, stomachs of the red-necked grebe contain a ball of red-necked grebe feathers, some of which they swallowed and some which they were fed when they were young. It is theorized that the ball acts as a ball valve to prevent fish bones, salamander bones, and other indigestible hard particles from entering the intestine. The feather ball reminds one of the hair ball of a cat or dog, or a bezoar of a cow.

Like other birds, red-necked grebes are creatures of habit, behaving the same year after year. Thus we could always rely on hearing its screechy squeal song at the same site on the same Breeding Bird Route in Canada. We couldn't see the bird because deciduous brush on the shore was too dense, but by having listened to tapes of bird songs again and again a birder can recognize a unique song that resembles no other, heard in the only surroundings in which that species utters it. Can you not recognize the voice of a friend over the telephone? The instructions for Breeding Bird Census takers expect them to identify ninety per cent of the birds by sound, not by sight.

What makes the red-necked grebe amazing and incredible? Its color scheme is copied closely by the ruddy duck. (Imitation is the sincerest form of flattery.) Its stomach contains a feather ball. Its young ride piggy-back. And it has the toe nails of a human being. And it has a very un-bird-like song.

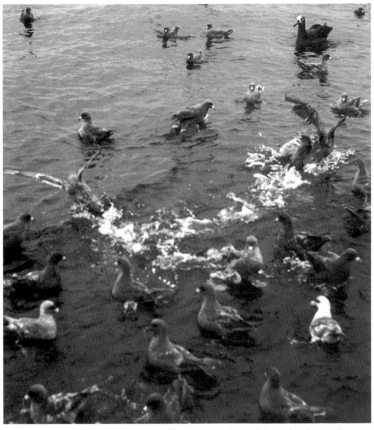

A lone black-footed albatross approaches a fulmination of fulmars feeding on chum.
Photograph by Kenneth J. Johnson

Fulmar

My first sighting of a fulmar was on a trip to St. Paul Island, one of the Probilof Islands. There in the Bering Sea a couple of them were flapping their wings stiffly with shallow wing beats, then gliding with flat outstretched wings. This was on July 21, 1971. The next time was on July 25, 1972 on a trip far out to sea, out of Westport, Washington.

The crew on our Westport boat put out some chum, a smelly bait of popcorn soaked in fish oil. As it floated next to our boat, the odor was wafted far away by the strong breeze. It was soon picked up by out-of-sight ocean birds, who quickly picked up the scent trail to our boat. Among them were a few fulmars.

Most specimens we saw were dark gray. In the Atlantic some of these birds, now reconsidered to be the same species, are white with blue-gray mantle, making them look like gulls. But gulls forage closer to land, and never have as stocky a build. The fulmar has a more muscular bull-necked build, likely the strongest flier, able to fly in the strongest gale with ease.

If the petrel pattering over the waves is a ballet dancer, the fulmar is a professional wrestler.

The scientific name of the fulmar is *Fulmaris glacialis*, where the specific name is from the Latin word *glacies*, meaning ice, since this bird summers and nests in the polar regions. The generic name is claimed to be derived from a Viking term for a stinky sea bird, in view of its habit of regurgitating foul smelling oily emesis on an invader of its nesting site.

The fulmar, I read, has stomach walls that secretes an oil that is foul smelling. If a dead fulmar is lifted up by its feet, this musk runs out of its mouth. If this oil gets on cloth or other material it permeates it with a stench that cannot easily be removed. Museum specimens have that same smell, which persists for decades.

What causes it? Its diet—for it eats dead fish and flesh, especially whale fat from corpses. When I visited Eskimo country and ate whale blubber the Inuit shared with me,

Fulmars. Photograph by Georg Bangjord

the blubber didn't taste bad, though, because it had not decomposed. While gulls follow fishing boats from seaports for the garbage they throw overboard, the fulmars have learned to follow ships far offshore that drag nets, since their nets, up to a mile in length, yield many creatures that fall off or are rejected when the net is pulled back onto the ship.

The fulmar seems to be the only bird that eats a medusa jellyfish. Observers note that when a fulmar can eat bountifully, it will gorge itself on its fatty food until it cannot fly, and must rest until it digests enough to be able to resume flight. During nesting season it goes off on hunting trips for a couple weeks at a time, to return to feed its young one so much food that it can thrive for a half a month until the next return to the nesting ledge.

The fulmar never drinks fresh water, for it is on the ocean its entire life except when it breeds on the face of a high cliff facing the sea, on a small tilted crevice where water cannot collect in a puddle. So it can drink only salty sea water, which would kill other birds or animals.

It is a member of the tubenoses – petrels, shearwaters, albatrosses, storm-petrels, fulmars. In the picture shown here of the pair of fulmars in flight, note the bump at the base of the upper mandible, which is the pair of tubes that dispose of the excess salt its special salt glands remove from its blood.

So, far out on the ocean this buxom bird that lives on fat, a virtual vulture of the ocean, thrives on an excessively high salt diet, and stinks.

Mother Carey's Chicken

The Wilson's stormy petrel's scientific name is *Oceanites oceanicus*. The Latin *oceanus* means the ocean, and the Latin suffix *–ites* means having to do with. In the species name *oceanicus* the suffix is Latin for belonging to. So this smallest of the ocean birds, between a sparrow and a robin in size, has to do with the ocean, and belongs to the ocean.

Alexander Wilson, the Scottish ornithologist, first described this species, so it was named after him.

It spends its entire life on the ocean, never coming to land except to breed, which it does in colonies only on the small islands offshore from Antarctica, when the Northern Hemisphere has its winter. The ocean surrounding Antarctica is abundant in its food of minute crustaceans, so its young one is well fed. The lone chick is hatched from an egg that is huge for the mother's body, almost rivaling the kiwi in that respect.

When the breeding season is over in February they move north to skim the waters of all the Atlantic and Indian Oceans and the South Pacific Ocean. There they continue their same diet but also concentrate on oily matter from dead sea creatures. They become so oily that when handled a musty smelling oily fluid ejects from their bill and nostrils. The natives of some islands have inserted a wick in the petrel's body, which when lit serves as a lamp as the oil-drenched corpse burns!

This opportunistic bird has learned to follow ships to scavenge the garbage, and relish castaway oily substances from fishermen's boats. They have learned to follow all sizes of vessels because the wakes that follow them stir up the small sea life, making it accessible onto

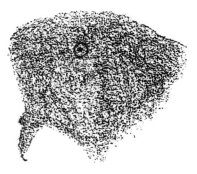

Frontal-side view of Wilson's stormy petrel, showing high forehead and tubenose.

the surface of the ocean. Before, during and after a storm the wind-driven water is more agitated to stir up more sea life to the surface, so the petrels are more numerous and come closer to the boat. So they acquired the name stormy petrels.

Then they patter along with wings elevated and dangling legs touching the surface of the water. This performance makes it look like they were walking on the surface of the sea, and reminded the good Christian sailors of St. Peter, who walked on the water of the Sea of Galilee, as recorded in Matthew 14:24-33. The name petrel is derived from that Biblical Peter because of his walk on the water. The sailors concluded that a little bird that walks on the water must be blessed by the Virgin Mary, so it must be Mother Carey's chicken. Mother Carey (Mater Cara in French) is referring to the mother of Jesus, and is part of English, French and Portuguese sea language and lore.

St. Peter's namesake walking on water.

Since petrels live only on the ocean when they leave their breeding grounds, and ocean water is too salty to drink, how do they thrive far away from fresh water? They belong to the group of ocean birds called tubenoses, the petrels, shearwaters, albatrosses and fulmars. These ocean birds have bulging nostrils at the base of their upper bill to accommodate an amazing gland which siphons off excessive salt from their blood to excrete. So they survive because they have a continually runny nose!

This smelly bird smells out its food when it is oil from a dead whale, or fish, or garbage from a ship's galley; and smelling its own nest is partly how it finds it in a colony of petrels in their Antarctic breeding ground.

It appears to have a bump on the front of its crown, which makes it look like it has a high forehead. Its body is a dark brown, with a wide white band over its rump and base of its tail. Most remarkably, it has bright yellow webs between its black toes, far brighter than the pale yellow wash on the nape of a jaeger, the only other ocean bird with any yellow on it. I believe no one has ever offered a theory as to why it has yellow webs. Perhaps the bright yellow attracts little fishes as the stormy petrel patters its feet on the water to disturb the odor-releasing crustaceans which are thereby brought to the surface by the pattering.

Wilson's stormy petrel is the leading candidate for the distinction of being the most abundant bird species on the face of the earth.

We added it to our life list when we saw them from the deck of the automobile ferry on August 16, 1965 as it sailed from Port aux Basques, Newfoundland, to North Sydney, Nova Scotia, as they were fluttering over Cabot Strait.

This tubenose, so oily it could be burned like a lamp, has a strong musty odor and lives by smelling its food from a great distance, as it continues to fly throughout the year, over thousands of miles of ocean, always on the move.

Its Bill Can Hold More Than Its Belly Can

That colorful rhyme, "A wonderful bird is the pelican; its bill can hold more than its belly can," makes note of that bird's most characteristic feature. Under its long lower mandible is a huge pouch or sac, used to collect fish. The pouch is flexible to stretch to accommodate more fish, and between the pouch and the lower mandible are muscles that stretch to further enlarge its capacity. When the pouch is full the pelican can squeeze out the water from it and swallow the contents into its gullet.

During courtship season the male expands his pouch, which attracts the female. During breeding season either parent regurgitates half-digested fish into its huge pouch, opens up its bill, and serves a fish soup to its eager young to eat out of its pouch. The entire head of the young bird disappears down the parent's maw as the soup bowl empties.

This bird's pouch is the subject of its scientific name, *Pelecanus erythrorhynchos.* The species name consists of the Greek word for red, *eruthros,* plus the Greek word for beak, *rhunkhos.*

The last thing a fish sees before being gobbled up. Photograph by Patricia Burke

But all the pelicans I've seen had yellow beaks. In A. C. Bent's *Life Histories of North American Petrels and Pelicans and Their Allies*, on page 284, he mentions this bird's "deep orange bill and feet." T. S. Roberts' *The Birds of Minnesota*, on page 163, describes a "huge reddish bill and orange pouch." Then W. E. Godfrey in his book, *The Birds of Canada*, page 29, says "yellow bill and feet." Since this is a Canadian bird with most of its range and breeding colonies in Canada,

I reckon Godfrey knows best, so he vindicates me. Next time you look at a pelican, bring a color chart along and you decide! The two species of pelican found in America have two different methods of collecting fish. The white pelican floats on the surface of the water to scoop up the fish. These birds often cooperate with each other to gather side by side and with wings splashing the water. In that way they herd the fish into a compact school, then engulf them with their opened bills–the avian equivalent of cowboys herding cattle!

The brown pelican, living near the ocean, flies up into the air, folds its wings, and dives speedily into the deeper ocean water to engulf the larger fish. The brown pelican is a year-round resident along the Gulf of Mexico shore of Texas and Louisiana.

The white pelican summers on certain larger lakes in North Dakota, Montana, Manitoba, Saskatchewan and Alberta, and winters mostly along the Coastal Bend of Texas. An unfailing spot for close-up viewing of white pelicans is the landing south of Rockport, Texas, where Gulf fishermen clean their fish. These wintering birds have learned to take advantage of the fish cleaning there, and can be approached to within ten feet.

The farthest north we've seen the white pelicans is at the roiling waters of the Saskatchewan River, just below the Squaw Rapids Dam that holds back Tobin Lake in Saskatchewan. Dozens of pelicans are there each summer, harvesting the mangled fish that have gone through the power plant's turbines.

The largest colony in America, located at Chase Lake in North Dakota, was the locale of a great mystery recently. In May and June of 2004 all 27,000 pelicans suddenly abandoned their eggs and young and disappeared. In 2005 only 18,000 returned, and only 280 young survived a massive die off. In 2006 over 34,000 returned to successfully raise young. 2007 was another successful breeding year, back to normal for the refuge.

Although clumsy on land, in the air a flock of white pelicans in flight are beautiful. They fly in single file or in a vee formation, flapping for several wing beats, then soaring

In flight, the heavier pelican folds its head back, but the whooping crane stretches it out.
Photograph by Patricia Burke

for a moment, but not synchronously. The flock often wheels and turns as they fly into the distance. At one instant in the high sky when they turn they seem to disappear, but then as they turn again they are easily seen as the sun reflects off their backs.

Every migration time flocks of whooping cranes are reported by various people. But whooping cranes are loners, flying solo, or at most as a family group of father, mother and only child. Both whooping cranes and white pelicans are large white birds with black wing tips, which confuses non-birders

So the avian equivalents of cowboys all have a built-in soup kettle.

Opossum Of The Bird World

The bittern got its name from the Latin *butorius*, meaning bittern. The scientific name, *Botaurus lentiginosus*, is derived from the word *bo*, a Latin word meaning to roar, plus *taurus*, a Latin word for a bull. The species name, *lentiginosus*, is from the Latin *lentiginis* meaning a freckle, and the medical term for a freckle. That is odd, for the bittern has stripes, not spots, and sounds like one of its nicknames, thunder-pumper, or stake-driver, and does not sound like a bull.

The amazing deep base song of the bittern has been translated into English as pump-er-lunk. But the method by which this bird produces these sounds is even more amazing and incredible. It hunkers down and gulps air into its neck and breast with gulping sounds and clicks its bill until that portion of its anatomy is distended. Then with apparently great effort and convulsive movements it gradually raises its body and head as it emits the pump-er-lunk sound. The air is deflated from the gullet and esophagus by the end of the lunk sound in its song.

The song, reminding some people of an old-fashioned wooden water pump, can be heard a half mile away because the sounds resonate in the air chamber the bittern creates in its neck and chest. This resonating phenomenon is the same as that described in my chapter, Auditory Afterthoughts, in Section VI Bird Curiosities. The sound waves are bounced around in the large air chamber and are reinforced and made louder, and, being low in pitch, travel farther. The size of the air chamber is made possible by the strong muscles in the wall of the neck and chest creating an effect like a bellows.

This pumping can be heard in spring, summer, or fall, so when it is heard during mating season it must be coincidental, not part of the nuptial display. Courtship activity with rival males sparring is even more amazing. Few people have ever seen it; I never have. One bittern followed about sixty feet behind the other, both crouching down with back arched, belly next to the ground, neck retracted over the breast, and bill pointed forward, as each bird glided smoothly along. Both birds showed a pair of plumes, or pom-poms, of pure white fluffy feathers, each enlarging to a four inch size. One came out from each shoulder of each folded wing and touched the other over the middle of the back. These ruffs remained in obvious sight for several minutes. Suddenly the pair of birds rose in the air and attacked each other, after which one flew away as the white disappeared on both birds. Nobody seems to know how those semiplume feathers compress together after the display, nor where exactly under the wing they get tucked away.

That is the fastest the bittern ever moves, for it always moves in slow motion. One bird was timed once; it took ten minutes to move twenty feet! It would stand motionless, then slowly move one foot ahead, then freeze again for a long moment. It seems it stands motionless for a long time until insects, frogs, and each such prey interprets its body as part of the harmless immobile scenery, and so they approach to within the bittern's easy striking distance. Such super-slow motion is also overlooked by predators, too, which are attracted only by motion when they hunt.

The bittern has two postures that are typical, the crouch just mentioned, and the upright. When danger approaches the bird stretches upright and stands motionless for minutes at a time. As it imitates a statue among the reeds, its striped plumage, identical in color to the reeds, camouflages it perfectly, so it becomes unrecognizable. If a breeze comes up and sways the reeds the bittern sways with the reeds in perfect harmony with the gentle motion. When the breeze

Typical postures of the bittern: foraging on left, "freezing" on right.

ceases the bittern stops swaying, too. That imitation of a post is the only time I have noticed the bittern, so I must have overlooked it many other times.

Its nest is a simple platform of several trampled stalks of reeds. But what is amazing is that the bittern tramples the reeds to form two paths—one leads to the nest, the other away from it. The bird always walks—or I should say creeps—on the path to the nest, and always leaves the nest on the exit path.

The opossum is a mammal whose survival tactic is to lie motionless as though dead when danger threatens. So the bittern stands motionless when danger threatens. That must come naturally, for it leads a life of slow motion.

Much of the above information is found in Bent's and Roberts' books.

Heedless Heron

We saw this on that small lake shore. This great blue heron stood in shallow water motionless, patiently waiting. Then in a flash it struck a fish, juggled it in its bill to face it into its gullet, and swallowed.

But this fish was several inches long and very plump, and jammed in the heron's throat. The heron tipped its head skyward so gravity would help drive the fish downward. The fish didn't move. The spines in the fins prevented the fish from being regurgitated. We watched, enthralled, to see what would happen. If it leaned forward to prepare to take off, it would surely fall flat on its face, because its center of gravity would then shift so far forward. Moments passed as it stood there. Then, very slowly, the big lump in the heron's neck crept down to its final destination in the stomach.

Did the inevitable painful stretching in swallowing damage the esophagus?

It is an axiom that a bird is aware of us before we see or hear the bird, so the heron knew we were watching it. I imagine, then, that episode of heedlessly trying to eat a fish too big for it must have been embarrassing for the heron, for it is such a dignified bird as it struts along the shore, or poses motionless and stately as it waits patiently for a fish to swim within striking distance.

The scientific name of this heron is *Ardea herodias*; *ardea* is Greek for heron, and *erodias* is Latin for heron. So that scientist must have been impressing us that the great blue heron is a heron that *is* a heron, the epitome of a heron.

In conformity with its majestic air, if disturbed by one's attempt to approach, it never loses its composure, but departs with slow, dignified strokes of its great wings, to land elegantly a distance away.

But in the early part of its life it behaves very differerntly. The young birds, gawky and ungainly, are fighting each other for position in the nest.

The great blue herons build their nests consisting of

twigs and small branches in the tops of trees as a colony on an island or in a swamp. The colony closest to my house is at Maclean Bottoms, which is a few miles south of Bismarck, N. D., south of the fishermen's dock on the Missouri River. Unfortunately the colony was abandoned when its cottonwood trees burned in a bottomlands fire.

Great blue heron.
Photograph by Terje O. Nordvik

An active colony is a scene of rabble and confusion. At the approach of a parent bringing food, the young stand up and clamor and struggle for their food. The parent bird stands erect for a moment, then bends its bill to pump fish soup into the young one's bill, if not onto the nest. Later the fish are placed on the nest for the young to pick up themselves.

As the young ones get older they become more restless and climb into adjacent nests, causing more fights and racket. If they stumble and fall to the ground the old birds abandon them to the predators on the ground.

If the predators attempt to climb the tree to the nest, they are met at the edge of the nest by liquid feces defecated on them by the nestlings, plus emesis regurgitated on them. This combination from both ends keeps the nest safe. However, in the past heron colonies have been wiped out by men with guns.

The Canada goose, the swan and the whooping crane fly with their neck outstretched, but the great blue heron flies with its long neck bent in an ess curve. It stands and strides with its neck straight, but as it is poised to strike its neck is flexed into its ess shape. As it strikes its neck straightens rapidly, with terrific speed and force, like the snapping of a whip.

I have never seen a great blue heron preen, but I am

informed that it is one of the few birds that has one toe serrated – the inner edge of the middle toe-nail – for use in preening. To add to its handsome appearance, one must mention its black plume off the back of the crown of its head.

The great blue heron was one of the birds that suffered from the onslaught of fashion-conscious women of the late 19th Century and early 20th Century who followed the crazy fad of wearing long feathers on their huge hats. Stopping that practice was a motivation for the creation of the National Audubon Society.

World Explorer

The cattle egret is the foremost world explorer. It originally lived only in Africa. Prevailing trade winds blow west from there, north of the equator. When the colonists from the Netherlands began clearing parcels of forest for grazing their cattle in Surinam, their colony on the northeast coast of South America, the cattle egrets which the trade winds brought colonized there in 1880. The adjacent coastal colony of French Guiana wasn't cleared, so was largely bypassed by the egrets.

Neither A. C. Bent in his 1922 books on life histories of North American birds, nor R. T. Peterson in his 1936 field guide, nor T. S. Roberts in his 1947 book on Minnesota birds, even mention the cattle egret.

As South and Central America in many places offered areas for settlers to graze cattle, the cattle egrets spread there in the early 20th Century. They reached Florida by 1940, and much of the United States in the 1950s. In North Dakota they were noted first at Long Lake National Refuge in July, 1978. Since 2000 they have become common in North Dakota. In North America today the cattle egrets now outnumber all the other egrets and herons combined!

Today it is in all of South America except Chile, in Eurasia, Australia, and Micronesia. It was first seen in New Zealand in the 1950s, and the first colony there in 1963. In each area their arrival was aided by prevailing winds. Throughout all the world it has spread on its own power, except where it lives on the Hawaiian Islands from Kauai to Hawaii. There a small group of Hawaiians have introduced the cattle egret because it fit their criteria of looking beautiful or singing prettily.

When we visited Dry Tortugas, which is 75 miles west of Key West, Florida, we found the cattle egrets that landed there were starving because the grass lawn inside Fort Jefferson there had no insects (or, rather, no creature to stir up the insects for them). As the birds became desperate for food,

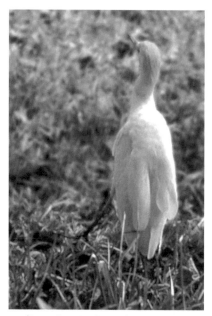

Staggering, starving cattle egret on Dry Tortugas. Photograph by Kenneth J. Johnson

some people have found, they have attacked the migratory warblers who have dropped into Dry Tortugas for a rest during their long journey between the Americas.

Bubulcus ibis is the scientific name the cattle egret has been given. That genus name, *bubulcus*, is Latin for a ploughman that plows with oxen. The giving of that name is logical, for the cattle egret follows the plowman to catch the insects disturbed by his activity, whether it be the bugs that fly or the grasshoppers that jump or the grubs exposed by the blade of the plow.

The cattle egrets in their native Africa hung around big animals such as the water buffalo or gnu or zebra, ready to pounce upon the insects flushed by the game animals' grazing. Some observers believe cattle egrets also like to ride on the backs of these beasts to pick off the parasites on their hides.

So when these egrets migrated to the New World, it was natural for them to adapt to the new herds of cattle introduced to grassy forest clearings and prairies. They likewise adapted to other grazing animals, such as the horse and sheep in Australia and New Zealand.

In the cattle egret's scientific name, the species name given to this bird is *ibis*. This is the name of an Egyptian bird. Neither the Egyptian ibis nor any American ibis can be mistaken for an egret, for the ibis is bigger and has a unique longer and down-curved bill. So the kudos I give the scientist for his generic name I must take away because of the inappropriate specific name.

There are two morals here. The first is fly with the wind, and great things will happen to you. But do not stop short of your goal – look at what happened at Dry Tortugas.

The second moral is stick with humans, and you will do well. Humans will always be drinking milk and eating beef and using wool. Domestic animals that produce those amenities will bring to light those insects you crave to eat.

The Mystery Of The Giant Canada Goose

Early settlers in North Dakota spoke about hunting and eating giant Canada geese which they had found on the surrounding prairie. These huge 45 inch long prizes were preferred and hunted intensively, so that by the 1890s they had been extirpated. The fond memory of these became a legend, perhaps a fantasy in the minds of tellers of tall tales.

However, the late Carl E. Strutz of Jamestown, North Dakota owned a captive flock of giant Canadas. These birds had come from eggs his father, a circuit preacher, had gathered from a nest near Streeter in 1893. In the 1940s National Wildlife Refuges secured stock for breeding from the descendants of these giants in the Strutz captive flock. But wild flocks were gone forever.

But then an amazing discovery was made in the 1960s. There was a wild, free-living flock of giant Canada geese wintering on Silver Lake Park, right in the center of the city of Rochester, Minnesota! Further investigation revealed that this flock summered in southern Manitoba, Canada. So the largest race lived farther south, and wintered farther north,

Canada geese. Photograph by Jon Arne Saeter

while the smaller races bred farther north, as far as the tundra, and wintered farther south.

Next followed a determined effort by wildlife personnel at Northern Prairie Wildlife Research Center, Jamestown, North Dakota,; and Sand Lake National Refuge, Columbia, South Dakota, to propagate giant Canada geese, in addition to or instead of their earlier efforts with the lesser races. Thirty years of dedicated research and application of their expertise have been successful in producing good numbers of birds, which have become free-flying flocks which go south in winter and return home next spring (A few of them have wintered in the Missouri River's open water warmed by the oil refinery and power plant in Mandan.)

The giant Canada goose is now a common bird in North Dakota. It is well known and well liked by non-birders, and prized by hunters. It is even multiplying to the extent that sometimes it is wearing out its welcome, such as by golfers who don't relish a goose or its droppings as a hazard. The home owners who live around the shore of Silver Lake in Rochester, Minnesota now barely tolerate them because of their polka dot lawns, which can't be walked on with clean shoes!

The game and fish people have done an excellent job of bringing those giant geese from being considered extinct to existing today as millions of wild birds in many free-flying flocks over North Dakota. Thanks to the game and fish people, we will continue to be able to get a thrill every time a vee-shaped flock of honkers fly overhead!

Refer to the North Dakota Game and Fish Department publication *Rearing and Restoring Giant Canada Geese in the Dakotas.*

Superabundant Snow Goose

This is an unprecedented environmental crisis. Never in recorded natural history has a species of bird destroyed its own breeding grounds. This is not a case of habitat disruption due to climate change, nor a case of civilization encroaching on nature to obliterate the life styles of the species that live there.

This is happening far from civilization, in the arctic tundra. The snow goose's breeding grounds are on the islands surrounded by the Arctic Ocean and on the mainland along Hudson Bay and James Bay. Only grasses and sedges grow on this tundra, and the snow geese pull the entire plants out of the ground, eat the roots, and discard the shoots and stalks. So the plants are destroyed, leaving a depression soon filled in by water to create a mire or a pond – shallow because the tundra thaws only inches deep above the permanently frozen ground. The mud and ponds then are exposed to rapid water evaporation which leaves salt behind, which retards re-growth of the grasses and sedges.

In the past, with a moderate number of snow geese present, only some of the grasses and sedges were grubbed out, and the remaining plants reseeded the bare spots. But with this population explosion, the more geese there are the less regeneration of plants can occur, and the more the other fauna and flora living there are affected.

In the last hundred years the population of the snow goose has exploded. A graph can show this more spectacularly than the written word, so consider these two graphs displayed here.

Godfrey's *The Birds of Canada*, published in 1966, gives us a revealing picture of the astonishing growth in numbers of the snow goose, for instance, that faithfully stop at a spot, Cap Tourmente, in Quebec south of James Bay, in their annual fall migration. This is shown in the adjacent graph of populations from 1900 to 1960. The graph from 1965 to 1995 is adapted from *Arctic Ecosystems in Peril: Report of the Arctic Goose Habitat Working Group*, edited by D. J. Batt; it records the number of snow geese in spring at St. Lawrence River, Quebec, from 1970 to 1995.

Data from the U.S. Fish & Wildlife Service shows a continued increase in population of the snow goose from 1995 to 2008, the year this chapter was written, enough for the line on the graph to keep pointing skyward. The population explosion includes the geese in central arctic Canada and Alaska and Wrangel Island (north of Siberia), as well as that north of Quebec.

When the superabundant snow geese migrate south to their wintering grounds, they damage crops by removing seedlings and seeds of grains, and graze the wheat, soybeans, hay and corn. If people have a so-what attitude that the arctic tundra vegetation is being damaged, they must become concerned now that in recent years snow geese have extended their wintering range from the Gulf Coast inland to the croplands of southern Iowa, Missouri, Arkansas, eastern Oklahoma and Texas, western Kentucky and Tennessee, and Mississippi and Louisiana.

It is an awesome sight to see, as I have in Texas, a large field solid white in color in winter, like it were covered with fresh snow, but hosting myriads of snow geese, jammed together so closely it would be impossible to squeeze a sparrow in between any geese.

So why are they so abundant? One observer blames the building of reservoirs that supply cities along their migration route, which provide rest stops for weaker birds who earlier could not have survived the long non-stop journey.

Another source attributes their expansion of their winter range from the Gulf Coast to nine states with land far inland, providing new areas of nutrition.

Another factor is the snow goose's ability to adjust and adapt to changing conditions, such as to move into new areas after they "eat themselves out of house and home" when they uproot and destroy all the grasses and sedges.

Hunting regulations have been blamed that are too restrictive and that need to be liberalized. A hunter tells me snow geese circle around too high to shoot, then drop sharply to the ground. Canada geese, on the other hand, fly in low so are easier to target. He says about the only way snow geese can be shot is if two flocks are on either side of the blind, and individuals fly overhead as they shift from one flock to the other.

The weather and other factors were favorable for snow geese. And there are other factors contributing to their abundance that we don't know about.

Since the snow geese are the only birds with a grin patch, they must do something with their bill that all other geese, ducks and swans don't do. The grin patch is the darkened hard edge of both mandibles, extending from the base of the bill almost to the tip

Grin patch on bill of snow goose.

of the bill. These two edges are further modified to present a row of short sharp serrations on the upper mandible. The snow goose feeds by tipping its head slightly, grasping a mouthful of grass or sedge with its grin patch, bending the stalks, and jerking upwards to uproot the plants, but then to eat only the roots. In a wheat field it uproots the grain and eats the entire plant. A Canada goose, by contrast, crops only the tops of the grass like a cow or horse, and does not disturb the roots.

A factor in this bird's population explosion which I have never seen mentioned is the shape of the grin patch. Since the serrated edge of the upper mandible is curved, not straight, it provides a wider opening when the bill is open, so a bigger mouthful of sedge stalks may be uprooted with each jerk of the head, hastening the denuding of the tundra.

The snow goose is labeled with the scientific name of *Chen caerulescens*, where *chen* is Latin for goose and the Latin word *caeruleus*, meaning dark blue, is joined to the Latin suffix –*escens*, translated as somewhat. A minority are of the dark blue phase or morph, which used to be called blue goose under the impression that it was a separate species; that explains the dark blue in the scientific name.

The Cree Indians, living in Manitoba, Ontario, and Quebec, call the snow goose wawa, and rely on it as one of their main items of food. There is a little city named Wawa in Ontario, situated by the northeast corner of Lake Superior.

The snow goose with its grin patch may look like it thinks something is funny, but ecologists don't think it's a laughing matter how it is destroying its feeding and breeding grounds.

Ruddy Duck

The sharp-tailed grouse and the prairie chicken have an inflatable air sac on each side of the neck, which is used in their nuptial displays. The ruddy duck has an inflatable air sac on the front of the neck, and for the same purpose. The chicken-like birds tip their heads down and forwards in their mating rituals, but the ruddy duck tips its head up and backwards when using its larger sac.

That is the only duck with an air sac. It is unique among ducks in other aspects, too. Bent, in his book on ducks, says its nest is shaped like a basket of interwoven reeds camouflaged among the dense reeds of the same color, a pile of reeds some eight inches high. A sloping ramp is built on one side of the basket so the female has an incline on which to slide down into the water when danger approaches. More reeds are arched over the top of the nest to further conceal it. When the female leaves the nest she sneaks away under the water unseen. When she surfaces after a long time only the upper part of her head shows up, and that only for a few seconds.

Ruddy ducks continue to swim with only the top of the head visible as long as danger is near.

Ruddy ducks act more like grebes than they do like other ducks. Most of their food they get from the plants growing on the bottom of the pond or marsh.

The ruddy duck's eggs are huge, the size of a turkey's egg, with a rough and granular shell, and as many as twenty in number. Several of them are laid in nests of other ducks.

One observer found a unique .instance where there was a muskrat's house on which three nests rested. One belonged to a canvasback, the second was on the other side of the house and belonged to a redhead. The third, on top of the house, belonged to a ruddy duck. Such an exposed site for a ruddy duck was not normal.

Its tail is unique. It is short, wide, and stiff. When swimming on the surface it is held erect at forty five degrees between horizontal and perpendicular, to point diagonally toward the rear. In mating display it is also erect but forty five degrees forward from perpendicular. When swimming under water the tail points to the rear, moving up and down and acting like a rudder. When floating calmly the duck may point its tail to the rear, resting it on the surface of the water.

FIG. 93. A Ruddy Duck in full display.
Picture from page 280 of
The Birds of Minnesota,
by T.S. Roberts

The plumage is unique among ducks in that the breeding plumage is bright, in contrast to its dull gray body at other times of year, more of a contrast than other ducks show. The bright brown body during breeding gives its name to the name of this bird, ruddy duck. Its cheeks are bright white. Its concave broad bill is bright sky blue. The crown and nape are deep black.

The male is also unique in that he stays with his mate during incubation and care of the young. But it has been found that the male accompanying the mother with her brood may not be her mate! The young leave the mother much sooner than do ducklings of other species of ducks.

Another observer noted another purpose for the inflated air sac during courtship, other than display. The male raised his head up, moved it backwards, and bent his bill down, patting it against the distended air sac faster and faster, making a noise each time the bill hit the bulge.

Another display was remindful of the western grebe, where the ruddy duck raised up and scooted over the surface of the pond rapidly, pattering over the surface with its feet. Roberts in his book, *The Birds of Minnesota*, described these actions. But the female did not join him, unlike in the performance of the western grebe.

The ruddy duck is a small duck that acts like a grebe.

Misunderstood Turkey Vulture

The turkey vulture needs to have a public relations agent to improve the bad reputation shared by the public under which this bird suffers. When European immigrants came here they called it a buzzard, since it looked and acted similarly to their buzzard of the old country. But that bird had strong talons to tear and grasp a corpse, and a strong beak to puncture a tough hide. The turkey vulture has legs too weak to walk well or hold a corpse with, and must find a soft spot in the hide with its weaker bill to gain entrance to the dead flesh. It can defend itself only by pecking, or by regurgitating its repulsive smelling stomach contents. It eats nothing until it is certain it is stone dead, so little dogs and their owners have nothing to fear from the turkey vulture, which is not like the buzzard that intimidates its dying prey.

The turkey vulture's scientific name is *Cathartes aura*; the generic name is derived from the Greek *katharsis*, meaning purification, because the bird acts as a scavenger. The specific name, *aura*, is Latin, which is modified from *auroua*, which is the phonetic spelling of the name Mexican Indians gave to the turkey vulture.

The turkey vulture got its common name because its red head, which is lacking feathers, reminded some people of our wild turkey, although that bird actually has a bare blue head with bare red nape and neck.

In August and September of 2006 the turkey vultures captured the attention of the public in Bismarck, N. D. by roosting in large numbers on the water tower by Tower avenue. In the late afternoon they would wheel about the tower, then after 7 o'clock would settle down to roost, each at a discreet distance from its neighbor, on the railing and on every protuberance available on the tower.

Some citizens wondered what their droppings would do to the soil around the base of the tower. Interesting question, for their stools have a unique characteristic. These birds eat over-age meat from dead animals, which contains nucleoproteins,

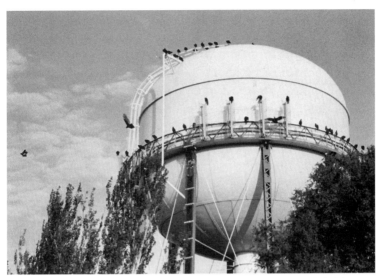
City water tower used as roost by turkey vultures. Photograph by Kenneth J. Johnson

which consist of purines. Purine is degraded to uric acid in the vulture's metabolism. That is excreted by its kidneys and bowels as uricaciduria, The feces, which includes the urine, contains so much uric acid that it kills bacteria.

If that were a human with that much purine in his system he would have gout; but has any veterinarian ever tested a turkey vulture for gout?

The vultures on the water tower behaved true to form, for on the morning it was cool, calm and cloudy they didn't leave but continued to roost until much later in the day when the sun came out and the air warmed up enough to cause thermals to form. These columns of warmer less dense air rose, enabling the vultures to hitch a ride in them to gain altitude up high enough to glide away.

In that way they conserved energy by flapping their wings only enough to move to the nearest thermal.

There is another crucial reason for riding thermals. These warm columns of air carry odors from the ground. Dead animals, of course, stink to high heaven. The vulture has an extremely high sense of smell. Its olfactory gland is huge for a bird, and the nostril opening on its upper bill is so big that a bird-watcher can see through the perforate nares from side to side.

It is the gas mercaptan produced by the decaying flesh of the dead animal that attracts the vulture to the odor it seeks in the thermal. Then the bird descends the thermal, wheeling and turning to keep smelling the odor to its source. Its keen vision then helps find the corpse. But the vulture alights and scrutinizes the body for a while until it is satisfied that it no longer moves, before it touches it.

How does the turkey vulture regulate its body temperature? When it is too hot it urinates on its legs. The urine cools the vulture as the urine evaporates. When the bird is too cold it spreads its wings. The sun warms the wings and thus its body. It also spreads its wings for the sun to bake off bacteria as the body warms to also dry off the neck and head for bits of the corpse's flesh to dry and drop off.

The Mexican village we visited had no paved road, sidewalks or curbing or sewer system. When an animal died there was no department of sanitation to dispose of the carcass, but the natives didn't mind seeing the smelly corpse lying in the main street. Turkey vultures were the disposal crew, and did an efficient job of cleaning up the street. The people and their animals were careful not to disturb the vultures in that valuable capacity.

The turkey vulture may be uncouth and indelicate, but it is indispensable in its place in Nature's cycle.

Cooper's Hawk In A City

A certain large bird has been seen in Bismarck, North Dakota several times. It is furtive, moves fast and silently, is gone in a few seconds, and is easily missed if you blink. Yet it is large, as big as a crow or larger, dark but not as black as that crow. The crow is much more sluggish than that mystery bird.

If one happens to be looking at the right spot at the right time, he notes this mystery bird has a long straight tail with rounded end, and fairly short wide wings with a space between the tip of each primary feather.

This opportunistic Cooper's hawk has adapted to civilization and now has taken up residence in Bismarck, where it has a monopoly on its prey of small birds, primarily house sparrows since they are the most abundant. This hawk is expert in speeding through foliage and past obstructions, curving and swerving with split-second movements, faster than the sparrow. I have read that a Buteo is able to catch its prey in one out of ten attempts; I suspect the Cooper's hawk is more proficient than that.

Cooper's hawk. Photograph by Patrick Beauzay

I vividly remember as a boy my first sight of a Cooper's hawk, perched upright as it posed on the cross arm of the telephone pole by my childhood home. Its blue back and finely red-barred breast invoked memory of the red-white-and-blue of our national flag.

For years a Cooper's hawk has been nesting on the state capitol ground, but few people seem aware of it there because its nest is well hidden and this *Accipiter* comes and goes so quietly. It may be best seen, but not easily, by looking out the south window of the hallway of the North Dakota Heritage Center on the capitol grounds. Another nest is in the Lions Hillside Park near its 16th street entrance.

This is the chicken hawk, the object of farmers' wrath. A. C. Bent, in his *Life History of North American Birds of Prey*, claims that the Cooper's hawk kills more chickens than all other birds combined, even returning again and again to clean out an entire flock of hapless chickens.

A Bismarck citizen told me he has a bird feeder that attracts many different songbirds which he took great pleasure in watching. But then the number coming to his feeder dropped dramatically. A Copper's hawk found his feeder, and with it a bonanza of easy picking. Faced with an empty feeder, he angrily vowed to scour the area for a mile around to find its nest. The next time I contacted him he said he found a young Cooper's hawk, too young to fly, laying on the ground in his back yard. So here that hawk's nest was proven to be right by his house!

In another bit of evidence of Cooper's hawk in Bismarck, this neighbor woman told me that as she abruptly came out of her back door a house sparrow fell almost at her feet. The hawk which had seized it was so shocked by her close appearance that it lost its grip on its prey and dropped the sparrow. As it flew off she identified the surprised raptor as a Cooper's hawk. The sparrow, bleeding and dying on the ground by her door step, shortly was surrounded by a circle of house sparrows – to commiserate and to solace, perhaps? Several other feeder watchers also testify to seeing their bird feeders being monitored by Cooper's hawks. These hunters, I expect, pay even more attention to house sparrows, but birders don't watch house sparrows much so aren't aware of that.

The sharp-shinned hawk is almost identical to the Cooper's except the sharpie is smaller. The end of the tail of the sharp-shin is square, while the Cooper's' is rounded. A memory aid to tell them apart is that the rounded end is C-shaped, C standing for city or civilization and Cooper.

So a large bird of prey has found security in our city, with an ample supply of house sparrows which are harvested efficiently, using surprise in its attack together with powerful force. This seems to be a national trend for raptors – consider, for examples, the peregrine falcon nest in Fargo, and the red-tailed hawk nest in New York City's Central Park. There undoubtedly are a number of other cities that are unintentional hosts to Cooper's hawks.

Mount Up With Wings Like Eagles

The Chosen People in the Old Testament were entranced with eagles. That is not surprising, for that huge bird commanded respect as it soared and wheeled about up in the sky, mounting higher up into awesome heights. And it did so not by frantic wing beats but by effortless casual movements of its wings. So it was that Isaiah 40:31 promised that "those that wait on the Lord shall renew their strength, they shall mount up with wings like eagles."

Being a naturalist, one would be curious to know the species of eagle Isaiah had in mind when he wrote. Research tells us there were and are some ten species of eagles and three species of vultures in the Holy Land. When Isaiah, or any of his contemporaries, gazed up into the sky they had no spotting scopes or binoculars to aid them in studying those distant birds so far up in the sky, so the species all looked alike.

If they did have those visual aids, and if they did patiently study them when they were on the ground, they would discover that some were not noble, and would not earn their respect. Old World vultures, for instance, are quarrelsome as they devour stinky rotting carrion, and they attack injured or aged animals while the animals are still alive. They are not timid or considerate enough to wait until convinced their prey is stone dead, like our New World turkey vultures do.

Some *Bible* passages about eagles must really refer to vultures. In Matthew 24:28, "Wherever the body is, there the eagles will be gathered together," fits the scenario in where a dead body lies, vultures gather to eat that carrion. The dead body here fits Jesus' description in the previous verses of false Christs and false prophets.

When Micah 1:16 says, "Make yourself as bald as the eagle," he must be referring to a vulture, whose neck and head have no feathers, an adaptation to its sticking its head into contact with rotten meat. Eagles have feathered head and neck, since they do not get in contact with carrion.

Of the thirty references to eagles that are in the *Bible*, they usually refer to some characteristic of the bird, such as its swiftness of flight, strength of wing, its nest being located high on a mountain cliff, or its long life.

In Psalm 103:5 "…your youth is renewed like the eagle's" refers to an ancient belief that when an eagle moults it miraculously becomes younger, which explains why it lives so long.

Scholars say the Hebrew word for eagle means a bird that tears flesh with its beak. So since the *Bible* does not differentiate between an avian eater of fresh meat or eater of carrion, we may be uncertain as to whether a verse of scripture is talking about a respected eagle or a disdained vulture. But whichever species of raptor was intended, it doesn't detract from the message the scripture conveys.

Avian Division Of Duties

The Harris' hawk demonstrates what has been described as the most sophisticated maneuvers in hunting tactics of any species of bird. While other raptors act singly, Harris' hawks cooperate as a group, each taking turns flushing out and chasing other birds, lizards and mammals, even jackrabbits, which they then share.

One technique is when two groups alternate flying ahead to scout until the prey is caught. Another method is when a hawk spies a prey, the group surrounds that victim, and one hawk attacks it, then all eat it. They wait for the dominant hawk, a female, to eat first. Then the others, by rank, eat in orderly fashion.

The members of the hunting group aren't strangers, but include young who stay with their parents for three years. They breed two or three times a year, which accounts for the size of the group of usually two to six hunters.

Falconers have exported Harris' hawks to England to practice the sport of falconry. Other raptors, such as the peregrine falcon, can be used only singly, for if two are used together they will fight each other. When Harris' hawks are used they work together to corner the mammal. These birds will even work with the falconer by following him, flying along with him until a rabbit comes into view, whereupon they act as a team to kill it.

The technique where this group hunting in packs works well is in their habitat of a desert of mesquite, cactus, and Spanish bayonet chaparral.

One person in the Internet (Time's Fool: The Harris Hawk) thought of the desert-dwelling Harris' hawk when she read about the desert hawk in Deuteronomy 32:10, 11: "In a desert land he found him, in a barren and howling waste. He shielded him and cared for him; He guarded him as the apple of his eye, like an eagle that stirs up its nest and hovers over its young, that spreads its wings to catch them and carries them on its pinions." (Actually Moses the author here was referring to the Children of Israel wandering in the wilderness and being protected by the Lord.) That same Internet person, when visiting the Cotswold Falconry in England, bonded with a Harris' hawk there as they stared at each other for a long time, each repeating the hawk's odd-sounding moan or purr.

In America the Harris' hawk is so tame it continues to perch on the saguaro or telephone pole when approached, instead of flying away as other hawks do. So because of its tameness it became extirpated in the 1960s. Fortunately, attempts to reintroduce it later have been successful. Today it is easy to see in Arizona and west Texas. Our first sighting of it was in Choke Canyon State Park, Texas.

Its common name was given it by John James Audubon in honor of his friend Edward Harris, a fellow birder who subsidized Audubon. The scientific name of this amazing bird is *Parabuteo unicinctus*. The Greek *para* means near or beside. The Latin *buteo* means a certain kind of hawk. The

Harris' hawk. Photograph by Norton R. Johnson

Latin *uni* means once; *cinctus* means girdled. So the scientist who named it regarded this as the bird similar to a Buteo that has a prominent white band across the base of its tail. It also has another white band across the end of its tail. The body is a dark chocolate color, with dark red wings and tibia, and yellow legs and bill.

The Harris' hawk with its outstanding skill in hunting as a member of a team easily qualifies it as an amazing incredible bird.

Old World's Answer To The Passenger Pigeon

In the early 1800s, when there were enough settlers in Middle America to witness the phenomenon, passenger pigeons were so abundant that a flock was huge enough to darken the entire sky. Audubon calculated there were 1,150,136,000 passenger pigeons in the flock that passed over him one long autumn day in Kentucky in 1813 (T. S. Roberts, in *The Birds Of Minnesota.*).

In Old Testament times the *Bible* records similar happenings of one species of bird appearing in a massive flock of mind-boggling numbers of birds. These quail, as described in Numbers 11:31, came on a wind off the sea in such numbers that when they fell exhausted in the Children of Israel's large camp they covered the entire campground plus the ground for a distance of a day's journey on both sides of the camp, which camp consisted of thousands of men plus their families plus their livestock. Reckon how many millions of quail would be in a flock of that size!

The Old Testament also records other incredible flocks of quail. The Jews and their families and belongings and livestock, having escaped from slavery in Egypt, were wandering in the wilderness and complaining. So the Lord promised to send them flesh in the evening and bread in the morning. Exodus 16:13 says quails "came up and covered the camp" in the evening, and in the early morning fine flakes of what the people called "manna" appeared on the bushes and on the ground. Since the site of the camp mentioned in both Exodus and Numbers consisted of the same people and their belongings, the evening flocks of quail must have also numbered in the millions to have covered that huge camp.

Incidentally, nutritionists say protein, such as quail, is needed for sleep time repair and nourishment of body tissues; and carbohydrates, such as the sugar mannitol from the manna from the bushes, experts have deduced, are needed for daytime energy. So the timing was perfect for the appearance of the quail and the manna.

This migratory quail crossed 500 miles of sea, aided by a tail wind.

If we consider these events chronologically, the passenger pigeon is the New World's answer to the quail, not the other way around, since the *Bible* was written thousands of years before America was discovered. In any event, it behooves us to learn more about this remarkable quail.

This was the Coturnix quail, scientific name *Coturnix coturnix*. The Latin word *coturnix* means quail. Our North American quail are all resident, but the four species of the genus *Coturnix* are all migratory. The *C. coturnix* of the *Bible* is the best known. It is 7 inches in length, the house sparrow is 6-1/4 inches, our American robin is 10 inches. This quail lives in Europe and western Asia, migrating south across the Mediterranean Sea into North Africa.

So when the Biblical quail reached land it was the north shore of Egypt, in the Sinai Desert. The Children of Israel camp was at the exact spot where that autumnal southward migration flight became grounded. The people harvested the quail for only two evenings, researchers say, but the manna appeared for forty sunrises. People can live on animal protein intermittently, but need carbohydrates daily to thrive.

Unlike manna, this quail was recognized by the Israelites as the same bird that had come to Egypt every winter for centuries, where it flew 3 or 4 feet above the ground, or scurried about in the ground vegetation. Flying or hiding, they were easily caught in nets and eaten with relish.

As late as the early 1900s, Egyptians were still netting them and exporting the surpluses to Europe, over two million annually, even three million by 1920. This slaughter and lack of any thought of conservation decimated the population and threatened to result in the same fate as America's passenger pigeon.

What is the status of the Coturnix quail today? *Birds of the World* ,authored by O. I. Austin, also says that the Japanese raise this bird both for food and also for its eggs.

In the 1950s they were brought to the southern United States and released. Here they grew until autumn, when they migrated southeast (the direction with which they were imprinted), only to drown in the Atlantic Ocean or Gulf of Mexico.

Go to the Internet, ask Google to find "Coturnix quail." There I was surprised to find apparently all four species in the *Coturnix* genus. This quail is sold ready-to-eat or live to use as pets or for breeding. Imagine having an egg-laying pet, or having a dinner eating the exact same bird the Israelites ate when in their forty year journey in the wilderness!

Chukar

In May, 2007 we saw a loose covey of five chukars outside our dwelling place in Bismarck. They visited our bird feeder at the bottom of the hill, then strolled leisurely in a loose file along the side of the hill.

Bird field guides all agree that chukars do not live in North Dakota. Then how and why were these wild free-roaming birds here? The small game bird specialist at the state's Game and Fish Department had the answer to this mystery. It seems there is a person living north of this city who raises chukars, and they escaped. They were seen in two other locations in my neighborhood also.

Game and Fish introduced chukars once in the Logging Camp Ranch area of the North Dakota Badlands, but after two years the colony disappeared. The Badlands might be appropriate for this bird, for its natural habitat is rugged hilly mountainous country. It has been introduced several times in the United States since 1893, but the only place these attempts have succeeded is in the West, especially in the Great Basin of Utah. Sibley's range map shows it is entrenched now in western Colorado and Wyoming, all of Nevada, and much of Idaho, Oregon and Washington, as well as in all of Utah.

The chukar is truly a mountain bird, for all of its homeland is mountainous Pakistan, Afghanistan, Russia, China, India, Turkey and Greece. True to instinct, it is at home on the barren slopes of the volcanoes on Maui and Hawaii in the Hawaiian Islands.

Why has this bird been introduced to the

These two field marks make the chukar different from any other bird.

The chukar prefers to run, not fly. Photograph by Ravn David Saeter

U.S. so many times? Because hunters enjoy this game bird so much, but also because it is popular for game farms to raise.

Game farms provide thousands for release for sport. The hen is a breeder almost as prodigious as the barnyard chicken, since she will produce maybe fifty eggs, which are placed in incubators or set under brooding bantam hens to hatch. Eggs or chicks are sold to fanciers to raise as a hobby, such as the man living north of Bismarck. Chukars are excellent eating.

The chukar's scientific name is *Alectoris chukar*. Its generic name was derived from the Latin *alectorum*, pertaining to a cock. Its species name is from the bird's name, which is a human's translation of what its call sounds like.

So, apparently those chukars I saw were attracted to the hill I live next to, the feeble imitation of a mountain the chukar's genes and instinct drove it to seek.

My Love Affair With The Chicken

It was long before I was old enough to go to kindergarten. An older little boy invited me to go with him on a walk of exploration. We were gone a good part of the day, on a long, long walk. At the end of our journey we saw a yard where there was a pen a little over a foot high, shaped like a miniature A-frame, bottomless and movable. Each slanted side of the "A" was solid wood; each end of the pen was open with horizontal narrow slats some 1-1/2 inches apart. Inside was a brown mother hen. Her chicks roamed freely in and out of her pen. I stood entranced.

When we finally returned to my house, there was my frantic mother, who had called the police to help find a lost little boy. In retrospect, the mother hen lived only two blocks away!

Several of our neighbors kept chickens in their garage or chicken coop. All our farmer relatives had chickens roaming freely in their farmyards. My parents raised a pair of Black Minorcas, until they were eaten. As I grew older, they bought a pair of Easter baby chicks and entrusted them to my care. They matured into White Leghorns, a pullet and a cockerel, and became my pets.

I took very good care of them, watching over them daily. As they grew older, the cockerel didn't like my holding him, but the pullet never did mind my holding her in my arms, even as she became a hen. With the male it was more difficult, but with the female it was rather easy to hypnotize her. One way was to rotate my finger in the air around her bill as she faced my finger. The other way was to point my finger toward her face and gently touch her bill. She would sit motionless until any slight movement broke the spell. When I pressed down on the hen's back and patted gently, she uttered the same trill a hen expresses when mounted by a rooster. This stimulates her to lay an egg, I surmise, just as it simulates the activity of a rooster.

You may doubt me, but if you have the opportunities with the right chickens and in the right circumstances you may hear all their incredible repertoire of fifteen sounds.

Barnyard Chickens Have
Fifteen Different Voices

I feel sorry for chickens on a poultry farm. They live indoors all their lives, crowded like sardines in a can, and never set foot on terra firma. Of course, they are comfortable with every need tended to from cradle to the grave, like a welfare state.

But the barnyard chicken has a life – interests, adventures, dangers, excitement, rarely a dull moment. Discover that it will have a chance to use all its repertoire of fifteen different songs. I have heard all fifteen. What's a birder doing observing chickens? Well, they're birds, aren't they? In Hawaii, in Kauai National Park, jungle fowl, the ancestors of our poultry, roam free and wild as part of the native fauna. These are the descendants of birds brought from Asia or Micronesia a thousand years ago by immigrants whose descendants are today's native Hawaiians.

One sign of spring was in a rural post office – even in Bismarck – where a carton of baby chicks was awaiting delivery. Their loud incessant peep, peep, peep pervaded the entire small building, a pleasant sound to all the agrarian customers.

As it grows older the chick's song merges into the second one, a peep-peep conversation with other chickens. If one becomes lonesome or wanders astray the third song is heard – a plaintive peeeep with upward inflection. The mother hen utters the fourth song, a chick, chuck, chuck to call her baby chicks.

The hen sings number five, a drawn out ascending cuuuck? cuuuck? when she is curious about something. Listen for it when you are in the poultry barn at the county fair. When she is cuddling her chicks they are reassured by her number six soft clucking. Her sharp chk! chk! is an alarm note, number seven. She expresses her opinion of mating with number eight, a soft trill, when the rooster mounts her.

The rooster is best known for his crow, number nine,

rendered in English as cock-a-doodle-do, the farmer's wakeup call. When the rooster finds a juicy morsel he sounds number ten, a tk, tk, tk which calls the hens to share it.

When danger is near, either sex when upset will sound the alarm, number eleven, cut-cut-cudaw'-cut, with accent on "daw", the fourth syllable. As soon as the hen lays an egg it sounds off with number twelve, a cut-cut-cudaw'-cut very similar to number eleven, but less stressful. Does this imply that the hen is puzzled and mildly disturbed by seeing what she produced?

Any rooster worth his salt will protect his domain by vicious pecking strong enough to cut skin, hitting with the elbow of his wing, and slashing with his spurs. When he charges his foe his face reddens, his neck feathers erect, he lopes sideways toward his foe and utters number thirteen "rrrrr."

When a hen is attacked it cries number fourteen, a squawking. As it is being killed number fifteen is an agonal agonized screaming.

Tapes are on sale for the call of almost every species of bird. But the tape records only one or two calls of each bird, whereas most birds have several calls, one for each occasion. So if the lowly chicken, not recognized for its singing, has at least fifteen vocalizations in its itinerary, how many thousands must a birder memorize to be an expert in this field?

Kokee Jungle Fowl

In the 1700s Captain Cook, while exploring the Pacific, met a certain native chief on one of the small islands. Cook then sailed his ship to another small island over a thousand miles away, where he was surprised to meet that same chief! Those Polynesians were so proficient in studying the ocean waves and the stars that he sailed his little canoe faster than the Captain's state of the art sailing ship could travel!

The ancient Polynesians' expertise in sailing great distances on the Pacific Ocean explains how back in 400 A. D. (A. D. is Latin for *Anno Domini*, meaning "in the Year of Our Lord", referring to the birth of Jesus Christ) these adventurers took provisions, including native jungle fowl, from Asia in their canoes. When they landed on the Hawaiian Islands the jungle fowl became introduced there.

These tropical islands proved to be ideal habitat, resembling the Asiatic jungle to which their ancestors were adapted. How lush they were may be exemplified by this story: A World War II soldier once told me that during maneuvers they were struggling through the dense tropical forest in the mountains of Oahu, when he looked down and found himself twenty feet off the ground!

Long after the war my wife and I flew to Hawaii to visit the islands we had missed by having lived only on Oahu. On each larger island we rented a car and unrolled our bedrolls to sleep in the car, such as in a park, where we were close to Nature, so as to enjoy the bird life. In the early morning all was very quiet, until suddenly and simultaneously all the birds burst out in song in a dawn chorus!

On Kauai we got a rental car at Lihui Airport and drove half way around the island, then up into the mountains to visit Waimea Canyon and Kokee State Park. We camped in the parking lot at Kokee Thursday and Friday nights, March 25 and 26, 1971.

Two most attractive tourist sites on Kauai are the beach on the west coast called the Barking Sands, and Alakai Swamp

1. Jungle fowl cock finds morsel, samples it, calls for hen, using his "tk, tk, tk call.

2. Hen comes, inspects morsel, utters a soft clucking, and eats.

3. Cock leaves remains of food for hen after eating his share.
Photographs by Kenneth J. Johnson

high up in the mountains next to the summit, Mt. Waialeale, 5148 feet elevation. But for me the most noteworthy event was hearing a rooster crowing in the jungle at Kokee! I was hearing one of the feral jungle fowl!

Although wild and free-roaming, one hen was tame enough to come around the park headquarters building, lured there by the park ranger by choice tidbits of food. This hen had four little chicks that reminded me of those our domestic chickens have, but the jungle fowl chicks are a darker brownish yellow with black stripes down their backs. The chicks peeped as the mother hen herded them with her chick, chuck, chuck notes.

We parked in a far corner of the parking lot, under a small tree. In the evening at dusk we heard a hen sounding its alarm notes, and its cut-cut-cudaw'-cut. Looking all around, we couldn't see it anywhere. Finally, it had enough and flew away from the overhead tree branch where it had intended to roost for the night.

During the day, when parked, we tossed out a cracker to lure a rooster to our car for pictures. It cautiously approached to inspect the object. Testing it in his bill, it met with his approval (photo 1). So he called a nearby hen with his tk, tk, tk call, and gallantly showed it to her (photo 2), just as I had seen domestic roosters do back home in our Midwest. Then, having eaten a very large sample and finding it good, he graciously left the remains for his hen and majestically walked away (photo 3).

So we heard five of the fifteen voices the close relative, our barnyard chicken has, as described in my December 21, 2005 Birds Column in the *Bismarck Tribune*, although I recall the jungle fowls' voices, except for the cock's crow, were softer.

These jungle fowl we found were smaller than our domestic chickens but seemed larger than Cornish hens, maybe the size of fighting cocks. The Kauai hen had a mottled brown back and a brown proximal tail and a lighter plainer brown breast and neck; the distal half of her tail was black. The rooster's body was a very dark brown color with flecks and streaks of gold. His large tail was black with a few contrasting white feathers. A few of the tail feathers were falcated. The cock's comb and wattle were bright red. The hen's legs were dull brown; the cock's legs were bright yellow.

The jungle fowl's scientific name, *Gallus gallus*, is from the Latin word *gallus* for cock.

Pratt, Bruner, and Berreth in their 1987 book, *The Birds of Hawaii and the Tropical Pacific*, state that because of interbreeding with free-ranging domestic fowl on other islands, Kokee is now the only place where the descendants of the 400 A.D. birds are pure and untainted by domestic chickens. The Kokee birds are protected, and live far from domestic stock, up in the steep mountains of Kauai. Even the mixed-breed flocks elsewhere are declining, or have been extirpated. Jungle fowl were reintroduced to Waimea State Park in Oahu, but the Kokee fowl never needed reintroduction.

How lucky we were to have seen these rarities at Kokee!

When you visit Kauai, be sure to enjoy the jungle fowl living wild up in the verdant mountains.

Ring-necked Pheasant, A Favored Game Bird

The ring-necked pheasant is the hunter's greatly favored game bird, and has been so for thousands of years. Being larger, it provides more good eating than grouse or doves, and is much easier to see and shoot.

But the U.S. Fish and Wildlife Service says the mourning dove is the most heavily harvested game bird. They are in plain sight on telephone wires and fences, making no attempt to hide like the pheasant. Their range covers all 48 states, whereas the pheasant is restricted mostly to the Upper Midwest. If we equate favoritism with the amount of money governments and game breeders spend on these game birds, though, the mourning dove takes care of itself by its fecundity, but the pheasant must be coddled and subsidized repeatedly in order to maintain its numbers; so humans must favor the pheasant, then.

Bobwhite are in the southeast quadrant of the United States; their supply is also supplemented by governments and game breeders. *Beef Magazine* says private game preserves charge $250 to $500 per gun/day to harvest bobwhite, and $275 to $400 per gun/day to shoot ring-necked pheasant there. The Internet's GameBirdHunts.com claims that pheasant hunters outnumber all other Iowa hunters, and millions of ring-necked pheasants are harvested by hunters every year, more than any other game bird. These hunters' impact on the Iowa economy is almost a quarter billion dollars annually, it is claimed.

They have been raised on game farms and released across Mid-America countless times. Populations there may sustain themselves, or if they don't because of natural reasons or hunting pressure they are replenished by restocking, and supported by private groups such as Pheasants Forever.

A. C. Bent says the first ring-necked, or Mongolian, pheasants were introduced into America in 1881, when the American consul-general in Shanghai, China shipped some to Oregon. T. S. Roberts says the first importation into the

Ring-necked pheasant – a newcomer from Mongolia. Photograph by Torgeir Nygaard

U.S. was by Benjamin Franklin's son-in-law. This was a failure. The first successful importation into the Eastern United States was in 1887. In 1887 the owner of an estate in New Jersey shipped some from England. Pheasants were carried by the Greeks and Romans from Asia to Europe for food. The bird also reached England, thanks to gourmets of that time, because of its good eating. Although the bobwhite and the mourning dove were already available for hunting, the Americans preferred the pheasant so much they spent considerable money, time and effort importing the pheasant. More shipments were made in later years from England to various Northern States. (They don't thrive in the South.) South Dakotans think so highly of the pheasant that they made it their state bird. Fittingly so, since South Dakota is said to have more of them than any other state, and catering to pheasant hunters there is big business.

The pheasant's scientific name is *Phasianus colchicus.* The generic name *Phasianus* is Latin, derived from the river Phasis, which today is called the Rioni River. It flows into the Black Sea from Georgia, a part of the old U.S.S.R. The specific name is *colchicus.* Colchis is an ancient country between the Caucasus Mountains and Armenia, now named Kutaisi, a part of Georgia, on that same Rioni River. This must be the only bird species whose entire scientific name is derived from the place names of where its ancestors dwelled.

Our Game and Fish Department counts them by listening to their crows. If a counter tarries too long he will start hearing the same roosters repeating themselves. So they limit the time spent at each location. The cock's crow consists of a long note and a short note. If the bird is fairly close an observer can hear a flapping of the wings after the crow. If the bird is very close he can also hear a brief faint flapping of the wings before the crow as well. So when it crows it also tells you how far away it is by how much of its presentation you hear.

This pheasant is polygamous. Many areas where the game laws permit only cocks to be shot encourage polygamy by the surviving males. The male's courtship dance is similar to a grouse's where he steps and bows and raises his feathers and even inflates his little air sacs as his tail is spread.

A. C. Bent in his book, *Life Histories of North American Gallinaceous Birds*, among other observations, claims that the females are scentless. This explains why prize-winning dogs flush only males!

Why is its tail so long? It uses it as a brake by bending it down and spreading it as it is landing. It is useful as a rudder. It helps impress the female in the courtship dance. It provides balance. But it has been known to get frozen in the snow, trapping the bird to cause its starvation.

We almost got killed because of a pheasant once. Driving down state highway 55 in Minnesota during hunting season I saw a hunter on the left side of the road, and a pheasant flying up on the right side of the road. Just as the hunter was raising his gun to shoot, my car was about to cross his line of fire. I blew my horn desperately. The hunter had the good sense to hold his fire, so we didn't get shot. What the frustrated hunter said probably wasn't fit to print.

As a boy I recall my farmer uncle relating the time he was riding his mower when it flushed a pheasant and in doing so cut off its legs!

My locomotive engineer uncle was said to stop his steam locomotive in a rural area of South Dakota while his crew harvested pheasants out of season.

Just as my cousin was bragging about how he shot that pheasant clean through the heart, I bit down on a piece of shot in its drumstick I was eating.

Ring-necked pheasants are of interest to birders because they are so obvious in the field, are beautiful, spectacular, easy to identify by sight, and have a distinctive voice.

Rock Ptarmigan Of Attu

Attu, the small island that is the westernmost piece of North America, east and south of Siberia, is the ultimate place for avid birders to add rare birds to their life lists. It is also the hardest place to get to. There are no human residents. In World War II it was the only piece of American soil invaded and occupied by a foreign enemy, but the media were so occupied with the bombing of Pearl Harbor by Japan that the invasion and occupation of Attu by Japan was largely overlooked in the news. The Japs were chased out from Attu only after bitter fighting by our Air Force and Navy and the "Northern Force" of the 7th Division's Alaskan 4th Regiment, led by Lieutenant Colonel Al Hartl. He was later promoted to Major General. I knew Al Hartl personally, for he lived in the same condominium as I until his death. The U.S. Coast Guard's Loran Station, which was set up there after the war, is now obsolete and abandoned. Frequent violent Bering Sea storms, sometimes a williwaw, render a landing by boat or by airplane dangerous, unpredictable and infrequent.

The airstrip our Armed Services used was jerry-built by laying perforated metal strips on the soggy tundra. The Coast Guard now used an improved replacement made of paved asphalt. So it was fortunate that the chartered airplane of the Reeve Aleutian Airways (now bankrupt and extinct) was able to finally land on the Coast Guard's airfield in between storms, and leave immediately upon unloading the birding tour Attour, consisting of fifteen determined birders with their supplies.

The logistics needed were as detailed as for any expedition. All our food, clothing, equipment, heating supplies had to be carried in. We slept and ate in Quonset Huts abandoned by the U.S. Army from the Battle of Attu of World War II. Forty degree winds driving rains horizontally had to be planned for, since we would expect to be outdoors during the day, looking for birds.

During the May 17 to June 3, 1979 days we were there I

added 30 birds to my life list on this island alone. If the reader is interested in which birds they were, here is the list of them: bean goose, Eurasian wigeon, common pochard, tufted duck, smew, white-tailed eagle, rock ptarmigan, Mongolian plover, black-tailed godwit, spotted redshank, common redshank, green sandpiper, wood sandpiper, common sandpiper, red knot, red-necked stint, Temminck's stint, long-toed stint, ruff, rock sandpiper, common black-headed gull, eye-browed thrush, Siberian ruby-throat, Pechora pipit, olive tree-pipit, red-throated pipit, brambling, rustic bunting, yellow-billed loon, gyrfalcon. The lure of coming here was to see migrating Siberian birds blown off course by west winds. That was the motivation driving these birders. But in so concentrating on the exotics, the bird which is resident on Attu, which my notes called ubiquitous, was ignored, even considered a "trash bird," it seemed to me. Imagine being disdainful of a rock ptarmigan!

Of the three species of ptarmigan, white-tailed, willow and rock, the rock ptarmigan lives in the bleakest, coldest most barren land by far. That fits Attu, for I don't remember

Attu rock ptarmigan; male in breeding plumage, with female.
Photograph submitted by Kenneth J. Johnson

seeing a single tree or bush or dwarf willow on the island – only marsh, grassy tundra, and steep snow-covered mountains. During our visit we stayed near the shore or trudged across tundra, but never climbed any snowy mountain slopes.

The rock ptarmigan easily blended into the ankle-deep grass and was hard to see, but conforming to its name it was equally at home among the barren rocks. Its legs are covered with feathers, and unlike all other birds except the snowy owl, even the toes are thickly feathered for insulation. This adaptation to the snowy winter tundra means it has built-in snowshoes, so it doesn't sink in the snow as it walks. The raven, which also lives on Attu, is said to have extra thick callouses on its toes for insulation, yet it sinks in the snow.

The rock ptarmigan's scientific name is *Lagopus mutus*. The generic name is Greek for hare-footed, very appropriate for its feathered legs and toes. The specific name doesn't seem right, for this bird isn't mute. It clicks and croaks – a guttural sound that is very unlike a bird.

A. C. Bent in his book, *Life Histories of North American Gallinaceous Birds*, considers the Attu rock ptarmigan a separate subspecies. Isolated on this island, it has evolved black feathers in the male's breeding plumage. My picture shows the male with a black breast; *The Sibley Guide to Birds* shows the Attu bird with all the colored breeding plumage feathers to be black. The rock ptarmigan in other Aleutian Islands or in Arctic Alaska and Canada shows the male's colored breeding plumage feathers to be brown.

Do you think it would have been easier to have searched for the rock ptarmigan in another part of its range? It breeds only in the barren, rocky tundra of the Alaskan mainland, British Columbia mountains, and Canada's far North.

Prairie Chickens Have A Unique History

2004 is a memorable year, for during October 9-17 a hunting season in North Dakota resumed for an upland game bird that had been predicted to be headed for extinction.

The history of the greater prairie chicken, also known as the pinnated grouse, has been not only that of cycles in its population, but a massive movement of the entire species from east to west over the years.

Before America was settled the greater prairie chicken lived in what is now Kentucky, Michigan and western Pennsylvania, but not west of what is now Indiana. Then as settlers moved west they cleared trees and planted grain fields ideal for the prairie chicken and displacing the sharp-tailed grouse. This happened during the early 19th Century. Records show prairie chickens were not in the Red River Valley in 1873, but appeared there in 1881, and were abundant there by 1885. The new railroads built westward greatly aided that movement. Through 1890-1910 these birds were North Dakota's greatest game birds. But after tall grass prairie became scarce, and early farming progressed into intensive farming which left less grain lying in the field after harvest, the prairie chicken became scarce.

So the hunting season had closed by 1946. But since our Game and Fish Department was releasing prairie chickens in Grand Forks County from its stock during the last decade of the 1900s, their population thrived there once again, and these birds also had appeared in the Sheyenne National Grasslands area by 1962.

The sharp-tailed grouse was wilder and less adaptable to civilization. Both birds are at home on the prairie, but the prairie chicken also loves grain fields; it is claimed to eat more grain than any other gallinaceous bird. The sharp-tailed grouse tends to prefer brush lands and open areas among stands of trees more than it likes the open prairie. The sharp-tailed grouse and the male prairie chicken are permanent residents, while the female prairie chicken may migrate south for a ways. This is consistent with the observation that when flushed the prairie chicken flies much farther than the "sharp-tail."

The easiest place I know of to find the prairie chicken is on Nature Conservancy land immediately south of Buffalo River State Park, Minnesota which is twenty miles east of Fargo, North Dakota. The largest number of birds I have heard booming is east of Lisbon, North Dakota in the Sheyenne National Grasslands area, just as the sun is coming up.

W. J. Breckenridge took motion pictures of a male displaying, illustrated in T. S. Roberts' classic *Birds of Minnesota*. That movie shows that the male leans forward as he begins his dance. As the male leans forward the "neck-tufts" (as Roberts calls them) move outward laterally and the sac begins to inflate and the boom commences. Then the neck-tufts move forward horizontally to swing out laterally as the sac enlarges. Next the neck-tufts rise upwards and forward with the sac fully inflated. Finally the neck-tufts point upward, then backward as the sac deflates, the head raises, the booming ends, and the neck-tufts return to the side of the neck to point downward and diagonally backward against the neck, the resting position of the pinna.

So the moving pictures showed that during the booming the pinna describes a complete circle, and the booming continues during both inflation and deflation of the sac. Roberts writes that the first syllable of the three-syllable boom starts with the pinna out sideways, the second syllable sounds as the pinna points forward and diagonally upward, and the third syllable booms when the pinna is pointing perpendicularly upward and the sac is inflated maximally and then deflates. (Some people allege that the booming comes only as the sac deflates.) There is no other bird that can move any of its feathers in that many directions. Prove I'm wrong!

So while tipped forward, moving his pinnae, working his sac, and booming, this grouse is also jerking his head, clicking his bill, moving his tail, and stomping his feet. That's quite a performance! If he were human, he surely could do more than chew gum and walk at the same time; he would be a one-man band.

Its scientific name is *Tympanuchus cupida* from the Latin words *tympanum* for membrane, referring to its air sac, and *nucha* for neck, the location of that air sac. The species name *cupida* is from the Latin *cupido*, meaning passion. So the namer of this bird rightly regarded the impressive air sac that expanded only when displaying on the lek (dancing ground) as being a mating display.

The best advice on finding the prairie chicken, I've found, is in a book written for hunters, *Upland Game Birds*, by Dick Sternberg. The birds roost in grass fields, then fly out just before sunrise, maybe for several miles, to feed. After feeding in crop fields of small grains (wheat, soybeans, cut-alfalfa, winter wheat) they fly back to their grass fields. That same route, called a pass, is followed on its round trip an hour or so before sunset. So they are seen feeding in the crop field, and seen again flying following the pass. Since the ranges of the sharp-tailed grouse and the greater prairie chicken may overlap or adjoin, and the two birds look so similar, what do bird books offer to help us differentiate? The sharp-tailed grouse has a spotted breast, a pointed mostly white tail, and a small purple neck sac. The greater prairie chicken has a barred breast, a short rounded tail, and a larger orange neck sac. But to see the sacs on either bird, one must get up long before sunrise, drive to the lek, settle down in one's quiet car or blind, and crouch motionless for hours while wishing you had put on much warmer clothing.

Bird That Allegedly Lost By One Vote

It wasn't as important as the Declaration of Independence or the Revolutionary War, but one of the important things our Founding Fathers thought about in the First and Second Continental Congresses was creating a national seal, or national emblem. That involved the design for it, which involved a national bird. So just after July 4, 1776 the Second Continental Congress appointed a committee of three to see to it and report back. (Have you noticed, Congress is still appointing committees?) The three men chosen for it were Benjamin Franklin, John Adams and Thomas Jefferson.

Before Congress got around to voting on this, Ben Franklin was sent to France to enlist the aid of France, which was crucial for our new country's survival. While Ben was still there Congress finally voted, on June 20, 1782 – for the bald eagle to be our national bird, on our national seal. Franklin was dismayed and disgusted, for he had chosen the turkey.

His logic was that the turkey was a more respectable bird, and a native North American, honest and courageous. The bald eagle, by contrast, eats carrion and steals fish from the osprey, leading the life of a coward and bully. John J. Audubon agreed with Franklin, but he had no clout in Congress.

Perhaps because a committee of three was appointed, and one member, Ben Franklin, wanted the wild turkey, the legend arose that that bird lost by one vote. A number of web sites make this claim, but no one quotes any source for this. The printed word even states this one vote loss by congressional ballot, but offers no proof. The book in mind won't let me cite it because it reserves all rights including the right of reproduction in whole or in part or in any form.

The Digital Reference Team of the U.S. Library of Congress thoroughly searched through the Journals of the Congress and the National Archives, and found nothing about any debate or vote on this in the Continental Congress.

So by repeatedly misquoting each other, people have kept alive an untruth, though it appeals to us since it is so spectacular and dramatic.

Ben Franklin was portly of build, similar to the robust body of his favorite bird, but his looks could never hope to match the beauty of the turkey.

If the reader can work it into his itinerary, he must go to the South Llano River State Park near Junction, Texas. There find the blind with bench on which to sit to view through a huge glass window the elaborate array of bird feeders. Other birds discreetly make way for the huge turkeys when they visit. They slowly step before the birder, only six feet away, as the bird and the birder eye each other. Their beauty is awesome: red and blue head, barred green and brown body, barred black and orange rump and tail.

A turkey looks too pretty to eat, but I'll eat it anyway, for turkey is my favorite food. It is America's favorite feast on Thanksgiving Day, the holiday founded by Pilgrims to give thanks to the Lord for His blessings.

Remember John Madden, the famous football coach turned Thanksgiving Day football game television commentator, and his special huge baked turkey with four drum sticks?

Bent vouches that the turkey is "the largest and grandest game bird in the world, certainly in North America." Some think domestic turkeys are stupid, too dumb to come in out of the rain, but that wild turkeys are mentally sharp. Let me quote from page 335 in Bent's *Life Histories of North American Gallinaceous Birds*: "Five deliberately walked in front of hunters, mounted a fence, and disappeared leisurely over a low hill before they were able to decide them to be wild. No sooner were they out of sight, than they took to their legs and then to their wings, soon placing a wide valley between them and their new amazed and mortified pursuers."

But we can overestimate the intelligence of a turkey. A turkey pen is a trap whose sides and roof are made of thin logs. The dirt is scraped out from the bottom of one side of the house to create a sloping entrance. Corn or grain is sprinkled on this slope, on both sides of the entrance. Turkeys eat the grain as the bait lures them inside. When in the trap with the bait all gone, they look upward to leave, but find no opening. They can't reason to crawl out the same way they came in.

A turkey shoot is a marksmanship contest that originated in Appalachia. A turkey was placed in a pen with only a slit opening on top. When the bird stuck its head up to look around, the marksman reclining a respectful distance away attempted to shoot it before the turkey ducked its head down again. In the award-winning movie *Sergeant York*, about World War I, York won the contest back home by rendering a perfect imitation of a turkey call. The bait heard it, and got so curious the turkey stuck its head far up, so York's marksmanship won the contest.

The turkey's scientific name is misleading and confusing. In *Meleagis gallopavo* the genus name is from the Greek *meleagridos*, which is a type of guinea fowl, which the turkey is not. The species name is from the Latin *gallus*, a male poultry, plus the Latin *pavo*, a peacock; the turkey is neither of these.

Turkeys have earned themselves into our culture, To be a turkey is something undesirable. Blunt plain talk is talking cold turkey. To quit a bad habit abruptly is to quit cold turkey. Articulate clearly enunciated speech is talking turkey. Turkey trot is a certain dance step. If a stage play is a failure, it is a turkey. Turkey-beard and turkey blossom are herbs. The turkey-beard gets its name from an odd dense tuft of leaves reclining at the base of the stem, reminiscent of that peculiar tuft of long feathers hanging down from the breast of a turkey. Turkey corn is squirrel corn. Turkey red is a red cotton cloth. A pompous person is said to be proud as a turkey.

So the turkey, wild or domesticated, has won a firm place in our culture, even though it hasn't won any popularity contest.

II. PARLOR GUIDE TO MORE BIRDS

Combative Coot

This news item appeared in the *St. Paul* (Minn.) *Daily News* for Oct. 13, 1933, on page 13, column 5: "Basset, Nebr., Oct. 13–When Joe Murer goes hunting he doesn't need a gun. Crouched in a blind at Fish Lake Murer saw two coots coming from opposite directions at terrific speed. They crashed in midair and fell in front of him–the impact killing them both."

It implies that that hunter was hunting coots as well as ducks, but I doubt it, for the usual hunter disdains coots as food–unless he was hungry, needy, or not fastidious. It seems the reason for his prejudice is that coots are omnivorous, eating various plants, algae and slime, small fish, snails, worms, insects, even feathers off dead ducks. A creature's meat gets its taste from what it has been feeding on.

So hunters of waterfowl shoot ducks, which are eaters of grain and water plants, hence they don't threaten coots. As a result, when a birder visits a pond or small lake, as soon as his car stops the ducks fly off but the coots remain. When this happens even out of season, it may indicate to a game warden how many poachers visit that area.

When a coot does fly, two observations are noteworthy. One is that as it takes off it does not leap out of the water vertically, but splatters over the water horizontally with wings flapping and feet pounding the water, running some distance before being able to leave the surface of the water. And they must fly in a straight line, not veering to either side. In flight they must fly straight, not zig-zagging or twisting or turning like a swallow or flycatcher or mourning dove.

That trait caused the death of one coot I saw that was too unmaneuverable in its flight to avoid hitting a strand of a barbed wire fence strung across this pond. Its wing tangled with the strand of wire. There it dangled, struggling feebly

In migration, coots never fight, but live together amicably.
Photograph by Aaron Van Ningen

until death freed it from its agony.

Their inability to swerve will explain why that pair of coots crashed in midair as reported in the 1933 news item reprinted at the head of this article.

For the etiologically inclined linguists, the Latin word for coot is *fulica*, which explains the American coot's scientific name, *Fulica americana*.

A Midwestern slough is a noisy place. Most of the racket comes from the coots. If they aren't splashing across the water they are hiding in the tule or cattails or reeds, making outlandish sounds. People have attempted to describe them using words such as grunting, squawking, croaking, coughing, plunks, sawing, filing, kuk-kuk-kuk, grating, coo-coo-coo-coo. Each sound means something, and is used for some specific purpose, I am sure. This writer has not lingered there long enough to assign each sound to some specific action or circumstance. There are many other slough birds contributing to the cacophony of the wetlands, but the coot is the singer with the greatest repertoire.

The young coot is very active as soon as it is hatched. As

the chick runs around, it looks like a black ball of down, with very big feet and a brilliant red head, of the same color as that of a red-headed woodpecker. The crown is bald, revealing the red of the skin which is due to the red blood vessels, the same color as the red bill. If the young one dies the red of the bill and crown promptly disappears as blood circulation ceases. The side and back of the head is a similar red but due to red feathers. That seems to be the only patch of red color to be found on the marsh floor.

The adult coot, of course, is a drab dark slate-gray except for the bright white on its rear end, which the male flaunts during his courtship display, plus a gray white on its bill and frontal shield.

As the chick grows up the skin of the forehead seems to fade and thicken to form a callus (the Latin word for hard skin), which is now called the frontal shield. The Internet says the size depends on the amount of testosterone in the blood stream, which determines the aggressiveness of the bird.

Being aggressive, coots fight a lot, whether for mates, or to attack intruders, or to chase away potential rivals. If neither bird retreats the result may be "hand-to-hand" combat; they strike with their bills and feet and rake with their claws. They grab their opponents' feet with their bills, trying to hold the other coot under water to drown.

So the frontal shield is a badge of aggression, the white rump is used as a flag to arouse the female, and its muscular build used in fighting a lot with other coots. This bird is always unyielding in flight or in fight.

We Felt Sorry For That Sora

My father enjoyed taking our family for Sunday afternoon rides in his pride and joy, that 1924 Willys-Knight four-door touring car "with sleeve-valve engine." So it was on that sunny May 14, 1933 afternoon we were touring the country roads outside of St. Paul, Minnesota that I urgently called him to stop. I jumped out of the car to retrieve this bird I spied behaving strangely in the ditch beside the road, flopping and somersaulting, unable to control its movements.

I picked it up, put it in the car, and we drove home with it. I had never seen such a bird before. Our little pocket field guide, Chester Reed's 1906 book, *Bird Guide Water Birds, Game Birds and Birds of Prey*, identified it as bird number 214, the Carolina rail, or sora.

Monday I took it to my high school biology teacher. The *St. Paul Daily News* wrote an article about it on May 28. Upon its death the teacher took it to her mentor at the University of Minnesota, where it was confirmed that it was a victim of lead poisoning.

Lead shot, used by hunters at that time, is now illegal. Instead, steel shot is used today.

When shot is spent it ends up on or within the surface of the marsh, where the sora feeds on seeds, insects and other aquatic invertebrates, so it is natural for the sora to regard a piece of lead shot as a seed. Having a shorter bill than the Virginia rail, this Carolina rail would probe more superficially in the mud than its larger relative with its longer bill, so would concentrate on the level where shot lay.

It has been observed that the sora concentrates on eating seeds in late summer, which is the time that hunters are shooting, who drop shot in the mud for the sora to mistake as seeds.

Why is this marsh dweller, as with its close relatives, called a rail? The *Funk & Wagnalls New Standard Dictionary of the English Language*, copyrighted 1913, reveals that the word comes from the French *rale*, meaning rattle. The rales I have heard in my stethoscope using it as a physician sounded like a crackling. So these birds' name is an attempt to imitate the sound of their voices. The particular call of the sora that is recognized best is its whinnying, a rapid series of notes sung in a descending pitch. For every time I have seen the sora, I have heard its unmistakable whinny many times, for this common bird is secretive and very shy, creeping about among the dense reeds in the marsh, rarely coming out to an open place to show itself, then squeezing in between the reeds again.

Once, volunteering for the Canadian Wildlife Service, we were running the Breeding Bird Census out of Hudson Bay, Saskatchewan. We were on the last stretch of the route, where it went alongside a long reedy marsh, as the dirt road approached the Porcupine Hills. Each year we found this colony of hundreds of yellow-headed blackbirds. But this one year as I was listening to them there suddenly sounded a huge chorus of "descending trills," which commenced and ended abruptly. I attributed that to the blackbirds, but they don't have that song in their repertoire; it never occurred to me at the time that I was hearing soras! For all those voices, I never saw a single sora, which is typical–you hear them but you can't see them.

The marsh reeds grow very close together, so how can a rail slip in between them? Their bodies, it seems, must be laterally compressed, or flattened transversely. That would explain the expression, "skinny as a rail," a term old folks would give to a gangly teenager. Audubon claimed that rails can compress their body so as to squeeze between the stems of marsh plants. Other authors have also mentioned how the body of a rail is flattened, as well

"Skinny as a rail": side-to-side view and front-to-rear view of laterally compressed sora.

as how they will in addition to that press their feathers against their sides. Sibley illustrates this phenomenon on page 247 of his book, *The Sibley Guide to Bird Life & Behavior.*

The sora's scientific name is *Porzana carolina. Porzana* is a Latin name meaning crake. (Crake is an out-of-date name for the sora.) This bird is found all over temperate and tropical North America; the scientist who names it *carolina* must have found it in the area of North or South Carolina, since what is now our Midwest, or Canada, wasn't very accessible in those days for him to explore. Other wide-ranging birds have also been named for the small area in which the bird was first found. Consider, for instance, the Baltimore oriole, or the Cape May warbler.

The sora's body is flat, it hides in a flat marsh, and it falls flat if it eats lead shot.

Whoopee!

For anyone living in Oklahoma, Kansas, Nebraska, or the Dakotas seeing a whooping crane on its migration is a thrill of a lifetime. Each sighting justifies an article in the newspaper, since at this writing barely more than two hundred of these cranes are in existence. Then careful questioning is in order to make sure the observer wasn't looking at a pelican or swan or goose or sandhill crane or whatever.

My records show that 1967 was a memorable year, for I saw the whooping crane twice that year. At Long Lake National Wildlife Refuge, Moffit, North Dakota, seen across the lake, its huge size made all the other birds it was among look like toys. The other sighting was at Aransas National Wildlife Refuge on the Coastal Bend of Texas.

For anyone really interested in seeing whooping cranes, they must go to the Aransas National Wildlife Refuge. There a visitor may climb up the long ramp to the top of the observation tower, which is erected on the edge of the coastal marsh which is the sole wintering range of this biggest bird in the North American fauna. There one may peer through one

Pair of whooping cranes at Aransas National Wildlife Refuge.
Photograph by Patricia Burke

of the powerful telescopes provided, to spot a tiny white speck.

Such a sighting to me is unsatisfactory. Then to get not only a decent look, but to study this bird – a dozen or more of them – we have gone several times on one of the two whooping crane tour boats out of Rockport, Texas.

From port the boat goes out to Aransas Bay, which is between the mainland and the barrier island, San Jose Island. As we join the Intracoastal Waterway, that passage way for barges and other marine commerce that runs from Brownsville, Texas to Boston, Massachusetts, we turn left to follow the Waterway northeast.

Whooping crane standing in marsh grass in Aransas National Wildlife Refuge. Photograph by Patricia Burke

This Intracoastal Waterway runs along the shore of the Aransas National Wildlife Refuge. All along the trip the tour guide gives a running commentary on the rich bird life seen from the boat. But, of course, the climax comes when we see the whooping cranes. At a strategic point the captain runs the bow of the boat up onto the shore, and we feast our eyes on their activities. The beached boat is so close we scarcely need binoculars, and being a stone's throw away we can observe minute detail. By never stepping ashore, and by keeping quiet and moving slowly, the birds have learned to trust our proximity. The crane picks up a blue crab in its bill, savors it, and gulps it down. They walk slowly, majestically, watching constantly for animals but more for trespassing cranes. These birds, we are told, are very territorial. Each pair has a square mile of marsh staked out with very precise boundaries, and chases any other whooping crane that dares to trespass.

Each pair of birds escorts their new born chick, when strong enough to fly, from Wood Buffalo National Park on the northern border of Alberta, Canada. When the trio arrives at Aransas, they reclaim their exact same square mile. As the offspring matures it is no longer welcome and is chased away. The local experts recognize each pair, and have names for them. They mate for life. But one male broke tradition, divorced his wife, and wed another female!

As the population of whooping cranes increased in recent years, the pairs have run out of space on the refuge, and young birds forced out now show interest in the spoil banks formed by dredges which are constantly maintaining adequate depth in the canal, 7 feet or 12 feet, according to locale, for marine traffic. These new islands are formed on the ocean side of the waterway, and quickly become covered with vegetation the cranes should tolerate.

We have enjoyed these boat trips year after year.

Their scientific name, *Grus americana*, is from the Latin word for crane, *grus*. But since its range is restricted to North America, *americana* is appropriate.

So, if you really want to observe whooping cranes, go to Rockport, Texas.

Sandhill Crane

How the sandhill crane got its name is moot, so I herewith give my own explanation.

Firstly, it is named after the Sandhills of Nebraska. That is the largest area in North America occupied by sand hills – treeless hills of sand, held in place by a thin cover of grass and yucca, and covering the huge Ogallala Aquifer, that giant reservoir of sweet water that comes close enough to the surface to result in the presence of scattered lakes and marshes.

Secondly, Nebraska is the site of sandhill crane fossils, identical to today's sandhill cranes. These fossils were laid down in the Miocene Epoch of the Tertiary Period in the Cenozoic Era of geologic time. This makes the sandhill crane at ten million years of age the oldest known bird species still surviving today! Imagine being able to trace your ancestry back 10,000,000 years, even to the same spot on the surface of the earth on which you are standing!

There is a third reason for the sandhill crane to be associated with Nebraska, and that is the eastward flowing North Platte River, world famous because of this bird. This river valley is wide and flat. From late February to early April it harbors as many as 12,000 migrating cranes per half-mile of river. At night they prefer to roost standing in water six inches deep. We have found them in early morning or late afternoon in wet meadows along the river, in crowded dense flocks. Once we saw in their midst a pure white crane, too small to qualify as a whooping crane. It must have been an albino sandhill crane.

Three subspecies are recognized. All three use the North Platte River as a stopover to rest and refuel on their migratory journey. The greater one nests in Minnesota and Manitoba. The Canadian subspecies nests in central Canada from Hudson Bay through Saskatchewan west to the Rocky M/ountains. (We counted them in the Hudson Bay, Sask. and Squaw Rapids Tobin Lake Breeding Bird Surveys.) The lesser subspecies ends up on the tundra of Arctic Canada, Alaska and eastern Siberia. (I have seen this form passing over the Aleutian Islands' westernmost island of Attu.)

These cranes all spend a month on the Platte, where they spend their days flying out to glean farmers' cornfields, picking up kernels of corn which otherwise would have sprouted the next summer as the farmers' unwanted volunteers.

We found the easiest birding to be west of the city of North Platte, Nebraska along U.S. Highway 30, and between that highway and the North Platte River to the south, and by following local roads. Birders throughout North America, and world travelers of that persuasion, are aware of the fame of North Platte River Stopover rest area which presents the spring sandhill spectacle.

On our stays in Rockport, Texas we saw these same birds scattered over the flat moist plains. But their crazy courtship-territorial defense dance was seen best on the flat land along the shore of Tobin Lake in Saskatchewan. There two cranes face each other, spread their wings, jump around, stretch and bow. This ungainly performance seems ridiculous for such a stately dignified bird.

The largest sandhill crane is also the world's largest statue of any crane. It is located in Steele, North Dakota, sponsored and maintained by the World's Largest Sandhill Crane Foundation. The statue was

The World's Largest Sandhill Crane. My son, Bruce, is present to show scale. Photograph by Kenneth J. Johnson

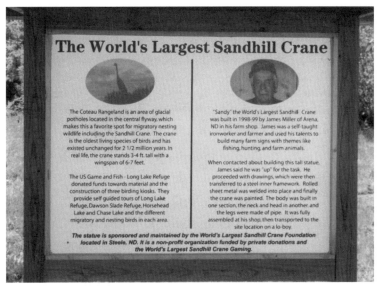

The World's Largest Sandhill Crane

The Coteau Rangeland is an area of glacial potholes located in the central flyway, which makes this a favorite spot for migratory nesting wildlife including the Sandhill Crane. The crane is the oldest living species of birds and has existed unchanged for 2 1/2 million years. In real life, the crane stands 3-4 ft. tall with a wingspan of 6-7 feet.

The US Game and Fish - Long Lake Refuge donated funds towards material and the construction of three birding kiosks. They provide self guided tours of Long Lake Refuge, Dawson Slade Refuge, Horsehead Lake and Chase Lake and the different migratory and nesting birds in each area.

"Sandy" the World's Largest Sandhill Crane was built in 1998-99 by James Miller of Arena, ND in his farm shop. James was a self-taught ironworker and farmer and used his talents to build many farm signs with themes like fishing, hunting, and farm animals.

When contacted about building this tall statue, James said he was "up" for the task. He proceeded with drawings, which were then transferred to a steel inner framework. Rolled sheet metal was welded into place and finally the crane was painted. The body was built in one section, the neck and head in another, and the legs were made of pipe. It was fully assembled at his shop, then transported to the site location on a lo-boy.

The statue is sponsored and maintained by the World's Largest Sandhill Crane Foundation located in Steele, ND. It is a non-profit organization funded by private donations and the World's Largest Sandhill Crane Gaming.

Sign board explaining the sandhill crane statue. Photograph by Kenneth J. Johnson

made by James Miller of Arena, North Dakota in his farm shop. It consists of a steel inner framework covered by pieces of rolled sheet metal welded together, and painted a true-to-life gray. The steel hoop on the back of the statue was hoisted by a crane (derrick) to maneuver the body of the crane (bird effigy) into position onto the legs.

The sandhill crane has a bald forehead. When the bird is relaxed and submissive, that area is a pale red. But when the crane becomes angry, the blood vessels dilate and fill with blood, so the forehead becomes a bright red. So now, as any sandhill crane flying by inspects this statue, we can imagine that its opinion of the statue will cause its bald forehead to become a pale red, indicating submission or approval, not a bright red from the relaxed engorged blood vessels, which indicate anger or disapproval.

Incidentally, any reddish-brown tint to the gray body feathers is due to iron oxide stain from preening with a bill that is covered with vegetation and mud, since the feathers themselves when clean are plain gray.

Killdeer, Avian Actor

For years I have pondered over one of my great mysteries of life. Wilson's plover, semipalmated plover, snowy plover, piping plover all have one black band on their neck, but killdeer has two black bands. Of course, the killdeer, being ten inches in size instead of six or seven, has more room on its longer neck for black bands. But the baby killdeer has only one black band when hatched, same as those other plovers. So when and how does the second band appear on the adult?

Ken Kaufman's field guide, *Birds of North America*, finally provided the clue to solve this mystery. It seems that as the young chick grows in size the lone neck band starts to grow a few white feathers down the middle of the black band, which feathers are joined by more and more white feathers, which then form a white band down the middle, splitting the black band into those two black bands that are sported by the adult bird. So now with that solved, we may proceed to more marvelous aspects of this interesting bird.

There are a number of species of birds that use the broken wing display to distract predators away from the nest and its eggs. Examples are plovers, killdeer, several grouse, and poorwill, in particular.

Bent describes the defense shown by a wounded poorwill. It opened its large mouth wide, hissed and blew, and flopped about, always facing the enemy. (*Life Histories of North American Cuckoos, Goatsuckers, Hummingbirds and Their Allies*, page 191.)

In Bent's *Life Histories of North American Gallinaceous Birds*, page 15, he relates an incident when a bobwhite flew up to the observer and "tumbled" at his feet uttering a shrill whistle, while its covey of young birds flew in all directions.

Again in discussing the protection the mountain quail provides its young he writes, "If the little ones are of a tender age and the need is great, the parent will fling itself down at your feet and go through the familiar decoy motions." (Page 47.)

In describing an exhibition of parental solicitude, this

account relates how a party came upon a brood of Montezuma quail. "At the moment of discovery, the parent bird rose up, and then, tumbling back helplessly to the ground, imitated so successfully the actions of a wounded and disabled bird that, for a moment, I thought she must have been trodden upon by one of our mules. Some of the men...attempted to catch her...until a dozen yards away...she rose and was off like a bullet." (Page 87.)

The American golden plover feigned a broken wing when the writer quoted by Bent came within sixty yards of its nest. (*Life Histories of North American Shore Birds*, page 196.)

The black-bellied plover also defends its nest by wing-dragging and distress calls (page 160).

But T. S. Roberts in his *Birds of Minnesota* declares the killdeer to be the most expert bird to perform the broken wing display. I cannot improve on his description of its acting ability, so I quote from Roberts' volume 1, page 465: "A few feet from the nest it falls flat on the ground as though hopelessly crushed, and crying piteously. If followed it revives sufficiently to limp along, dragging first one wing and then the other, tail spread widely, displaying the showy lateral feathers and the tawny rump in a most alluring way."

The nest, which is the object from which the killdeer lures away any intruder, is only a trivial depression on barren ground with a bleak scattering of debris nearby. Since the nest is exposed to the hot sun, the killdeer has been known to wet its belly with water to cool the eggs in hot weather.

Since civilization has eliminated some of the killdeer's nesting sites, this adaptable bird has occasionally taken to laying its eggs on the flat gravel roof of a building. This site seemed to suffice until it was time for the young to leave the roof. How do they get off the roof? But the young can jump fifty feet to the ground and scamper away unharmed, reminiscent of a wood duck nestling jumping out of the wood duck's hole in its tall tree, to land on the ground safely.

The killdeer is a very beneficial bird for the farmer, eating insects harmful to agriculture, plus an occasional angleworm. Roberts records an amusing incident. A small group was feeding on muddy ground. One of them was having a hard time dragging out a long angleworm, when it was attacked by one of its neighbors trying to steal the prey. Quickly the first bird placed its worm on the ground and sat on it until the second bird went away. Then it stood up and ate the angleworm.

Whereas only a few people have been fortunate enough to have witnessed its broken wing display, every prairie birder has heard the vociferous "kill-dee-a" repeatedly. The New Englanders who heard that call named the bird killdeer, since they cannot pronounce the letter ar. (Similarly, in the Easterners' dialect, the call of a crow is the same as the other name of an automobile, is it not?)

The scientific name of the killdeer is *Charadrius vociferous.* The species name certainly is appropriate for this vociferous bird. But the genus name is from the Greek *kharadrios* meaning a bird living in clefts, derived from the Greek *kharadra*, meaning a ravine. Such a misnomer is inexplicable.

A thought in conclusion: If there were an annual avian Oscar Award for best performing actor, the killdeer surely would be a nominee for its broken wing display.

A killdeer, the best avian actor, performing its broken wing display.
Photograph by Aaron Van Ningen

North Dakota's Loyal Peep

A peep, as any birder will tell you, is a small sandpiper. These several species of shore birds are all less than nine inches long, all look alike, and are constantly moving, so it is so hard to tell them apart that many birders give up and call all of them peeps, in imitation of their voices.

But one, the spotted sandpiper, deserves a special place in the hearts of North Dakota's birders. Other peeps show up in flocks from somewhere south of here, always in a desperate rush, never stopping their frantic feeding to pause, then disappear northwards to Canada. Then in late summer they repeat the same performance with the same attitude in their mad rush southward.

A number of the spotted sandpipers drop off in North Dakota, though, and stay here to breed and raise their young. So don't they merit our special admiration? The more we learn about them the more interesting this bird turns out to be.

Its scientific name, *Actitis macularia*, is derived from the Latin *actitatus* meaning quick and frequent action (that's a characteristic of peeps, isn't it?); and *macularia* is from the Latin for spot. The spotted sandpiper is the only one with large black spots on its white breast in its breeding plumage.

Unlike most other peeps, the spotted sandpiper never flocks, and the females winter farther north closer to the summer breeding area, so it can arrive there earlier in the spring to gain an advantage in choice of site.

For some obscure reason this species is continuously moving its tail up and down. A hatchling emerging from its egg even starts moving its tail that way. The only time this action ceases is during the courtship display. Then the suitor spreads its tail, erects its head, and calls weet, weet, weet. Next it moves its wings forward and downward, and prances rapidly toward the intended mate, who then preens its feathers unconcernedly. It was assumed by naturalists that the aggressor was male, until by shooting that individual and dissecting it, found it to be female! Up to five nesting sites are chosen, and this dominant female lays four eggs in each of them. Then she incubates one nest herself while each of the males she had chosen incubates his particular nest. On hatching, each parent protects its own hatchlings for a few days until the little ones can fend for themselves. This is polyandry at its ultimate.

Its flight is distinctive. It repeatedly says peet-weet as it flies with shallow stiff fluttering wings which are curved in profile, pointing downwards below the horizontal. When migrating or in crossing a sizable body of water, however, this bird reverts to the conventional method of flight, which is speedier.

Another unique habit is when being chased, in desperation the baby or the adult may dive into the water and swim submerged, or even walk on the bottom like a dipper or water ouzel! While submerged it can be traced by noting the shiny little air bubbles clinging to its body.

This loyal North Dakotan-born native is truly a fascinating peep. Some women's rights organization should adopt it as their mascot!

Long-billed Curlew

Curlew Valley is west of Almont, in Morton County, North Dakota. It was named by settlers in the 1800s because the valley contains Big Muddy Creek which winds around to create the ideal deep grassy hollows which long-billed curlews prefer for their nests.

Bent quotes records of ornithologists who told of huge numbers in the prairies in the 1800s, making wistful reading for one who finds no more of them today in their former habitat. For one reason, a fatal habit these birds shared with other shore birds was when a hunter shot a few the flock kept circling around to return to the same spot, each time losing a few more to the gun.

The female did the brooding while the male stood guard. When an intruder approached, the bird sounded a noisy alarm as it charged through the air at the disturber. When close to the nest, the curlew performed the same broken wing act for which the killdeer is famous. Little birds flushed from the nest would run a few feet and crouch motionless, the various shades of brown in the plumage rendering them invisible until they moved again.

Of course, the baby chick's bill is short like those of other baby chicks, but then it begins its odd elongation. The

LONG-BILLED CURLEW:
"SO IT HURTS TO PICK SOMETHING UP? WELL, I DON'T HAVE TO BEND OVER!"

bill ends up over three times as long as the head. Pinocchio, whose nose grew longer every time he told a lie, would have to become a confirmed prevaricator to match the long-billed curlew.

What's the logic for having such an excessively long bill? In the mixed-grass prairie of the Dakotas and Montana, we see no reason for it when the bugs and berries it eats are in plain sight. But in winter-time on the Gulf Coast prairie of Texas they spend their time near the beach feeding on the inter-tidal tiny invertebrates. Here their long bills can travel down long burrows, where the muscles in their flexible bill can maneuver the tunnel all the way to its prey.

In our experience the greatest trouble we had in Texas was in confusing the long-billed curlew with the whimbrel, for both birds were similar in shape, size and color; it develops that it takes time for this curlew's bill to grow longer than the whimbrel's bill. A better differential is to note the black and white stripes on the crown of the whimbrel, noted only if it tips its head just so. Most all the birds at Rockport and Galveston were curlews. In North Dakota a whimbrel is rarely seen passing through in late May or early June going to its home near the Arctic Ocean.

One of the whistles in this curlew's repertoire is the "curleuu" of three second duration, which gave it its name. The scientific name, *Numenius americanus*, is from the Greek word *noumenios* meaning curlew; *americanus*, of course, means American.

This summer you will no longer find a long-billed curlew in Curlew Valley. Try looking for it in back country near Marmarth, North Dakota.

With Eyes In The Back Of Its Head

An owl can see behind it by whipping its head around 180 degrees in a split second. The adult woodcock can see behind it without having to whip its head around, for the woodcock's eyes are set so high and so far back in its head that it can see behind very well without turning its head. Other birds can see behind by turning their heads to the side and looking with one eye. But the woodcock with bill pointed forward can see behind with binocular vision, since it can see behind with both eyes simultaneously!

View from above of nesting woodcock showing its eyes set far enough back on its head so it can see both forward and backward without turning its head.

Such a singular ability enables it to bore two inches down into muddy ground with its bill in its quest for food such as angleworms. By seeing behind it can keep watch for enemies, enabling it to extract its bill in time to fly away before it can be harmed.

With eyes set high and back on the head they are out of the way of splattering mud and vegetation as it explores boggy thickets.

On April 12, 2007 following up on reports that there was a woodcock cuddled up against the south-facing wall of the Heritage Center Building in Bismarck, North Dakota, I was told to look out of a certain window. Craning my neck I could see nothing, until I finally made out a pair of eyes. Extrapolating towards me from them I made out the back of the woodcock. It was motionless except for slight fidgeting, proving it was alive. Its protective coloring was marvelous. I was able to see its eyes by looking at the back of its head! It was able to subsist on life in the five inch wide thawed soil between the building and the frozen snow-covered ground.

Its narrow tubular bill, almost two inches long, has its terminal upper mandible flexible, so it can grasp angleworms in the soil. They are also detected by feel by the sensitive bill.

The American woodcock has its eyes set farthest back on its head of any bird.
Photograph by John W. Hoganson

The angleworms are first brought near the surface of the soil by stamping the feet to simulate patter of the rain.

Where and when the woodcock does this is marked by 5 mm. sized holes its bill makes in the muddy ground, which are called bore holes.

The woodcock is active after sunset, before sunrise, and during moonlight. I saw it once during the day, however, at Sica Hollow in northeast South Dakota during dark gloomy weather due to dense cloud cover, when it flew up abruptly, displaying its orange underside and tail as it rose.

In the woodcock's scientific name, *Scolopax minor,* the generic portion is from the Greek *scolopax* meaning woodcock. The specific name *minor* refers to the smaller size of the 11 inch American woodcock compared to the 13-1/2 inch sized European woodcock of the same genus. The latter bird that I saw at Bymarka, Norway on June 19, 1998 was much easier to observe, being in broad daylight.

The incredible complex courtship of this bird with strutting, flying up, flying down, making noise with its flight feathers, and singing I described in the chapter entitled, Birds That Make Sounds With Wing Or Tail. Unfortunately, this courtship display is performed only after dark, so it is very hard to see.

The woodcock is recognized by hunters as one of the best game birds, so in early days their large numbers were killed recklessly with no thought of moderation or conservation for future generations. Bent (on page 73 of his book, *Life Histories of North American Shore Birds*) records one sportsman as shooting 125 in one day. The person that shot the most birds was considered the biggest hero, and each hunter strove to outdo the other.

Predators have taken their toll for centuries without diminishing the population, and they took only the weak, the injured, and the elderly. But hunters take the robust, those most capable of preserving the vigor of the race.

On page 67 of his book Bent documents the odd trait of the woodcock, where in wet or cold weather both birds sit on the nest at the same time! Huddling closely, they face in opposite directions with bills pointing diagonally upwards. That unparalleled maneuver is fitting for this vanguard of early spring migrants, which must adapt to the cold weather.

Its incredibly remarkable camouflage is so excellent that the woodcock must feel confident it cannot be seen, so it may sit motionless on its nest regardless of how close a person gets. One photographer even removed two leaves which were resting on the bill of a nesting woodcock, so he could get a better picture.

So the woodcock is incredible for four reasons: (1) the eyes on the back of its head; (2) the narrowed stiff three outer primaries which whistle; (3) the flexible outer third of the upper mandible; and (4) the entire complex courtship display.

Bird With Zebra-colored Armpits

The most singular part of the plumage of the snipe is in the "armpits." The axillaries, the feathers of the axilla, are zebra colored, with stripes of jet black on a snow white background. Only the snipe and the long-billed and short-billed dowitchers have these surprising feathers, in a spot where one usually can't see them. I was first aware of them as I preserved feathers in my notebook on May 1, 1938 from a snipe. I had plucked them from a specimen I found "recently dead with eaten breast" near St Paul, Minnesota. This bird was not a dowitcher because

Feathers from Wilson's snipe, left to right: back, under left wing, tail. Life size.
Photograph by Kenneth J. Johnson

its tail feather had much red on it, and the edge of the back feather showed the white stripe of the snipe. (See photograph.)

What is the survival value of this unique feature, hidden from view? My theory is that in courtship the male struts about the female displaying by raising his wings to flash the brilliant black and white pattern before her galvanized eyes.

If so, this was a fruitful feature, for when our civilization came to North America snipe were "exceedingly abundant," to quote *Bent in his Life Histories of North American Shore Birds, part one.* But such a plethora of game birds was not to last, since hunters from 1850 to 1900 slaughtered them. Aside from the market hunters, so-called gentlemen sportsmen shot just for the fun of it as rapidly and as long as they could. One such game hog is credited with over 76,000 snipe. His best day was 366 snipe in six hours. That massacre came about in spite of the bird's habit of zigging and zagging in flight, making it hard for a marksman to hit.

The term sniper, used for a concealed sharpshooter who shoots individuals, originated from the marksman hunter able to shoot a snipe with ease.

The scientific name is a misnomer. *Gallinago gallinago* is from the Latin *gallina*, meaning a poultry hen. A snipe is not a gallinaceous bird and doesn't look like nor is related to a pheasant or a chicken. That ornithologist certainly blundered, it seems to me.

In my 1938 notebook I called it Wilson's snipe, its name at that time. Bent in his 1927 book called it Wilson's snipe, *Capella gallinago delicata*. Then the name changed to common snipe, the name used by today's field guides. Now as of 2006 it is being called Wilson's snipe, with its scientific name changed to *G. delicata*, as its European counterpart continues to be *G. gallinago*. The Wilson's snipe species name *delicata* is from the Latin *delicatus*, which means pleasing.

The main justification for splitting into a new species would be that the Wilson's snipe, the American bird, has sixteen tail feathers; the common snipe of Europe has fourteen tail feathers.

Wilson's snipe, with more tail feathers than any other shore bird, uses them to good advantage. When this bird winnows up high in the air, as it dives it spreads its tail feathers so wide that the outermost feather on each side makes almost a 180 degree angle with its counterpart on the other side. Then the narrow spaces of air between the feathers cause the barbules on the vane of the feather to vibrate, to make that tremulous whistling sound called winnowing.

One of the great thrills in birding is to hear the so-called winnowing of a snipe. In the early morning especially, hear that faint tremulous whistle from high in the air. Searching the sky carefully one may find the barely visible bird. This repeated performance is interpreted as a courtship display. Somewhere in the marsh below is a female.

When I was a boy, Boy Scouts had a custom when

camping to persuade a greenhorn to go out at night in a marsh with an opened gunny sack to catch a snipe.

That lad needed both hands to hold the sack open for throwing over the snipe, so he could not manage a flashlight. Stumbling in the dark, if he did approach a snipe it would stay well hidden (even if it were broad daylight) until nearly stepped on, then flush abruptly before the lad could snare it.

In spite of all adversities, Wilson's snipe has been able still to be regarded as common.

Ferocious Feces-Eater

The three species of jaegers all nest circumpolar, on the Arctic tundra in both hemispheres. They are closely related to gulls. Although about the same size, they are pirates that prey on the gulls, eating their eggs and young and robbing the adults of their food. Instead of the blue or black mantle of gulls, juvenile jaegers are dark brown, while adults have dark brown tails and backs, yellow necks, and white bellies.

The scientific name of the long-tailed jaeger is *Stercorarius longicaudus*, in which the genus name is from the Greek word *stercocarius* which pertains to feces and carrion, or the Latin *stercoris* meaning feces or dung. The species name *longicaudus* is a combination of the Latin *longus* for long and the Latin *cauda* for tail.

But calling the long-tailed jaeger an eater of feces is an exaggeration, since dung and offal are just a minor part of its diet. It eats much more carrion, which is decaying meat. It also hunts lemmings, mice and other small mammals, and eggs and small birds. There is a thin line between game, flesh and meat on the one hand and carrion and offal on the other hand. The former becomes the latter as soon as decay sets in, which is very shortly after death.

The most typical memory a birder has of this bird is of it chasing a flying gull and harassing it until the gull must regurgitate its food. The gull then escapes as the jaeger concentrates on eating the gull's meal. A rare feature that makes the jaeger such a superior flyer is the tuft of projecting feathers at the elbow of the wing. This advancement has been found to prevent turbulence over the upper surface of the wing. The

A long-tailed jaeger (Stercocarius longicaudus) in flight.
Photograph by Tore Wuttudal

illustration on the previous page shows this clearly.

If a jaeger is shot and is badly wounded, other jaegers have been known to attack it, kill it and eat it (page 26, in Bent's Life *Histories of North American Gulls and Terns*).

Such a vicious and aggressive nature is carried over to its nesting grounds on the tundra, where it will attack anything that approaches its nest that contains eggs not yet hatched. Even humans are attacked, the jaeger flying into the person's face, swerving only as it is about to strike. After the young hatch they are active and capable of hiding, so the parents are less aggressive in their defense then.

The English name, jaeger, is more accurate for this bird than the scientific genus name, for jaeger is Norwegian for hunter. Being Norwegian, the word is pronounced yayger. In Europe jaegers are all named skuas.

The field guides all list three jaegers. As for me, every jaeger I see becomes a struggle as to which jaeger it is. They all look alike, and the one at hand never lingers long enough for me to scrutinize details to diagnose which species. Of course, if it has that ridiculously long tail that is as long as the rest of its body, which distinguishes it from the pomarine jaeger and the parasitic jaeger, there is no problem, But juveniles and non-breeding ones of that species don't have that long tail.

Maybe the range of the species will be an aid to its identity. Take the jaeger I saw cruising over the marsh west of the water tower, on the Laguna Madre side of South Padre Island, Texas north of the city on January 11, 1999. Sibley would call the long-tailed jaeger rare at that location. Sibley says the parasitic jaeger is regular there in the winter time, but the pomarine jaeger's winter range is regular only far off shore, not visible from shore. So would one lone bird be a lucky rarity or a common one?

There is no question about the identity of the long-tailed jaeger we saw in Alaska's Mount McKinley National Park on July 22, 1959, however. Sibley's range map shows the summer range of the long-tailed jaeger extending into that national park. Neither summer range of the parasitic or pomarine jaeger comes close to extending into the interior of Alaska. The closest limit of the parasitic jaeger's summer range is over 300 miles away to the west from the park. The closest that the summer range of the pomarine jaeger to the north comes to the park is over 500 miles away. And seeing the long-tailed jaeger in July in the national park is the best time a birder can enjoy the sight of that long tail that is the feature of its breeding courtship plumage.

Unfortunately, a tourist today is severely restricted as to where he can travel in the park. He must travel in a crowded scheduled bus along the highway and cannot wander away from it. In 1959 we drove our car alone, unhampered as to where we could walk.

Jaegers, and only adult jaegers, are the only adult ocean birds that sport yellow in their plumage. The neck has a strong but pale yellow tint, making it easy to distinguish them from other birds of the ocean. Wilson's storm petrel has brilliant yellow on the webs between its toes, but no yellow in its feathers.

Our opinion of jaegers is that they have a repulsive choice of food and obnoxious behavior, but make a prized addition to a birder's life list.

Pacific Islanders' Best Loved Bird

It was during World War II that I first knew about the fairy tern. On our way to the Battle of Okinawa, our troop ship rendezvoused at an atoll never mentioned by news media. There a fortunate few of us managed to enjoy shore leave. The wind-blown palm trees were leaning far over. On the bare trunk of one palm a small egg was resting, defying gravity by not rolling off.

Tending to it was this pair of small snow-white birds, whose every movement in their flight as they hovered there exuded daintiness and elegant beauty. What a respite from war!

My reaction to this bird was like that of everyone else who is privileged to make its acquaintance.

The first thing noticeable is its brilliant white plumage, with never a dark or off-white feather to mar the pure whiteness. This is further set off by black feet, black bill, and black eyes accentuated by the jet black ring around each eye, giving the eyes a soulful look.

Then their every movement confirms an air of elegance and grace as they flap their wings noiselessly, flutter about daintily, or hover in one spot magically.

They endear themselves as they sometimes seek out and follow people, hovering just above one's head as they murmur pleasing musical sounds as if they were crooning affectionately.

And after studying their ways and actions, men have found no disgusting or distasteful habits to criticize.

But scientists are matter-of-fact and all business, not romantic or poetic. So the fairy tern's scientific name became *Gygis alba*, from the Greek word *gugis* for a water bird, and the Latin *albus* for white.

This tern is also called the white tern, or love tern.

When I was on Oahu before assignment to the U.S. Tenth Army for shipping west to combat in Okinawa, I saw no fairy terns. And when my wife and I lived on Oahu after the war was over, we saw no fairy terns there. But today, the Internet says, fairy terns are the most common and most loved seabird on Oahu. It seems these opportunistic birds since the 1960s have found nesting sites in many places in Honolulu and elsewhere on the island. A main reason is that humans have planted ironwood trees here – a pine-like species of tree that grows wild on Western Pacific islands. This is one of this bird's favorite trees for holding its eggs.

It appears that Oahu is promising to have a population boom for this bird, for it has been noted that some pairs stay there year-round and nest twice or thrice a year, using nesting sites so much more favorable for their egg that their broods' survival rate is much higher than in Western Pacific islands. So it is not surprising that in 2007 the mayor of Honolulu announced the designation of this white tern as the official bird of that city.

Oahu is not the only island where this phenomenon, the extension of its nesting range, is taking place. In the U.S.A. Trust Territory of the Mariana Islands, my friend, R. S. has lived part time for several years, specifically on the island of Saipan. While there he noted there are a good number of pairs of fairy terns. They are in town, in parks and among trees in yards, in addition to their historic brushy habitat. The ironwood is native to Saipan, but when Americans built their houses they planted ironwoods in their yards, which brought the fairy terns into close proximity.

They feed on minnow-sized fish which have been driven to the ocean's surface by large predaceous fish. The little fish are caught either by dipping the surface or by plunge diving.

The dexterity of its bill is remarkable, for it can catch small fish one at a time, line them up crosswise in its bill, carry them a long distance back to its fuzz-ball chick, and feed them one at a time to it without spilling!

While breeding they remain near by, to shorten the trips to feed the young one. But after it has grown the western islanders disappear, no one knows where, the same ones only to reappear at the same nesting site next year.

The pictured award-winning photograph was taken by the late professional photographer and bird lover, Bower Rudrud, of Bismarck, N. D. when he was on Midway Island researching material for a wildlife film.

In conclusion, here is a pearl for the birding aficionado: What do fairy terns and polar bears have in common? They both have black skin.

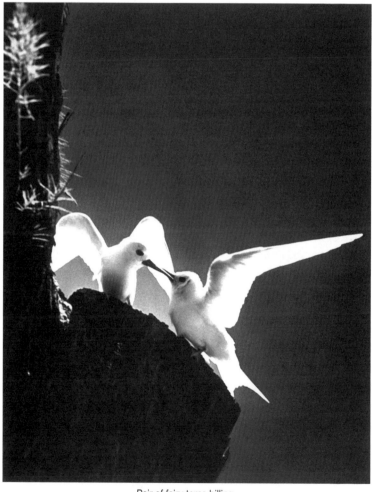

Pair of fairy terns billing.
Award-winning photograph taken on Midway Island by Bower Rudrud.

Presentation Of Profound Prognathism

A facial surgeon told me he would probably be shocked and challenged if he saw a patient whose lower jaw stuck out 1-1/4 inches beyond the upper lip of his face. That is the comparable degree of prognathism the black skimmer has.

How does such an oddity come about? How does the bird with such a phenomenon adapt to it? It seems that the black skimmer hatchling has a normal bill, and picks up the regurgitated fish its parent presents for it from its opened bill, or from the ground. Later they are taught to eat more solid food, such as small fish, the conventional way.

The longer lower mandible of the adult does not develop until the young one nears adulthood and has learned to skim the surface of the water as demonstrated by the adults. Then the lower mandible quickly starts to grow longer and longer, until the skimmer can no longer peck like other birds. However, if need be it can still pick up food from the ground by tipping its head sideways and closing its bill on the food like a pincers. It is believed that friction from the lower bill skimming the water wears down the lower bill, so Nature compensates by stimulating the bill to grow faster.

The adult feeds on the wing by skimming the smooth water with its long rigid lower mandible. As animal food touches the inside of the lower bill it is felt, and the movable upper bill opens and closes on the morsel.

It is said that the black skimmer feeds mostly at night, but during broad daylight we have enjoyed watching it skimming the water of Bolivar Pass, along the ship channel at Galveston, Texas. While there we also enjoyed watching ships from all over the world passing through the Bolivar Pass ship channel to visit Texas City and Houston on Galveston Bay.

The black skimmers were prominent sitting on the sandy shore of the channel, in a tight flock, all facing the same direction, all in their colorful plumage of black tail, back and crown; white nape, forehead, neck and breast; huge bright orange bill with black tip; and small red feet.

Adult black skimmer, with jutting lower bill. Photograph by Patricia Burke

The scientific name, *Rynchops niger*, is fitting, for *rhunkhos*, its generic derivative, is Greek for beak, and *ops* is Greek meaning appearance, since the appearance of a person is determined largely by the look of their face. The Latin word *niger* is translated as black.

The black skimmer is one of the birds that are amazing and incredible.

Tufted Puffin

Nine species of shearwaters all have *Puffinus* as their
generic scientific name, which is a Latinized form of the
English word puffin. Why this is so is a mystery locked up in
the mind of the scientist who used the name, since about the
only similarity of the two, shearwater and puffin, is that they
both are ocean birds. The true puffin is named so because it
has a puffed-out beak, which shearwaters lack.

That puffed-out beak is an
understatement, for during the breeding
season the beak of the tufted puffin is 2¼
inches in diameter, massive for a bird 15
inches long. It is not surprising that people
have called this bird sea parrot and clown
of the sea. The outer half of this huge
schnozzle is bright red, the same color as its
feet. The inner portion is brownish orange,
except for a spot at the corner of the mouth
which is its black skin, matching its black

Above: Winter,
non-breeding
Below: Summer,
breeding

body. This inner portion of the bill is large and high enough
to form a straight edge from the red part up to the top of the
head. After the breeding season this orange part falls off to
reveal the permanently narrower portion of the inner bill,
black to match the black body. The entire bill is very flat for
its size, laterally compressed.

The purpose of this monstrosity, I surmise, is to attract
a mate. But both species grow this odd attachment, and in
other birds it is only the male that has a courtship adornment.
Perhaps it provides a longer edge to the bill so more fish can
be carried to the nest. The puffin is expert in holding a dozen
fish side by side between its mandibles. That way they can
make longer foraging trips and take home more food to their
young one. In courtship this puffin rubs the long bills together
to male a sound that must please the mate.

The lone chick may be hidden in one of two types of
nests. If the steep shore which the puffin chooses has soil, the

baby may be at the end of a burrow some four feet long. This is tunneled out by using the claws of their webbed feet. The inner claw is largest and the most curved, making the moving of dirt most efficient.

The other type of nest is in a steep rocky shore. Here the puffin lays its lone egg far in between the large rocks or boulders. One visitor to the colony related how on approaching in a boat each young one peeked out from between the large rocks, their white natal fuzzy feathers making them look like a group of little old whiskered men. Such a haven among immovable boulders was safe from all predators except rats dropped off when men came ashore. After men visit an island where these puffins nest, the rats and cats left behind exterminate the birds.

Puffins nest in colonies, but during the rest of the year they spend all their time far away from land. At sea they stay in flocks, feeding when awake and floating when asleep.

The tufted puffin gets its name from the long curved tuft of yellow feathers arising from the side of the head. This tuft, reaching down past the neck so far as to touch the back, falls off after the breeding season, leaving only a few short strings of dark yellow that are hard to see. Although the tuft is less conspicuous than that huge gaudy beak, the man that gave it its scientific name mentioned the tuft but ignored the beak.

In the scientific name, *Fratercula cirrhata*, the specific name is from the Latin meaning curled, referring to the curve in the long tuft. The generic name is also from the Latin, meaning little brother. It also means a friar because this puffin clasps its feet together in its flight after it rises from the sea. The person who named it must have been of a religious bent, for that peculiar trait reminded him of a friar clasping his hands together in prayer. If the puffin really were thanking the Lord for becoming airborne, it would be because it has such a hard time taking off.

Puffins are built for underwater swimming. They flap their short wings to move fast, and clasp their feet as a rudder, or use them as paddles. To leave the water they must run along the surface for a long way, flying right through waves as they do when swimming below the surface. Gaining enough speed to rise above the waves is a struggle.

The first time we saw this bird was in the Strait of Juan de Fuca, when riding on the ferry between Washington state and Vancouver Island, British Columbia, in July, 1970. It lives year round along the shore from California to the Aleutians and lives out to sea as far as 460 miles off shore.

This bird with the puffed face sheds its gaudy mask of the horny plate each year, to reveal an ugly face. Then it abandons its young one, after viewing it in a good light, having never looked at itself in a mirror.

Mourning Dove Need Not Mourn

A most distinctive cry of any bird is that of the ubiquitous well known mourning dove. Its sad song, in a minor key, translates as, "Oh, oh', boo-hoo-hoo," a drawn out wail. Roberts diagrams the song as __^__ _ __, where the second note is at a higher pitch and sounds like the breath is being inhaled instead of exhaled, and the tail is dropped downward instead of jerked upward, as with the other notes.

To our human ears it sounds like this dove is mourning, but we can discern nothing for it to be sad about, for it is one of the most successful species of bird. Its numbers are huge, it has adapted to environments from sea level to 7000 feet altitude, it is comfortable around civilization, wilderness, woods, prairies or desert.

This mourning dove is a member of a very exclusive club of birds who breed throughout all the contiguous United States. Only eight birds can lay claim to that distinction. Three of them, rock pigeon, starling, and house sparrow, are foreigners from Europe who were introduced unwillingly or unwittingly, and found no impediment to their dispersion across the continent. The other four, red-tailed hawk, killdeer, great horned owl, and red-winged blackbird, are all native and proven to be very adaptable. The red-winged blackbird is the most extreme example of this, for it has spread from its marshy home onto drier land now, and is said to be the most abundant native bird in America.

(Four other natives almost qualify for this club. The turkey vulture doesn't breed in northeast Minnesota; the cowbird is absent from southwest Arizona except in winter; the house finch hasn't reached southern Florida yet; and the rough-winged swallow reaches the tip of Florida only in the winter.)

Because its nest is so skimpy, it can barely keep an unattended egg in place, so the female picks a level site, often on the flat branch of an evergreen tree or on a window ledge. There she sits as the male brings her one stick or one twig at a time. If he drops one stick *en route* he proceeds to the nest with an empty bill before going back for another stick! Each trip to the nest is by the same route from branch to branch. If the female leaves the construction site the male pursues her and pecks at her until she returns – unless it is 10 or 11 a.m., when building ceases for the day.

After the eggs are laid the male incubates them from 10 a. m. to 3 p.m., and the female covers them from 3 p.m. until the next midmorning.

The young are fed pigeon milk – a predigested liquid made from seeds. Both parents feed the young. The nestling puts its bill into the opened bill of the parent. The parent closes her bill, pauses to summon up her strength, and slowly pumps with her throat muscles to regurgitate the contents of her crop. The procedure seems to require great effort with body contortions by both birds.

The mourning dove's tail is distinctly different from that of other birds. When sitting on a telephone wire, its streamlined body ends in a long pencil-shaped tail. But when

this dove flies, its tail fans out into a quadrilateral. The longer two sides of this geometric shape are toward the rear of the bird and display prominent bright white spots, each accented by a black border, at the end of each tail feather. This is a scheme, it has been theorized, to divert a predator distracted by the white spots to attack the tail instead of the body, allowing the dove to escape to live another day.

The mourning dove's tail is also used in courtship. The male struts around the female spreading his tail feathers. Then he raises the tail as his body tilts forward for a better view of the tail, as he opens and closes his tail. This displays the white spots more conspicuously than a steady display of them would.

White spots on this tail distract predators.

Another feature of the mourning dove is the noise from its wings. There is a noisy flapping of the wings when the wings strike each other above the back, observed rarely in its courtship, but commonly heard when surprised and flying away from danger. Then there is the whistling when flying, caused by air streaming past the leading edge of each wing. This sound is much louder than that heard from most other birds.

The mourning dove is equally at home in dense woods, open woods, farm yards, cities, prairie, stream margins, desert, oasis, or mountains. It is the avian model of the adage, "Bloom where you are planted."

Snow White Doves

Close to the end of his life, the late Pope John Paul II symbolically tossed white doves out his window. Instead of flying off as expected, they turned back and flew inside again. It seems it was not quite time yet for the pope to depart this life, since the performance of releasing a dove is symbolic of releasing one's soul from this life to the hereafter. It is a symbol of a spirit soaring free, a symbol of hope, a way of saying farewell, of purity, gentleness and peace, an emblem of love.

The White Dove Company, in the United Kingdom, is associated with a society of funeral directors. That company's vocation consists of providing pure white doves for release at funerals and memorials. They signify the Holy Spirit, just as the Holy Spirit descended from heaven as a white dove onto Jesus Christ at his baptism (John 1:32-34). The organization brings a white basket to the solemn ceremony, and at the climax the lid is lifted and the pure white dove(s) fly out and away.

The Sacred White Dove is the white color phase of the ringneck dove, or ringed turtle-dove, or laughing dove, or Barbary dove, or Java dove.

It has been concluded by biblical scholars that the pair of doves brought by Mary and Joseph (Luke 2:24) to the Temple for sacrifice in accordance with the law concerning the birth of a first-born male, were Barbary doves. This makes them *Streptopelia risoria*. This species had been kept in captivity for availability for sacrificial use in Biblical times. That Jewish law was decreed by the Lord in Leviticus 12:1-8 as a sin offering on 40 days after birth (circumcision 7 days after delivery, then 33 days later). Joseph and Mary were supposed to bring a lamb for a burnt offering along with the dove, but the law allowed them to substitute a second dove instead of a lamb, since they couldn't afford to buy a lamb. So Jesus was born to very poor parents.

Searching the Internet reveals that the ringed turtle-dove

had been domesticated and bred for over 3000 years, with fanciers trying to produce a snow white bird by inbreeding and crossbreeding. Its ancestors lived in the Sudan and Arabia, it is thought, In later years they were kept in southern Europe. It is still a garden bird in the British Isles. From captive Caribbean birds of the 1880s, caged birds were transported to Florida and California. Escaped birds or released birds have established populations in North America which are very dependent on human civilization. The Second Edition of the American Birding Association Checklist recognized the ringed turtle-dove as a legitimate member of our avian fauna, so we got our lifer at the place the A.B.A. recommended: Olivera Street in Los Angeles. There the *S. risoria* specimen we saw on October 15, 1975 running around on the pavement among pedestrians acted like it was afraid of its own shadow, consistent with a bird comfortable only in its own open-door cage.

Be assured that if a white dove is tossed out of a Vatican window, or released out of a hat by a magician, or released out of a basket at a memorial service, it is the same species that ancient Jews offered up to God as a sin offering. Why couldn't it be another species of pure white dove, perhaps an albino rock dove? Because only *S. risoria* after millennia of taming is docile enough to be trusted to crouch quietly in a confined space.

The *Sibley Guide to Birds* shows two look-alike doves from the same genus on the same page – the ringed turtle-dove *Streptopelia risoria* and the Eurasian collared-dove *Streptopelia decaocto*. This Eurasian collared-dove has a history just as amazing as the history described above for the ringed turtle-dove. The Eurasian collared-dove originated in India, then expanded into Asia Minor, then the Balkans in the 1500s. As years went by it appeared in Europe, then Russia and Spain, preferring cities and villages.

In the 1970s this Eurasian collared-dove was imported into the Bahamas by suppliers catering to keepers of doves. After some escaped from an aviary they multiplied in the wild and spread to Miami, Florida in the 1980s. By the start of the 21st Century they appeared in Bismarck, North Dakota.

In translating the scientific name of the genus *Streptopelia* the *Strepto* is from the Greek *strepto*, twisted, or *strepho*, turn; and *pelia* is from the Latin *pilus*, hair. The ringed turtle-dove's specific name *risoria* is from the Latin *risor*, laughter. The explanation of all this is that the generic name refers to the many variations in "pelage", or color, that occur in the various strains of doves in this genus – blond, white, ivory, peach, orange, rosy, fawn, etc. The specific name refers to the ringed turtle-dove's call, described as a soft nasal jeering laugh.

The Eurasian collared-dove scientific species name, *decaocto*, comes from the Greek *deka*, ten, and the Greek or Latin name *octo*, eight. At the end of the underside of its tail there are five white spots on each half of the tail. Between each conspicuous white spot is a narrow black line. So there are altogether ten white spots and eight so-called "spikes."

In retrospect, the caged birds we saw in 1999 at the Mo Ranch near Hunt, Texas were *S. risoria*, while the free roaming doves we saw in 2000 at Moody Mansion in Galveston, Texas were *S. decaocto*.

So when you see one of these newcomers to North Dakota, the Eurasian collared-dove, be impressed by the remarkable travels of its ancestors, for this bird species to have finally arrived here!

When Migratory Birds Can No Longer Migrate

The rock dove's name has been changed to rock pigeon in 2006 by official decree of the American Ornithological Union and its British counterpart.

The homing pigeon is a race of the rock pigeon that has been bred by fanciers for almost a thousand years so as to be able to find its way home to its loft when released from as far as over 1500 miles away.

How can this bird accomplish such a feat? One theory is that it does so by smell. But pigeons whose olfactory nerve has been cut can still fly home as fast as those with an intact sense of smell.

The map-and-compass theory claims they have an internal clock and an internal sense of compass direction home which depends on the position of the sun. But on cloudy days they get home as fast as on sunny days.

Some people think they navigate by memorizing the landscape, such as hills, highways and railroad tracks. This could explain when they're close to home, but not when they're released far beyond the horizon, over new terrain.

The best explanation is the magnetic theory, where they follow the earth's magnetic field. It was known that their brain contains a trace of an iron oxide called magnetite, but new research finds that their upper bill is covered by a very thin layer of cutis. This tissue contains ultra-microscopic particles of atomic size magnetite. When the upper beak is anaesthetized, or when the ophthalmic branch of the trigeminal nerve, which carries messages from these nanocrystals to the brain, is cut, or a magnet is attached to the cere, the bird can no longer find its way.

What are these tiny, tiny super magnetic particles in their upper beak? They are nanocrystals, arranged in elongated structures which are in contact with nerve tissue on the upper beak.

So rock pigeons are dependent on the earth's magnetic field to find their way over long distances. By inference, other birds use the same way to migrate. But now comes a complication. Scientists find that these magnetic lines running from the north magnetic pole to the south magnetic pole shift a little from east to west or *vice versa*. And over eons of time the N-S orientation of today has flip-flopped to S-N, and back again. This switching occurs gradually or abruptly, as certain areas of the magnetic field weaken or become neutral, and may be of opposite poles in certain areas of the earth on a given day. One strain of homing pigeons is confused by a magnetic anomaly more easily than another strain, it has been noted.

When bedrock is laid down and hardened, magnetic particles are polarized in it permanently, according to the magnetic field at the time. Upon studying a series of rock samples drilled serially in a vertical row of borings at one spot in the earth's crust, scientists have found layers of bedrock with N-S or S-N orientation at various levels, which confirms the magnetic field's vagaries.

So when migratory birds are adapted to one polarity, and it shifts or weakens or switches orientation, will they not lose their ability to find their way? Now suppose in the summer the magnetic poles switch. Then when fall comes and migratory birds head to their winter home, they will fly to Canada, then to the Arctic Sea, to starve and freeze to death since they were orientated to fly south in the fall, but the South Pole they knew is now in the opposite direction. Luckily, this won't happen yet in our time, we hope.

In the rock pigeon's scientific name the genus name *Columba* is from the Latin *columba*, meaning a dove or pigeon. The species name *lividus* is also Latin, meaning bluish grey.

The ancestral home of the rock pigeon was around all sides of the Mediterranean Sea and in southwest Asia, where natural cliffs provided nesting sites. They were introduced to North America in the early 1600s into what is now Nova Scotia, and are abundant now in cities all over the world, where they have found high buildings a perfect substitute for their ancestral cliff dwellings.

City people delight in feeding them stale bread and seeds as flocks of rock pigeons become tame and congregate in city

Statue of man feeding rock pigeons.
Photograph by Kenneth J. Johnson

squares and parks. The pictured statue, "Old Friends," sculpted by George Lundeen, resides in the main hallway of Bismarck's Medcenter One. There it is safe from the indignity of its head being whitewashed by pigeon droppings, a common fate of all city square statues.

The swelling population of city pigeons is held in check by raptors such as peregrine falcons, who also have found that a high building can provide an excellent nesting site. In one of his books, Ernest Thompson Seton writes of a certain raptor in whose nest was found the leg band of a prized racing pigeon. That finding solved the mystery of why that champion homing pigeon never arrived home from one of pigeon fanciers' races.

Slinky Bird

The black-billed cuckoo's scientific name is a mouthful. The name of its genus, *Coccyzus*, is Greek *kokkuzo* for cuckoo cry, from the Greek *kokkus* for cuckoo. The name of the species, *erythropthalmus* is from the Greek *erythros* for red, plus the Greek *ophthalmos* for the eye. The eye itself is actually black, but there is a red ring around the eye. That red is not from feathers, but is from bare skin, which is odd.

Another odd feature of this bird is that its foot has two toes facing forward and two toes pointing backward, the same as woodpeckers. As a result, this feature is fine for perching, but the bird can barely hop or walk. The feet of the young are so strong that if a person attempts to lift one out of its nest it can grip the nest so tightly that some of the nest may come along with it. Unlike woodpeckers, it does not climb tree trunks, since its tail feathers aren't capable of functioning as props like a woodpecker's tail does.

Another odd feature is on the roof of the mouth of the hatchling, for the dark roof contains some white pads which the young one uses to secure a tight grip on the top of the adult's smooth bill. The parent bird brings the cuckoo's chief food item, a live caterpillar, to cram down the maw of the baby. The squirming caterpillar is resisting, so as the parent pumps and pushes and the baby sucks it takes a full minute

Nest with European cuckoo's egg in it. Photograph by Per Harald Olsen

for the caterpillar to arrive in the stomach of the young one. Those pads might be considered Nature's original Velcro!

Spiny caterpillars shed their spines onto the lining of the stomach of the cuckoo. But the cuckoo is able to shed the stomach lining and grow a new lining.

Whenever there is an invasion of caterpillars cuckoos mysteriously appear from nowhere to eat them and save the threatened plants. How the cuckoos find out about the plague is a mystery.

The cuckoo gets its name from its voice, a series of low-pitched cow-cow-cow or kuh-kuh-kuh. Some people call it the rain crow because it is more noisy before a rain.

My first introduction to the cuckoo was when I walked over the countryside some distance from my boyhood home in Minnesota. In an open oak woods I heard this cuckoo calling but could not find it.

The mother who reprimands her kid to "Sit up straight! Don't slouch!" would be driven to distraction by this cuckoo, for as it perches it leans farther forward than other birds. This gives it a furtive look, in line with its hiding in dense foliage and retreating into underbrush when approached.

But it didn't run true to form once when we were canoeing in the bottomlands of the Missouri River, where the water, backed up from the dam, formed Lake Oahe. Out among the scattered drowned cottonwoods, shorn of their leaves, was this black-billed cuckoo singing. I found its notes were easy to imitate, for upon hearing me try it became greatly agitated and flew toward the canoe to challenge the perceived intruding cuckoo.

The European cuckoo is notorious for its reputation of being a parasite by laying all its eggs in the nests of other birds, and having the victims feed and raise the baby cuckoo. I thought American cuckoos are superior to that despicable trait, but I read in Bent's *Life Histories of American Birds* that that is not quite true. Our cuckoos on occasion have been found to have laid their egg in another bird's nest. Those species victimized have included the chipping sparrow, yellow warbler, pewee, cardinal, catbird, cedar waxwing, wood thrush, robin, yellow-billed cuckoo, mourning dove. In this cuckoo's case, however, the mother bird hovered about watching to see that the foster parents took proper care of her offspring, whereas the European cuckoo completely abandons her egg and ignores what happens to her young one.

The black-billed cuckoo is one of our most beneficial birds, most self-effacing, and possessing odd features that set it apart from other birds.

Quasi Bird

The hoatzin can claim to be a quasi bird more than any other feathered creature because it has important features not shared by other avian species.

Taxonomists cannot agree on where to place it among the other birds; among all the differing opinions one considered it closer to a dove and another thought it seems closer to a cuckoo. What features make this bird so weird?

By being on a strictly vegetarian diet, they have developed two huge stomachs. Their double crop occupies so much space that it has displaced some of the breast flight muscles and the part of the sternum to which they attach. The first crop receives the leaves they eat, which are fermented by bacteria there to cause a musky odor, justifying one of its other names, stinkbird. The second crop further digests the mash to what looks like pea soup. This mess passes into the intestine, or is regurgitated as food into the maw of the eager young. The bacteria break down the plants' cellulose into sugar.

The huge size of the stomach is necessary since so much more volume of greenery is necessary to obtain enough calories, which are still fewer than what a meat or insect eater gets from a small volume of meat or carrion. Just as a cow eats grass in the morning, lays down to chew its cud, and eats grass again later in the day, so the hoatzin forages in the early morning for a half hour, rests at midday when the weather is hottest, then forages again for a half hour in the early evening.

The huge crops distend the belly so much that the hoatzin has developed a nubbin or rubbery callus on its breast, on which to rest the weight of the huge heavy crop. This forms a tripod with its two legs when it perches.

Its wings are not as aerodynamic as a songbird's, nor as strong as one of the raptor's which prey on it. It is a clumsy flier, where it flies for only a few yards only to crash land.

Its outstretched wing presents a round silhouette, somewhat like a grouse's wing, not an oblong one, as most other birds have. That bending to the rear of the primary feathers instead of out to the side makes it easier to slip between the branches and twigs of the dense rainforest, where it flies and clambers about.

When it hatches it can't fly yet, but clambers about by crawling with the aid of two hooks or spurs on the leading edge of each wing. Read the chapter titled, "Making A Dinosaur From A Bird's Egg" for more about this.

The sketch shows a silhouette of the adult hoatzin, with its rounded wings for flying through narrow gaps in the dense rainforest ground cover in South America's Amazon River watershed. The hoatzin illustrated has one of its claws still attached.

This colorful bird has red eyes accented by surrounding blue skin, a red crest, dark brown back, and red on its flanks and dorsal side of its primaries, with pale yellow breast and sides.

The hoatzin gives us a clue as to what dinosaurs might have sounded like. It is said these birds hoot, yelp, and wheeze. It is two feet long, a large bird but hard to see since its colonies of nests are not numerous, and the rain is pouring, mosquitoes are swarming, and the dense foliage obscures one's view during its breeding season.

The scientific name is appropriate. *Opisthocomus hoazin* means one with long hair behind, in reference to its crest. The *hoazin* portion of its name is from the Spanish *uatzin*, the name given to it by Spanish conquistadors.

This quasi bird eats like a cow, clambers like a lizard, and sounds like what a dinosaur probably sounded like.

Owl That Hissed

It was on March 28, 2002 during our annual Texas winter birding tour, we were visiting High Island, Texas, the world-famous haven for spring migrant warblers in which to rest after their exhausting trip across the Gulf of Mexico. There on the bulletin board at the visitors' entry station was pinned a clipping from a distant Texas big-city newspaper. The feature article told about a snowy owl that landed in a field out of the town of Tye. But Tye, on the west side of Abilene, was over 400 miles away as the crow flies. Would that snowy owl still be there by the time we got there to add it to our Texas life list?

Birding on the way to Tye, we arrived by April 5. Inquiring at the local truck stop, the waitress there knew exactly where it was, for by now it was famous and well-known, even among non-birders. Following her directions, we drove down this two-rut road among farmers' fields, and there it was.

It sat motionless. I wondered if it were dead, until it turned its head to look at me, a genuine snowy owl. Even up in the Texas Panhandle, next to Oklahoma and New Mexico, this visitor is rarely seen, and then only in a severe winter.

Other migratory birds go south in the winter because daylight grows shorter or it gets too cold for them. This snowy owl is adapted to life at night, like a typical night owl; and it can stand the coldest winter, so it can stay in the Far North all winter. So why would it go south to southern Canada and northern states in winter? The snowy owl moves south in winter when the variable rodent population crashes, so its food supply gives out. But couldn't this Tye owl find any mouse or rabbit in the Upper or Lower Midwest? Maybe its sense of direction wasn't working right.

The snowy owl is circumpolar, nesting on tundra in Alaska, Canada, Greenland, Iceland, Scandinavia, Russia and Siberia north of the taiga. It comes south of that area only in winter, how far depending on how few are the lemmings,

Snowy owl. Photograph by David Cahlander

voles, hares, rabbits, ptarmigan that are its prey. Incidentally, when transporting its prey it carries a lemming in its bill, but carries a hare in its talons.

To find its prey, it sits on a small elevated vantage perch such as a pingaluck (a small hillock in the flat tundra). Farther south a boulder serves well as a roost. So when it reaches civilization it adapts a hay stack as its vantage point. When I visited Attu, the western-most island of the Aleutian Islands, it preferred the cornices of a building left over from World War II's Battle of Attu or from the Coast Guard's Loran Station.

When I was on Attu with Attour, the birding tour, one day I left them and wandered alone on the tundra There I came upon a snowy owl sitting in the grass. As I approached it, when I was fifteen feet away, the female hissed at me. (Only the female incubates – the male only brings it food then.) Authors have described the snowy owl as being bigger and more vicious than the great horned owl, prone to attack when threatened, so, discretion being the better part of valor, I cautiously walked away.

Bird guides and other books I have seen described the various voices of the snowy owl, but they never mentioned hissing. Nevertheless, books or no books, this one hissed at me menacingly.

On Attu, that was the only nest of the snowy owl I found. But when we took the bus to visit Prudhoe Bay on the Arctic Ocean, we found some twenty-five snowy owls nesting on the tundra right by the oil company's complex of temporary structures laid on the permafrost. Maybe they were attracted by Norway rats from the oil workers' kitchen and bunk shacks? Those rats always accompany humans wherever they go.

Wildlife other than snowy owls weren't spooked by the oil field activity either, inasmuch as the caribou walked under the elevated pipeline unconcernedly.

Has an owl you seek been using that boulder or rock pile or hay bale for a roost? Inspect the ground at the base of it, where it would regurgitate pellets of indigestible fur or skeletal bones. That would be a clue to its return to its lookout.

Canadians think highly of the snowy owl, for they put its picture on their paper money, a $50 note. Just as each of the United States has adopted a specific bird as its state bird, Quebec has chosen the snowy owl as its official provincial bird.

The scientific name is *Nyctea scandiaca*. The *scandiaca* part obviously is the Latinized form of Scandinavia, where the snowy owl was most easily found by early ornithologists. *Nyctea* is from the Greek *nukteros*, meaning by night, which must be a blunder, for its northern home has 24-hour daylight summers, and when the bird comes south it does its hunting by daylight.

Finding The Boreal Owl's Nest

The boreal owl is barely the size of a robin, nocturnal, scarce, and is a Canadian. *The Sibley Guide to Birds* reveals that its winter range in the United States is the smallest of all the owls, even smaller than that of the snowy owl, great gray owl, or northern hawk owl. As for the breeding range, in the States east of the Rockies it nests only in the northeastern edge of Minnesota. It is a prize for birders to see this species, especially to find one on its active nest.

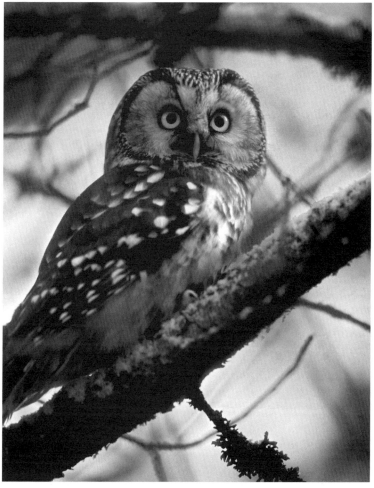

Boreal owl. Photograph by Dag Roettereng

A professional doing research on boreal owls invited us to join a group to go out in the field to find its nest, which had been staked out in advance. Our base camp was in Isabella, a village in the Superior National Forest. I don't know the temperature, but it was a very cold and cloudy day but not windy. Everyone was warmly bundled up. We drove some distance through the partly logged mixed coniferous woods, along narrow forest roads through ample snow, but not deep enough for us to get stuck.

Finally the cars stopped, we got out and started walking. It was noteworthy to find tracks of the timber wolf, but we didn't see any wolves, although I'm sure they watched us. Then we turned and followed an imaginary trail through deep snow. At one spot a fat young woman crashed through the crust, sinking up to her knees. There she was stuck. Another man and my wife and I pulled her out and helped her along. My petite spouse did not fall through.

We soon arrived at one of the scattered trees and told to turn to face looking at a certain dead tree trunk some thirty feet away, and were warned to remain quiet. About fifteen feet from the ground was a hole in that tree maybe three or four inches wide. While we watched, the leader trudged over to the base of the tree. He delivered a sharp blow to the bark. Promptly there appeared at the opening of the hole a boreal owl! It stared at us intently, as we murmured excitedly under our breaths.

I consulted the picture in my pocket field guide to confirm that this unquestionably was a genuine boreal owl.

That evening back at Isabella we congratulated everyone on our mutual good fortune as we enjoyed a warm supper in the lodge.

This occurred on April 2, 1994.

The significance of that sighting was impressed on me when I discovered that T. S. Roberts, in his exhaustive *Birds of Minnesota*, stated that there was no evidence of this Richardson's owl (as it was called when he wrote his book) nesting in Minnesota!

Ernest Thompson Seton, the Canadian naturalist, described its song as sounding like dripping water, at the rate of two drips per second, going on for minute after minute without a pause. It reminds me of a badly leaking faucet. This ten inch long chubby little owl is brownish black, with rows of prominent discrete white spots on its back and rows of prominent white spots tending to run together as stripes on its breast. Its facial disc is white.

It seemed odd to be tramping through the snow to see a bird on its nest, but some owls do lay their eggs that early in the year. The northern hawk owl nests in April in Canada but not in the United States, it seems. The barred owl nests in March, the great gray owl in April, but the great horned owl is the earliest, nesting in February!

The Doomed Burrowing Owl

Pioneers on the Great Plains told of communities of prairie dogs, rattlesnakes and burrowing owls living in burrows as close neighbors.

Today these colonies are but a memory. What happened? The government encouraged railroads to bring in settlers to populate the land. Each farmer was allotted a limited acreage, so to make a living off the land he had to utilize every bit of it. My forebears referred to a marsh disparagingly as a slew-hole because it couldn't be cultivated. Ranchers viewed a colony of gophers or prairie dogs as varmints because its occupants kept the area devoid of vegetation so it deprived the livestock from grazing there. So logic required the prairie dog towns must go. This abetted sportsmen and farm boys to make use of their shooting arms. Remember the annual Great Prairie Dog Shoot at Breien, N. D,?

The fate of the burrowing owl is tied to the fate of the prairie dog, since it is rare that this owl nests in a cavity other than a prairie dog's, although this owl allegedly can dig its own burrow, or use one made by a badger or a Richardson ground squirrel. In North Dakota prairie dog colonies were all west of the Missouri River; if a colony of varmints was east of the river it was created by the Franklin ground squirrel.

Unfortunately, the burrowing owl is easily mistaken for a prairie dog, for they both have about the same size, shape, color and posture, and prairie dogs far outnumber the occasional owl in the colony. So, the shooter doesn't differentiate between them, and aims at whatever resembles a prairie dog.

States within the range of the burrowing owl have placed this bird on the endangered or threatened list. If such drastic action seems unjustified, explain what happened to those birds that used to live in Burleigh County's Wildrose Township Section 29, by the northwest corner of 141 Ave. SE and 392 St. SE. Or those that were in the large pasture in Telfor Township northwest of the junction of 102 Ave. SE and 158 St. SE. Or the large group living among the Franklin ground squirrel colony by Sterling Corners, northeast of the junction of Highway 14 and Interstate 94. Or those in the prairie dog town south of Belfield that was on the west side of U.S. Highway 85, in the pasture containing an old abandoned automobile. Or that pair that lived on the north shoulder of the highway northeast of Pierre, S.D.

Is the demise of the burrowing owl due to the demise of the prairie dog or ground squirrel? The prairie dog colonies in Theodore Roosevelt National Park are thriving and expanding. Burrowing owls had been found quite regularly there in the past, but in recent years only one pair has been found and that not lately. This implies that there are other reasons for their decline. N.D. game and fish personnel have been conducting an ongoing study to ascertain what these reasons are.

If you yearn to see a burrowing owl yet, the only place I know of where a sighting of a wild uncaged specimen can be assured without trespassing is in Lubbock, Texas. The city park there has protected a prairie dog town, a famous tourist attraction, in which reside a very few burrowing owls. But in 2003 the Texas Commission on Environmental Quality was starting a program in Lubbock to capture and remove the prairie dogs because they "overgraze and burrow, which could contaminate groundwater." When they go, those burrowing owls will also be gone.

Efforts are being made here in North Dakota to save the burrowing owl. A bird house design made of wood has been proposed by the N.D. Game and Fish people. It consists of a hole in the ground with a long wooden tunnel leading to a chamber. This owl in desperation has even tried using a culvert as a sanctuary. A wide crack in the sidewalk at Riverside High School in El Paso, Texas is home for a family of burrowing owls, as of this writing.

That casual look-alike, the short-eared owl, is the only other diurnal owl in the U.S. that can be confused with the burrowing owl. They do share owls' unique ability to turn their head completely around.

Repeat this experiment I performed. While a great horned owl was watching me, I walked to its right and around to its rear. It followed me intently with its eyes. At its rear, I kept walking around it. In a split second it whipped its head around counter-clockwise to resume its intent gaze at me as I came around its left side to its front. If I hadn't watched carefully, I would swear it had continued turning its head in a complete circle, as it has been claimed it does. But to turn its head completely to the rear in either direction is still a remarkable feat. Note this picture of the short-eared owl doing just that!

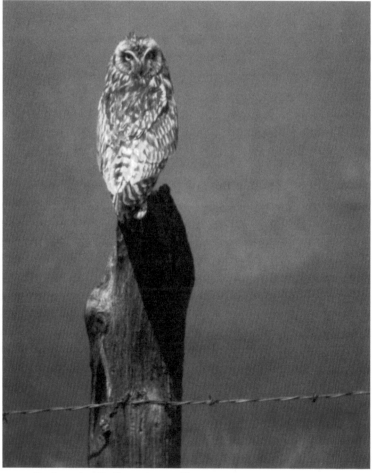

Short-eared owl looking to the rear. Photograph by Judith Ekberg Johnson

Poorwill Can Become Torpid And Hibernate

People have been reporting hibernating poorwills for over two hundred years, but such a ridiculous idea, contrary to logic and experience, was not given credence – until 1946 when a poorwill was found nestled in a depression in a boulder in southern California, and validated that it was truly in a torpid state, and remained healthy.

In the last few years bird scientists have taken an interest in torpor and hibernation of the poorwill. They use a special thermometer which can be affixed to the bird, and record temperature changes much more rapidly than ever possible before. The results are astounding. These birds can lower their body temperature down to 27.4 C and still fly, and down to 5 C to become torpid and recover. This is the lowest for any bird! However, heating them quickly when in torpor, such as with a heating pad, kills them.

One clue to their adaptability to cold is said that they eat mostly beetles, which are high in unsaturated fat. This fat remains liquid and still available to metabolism as the body cools down.

How often do they lower their body temperature? While ordinary birds migrate south as nights get cold, poorwills have the option to do so too, but take advantage of their singular ability, so customarily chill down every night. So they are diurnal and may sleep through the cold night.

It is to be expected that the poorwill can stay torpid for days at a time – that is, it can truly hibernate, but as of the date of this writing researchers have never followed any through an entire winter under natural conditions to prove this. So far, the poorwill has proven to hibernate for two months duration, and a population wintering in Tucson, Arizona is being studied throughout the entire winter season.

The *Archaeology Southwest* publication, vol. 21, no. 1, for Winter 2007, on page 7 points out that the Pima Indians of Arizona have known for generations about the poorwill hibernating all winter long. They would find it lying on the desert flats in winter, motionless, seemingly dead. But when picked up it was alive, and if watched stayed that way until when spring heat aroused their insect diet for them.

The poorwill has a huge mouth, for it can open it wide both vertically and horizontally. The insect collecting capacity is embellished by an amazing row of long hairs all around the mouth, which are called rictal bristles. The nighthawk does not have them.

Its huge maw is also used to open wide to discourage predators, enhanced by hissing and swaying the body and clicking the bill. This scary technique is used by young ones threatened by predators, by adults discouraging invaders of the nest, and

Poorwill (upper bird) is only two-thirds size of nighthawk (lower bird), and has only one white spot. Nighthawk has three white spots.

by a poorwill of either sex held in the hand. Near the ground nest the poorwill also flies about the head of the investigator, snapping its bill and clapping its wings.

The nighthawk spends its feeding time flying overhead and catching insects on the fly, but the poorwill spends its feeding time mostly on the ground with forays a few feet off the ground catching low flying larger insects.

The poorwill belongs to a very select group that grooms with the toenail of its middle toe! There are four stages of development of this feature in different species of birds. The most primitive, in the barn owl's middle toe, has only some lines, or shallow grooves, on the inner side of the nail. The second stage, on the foot of a heron, also on the inner side of that same nail, has a comb with narrow spaces between each tooth of the comb. The third stage, on a nighthawk, has thicker teeth with a wider space between each tooth. The second and third types of combs are pictured here, the sketches shown from Roberts' book. The fourth stage, not pictured here, is on the middle toe of the poorwill. It probably uses the left toe for one side, and the right toe for the other side, of its unique insect catcher surrounding its huge mouth. So it combs its rictal bristles to keep them in optimal working shape. I am reminded of the vain dude using his little mustache comb on his little mustache, but the poorwill has a practical utilitarian use for its toe nail comb.

Fig. 50. Foot of a Heron, showing the comb on the inner edge of the middle toe-nail.

Picture from page 172 of
The Birds of Minnesota, by T.S. Roberts

The poorwill's scientific name is a clever choice. *Phalaepoptilus nuttallii* is from the Greek *phalaina* for moth, plus the Greek *ptilon* for feather or wing. The person who named the poorwill was referring to its flight, for it flies erratically like a moth, the more efficiently for catching more insects. The *nuttallii* species designation is named after the English ornithologist. Nuttall spent the second half of his life, until 1859, in the U.S. studying birds.

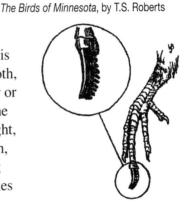

Fig. 264. Foot of Nighthawk, showing comb on inner edge of middle toe-nail.

Picture from page 637 of
The Birds of Minnesota,
by T.S. Roberts

The range of the poorwill is the western half of the U.S., and into Mexico. North Dakota's Badlands are the extreme northeast in which it lives, and where we've seen it in Theodore Roosevelt National Park. It joined our life list earlier in the Basin of Big Bend National Park, Texas.

While working in the Medora, N. D. zoo during university

student summer vacations, this youth used the poorwill in his romantic dating days. He invited interested coeds for a ride in his convertible car with him to see the poorwill after dark on the loop road of the South Unit of the adjacent Park. Read details about this in the paragraph "Poorwill and the Girls" in the chapter "There is Humor in Birding."

The poorwill is a species that shows us how little we know about many of these amazing incredible birds.

Nighthawk Really Isn't A Nighthawk

Strictly speaking, nighthawk is not a good name for this bird, for with the name hawk we think of a raptor, the eater of birds or mammals, and this bird eats nothing bigger than an insect. And it isn't a bird active at night, for when it gets dark it lands and goes to sleep, not to reactivate itself again until early morning at first light.

So the saying, to be a nighthawk, to refer to a person who stays up late at night, would not be accurate.

Ehrlich, Dobkin, and Wheye in their book, *The Birder's Handbook*, copyright 1988, claim that the common nighthawk "feeds at dusk, night, and in day." Bent in his 26 volume *Life Histories of North American et al* series of books, copyright 1940, makes no mention of the common nighthawk feeding at night. Rather, he relates to a study wherein observers maintained a constant 24 hour watch on this nighthawk's nesting site in June, 1921 at the northern latitude of Brunswick, Maine. At 3:24 a.m. the male awakens from his perch on a nearby elm branch. At 3:30 a.m. on this graveled roof the female stirs as dim light in the east grows brighter. Then follows a day of activity. At 9:22 p.m. the female returns for the last time and settles down to brood for the night. Activities began again at 3:40 a.m. on the next day. I believe Bent is more convincing — they don't feed in the dead of night.

This is truly a diurnal bird, since it needs light to see its insect prey, and it surely does not find them by smell. As to light, someone reported a case where a nighthawk caught a bunch of fireflies on the wing. Upon opening its mouth to feed its young, this observer saw in its wide open maw brilliant light, like a flashlight shining out of its mouth!

The common nighthawk has a huge mouth, as wide as its head, the wider to catch more insects as this bird flies erratically through the air, digressing to catch more bugs, seemingly never getting stung by a trapped bee or hornet or wasp as it sets records among birds for highest numbers of mosquitoes and ants eaten. A government worker counted 500 mosquitoes in the stomach of one bird. In another nighthawk were found 2175 flying ants – females about to start new colonies of ants. The nighthawk has an enormous stomach, which supplies enough food for its two fledglings, fed by regurgitation, just like the rock pigeon, which also has an enormous stomach for feeding its squab that similar way.

In the common nighthawk's scientific name, *Chordeiles minor*, the generic *Chordeiles* is from the Greek, which is interpreted as music in the evening.

Music in the evening here tries to describe the loud buzzy peent...peent the common nighthawk utters as it flaps its wings arrhythmicly, coursing about in the evening air. Musical is not an accurate description of this note, but it must be accepted in view of some of the modern symphony orchestra's sounds.

The most well-known sound from the common nighthawk is not vocal but produced by the forces of physics. The male bird quietly flies up high in the air, then dive-bombs, or drops downward in a rush. At the end of its rapid descent, as it gets down to a few feet off the ground, it turns upward abruptly as it thrusts its wings forward. Air whips between its primaries, causing each feather to vibrate, making this booming sound. One reason for this odd behavior is that that is the male's way of impressing the female, who is crouched on the ground at the spot where he turned upward sharply. After this showing-off, a courtship dance takes place, then copulation.

The other reason for this odd performance is to intimidate any intruder or predator. This is an effective way of scaring away any stranger that might be a threat.

My father grew up on a homestead in western Minnesota, and he vividly recalled wandering on the open prairie and being accosted by the nighthawk in this manner. In like manner I have shared this experience on the North Dakota prairie, where the female historically has found a small bare spot to lay her two eggs.

Since the coming of cities with buildings with flat tops

covered with asphalt overlaid with gravel, the nighthawks have adapted to them by laying their eggs on the gravel roof, generally one pair of nighthawks to each building. This was hastened by the prairie becoming diverted to crops and overgrazed pastures and feral cats.

The building top is inferior to the prairie, though, when the hot sun heats up the roof to 115 degrees F. The suffering young one, unable to fly yet, pants to cool off enough, and may not find a cooler shady spot, so it dies.

In Washington State west of the Cascade Mountains nighthawks have been driven off graveled flat top buildings by glaucous-winged gulls. Being more aggressive and predatory, the gulls had the advantage, but also because their hatchlings, being more semiprecocial because of having stronger legs than the baby nighthawks, were much better able to move to a cooler shady spot on the sun-baked roof.

To determine whether a nighthawk has nested on a graveled flat top, look for a faint straight line, formed when larger pebbles have been forced to one side. That happened gradually. The line is straight because when the female landed she always came in from the same direction. Each time the female pushed the eggs under her breast they moved and turned a little bit. That prevents the yolk from settling; other birds preserve their eggs by turning them with their bills.

Nighthawk prefers to perch lengthwise on a branch or railing, unlike other birds that perch crosswise. Photograph by Judith Ekberg Johnson

Wings That Beat Alternately

A few birds are flitting about overhead on this summer day. They are odd-looking, with a small cigar-shaped body, short square tail and sickle-shaped wings held stiffly. But watching the wings we note something strangely unique – first one wing beats, then the other one beats, in rapid succession. Why?

Chimney swift, the "flying cigar"

How can that be? No other bird flies that way.

For years people have puzzled about this. Finally somebody took slow motion pictures of their flight, which proved that the wings do not beat alternately. Then why does it look like they do?

The bird is tilting rapidly to the right and to the left. When it tilts to one side only its right wing is seen as the left wing is hidden from sight; then when only the left wing is seen the right wing isn't seen because it likewise is in the same line of sight as the body. Yet both wings beat at the same time. By tilting rapidly to the right and left, it seems, more area is covered to ensnare more flying insects. This clever maneuver of this bird, the chimney swift, intrigues us to investigate what else is distinctive about it.

For example, the chimney swift never lands on the ground! It never lands on anything, Bent says, except on the inside wall of a chimney – unless a few still nest in a hollow tree, as they used to before the days of chimneys. They obtain twigs, the component of their nests, by breaking them off while in flight, never landing on the tree. They build their nest on the inner side of the chimney by gluing each twig in place using their sticky saliva, as they cling to the chimney with the aid of their stubby claws and short bristly tail, the tail feathers ending as long naked spines which they use as props.

An Asiatic cousin to the chimney swift builds its nest the same way, and the Chinese harvest these nests to make delicious (?) soup using the leached saliva! Neither whites nor Indians in America avail themselves of this delectable (?) delicacy.

The National Audubon Society has listed the chimney swift as one of our birds whose population has decreased significantly, down to about half of what it was. In the Bismarck area it was found in the old Wachter's feed lot area northeast of the Washington street and Burleigh avenue intersection, but a housing development there cut down all the hollow cottonwood trees, thus eliminating the chimney swifts. And the old Bismarck Hospital housed a huge colony in its huge chimney, but when the chimney was torn down as the hospital morphed into Medcenter One the chimney swifts vanished.

A chimney seems an unnatural place to roost overnight, especially in which to nest. Each winter soot accumulates; doesn't it bother them? Yes; when a large flock comes in to roost, they have been known to dislodge the soot, which smothered them and caused them to fall down the shaft into the house. Also, in an unseasonable cold snap before migration south, the people lit a fire in the fireplace. The hot fumes asphyxiated the birds, whose corpses had to be removed from the flue.

A rare spell of cold rainy weather has been known to clear the air of flying insects, causing the absence of the swifts' sole source of food, causing the swifts to starve to death.

Since saliva is water-soluble, a heavy rainstorm can dissolve the saliva-glued nest to loosen its grip on the wall and to crash. The fledglings fall down the chimney too, but by using their claws and spiny tail they climb up the chimney wall again. Using a hollow tree, with its entry hole on the side of the tree, would avert this disaster.

When feeding their young the parent bird regurgitates its food into the mouth of the young, like the homing pigeon, or rock pigeon, does, but here while the young clings to the wall, the parent bird crawls up the wall behind it and pumps the food into its mouth as the young turns its head!

Now since so many calamities have happened with living in chimneys, why do chimney swifts still nest there? They have no other choice, since hollow trees are chopped down by man.

At their nesting area they fly all day long, never landing to rest, Bent says. In migration north they fly only in the daytime, and then fly in loops, flying north then turning aside to fly south, then turning again to resume flying north. At dusk, the swifts find a hollow tree or chimney to crowd into. That's what I gather from A. C. Bent in his book, *Life Histories of North American Cuckoos, Goatsuckers, Hummingbirds, and Their Allies*. In their southward migration their destination was a mystery until their winter home was finally found in Peru.

The chimney swift truly is a bizarre bird.

Black-chinned Hummingbird

Embark with us on a power boat at Page, Arizona for a day-long trip, and cruise upstream on the Glen Canyon Reservoir. On the way to our destination stop in an alcove and cool off with a brief swim in the water. After more panoramas of beautiful cliff walls rising high above the drowned Colorado River, we arrive at a tiny, easily overlooked landing on our starboard side at the mouth of a side canyon. There we disembark to follow a trail up the canyon to our destination, Rainbow Bridge National Monument, in southern Utah.

On our hike up the canyon we stop for a picnic lunch. Looking about at the scenery, we spy an amazing thing; under a projecting overhang, growing out of a crack in the rock, a tiny shrub is holding a tiny nest on which is nestled a tiny bird. Such an odd site in such an area of the country means that type of hummingbird has to be a black-chinned hummingbird. But this mite has a white chin. The female of the species has this plumage, and it is the female that incubates the two tiny eggs it has laid.

She had constructed the nest, less than two inches in diameter, of plant down, held together and held securely in place on a fork of that bush, by spider webs. The nest is semiglobular, more than half of a sphere. The rim is curved inward at the top, which feature prevents the eggs or the young from falling out. As the young increase in size the flexible top can expand to accommodate them. When building the nest the female twirled around with a shivering or trembling motion to make the inside round. She often whirred her wings to change her position, or sat on the rim to shape the nest with her bill. Bent in his book quotes observers who had witnessed this construction. Could humans make a structure as functional as that?

The tour guide was amazed when we pointed out the nest to him, for he had passed it daily without noticing it. He was thrilled to add it to his commentary of interesting things

Female black-chinned hummingbird on nest, hidden under overhanging rock face of canyon wall. Photograph by Kenneth J. Johnson

to point out on future trips, being cautioned not to let any tourists disturb the bird on its nest.

Bent quotes an observer who witnessed a surprising incident. This black-chinned hummingbird found itself trapped in a porch enclosed by a wall of chicken wire with meshes only one and a half inches in diameter. After inspecting carefully for an escape opening and finding none, he decided to dart through the mesh. In doing so, he furled his wings just as he passed through the mesh, then resumed the normal wing spread as he reached the other side of the screen.

All hummingbirds share many remarkable attributes, noted in the next chapter.

Bird With Double-jointed Wings

Hummingbirds are birds of the tropics, flourishing best in the South American rain forest of the Amazon Basin. The dense vegetation, from forest floor to 200 feet tall trees, makes discovering new species difficult. Over 300 species have been validated, and new species of hummingbirds have been described, even since the birth of our younger generation.

Outside the tropics several species are now found in North America, notably in the Southwest, but the ruby-throated hummingbird is the only one to breed only in the eastern half of the United States.

There this species with its adventurous ancestors has continued the same symbiosis between plant and bird that

Male ruby-throated hummingbird. Photograph by Patricia Burke

other hummingbirds enjoy. For it is now believed that the nectar the hummingbird seeks acts as a lure, for the plant to deposit its pollen on the feathers of the chin and crown as the bill burrows deep into the tubular flower to reach the nectar. Then the bird goes to the next flower, depositing the first plant's pollen onto the second plant.

How does the nectar get up into the bird? It is not sucked, researchers find. The distal part of the hummingbird's tongue is split. As the tongue is stuck out of the bill into the nectar, the liquid runs up the fissure between the split halves by capillary action. The tongue is then withdrawn back into the bill, and the nectar is swallowed.

Nectar is pure carbohydrate, fitting for a quick source of energy. Hummingbirds need a lot of it, for they have a high rate of metabolism, being very hyperactive. Their body temperature is 106 degrees Fahrenheit. They breathe 250 times per minute and beat their wings 50 times per second. Their heart beats 1200 times per minute when feeding, but only (!) 250 beats per minute while at rest. Such hyperactivity demands their descent into torpor at night, even down to 50 degrees Fahrenheit, more so during cold nights, so energy won't be wasted maintaining that high daytime temperature.

Their dietary need for protein is met by an occasional insect for the adult, but the nestling needs and gets a diet of insects for body-building, even though it was hatched from an egg only as large as a navy bean, which was laid in a nest only as large as a walnut shell, by a bird less than 4 inches long.

Hummingbirds can hover more expertly than any other bird. Their humerus, the bone that attaches the wing to the body, is modified so that the wings can rotate almost 180 degrees. A person may say it is double-jointed. The wing can extend out to the side with the underside facing down to the ground as in other birds, but it can also twist backwards so the under surface faces to the rear, or forward so the under surface faces forward. So now this bird can fly forward and backward, straight up and down, or sideways. The wings need beat less rapidly when the bird is moving backwards (60 times per second), and least rapidly when hovering (55 times per second).

The sketch shows how the hummingbird flies backwards. It assumes a vertical position, its belly facing the flower or feeding tube of the feeder, and its tail pointing downwards to the ground and diagonally forward. Then with a ventral stroke of its wings towards the tube, each wing's flat under surface pushes towards the tube, moving the bird away from it. Then with a dorsal stroke of the rotated wing the wing moves behind the bird and the flat under surface of each wing pushes the bird upwards against the force of gravity. Then the wings rotate back again to the first position. This cycle is repeated some 60 times per second!

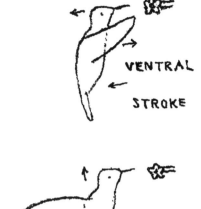

Being such a tiny size involves amazing incredible facts, but also results in some horrible happenings. Bent's book, *Life Histories of North American Cuckoos, Goatsuckers, Hummingbirds and Their Allies, part two*, describes them:

A certain man heard persistent notes of a hummer, and sensing something wrong, investigated. There hung the bird in a spider's web, and a big yellow and brown pot-bellied spider was turning the hummingbird over and over, winding its web around it! The wings and legs were tightly bound, but the head was still exposed for the victim to still cry for help. The man killed the spider, and very carefully unwound the bird.

On a calm day another man noticed a pasture

thistle waving. On investigating he found a male ruby-throated hummingbird impaled on the prickly purple flower by his stomach feathers but not his wings. He cut off the flower, carried the pair home and carefully removed the bird. The hummer flew away unharmed, minus a few feathers.

A bass was seen to jump out of a pool to swallow a hummingbird that hovered over the water.

A record was reported where a ruby-throat was found in the stomach of a merlin.

A couple walking in the woods investigated a rattling noise to find a large dragonfly on a hummingbird's back. On chasing the insect away, the bird, after resting for a while on the palm of the hand, could fly away.

Frogs have often been observed capturing and swallowing ruby-throated hummingbirds.

No bird merits a place among amazing incredible birds more than this hummingbird.

Halcyon, The Kingfisher

A halcyon is a kingfisher, thought to have a calming influence on the sea. The scientist naming the belted kingfisher was engrossed in the concept of halcyon. In *Ceryle alcyon*, the bird's scientific name, the genus name is from the Greek *kerulos* for halcyon, a sea bird. The Greeks did not know of the nest-burrow this bird digs in banks; they thought its nest was on a small raft out to sea, and the gods kept the sea calm to protect the nest. Hence the expression "halcyon days" meaning calm tranquil days. The specific name *alcyon* obviously is from the same word halcyon.

In my youth I met a girl named Halcyon Dudley, who accompanied her father in his sailboat, and presumably she did calm the waters, more or less, as they sailed along. For when I sailed with another captain in his sailboat, we capsized.

The belted kingfisher is the blue and white bird with a large head and bill. The big bill is used to dig out its burrow, at the end of which an enlargement serves as a nest. The tunnel, started a foot below the top of a bank, is at least four feet, sometimes twelve feet, long! Roberts in his *Birds of Minnesota* explains how this is done. Both spouses dig. One bird would go in, stay for about three minutes loosening dirt from the end of the burrow, then push the loosened dirt out to the beginning of the burrow, then climb out over the pile of dirt. Next the other bird would enter, throw out the dirt the first bird had left at the entrance, then go deep into the

FIG. 277. Bare lower tibia and foot of the Belted Kingfisher.

Sketch from page 657 of Roberts' *Birds of Minnesota*

tunnel and lengthen it some more, and push out the loose dirt to the entrance, climb out over it and fly off. This continued day after day, sometimes for almost a month.

One observer found a burrow which branched from its opening into a short smaller side tunnel for a rough-winged swallow, plus the kingfisher's much larger (about 4 inches wide by 3½ inches high) main burrow.

When the eggs laid at the far end of the tunnel are hatched, the hatchlings orient themselves to face the entrance, so as to receive food. There they stay pointed in that direction in virtual total darkness, eating by feel and touch. During the feeding of the young, the passageway develops a central ridge with a furrow on each side of it, as the kingfisher's feet move its body along. The nestling consists mostly of a big head with a large bill and strong wings, very top-heavy.

This body-build persists throughout life, with an oversized head and beak and undersized underpinnings. The huge beak, used to digging its nest burrow, is also necessary to spear big fish, aided by the big head, and neck muscles needed in controlling the struggling fish. I have never seen a kingfisher walk; I don't think they can.

The kingfisher's lower tibia has no feathers. All perching birds, woodpeckers, cuckoos, hummingbirds, and parrots have feathered tibias. Together with this bird's short tarsus, that

Caricature of the kingfisher with its oversized head and beak and undersized underpinnings.

may explain its ability to scrape its loosened dirt down to the entrance of its burrow.

When one investigator dug out the sod and dirt above the nesting chamber for studying the young, then replaced its roof with a stone, the adults filled in that chamber as they excavated another chamber in the same tunnel.

Being inches below the surface, this underground nest is rather chilly, and the newly hatched young are naked, so they cuddle together as close as they can, in a tight ball.

For the first week the young are fed fully digested fish by regurgitation. Then the mast contains more and more recognizable fish, then only undigested fish as the young grow.

The nest is kept quite clean by the parents removing regurgitated pellets, although fish bones and scales litter the floor.

After the young leave the nest the adult feeds them as they perch on a limb. Then the parent beats a fish unconscious and drops it on the water. The young perched on the limb sit looking at it. When they get hungry enough one finally dives for it. Missing the target, it flutters in the water until it gets the fish. It eventually becomes able to hit the fish in its dive, and switches to diving for live fish. When the offspring are able to return to their perch, whack the fish, toss it in the air, catch it and swallow it, the parent forsakes them.

The belted kingfisher belongs to that exclusive group such as the phalaropes where the female's plumage is more colorful than the male's. With brown on part of her white belly, the female is more brightly colored than the male with its all white belly.

So it is that halcyon, the kingfisher, spends its early life in a cool black hole, is taught by its parents how to survive by diving for its food, and catches fish for a living.

Three-toed Woodpecker

The birds of North America are one thing and the birds of Europe and Russia are something else, and each fauna requires its separate field guide. Quite a number of birds resemble a similar species on the other side of the world, though, like the American robin and the European robin. A few seem identical, such as the magpie, but have been declared separate species by scientists. A few, such as the house sparrow, have been deliberately or accidentally introduced here from Europe. The cattle egret introduced itself here without our knowledge or help. A true rarity is a bird found on both sides of the world, that belongs to the same identical species, yet both are non-migratory residents of their continent and unable to commingle. Such a bird is the three-toed woodpecker.

The scientific name of the three-toed woodpecker is *Picoides tridactylus*, in which the genus name is a combination of the Latin *picus* meaning woodpecker, plus the Greek word *eidos* meaning shape or form. The species name *tridactylus* is a combination of the Latin word *tri* which means three, and the Greek word *dactulous* which means toe.

The other *Picoides* woodpecker, the black-backed, also has three toes; all other woodpeckers are blessed with four toes. The foot with only three toes has the inner rear toe missing, with the other rear toe unable to turn forward. In the foot with four toes the

This female Norwegian bird has a white back, the same as the Rocky Mountain form of this same species.
Photograph by Per E. Fredriksen

outer rear toe can rotate forward. Why the three toe bird has a toe missing is a mystery. Which bird has an advantage?

When this bird approaches it comes in low and swoops up as it lands on the trunk of a spruce tree. It doesn't descend easily because its head faces upward and its tail has stiff feathers that are props against the trunk to prevent falling. Then it moves up the trunk spirally. When it pounds the bark with its bill it closes its eyes as the bill hits the tree, to prevent pieces flying into its eyes, presumably. But much of its attack on the trunk consists of prying loose the bark for access to wood-boring beetles.

It leaves a wide zone of the trunk devoid of the dark bark, exposing the light colored wood around its nest hole, making its nest entrance easy to find. The hole is two inches wide. The gourd-shaped nest cavity expands downward, four inches wide and ten inches deep, with loose wood chips lining the bottom.

It locates the grub in the wood by hearing its gnawing. We remember hearing the loud crunch, crunch of larvae chewing deep inside logs in a stack of firewood at a camp in the evergreen forest of Canada. As the woodpecker drills its bore hole accurately to the larva it slides its long tongue deep down the hole for the sticky barbed tongue to extract the worm.

It is amazing how long the tongue is. It is stored in the woodpecker's head, in a long tube that extends back under

ARCTIC
THREE-TOED
WOODPECKER

AMERICAN
THREE-TOED
WOODPECKER

Illustrations from page 683 of T.S. Roberts' *Birds of Minnesota*.
Skull of black-backed woodpecker on left and three-toed woodpecker on right
showing how far behind and over the top of the skull the long tongue extends.
The common names have changed since Roberts published.

the skull, up the rear and over the crown of the skull to a spot between the eyes! The drawing in Roberts' book illustrates this phenomenon, although the common names of these woodpeckers have changed since his book was published.

The three-toed woodpecker is taciturn and tame. It may sit on the side of a spruce tree for minutes, and moves slowly. It sees the birder approaching but doesn't fly away as soon as do other woodpeckers. The bird lives in spruce and fir forests which don't see many humans, especially in those areas which have burned from forest fires or are severely infested with the larvae of wood-boring beetles. These two small areas are the only places where these boreal birds can be expected to be found. In America that is in the so-called Canadian Life Zone.

It is easier to drill out a nest in a dead spruce than a live one, because the wood is softer. But the woodpecker often chooses a live tree with its firmer wood that is much harder to chisel. The reason it chooses a living tree for its nest, it is believed, is that the black bear in attempting to bite the wood away to expose the nest in the living healthy tree finds it too hard to do.

A woodpecker with only three toes is unique in having yellow in its plumage, but the yellow is only on the forehead of the black-backed, and only on the adult three-toed male. The white bars on the back of the three-toed, and the all black back of the black-backed, are easier to see as field marks.

The three-toed woodpecker's range only comes close to the northeast corner of North Dakota, but we have recorded the black-backed woodpecker in the U.S. government's experiment station south of Mandan, N. D. on October 23, 1965.

III. PERCHING PERFORMERS

Eastern Wood-Pewee

A favorite treasured memory of my early childhood is my leaving the house in which I was born, crossing the street, walking past the neighbor's house, and entering an open oak woods. The large oak trees, not crowded together, shaded an open forest devoid of underbrush and carpeted only by long silky grass. In this atmosphere of awe, even reverence and peace, were heard two species of birds each singing its soft dreamy song. The eastern bluebird was easy to see in its bright blue plumage. The eastern wood-pewee blended in too well to be obvious, but its song, a leisurely pee-a-wee, was most wistful, dreamy, even plaintive. Sometimes it varied as to sound like pee-ur.

The eastern wood-pewee, along with the red-eyed vireo, are the last to arrive from the south each spring. Together the two birds continue to sing their repetitive songs in the summer after other birds have mostly fallen silent. And they complement each other as the vireo stays high in the trees chasing its insect prey as the pewee concentrates on the insects lower down around the tree.

A further division of the edibles is the harmony where a larger song bird, such as the kingbird, is specializing in larger flying insects, as this pewee is concentrating on little flying insects, many so tiny they are invisible to our comparatively dull eyes.

The pewee does not harvest every insect by sallying out, catching it in mid-air, and returning to its favorite lookout; it has been observed stealing freshly trapped flies from a spider's web!

Bent on page 275 of his book *Life Histories of North American Flycatchers, Larks, Swallows, and Their Allies* has shown that many musicians have admired the song of the eastern wood-pewee. Some have even spent years studying it. In the half light of the dawn and evening dusk the daytime pewee notes are arranged into a rhythmical twilight song that has merited the admiration of musicians.

Go to the C note that is two octaves above middle C. Then go to the E note that is two notes above that high C. The sounds we translate as pee-a-wee is sung by this pewee as E, A, C, in leisure timing. The twilight song has been interpreted as a four line ballad. The first line is E, A, C, followed in rhythmic beats by five rests. The second and third lines are the same. The fourth line is E, B, followed by six beats. The first three lines' notes end in an upward inflection. The B note in the fourth line ends in a downward inflection, sounding

The ballad of the eastern wood-pewee.

like a doleful minor note, creating a feeling of wistfulness and sadness, yielding a more romantic effect.

So this ballad states a musical theme for the first line, an answering theme for the second line, a repetition of the first theme for the third line, and a repetition of the second theme but ending with the keynote, for the fourth line.

This is a higher technical rank than any other bird music, and qualifies the eastern wood-pewee to join the ranks of amazing incredible birds.

Say's Phoebe Doesn't Say It Feebly

We were introduced to the true American West on June 19, 1955 when we stayed overnight in a motel in Belfield, North Dakota. The bright early morning sun was shining into the east facing windows of our unit, when we were awakened by a shrill bird song, very loud and piercing. Its source proved to be this Say's phoebe, which had built its nest under the eave directly at the front of our unit. Its repeated calling prevented any more sleep, arousing us to add this new bird to our life list.

This flycatcher is smaller than a house sparrow. It has a black tail. Its head, back and breast are gray, but its belly is a distinctive red brown, the same color as the scoria of North Dakota's Badlands, with which Badland roads are covered. So it fits Badlands décor.

What endears Say's phoebe to us is that it wholeheartedly has accepted ranch buildings as its nesting sites, and often livens up an abandoned school house or old family dwelling with its presence.

Out in the Badlands area where the unique columnar cedars grow, the campground's outhouse sheltered this pair of Say's phoebes under its eave. At the second stop on the Bowman (N. D.) Breeding Bird Census route, we always anticipated hearing the Say's phoebe's unmistakable call each year, loud enough to wake up the sun and cause it to rise above the horizon.

It doesn't flock or form colonies; it is a loner.

It is a bird of the West, west of the Missouri River in North Dakota; but on occasion one does nest east of the river, always in or on a building, at the eastern edge of its range. But buildings appeared only since European immigrants erected them; where did they nest before that? A. C. Bent's book, *Life Histories of North American Flycatchers, Larks, Swallows and Their Allies*, records that they have nested on cliffs under overhanging rock, and on ledges in caves, or in cavities in trees. So this phoebe learned to move to crevices in abandoned mine shafts and wells, and took advantage of the similarity of an eave of a building to a natural crevice.

This bird nests farther north than other flycatchers. Its adaptability was demonstrated when the Alaskan Pipeline to the Arctic Ocean's Prudhoe Bay was built, Say's phoebe quickly learned to build its nest on the pipe's exposed support!

The male acts as a lookout as the female incubates her eggs for half a month. During this time the male feeds his mate insects which he catches. The young ones are fed a pure insect diet, by regurgitation at first, then by direct feeding of insects by the male, who teaches them to fly and catch insects when they are ready. With the second brood, the female teaches them to fly and catch their own insects.

Being on a diet of insects only, the rancher would welcome Say's phoebe to his spread.

It seems unusual for this bird to feed its newborn by regurgitating predigested food, but even more so to learn that it forms pellets of indigestible parts of the bugs and regurgitates them onto the ground below the nest – like an owl does!

It is said that a large flycatcher, such as a western kingbird (8-3/4 inches long), catches large insects; Say's phoebe (7-1/2 in.), medium sized insects; and a small flycatcher, such as a western flycatcher (5-1/2 in.), small insects. So they don't compete with each other. But they all sit on a perch watching, dart out to catch their specialty, and return to their perch.

Flying insects will always be around, and the West's low humidity preserves wood in old buildings much longer than in the more humid range of the eastern phoebe, so I trust the adaptable Say's phoebe is assured of a secure future.

Charles L. Bonaparte (a gull was named after him) gave Say's phoebe its name in honor of the famous American ornithologist. The bird's scientific name is *Sayornis saya*; *ornis* is Greek for bird, so *Sayornis* means Say's bird. The species name *saya* is derived from Thomas Say's surname. This may be the only creature whose scientific name uses the bird's common name twice.

Shrike, The Passerine Raptor

The passerines, or perching birds, comprise the largest order of birds, and include all the song birds. They look pretty and perch on a limb and sing. Insects are their main diet.

But one passerine is a renegade. Few people have heard it sing, for it sings its musical song very rarely. And it often abandons its insect diet to attack and eat other birds. Here is a songbird that eats other songbirds!

How long has it been acting this dastardly? Long enough for its ancestors to have evolved a prominent hook on the tip of its upper mandible, like the bill that typical raptors have, which they use to rip shreds of meat off birds' corpses.

It is often seen sitting motionless on a prominent branch or fence or telephone wire, scanning the landscape with its very keen vision. When it sees its prey, perhaps a grasshopper or a dickeybird, maybe 60 yards away, it drops off its perch and flies close to the ground in a straight flight with rapidly beating wings. As it approaches its goal it rises up higher, then pounces. It aims at the nape of the bird so strongly that the neck is broken or dislocated. It bites its prey by snapping the tip of its lower mandible against the sharp cutting edge of the upper mandible, like a scissors.

Now the raptor-bound evolution of the feet did not match that of the bill, for its feet are songbird size and strength, far too weak to clutch or hold down its prey. So with its bill it carries the victim by the neck to a sharp projection, such as a thorn or barb in a barb-wire fence, and impales the bird or bug by its neck. Oddly, it never jabs the body of the prey through its center of gravity. By impaling the bird through its neck, I surmise, the head is held rigid so the shrike can extract its favorite food, the brain, most easily, from the back of the skull. There the prey hangs, perhaps until

Sketch from page 161 in Roberts' *Birds of Minnesota, Vol 2.* Note zigzag edge of end of upper bill, whose sharp edge acts with lower bill as a scissors.

desiccated, for much of the time this butcher bird eats it much later or forgets and abandons its larder.

What happens if the shrike cannot ingest a piece of food that is too big and gets stuck? It either disgorges it, or passes its foot along the side of the head, and the claws catch the projecting part of the food at the side of the mouth.

The young and the parents regurgitate pellets of undigestible parts of the prey. Both young and parents also defecate; the young in the nest produce fecal sacs which the parents carry off.

The shrike is no shrinking violet. One observer saw a shrike attack a canary in its cage on a porch. Or a shrike has even entered a room through an open window to do this, even while humans were in the room. In each case the canary panicked and tried to escape by sticking its head out between the bars of the cage, making it easy for the shrike to snip its head off with its powerful mandibles.

Another observer found a shrike which had caught a garter snake. The snake then coiled around the body of the shrike, threatening to strangle it until he released the shrike.

A bird bander once noted that after he banded the leg of a nestling the mother bird noticed it and tried to treat the band as a fecal sac. She pulled and tugged, lifting the band and leg of the young one out over the edge of the nest. Finally she lifted the entire bird out of the nest and flew some six feet with the band in her bill and the young one dangling beneath, before crashing to the ground with the weight. Both parent birds hovered over it, greatly upset and crying loudly. After the female finally returned to the nest, the bird bander returned the young to the nest. Thereafter, several times the female left the nest to return to the spot where the young one had lain on the ground! It seems this bird cannot count, and returned to that spot by reason of memory, not because of where the young is seen or heard.

North America has two very similar species of shrike. The northern shrike, *Lanius excubitor*, breeds in northern Canada and winters in northern United States. *Lanius* is Latin for butcher, fitting for this butcher bird. The *excubitor* is Latin for sentinel, since its custom of sitting on a post is reminiscent of a sentinel.

The other shrike is the loggerhead shrike, named for its big head. In its name *Lanius ludovicianus* the Latin specific scientific name seems to be named in honor of a German named Ludwig, whose name was Latinized, and whose last name was a village, the Latin being *vicus*. The suffix *–us* is masculine, since Ludwig was a man.

Cherokee Indians have confused the shrike with its look-alike the mockingbird by naming them both the head-eater. So they thought the mockingbirds' calls mimic songs of other birds because they ate heads (containing singing acumen) of other birds.

In the Upper Midwest any shrike seen from November 1 through March 15 is a northern shrike. A shrike seen in October and from March 15 to May 1 may be either a northern or a loggerhead shrike. The larger northern shrike has a lighter lower bill and faint barring on its breast. The main difference between the two species is that the northern shrike eats more songbirds.

So this songbird lost interest in singing and developed a raptor's hooked bill to rip and cut the necks of other songbirds.

Canada Jay Has Cheek

The most striking trait of the Canada jay is its extreme tameness or boldness.

To best see this bird go to Canada, where they live in the Boreal Region, which consists of the Hudsonian Life Zone (Alaska, Mackenzie River Delta, south shore of Hudson Bay, and Labrador) and the Canadian Life Zone (Alberta, Ontario, Maine, and northern Minnesota). There you need not search hard to find one of these gray jays, for it will come to you.

The black-capped chickadee is the bird with the greatest curiosity in the deciduous woods of the United States, and the Canada jay has that position in the coniferous woods of Canada.

If, perchance, the Canada jay does not greet you, it may be because you are earlier than the tourist season. They are quiet and secretive during their nesting season. The nest is built in February and the eggs are in it by April. To be insulated sufficiently while there is still deep snow on the ground with below zero weather, the outer nest consists of

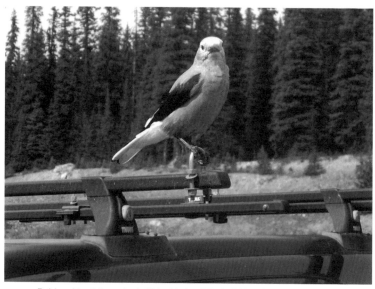

Bold parking lot greeter in Yoho National Park, British Columbia, Canada.
Photograph by Norton R. Johnson

sticks, moss, old spider nests, and bark, placed in a spruce tree. The inner portion is completed with the same material but of finer grade, plus gray jay and local grouse feathers. When the jay is snuggled down in the close-fitting cup the interior stays warm even in bitter cold weather. While the incubating female carefully keeps the nest perfectly clean of any filth, the male effectively removes from the ground any fallen particles during nest construction, and all food particles and feces dropped by the young. So no trace of the nest is there to reveal its secret presence.

After the fledglings have flown the nest the family resumes its activities of patrolling the North Woods.

For the campers, they barely select a site in the campground before the gray jays find them, looking to satisfy their nearly omnivorous diet. They invade the tent, raid the picnic table, open boxes and cans, eat from the frying pan and lunch plates, even landing on the camper's knee or hand.

The back-woodsman tramping or snowshoeing through the woods is not alone, for he is accompanied by the Canada jay, watching his every move. When it is meal time the jay joins him, being very tame, and eagerly shares his food without any invitation to do so. Likewise with his cabin. It enters the cabin to open every container and eat. Every unprotected edible entity is eaten or carried off, and the jay spoils whatever is left behind. The lumber camp is in the same situation.

The trapper finds bait removed from his traps, and any animal caught in the trap is eaten. If an animal carcass is hung on a tree the jays will peck holes in it and dig down in each hole to eat the meat, thereby destroying the quarters.

What do the birds do with the food they steal and don't eat where found? They cache it. To make the trip worth while, they take as big a load as possible, such as carrying three baked beans in the throat with one in the bill.

The cache site can differ with each trip. A horizontal hemlock branch may hold a mouthful of oatmeal. Bread crumbs may be in a crotch of a tree, and overlapping fir twigs will secure a chunk of bread. Four beans may rest on a flat surface. A storehouse of a handful of biscuits may be in a tree stub. Berries have been found in hollow trees.

If the birds notice a person looking at a cache they would empty it and move it to another depository. These jays have a remarkable memory, for they retrieve over a thousand seed caches each year, in times of need.

Bent in his Life Histories book on jays relates Canada jays' encounters with other spruce woods dwellers. We paraphrase.

They like to associate amicably with adults of yellow-rumped warblers, winter wrens, chickadees, and purple finches.

They attack all hawks and hawk owls and boreal owls.

A robin tried to drive away this gray jay attempting to steal the robin's egg.

Two jays repeatedly dive-bombed a weasel. Its white fur was soiled with blood, and it was running between patches of snow trying to disappear. When the head and neck of the weasel showed up out of a hole in the snow, the two gray jays alternated in swooping down and slashing with its beak. Blood spots appeared on the snow. The weakened weasel finally found refuge in a pile of brush. That pair of jays in protecting their nest with its young birds bested one of the fiercest fighters in the woods.

A woodpecker was chased away from a worm it just pulled out of the hole it had chiseled in the tree.

One observer watched two ruby-crowned kinglets darting at two jays, each of which was holding a nearly grown kinglet in its claws. Each jay opened the stomach, ate all the viscera, pecked at the head, and devoured the nestling.

They have also been seen carrying nestling Audubon's warblers.

But the Canada jay has its positive aspects as well. All woodsmen are not antagonistic to it. Those native islanders on Anticosti Island in the Gulf of St. Lawrence have a friendly attitude. In the cold winter when supplies are low poachers come to get deer. But Canadian game wardens listen for the chatter of the jays enjoying their habit of being camp followers, track those sounds to the poachers' camps, and arrest the poachers and salvage their booty.

Spruce woods are huge, desolate, monotonous, and quiet. So when this robin-sized bird with dark gray back and pale gray belly breaks the stillness and flies along with the trapper, he likes to have a companion.

I'm sure a moose likes them, for when a hunter approaches, the gray jay accompanying it sounds an alarm which warns the moose.

Tough Nut To Crack

The most apparent activity of Clark's nutcracker is that it cracks nuts, hence its name. The scientist who observed it thought so too, for now its scientific name is *Nucifraga columbiana*. This was derived from the Latin word *nux*, which means a nut, and from the Latin word *frango*, which translates as, "I break in pieces."

The specific portion of its name, *columbiana*, is named after the region where this nutcracker lives as a mountaineer, in Colorado, Wyoming, Idaho, Washington, and into Canada. The English named their Canadian portion of its range British Columbia.

This nutcracker was named to honor the co-leader of the 1804- 1806 Lewis and Clark Corps of Discovery expedition, which first discovered it and described it.

The nuts it cracks are from the cones of the Douglas fir and limber pine and other pines, as well as seeds of the cedar and juniper. Seeds are tough to crack, but Clark's nutcracker is up to the task. It has a very strong bill, having been compared to a crowbar.

Speaking of crows, taxonomically Clark's nutcracker is

As Clark's nutcracker scrutinizes my offering to it,
it seems to say, "Do you call that a nut?" Photograph by Kenneth J. Johnson

a specialized jay belonging to the *Corvidae* family of birds that includes jays, crows, magpies and ravens. So it shares the family traits of being strong, rugged, vocal, bold, brazen and intelligent.

Like a gray jay, it is a camp robber, but it carries the gray jay's chutzpah farther up the mountain side. The nutcracker lives at elevations from 3000 feet up to 13,000 feet, and breeds from 6000 to 8000 feet, between the lower edge of the coniferous forest up to the timber line.

In its well built foot-sized nest, hidden high in a pine tree, the fledglings hatched in April are fed partially digested pine seeds by regurgitation. Later they are fed the seeds whole. As they become feathered they are lured from the nest by having to come to the parent to be fed.

Finding an active nest is a challenge, for at over 6000 feet elevation in April one would have to plow through snow up to four feet deep.

To function at that height in winter conditions, and raise a brood doing so, the bird would need to use its energy wisely. So the parent collects the seeds by storing them under its tongue and in its throat. The pouch that is formed there has been found to hold over fifty pine seeds. To carry that weight this bird has to be a powerful flyer.

In summertime before the pine seeds ripen the nutcracker eats insects, often caught like a flycatcher does, by sallying forth to catch them on the wing.

Since the pine seed harvest isn't year-round, the Clark's nutcracker caches the seeds in crevices, and even in the ground, where some are never retrieved. In this way new pine trees are grown, to eventually yield more pine cones in due time.

We found that these birds, being camp robbers raiding campgrounds for food, are easy to attract by feeding them. They are bold enough to approach almost to arm's length, as my picture demonstrates. We got our best view of a Clark's nutcracker in the tourist campground in Mount Rainier National Park in Washington.

Perching Performers • *177*

Clark's nutcracker doesn't migrate north and south like other birds, but migrates up and down mountain sides. So in winter it may venture out onto the plains. It has been recorded several times in the North Dakota Badlands, and once in Belfield, N. D. It has shown up in the annual Christmas Bird Count held at Medora, N. D.

Besides being bold, these are raucous birds, and can afford to be, for they seem to have no enemies to fear. When you are visiting the high mountains in Western United States watch for a noisy flock of foot-long light gray birds with black wings.

Meet The Magpie, The Most Brazen Bird

The prairie dog, antelope and magpie are considered to be West River denizens. But unlike the mammals, magpies can fly, so look for one east of the Missouri River. At each Christmas Bird Count our club members from Mandan were considered remiss if they failed to add the magpie to the list, but our Bismarck members were excused if they failed to do so. To find this bird in Burleigh County, this writer recommends going to the Glencoe Presbyterian Church on south Highway 1804, then drive west on the boundary road between Burleigh County and Emmons County.

The magpie is found around the world in the boreal latitudes of the Northern Hemisphere. The early English name, magot pie, was contracted to magpie. The mag part of its name is a contraction from Maggie, or Margaret, which was the name of a chattering female, in reference to its voice. The scientific name given to this northern bird is *Pica pica*. *Pica* is Latin for magpie and also for an omnivorous bird, because it seemed willing to eat everything. Pica is now a medical term for a condition where the patient has a morbid appetite for unusual food. The Latin *pica* also refers to black and white coloration, which is the magpie's color scheme.

But now again the lumpers and the splitters got busy. These taxonomists decided that the American magpie was a subspecies of the Eurasian magpie, so it was named *Pica pica hudsonia*, since *hudsonia* referred to the Hudsonian Life

MAGPIE: "I'LL GET THAT BUG OUT OF YOUR EAR"

Zone, which extends from Alaska to Canada's Hudson Bay. The Hudsonian Life Zone is a division of the Boreal Life Zone.

In the last few years our magpie achieved a full species status – it is now *Pica hudsonia*!

Magpies have always captivated humans, who have given them over 400 names. They have appeared in folklore and in superstitions. They are attracted to civilization. In camps of Indians and later in the Lewis and Clark expedition, magpies would enter tents, snatch food from dishes, and steal pieces of meat from game which was being dressed. Such piracy, of course, resulted in men hating magpies and trying to kill them. One rancher whose spread is south of Medora has the side of his barn decorated with a row of dead magpies, hung side by side in a row. He likely was motivated by noting the birds' habit of killing and eating his young barnyard chickens. He also may have observed them picking at his cattle's ears, thinking the cattle were being harassed. The cattle actually were pleased to get ticks removed from their ears, just as deer and elk also benefit from this practice. Maybe he had witnessed a darker side of magpies, when they have been known to open sores or cuts and eat the flesh of an injured cow or horse or sheep, even persisting to the death of the animal.

Meriwether Lewis when westbound with his and Clark's Corps of Discovery shipped back to Washington, D.C. from North Dakota a collection of things to show what the corps had found. Among the artifacts were a prairie dog and a magpie, in separate cages, of course. President Jefferson kept the magpie in his home as a pet.

It is agreed that the *Corvidae*, the family of jays, crows, and magpies, includes the most intelligent birds, and the magpie is probably the smartest. It is too clever to be caught in a trap that ensnares other birds. Its loose colonies are situated near best food sources; they have been quick to note the abundance of their food around horses and barns. Captive birds kept as pets have imitated words they hear spoken. They engage in mobbing, where a group will engage in dive-

Magpie, camp robber, escaping with cheese. Photograph by Jon Arne Saeter

bombing and pecking a predator. They may move one of their eggs to another magpie nest as insurance in case one nest is destroyed, so some progeny will survive for posterity. While the female is incubating the male is solicitous in keeping her well fed, but at the same time philanders among other females, increasing the odds his genes will be passed on.

This 20 inch long bird, whose length includes a 10 inch long tail, builds a most unique spherical nest two feet in diameter. It is made of stiff twigs, preferably thorny. The hollow interior is accessed by two openings. The floor of the inside cavity is made up of mud or cow dung, on which is laid five to ten eggs. Occasionally another bird, such as a black-crowned night heron, may build its nest on top of that ball of twigs! Song birds often take refuge inside an empty nest, such as during a storm or when being chased by a raptor.

So if being brazen will get you far in life, the magpie surely has a secure future.

Raven

In the world of birds, the raven is in a class by itself. No other bird has all the attributes that men have ascribed to it.

The raven appears several times in the *Bible*. In Genesis 8:7 Noah released a raven from the ark to look for land. In 1 Kings 17 because Elijah gave wicked King Ahab a dire prophecy Ahab sought to kill Elijah, so God directed him to go into hiding by a brook. There a raven brought Elijah food twice a day. Proverbs 30:17 warns that one who disrespects his parent will have his eye plucked out by a raven. (They have been known to do this to animals.) In Job 38:41 God admonished Job by stating that one of the myriad of things He does is to provide food to the raven. Psalm 147:9 confirms God's care for ravens. For the third time in the *Bible* Luke 12:24 reiterates how God feeds the raven; so could it be God's favorite bird?

Over two thousand years ago the Celts embellished their weapons with depictions of ravens, which they revered highly. An old saying warns that if the ravens ever abandon the Tower of London England shall fall to her enemies. Today the British still maintain the presence of ravens there by a full-time caretaker, the Raven Master. This author witnessed two ravens at this tourist attraction. The area contains a castle built during the Medieval Age by a Norman invader, and named Ravenscroft after the dense woods and hill where ravens lived.

Through the centuries successive owners of Ravenscroft met tragic fates, attributed to a curse by the ravens, an omen of death. A white raven is a Celtic symbol of peace. Refer to the Internet website by Google, by clicking ENGLISH+CASTLE+RAVENS.

The Murdoch of Cumloden coat of arms depicts two dead ravens, side by side, joined by an arrow piercing the neck of each raven! Hear the story of how this came about. In 1307 King Robert the Bruce and his group were fleeing from the English. He sought lodging in a widow's house, who shared her meager food. Eyeing her three stout sons, he asked them

Raven. Photograph by Anders Lamberg

to join him if they could show their skill in archery. The eldest son shot an arrow at two ravens perched on a high pinnacle and shot them both through their heads. These three men followed King Robert as he threw the English out of Scotland. In reward they received title to the area of Cumloden.

In one of the greatest poems ever written, *The Raven*, Edgar Allen Poe was dozing in his library one December midnight, sorrowing for his lost Lenore. Answering a tapping on the window, Poe opened it allowing a raven to fly in. When he asked the bird its name, "quoth the raven, 'Nevermore.'" When Poe pined for respite from memories of his sweetheart Lenore, quoth the raven, "Nevermore." When Poe asked if there was any rest from the horror haunting him, quoth the raven, "Nevermore." Poe then asked if he would ever meet Lenore again, quoth the raven, "Nevermore." Then Poe shrieked at the raven to get back outside into the winter tempest, but quoth the raven, "Nevermore." (Ravens have a rich vocabulary, so Poe's raven is credible.)

A thousand years ago the Vikings' god Odin had two ravens who went out in the morning to fly over the world using their sharp eyes to observe. Then in the evening they returned and reported all the day's happenings to Odin. Today the Norwegians often name their boys after the raven because of respect for it, or to honor how smart the raven is. Today in Norway, I am told, there are over fifty men named "Ravn" in the phone books in that small nation.

Iceland has a legend that a raven saved a girl from an avalanche. Inuits are convinced ravens help their hunting by pointing with their wings toward the caribou, polar bears, or seals. Tibetans believe the raven is the messenger of God. Irish felt that ravens knew everything.

The Indians along the Pacific Coast in Alaska and British Columbia had legends about the raven, and this bird was at the top of totem poles carved by Indian tribes, such as the Tlingit.

The ravens are avian acrobats. They have twisted, tumbled, somersaulted, and flown upside-down as they grasped talons. They have tossed an object in the air to catch it again, or tossed it to each other repeatedly. They have hovered with wings steady, or risen to great heights to dive bomb, and have mobbed foes. They have teased a pursuer by staying out of reach, or turned aside just as it was attacked, and have pulled the tail of a wolf. They can slide in snow or drop rocks on someone, or drop a nut or shell onto a hard surface to expose its meat.

A trap can be robbed, food can be stolen, prey can be taken from a predator, eggs and young can be taken from a colony of gulls or herons, hawks can be made to give up their catch. In Arctic villages where they are not harassed they are extremely tame but stay just out of reach as they keep the village clean.

Ravens have been known to solve problems, such as reeling in a string to which food has been tied. They avoid a carcass if wolves are absent, but join them where the wolves are eating their kill. Ravens alert wolves to danger and to sources of food. They store food and return later to eat it. They know how far a gun can shoot. A raven can count to seven.

So, throughout the history of mankind, some peoples revered the raven, some peoples reviled the raven, and both respected the raven's super-intelligence.

When A Crow Calls,
Each Caw Means Something

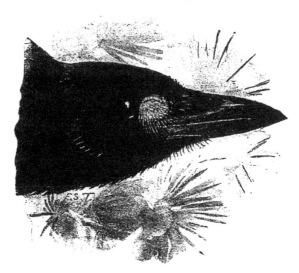

Silverspot.

E. T. Seton's sketch of Silverspot, who could always be recognized.

My boyhood favorite author was Ernest Thompson Seton. In one of his books, *Wild Animals I Have Known*, this naturalist described a certain crow, a leader of his band, whose language included over ten distinct messages, one for each purpose.

Each call in Seton's book was written on the treble clef musical score. The first call was two F quarter notes, one each to a measure of music. Playing it on my piano, it seems Bismarck crows sing it three notes lower, at middle C note pitch. Seton was listening to Toronto and Manitoba crows. Nevertheless it seems all ten messages are valid. This no. 1 caw caw message says, "All's well, come right along!" as the crow leads his band in flight.

No. 2 call was one caw half note D ending as an abbreviated quarter note a step higher – E. It means, "Be on your guard," sent when the crow spotted Seton.

Once when it noted that Seton carried a walking stick it

Caw **Caw**
Call no. 8, "Goodday." is for
making contact.

Ca
Call no. 3, "Danger," is for
sounding caution.

ca ca ca ca Caw
Call no. 4, "Great danger," is
shouting an alarm.

Caw   **Caw**
Call no. 1, "All's well," is
announcing an all is clear.

Musical scores written by E. T. Seton.

uttered call no. 3, a brief caw quarter note four steps higher in pitch–B. This meant, "Danger." (Have you noticed that when a bird is in stress, its call is in a higher pitch? And in extreme stress, even agonal, it approaches a scream? In stress the syrinx throat muscles tighten to narrow the airway, causing a higher pitched sound to emerge.)

When Seton carried a real rifle, this crow gave call no. 4, four quick staccato cacacaca eighth notes, followed by a quarter note, all at the same pitch–B–as call no. 3. This call for retreat meant, "Great danger–a gun!" The others in the band immediately repeated this call as they scattered and flew out of range.

When a red-tailed hawk appeared, this leader crow cried, "Hawk, hawk," as call no. 5, consisting of a half note E caw with a short downward deflection quarter note two steps lower–C, followed in the next measure of music with the same two tone combination. This caused the flock to mass in a solid body as they flew past the hawk.

Call no. 6 was reserved for extreme danger but was written on the music text in Seton's book the same as call no. 4–all B notes. However, he claimed to recognize many other calls he didn't describe, noting that very little difference in sound makes a very great difference in meaning.

While no. 5 meant hawk, the same combination of two downward caws but now D-C instead of E-C, followed by four rapid staccato notes two steps lower in pitch, was labeled no. 7. This means, "Wheel around." So no. 7 is a danger message similar to no. 5, followed by a retreat order similar to no. 4.

No. 8, caw, caw with each half note F caw slurring down to a shorter quarter note only one step lower–E–meant, "Good day," a friendly greeting to a crow some distance away.

No. 9, meaning "Attention," consisted of three short quarter notes A, one in each measure of music, each separated by a musical rest.

No. 10 was heard only during courtship. One crow, a male, would lower its head, ruffle its feathers, come face to face with another, a female, and gurgle out a long sustained tremulous "C-r-r-r-a-w" in a descending musical pitch of half notes. Seton didn't mention the prolonged nasal whining cry of the young bird at the nest, meaning "Feed me!"

Bismarck, North Dakota crows are living in a corvine paradise. They have plenty of food and shelter, and as long as Bismarckers love tall trees there are plenty of nesting sites. Bismarck crows never see a rifle, nor a red-tailed hawk in town, and are always in sight of humans who are harmless, so they may not need to sound their most desperate alarms. That is consistent with the central C pitch of our relaxed crows, contrasted to the higher F pitch of Seton's stressed crows, since stress causes higher pitch.

But once I heard our? crows – or migrating strangers? – use a pitch higher than C; at dusk instead of settling down to roost they milled around repeating call no. 7 "Wheel around," because of a danger undetermined to me.

I have often heard the no. 1 "All's well" call, and the no. 8 "Good day" greeting, and the no. 9 "Attention" message.

Listen closely to each crow you hear, and translate what it says into English! To break the code, keep three things in mind: how high each note is, how long each note is sung, how long a time between each note.

Seton was able to crack the code in crow conversation because he listened to his crow, Silverspot, day after day, year after year. He was able to hear that same crow, the leader of his band, because he could always identify that same individual. It had an identifying mark, a distinctive white patch, before its eye. Silverspot stood out with his white spot, and was always the lead crow in the fly-by.

A crow with a small cluster of white feathers in its plumage is a rarity, but such a marked raven or grackle has also been seen on occasion.

White feathers on a crow are rare. Photograph by Kenneth J. Johnson

Cliff Swallow

Cliff swallows built their nests on cliffs before civilization came to America. In the 1820s and 1830s they discovered that eaves of buildings provided excellent nesting sites, so their nests first started to appear there. As buildings multiplied, so did the swallows. Then many years later in the Midwest the prairie offered few buildings, but section line roads resulted in bridges over creeks. The innovative birds found ideal nesting sites on the undersides of bridges, which also provided protection from vandalism by the creek water forming a barrier to approach to the nests. And the creek provided a handy source of mud for nest building.

So today a bird watcher exploring the prairie which has been turned to over-grazed pasture and barren tilled fields, and bored by the resultant paucity of bird life, has his heart thrilled by this cluster of birds about the bridge.

A complete demonstration of nest building by the cliff swallow is the easiest to watch of any bird I know. The side of the building offering optimal protection from wind or rain or hot sun is skillfully chosen. On a warm sunny day the swallows find a nearby mud puddle. The swallows cluster about it, their feet barely touching the ground with their tip-toes. Their wings extend backwards and skywards and flutter constantly as the birds maintain a soft twittering. Their bodies tip forward to allow their open beaks to mouth a glob of mud around in their mouths. After a pellet of mud is formed, presumably with their saliva as a binder, they fly up under the chosen eave and deposit the glob of mud. Successive globs of mud gradually form a hollow gourd shape, finished off by a small hole just large enough to allow entry and exit by the bird. Each pellet dries quickly before it receives the next pellet. Bent recorded the case of a lazy swallow that stayed by her nest waiting until her neighbor deposited a pellet for her nest, then she reached over and moved the neighbor's pellet to add to her own nest!

The only time a cliff swallow is on the ground is when it copulates. The black swift even has sex while flying.

Cliff swallows in and on their nests. Photograph by Kenneth J. Johnson

When nests are adjacent, a female may easily lay her egg in a neighbor's nest, deliberately or by error. Cliff swallows have been known to carry an egg from one nest to another, in their beak.

Once they were observed to plug up the entry hole to one nest, and build another nest on top of it. After the birds had finished raising their young and had departed on their southward migration, the observer broke open the sealed off nest and found a dead cliff swallow, which had died a natural death while in the nest, and of course could not be removed by the survivors.

These birds are entirely insect eaters. When feeding their young they provide soft-bodied insects, such as flies, by regurgitation. When eating for themselves they also eat hard-bodied insects, such as beetles. But their food is all air-borne, caught when they are flying. If a bird can't find insects it may follow another who was a successful forager.

I have never known a swallow to get hit by a car. They are far too nimble a flyer for that ignominy.

Bent in his book *Life Histories of North American Flycatchers, Larks, Swallows, and Their Allies* has revealed that while warblers fly at night non-stop across the Gulf of Mexico, cliff swallows in their migration fly around the Gulf feeding on insects by day, to roost in trees and bushes at night.

The swallows of San Juan Capistrano Mission near Laguna Beach, California are internationally famous for their arrival there on March 19 of each spring migration. These are cliff swallows.

Its generic name, *Petrochelidon*, is derived from the Greek *petro*, meaning a rock, plus the Greek *chelidon*, meaning a swallow. The specific name used to be *albifrons*, from the Latin *albies*, meaning white, with the Latin *frons*, meaning forehead. But then someone tinkering with what is supposed to be the immutable changed the specific name to *pyrrhonota*; *purrhos* is Greek for red, *noton* is Greek for the back, because (only) the rump is red. The white forehead by far is more logical as a noticeable distinguishing characteristic for use in a scientific binomial. Scientific names were created to be changed only if some new discovery proved the original name to be inaccurate. Perhaps it was justified because a few foreheads were found to be pale buff, not pure white.

Our Faithful Winter Friend

Dorothy Moses (a grade school in Bismarck, N. D. is named after her) once told me her favorite bird was the much maligned house sparrow because it is faithful and stays with us while the songbirds all desert us and fly south for the winter. She could have chosen the white-breasted nuthatch instead, for it is our faithful winter friend, and, contrasted to the house sparrow, no one has ever had anything bad to say about it.

In the summer it patrols tree trunks unobtrusively, its soft nasal yank-yank voice drowned out by all the more conspicuous and louder songsters. Then in the cold winter when the woods and suburbs are quiet we can hear its soft song which was unnoticed or drowned out the summer before.

Two little birds spend their time on tree trunks during North Dakota winters. The brown creeper has a stiff end to its tail to use as a prop as it climbs upwards looking for hibernating insects. The white-breasted nuthatch has the conventional soft tip to its tail as it creeps down and around on the trunk looking for similar prey. While it looks into upward facing crevices, the brown creeper looks into downward facing crevices. So they don't compete with each other.

A nuthatch is the only bird that can descend a tree trunk head first. What keeps the nuthatch from falling to the ground as it descends the tree trunk? While one foot is moving forward, the other

Avian acrobat doing the splits.

foot is turned backwards to the rear as its claws dig into the bark for support against the pull of gravity – an avian acrobat doing the splits!

The brown creeper is colored to blend in with the tree trunk, but the black, white and blue white-breasted nuthatch stands out. Perhaps someone who reads this can explain why.

T. S. Roberts says this nuthatch visits a farmer's corn-crib to transport a corn kernel to a crevice in a fence post or tree trunk, where it wedges the kernel into the crevice so it can break it apart into small bits, the same as it does with nuts.

A. C. Bent says they mate for life, and throughout the year are within call of each other. Their yank, yank song is mostly a call to keep in touch with their nearby mate. If one bird dies, its place is promptly filled by an occasional wandering single bird. What a model for today's society, with its high divorce rate!

Some American Indians thought this white-breasted nuthatch was deaf because it tolerated such close contact with humans. This trusting nature explains why it is easy to hold nuts or suet in one's hand to entice the nuthatch to land and feed while perched on the outstretched hand.

How did the nuthatch get its common name? It is a combination of nut and hatch. Hatch came from the French *hacher*, which came from the German *hacken*, which means to cut. The bird typically uses its bill to chisel apart a nut into little pieces to eat.

How did the nuthatch get its scientific name, *Sitta carolinensis*? *Sitta* comes from the Greek *sitte*, which is the Greek's name for a nuthatch. It seems apparent that the Carolinas, North and South, were on the mind of the ornithologist who named this sittine bird.

Every feeder watcher who puts out suet in his bird feeder is familiar with this friendly little bird.

Perky Pugnacious Wren

The house wren is no shrinking violet – quite the opposite. When the male arrives in the springtime he selects a piece of land an acre in size and declares it as his exclusive territory. If another male wren intrudes, the stranger is scared away by his territory song. If another species of bird establishes a nest, the nest, eggs and young are apt to be destroyed by the wren.

The territory song is also for attracting a female. She will choose a mate by deciding which male's song sounds most attractive to her. While singing the male has also been selecting twigs and sticks and grass, with which he builds a nest to present to the female.

I know of a man who built a mansion in Rockport, Texas as a surprise for his wife. When finished and he presented it to her, she was so dissatisfied with it and so outraged at his secrecy that she divorced him. That was almost like the male wren who built a nest in a nest box and presented it his bride. She strongly disapproved of his taste and proceeded to throw out his nesting material, stick by stick. Thereafter, thoroughly chastened, he contributed very little to the final nest, and spent his time singing and defending his territory. He also started constructing a dummy nest on which to vent his hyperactivity. The dummy nest, so often built, has also been explained as a device to confuse a predator seeking to invade the active nest.

Before the age of wren houses and nest boxes, wrens used tree stumps, upturned tree roots, fallen logs or other cavities. Humans have provided other odd sites unwittingly, such as an old boot, sprinkling can, jacket pocket, farm machinery, or deserted nest of another bird, etc.

The wren house with its opening too small for a house sparrow to enter, presents a challenge for the wren to move twigs, perhaps four inches long, into the house. The wren has learned how to do this by thrusting one end of the stick into the entry hole, then using its bill to move the rest of the stick through the entry hole inch by inch until the stick drops inside. Then it moves inside the box to arrange the stick among the other sticks. When the box is quite full, it rounds out the middle of the sticks and covers them with a lining of rootlets, feathers, grass, cotton, paper, and cocoons. Some of the sticks have egg sacs of spiders attached to them. One observer noted a nest where too many spider egg sacs were attached to the sticks, so when they all hatched before the wren eggs were laid the nest box was swarming with baby spiders. The wrens were forced to abandon their nest.

Some observers have recorded house wrens that failed to raise their own brood, or who didn't succeed in mating, relieve their nurturing energy by feeding other birds, whether young or adult. Thus this frustrated wren in question kept feeding caterpillars to a nesting female grosbeak, who then fed them to her young. When the male grosbeak replaced his mate on the nest, this house wren fed him, who likewise gave the insect food to the young grosbeaks. After the young grosbeaks left their nest this wren fed them directly. After the young matured and flew away this busybody fed a family of house sparrows.

The Chippewa Indians' name for the house wren when translated means "a big noise for its size." Our next door neighbor likely would have considered this an understatement, for this woman hated the wren that lived in our bird box because it sang so loud so early in the morning that she couldn't sleep late. (That was the woman who owned the cat that sneaked over to our sand box to use it as an outhouse, so that we could no longer allow our little children to play there any more. See chapter "Cats Versus Birds.")

The house wren's scientific name is quite apropos. The generic name is *Troglodytes*, which combines two Greek words consisting of *trogle* (a hole) and *dutes* (one that delves into). The species name, aedon, is Greek for a singer. So the namer correctly called this wren one who enters a hole and who is an accomplished singer.

The position of a male house wren's tail reveals how excited he is. If the tail is horizontal, pointing to the rear, he is as calm as he ever gets, such as when he is foraging for food. If the tail is pointing diagonally upward he is singing a courtship song. When he is more excited, such as when scolding, his tail is vertical. When pointed slightly forward he is copulating.

The house wren is a bird of extremes. In defending its territory it may even destroy the domain of another bird. Or if for any reason it can't raise its own offspring, it has been known to adopt birds of another species and feed them. When it builds its nest, it often builds two or three, yet uses only one.

Positiion of tail indicates mood. From top to bottom: foraging, singing, scolding, copulating.

Why There Are So Many Robins

Why are there so many robins? There are some birds that are rarely seen, many species that are uncommon even in their narrow niche. Then there is the American robin, with whom everyone is so very familiar. Here are several reasons we have found for this:

1. When men felled trees and erected buildings they provided the robins with many more sites that give enough support for the bulky nests it builds. Being poorly concealed doesn't matter, for the robin is very capable of defending it.

2. The robin accepts man as a neighbor, adapting to the dense population of a large city.

3. Before settlers arrived there were no earthworms here. When these settlers came, they brought with them potted plants and shrubs with soil containing earthworms, which were and are a major item in the robin's diet. Witness the robin pulling an earthworm out of a mowed lawn.

4. The robin has been typed as being very nervous, even bordering on hysterics, and being almost fearless. It defends its nest and young from meddling birds and mammals, and

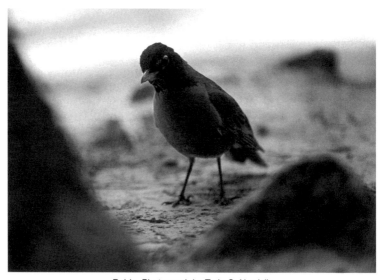

Robin. Photograph by Terje O. Nordvik

even attacks humans if they encroach. Being belligerent pays.

5. Robins typically throw out a cowbird's egg, being strong enough to do so, and are able to recognize that egg as not one of theirs; the cowbird's egg is white, the robin's is robin's egg blue.

6. These birds avoid the life-threatening trauma of migrating across the Gulf of Mexico, and eschew the distances to Central or South America. They do so by wintering in our Southern States. They are hardy enough to endure a rare winter freeze in the Deep South.

7. They raise more than one brood a year, doubling their chances for maintaining their numbers. The male cares for the fledged first brood as the female incubates the second brood, with full time care ensuring maximum success for both broods.

8. People like robins. They think they're cute and charming. Robin Redbreast enjoys a soft spot in humans' hearts because they have a pleasing song singing, "Cheerily cheer up!" They are a welcome harbinger of spring after a harsh winter, and they have a trusting nature to nest in dooryards so close to mankind's activities.

9. They make good neighbors. The fledglings produce fecal sacs, which the parent bird carries away to dispose of elsewhere. The barn swallow, by contrast, is prone to place its nest under an eave, where the young drop their feces on the sidewalk and doorstep, which is unacceptable. The house sparrow makes a huge unsightly nest, its voice is an unmusical harsh chirp, and it steals earthworms from the robin as it pulls them out of the ground.

10. Our culture is conducive to raising robins. The limiting factor in the abundance of a bird species is the availability of nesting sites, and there are plenty of innovative sites for robins still available around our habitations. And our manicured lawns are earthworm factories, producing a plethora of robins' favorite food

Virtuoso Veery

For years many people have been mystified by hearing nocturnal migrating birds sing call notes described as soft mellow whistles. These notes were different from any diurnal birds' notes. This puzzle as to which bird was singing them was finally solved by ornithologist William Brewster in 1907.

In the early morning Brewster heard this call note in the distance come closer and closer until this mysterious bird landed in shrubbery by him. The bird continued to call, but gradually changed the character of the note until it changed into the familiar call of the veery.

The veery's name was derived from its song. The song of the veery has been called one of the strangest sounds in nature. An effort to translate it into English sounds like wheeoo, wheeoo, wheeoo, wheeoo, a series of downward inflected phrases, each a little lower in pitch than the previous phrase. But this ethereal song has qualities that raise it higher above the song of any other bird. Bent in his life histories book on thrushes feels that it "expresses a calmer, deeper, holier emotion, like a hymn or a prayer."

One measure of a robin's song is below the veery's song, but only one fourth of a measure of the veery's song can be shown. To accommodate an entire measure with all of its 1/64 notes, this page would have to be four times as wide.

That it evokes a feeling of sanctity seems due to the technique of harmony, or the curious effect of so-called vocal double-stopping, or arpeggio. Some people have sensed an effect like ventriloquism, when it sounds like there were veeries in every tree, singing in chorus. Other people feel like they are listening to chords or broken chords.

Only by slowing down a tape of the veery's song was it appreciated that it sings 1/64 notes, maybe 1/128 notes, closer together than in any other bird song! To impress the reader with the significance of this, we have tried to compare one measure of music from a robin's song with one measure of a veery's song. But the 1/64 notes took up so much space that we could fit only a fourth of a measure of the veery's song on one page of this book, since it takes 64 of these notes to fill up one measure of musical score.

If any reader is unfamiliar with the symbols used by musicians to record their music, this diagram is presented. A whole note represents one musical note, lasting long enough to occupy one entire measure of time. A half note represents a tone lasting half as long as the whole note, so two of them will fill up one measure. The robin's song pictured shows quarter notes, three of them in one measure plus the musical symbol for rest, a pause of brief silence. So it takes four quarter notes to fill one measure. Each successive note in the diagram takes half as much time as the previous note.

The veerys song is unique, but the deliverance of the song is not unique, for the veery is like many other species in that when the bird sings in the evening it has its favorite singing perch to which it resorts day after day. Bent records that when the veery sings there every evening it always faces northwest on the very same twig!

Its nest is about a yard off the ground, in moist or wet woods, and is made of wet dead leaves on the outside but lined with dry weed stems, stalks of grass and strips of bark on the inside. Mrs. Harding reports what she found when she witnessed a hatchling coming out of its shell. It methodically drilled a series of holes around the large end of the egg, then expanded its body until the shell began to crack open. As the two halves separated the nestling raised up with the shallow cup-shaped piece of egg shell resting on top of its head like a blue hat! The baby bird played the role of a comedian for only a few seconds, until the avian helmet (reminiscent of a World War I helmet) fell off.

The robin browsing for food runs a few feet, stops to cock its head to listen for earthworms, then stabs one. The veery progresses by a series of springing jumps, then pauses with body upright, looking about for insects.

So the nightingale may claim to have the most beautiful song, and the mockingbird may claim the largest repertoire of songs, but the veery sings the fastest notes to produce what people have considered the most ethereal feeling of a hymn or a prayer.

The Deep South's Favorite Bird

The U.S. Postal Service held a nation-wide contest for everyone to vote for their favorite bird. Every state's choice would be pictured on a commemorative first class postage stamp for that state. The idea was a great success. When the fifty stamps were all issued in 1982, it was interesting to see which were the most popular species of birds.

The cardinal was chosen by mostly mid American states: Illinois, Indiana, Kentucky, North Carolina, Ohio, Virginia and West Virginia. Five Deep South states chose the mockingbird: Arkansas, Florida, Mississippi, Tennessee and Texas. The western meadowlark was the choice of six Western states: Kansas, Montana, Nebraska, North Dakota, Oregon and Wyoming.

Five Deep South states didn't pick the mockingbird. Alabama voted for the flicker, Georgia the brown thrasher, Louisiana the brown pelican, South Carolina the Carolina wren, and Maryland the Baltimore oriole.

But that should not unseat the mockingbird as Deep South favorite bird. South Carolina chose the Carolina wren because it has Carolina in its name.

Two hundred years ago Mark Catesby, a pioneer ornithologist, found the mockingbird in the Carolina Low Country in the region around Charleston, and it has become recognized as the bird most closely identified with South Carolina ever since then.

It is completely at home along the barrier islands hearing the Gulf Stream rollers, the pines and cypresses, the live oaks and magnolias inland, and the old city with its garden walls and homes. Most of the mockingbirds live in towns and cities.

Jean Berry, a resident of Charleston for over 35 years, tells, "of living on James Island, a heavily wooded barrier beach land that stretched east along the Ashley River and curved to form the southern part of Charleston Bay toward the tip of Charleston and the Fort.

"The mockingbirds nested in the pine trees and tall, deep

America's mockingbird is the greatest songster of all the birds.
Photograph by Patricia Burike

hedges – or under overhangs of buildings. A mocker daily set up a call that sounded like baby kittens or very young cats. The family mother cat, who recently had her only brood of kittens, kept a constant search for missing babies – in the wood pile, by tool shed or garage and shop walls, as the teasing bird lured her away from his family tucked under the eaves of the garage. The family elder cat, a neutered male, finally spotted the mockingbird as it flew from oak tree to pines, away from the garage. Yet neither cat ever spotted the mockingbird nest!"

Bent in his *Life Histories of North American Nuthatches, Wrens, Thrushes and Their Allies* also recognized what he called the spirit of play in the mockingbird, but only near its nest. It bedevils cats and dogs nearby, diving on them as they napped, or landing on a dog's back to peck savagely, eventually driving them away with their tails between their legs. The mockingbird is known to attack anything that gets near its nest, even its reflection in a shining hub cap or other chrome on a car.

The greatest fame of the mockingbird is its voice. This was acknowledged in its scientific name. *Mimus polyglottis.*

The generic component means mime. In the specific name *poly* means many, and *glottis* refers to tongue or the narrow opening between the vocal cords in the larynx, which modulates the voice. So its scientific name means "the many-tongued mimic."

And so it is. This mockingbird is agreed to be the most versatile, most capable singer among all the birds. It has been documented that it has sung some ninety different songs in rapid succession! Every species of songster to which it has heard can promptly be mimicked, and even be improved upon by embellishing, made richer in tone and fuller.

Edward Bok, creator of the famous Singing Tower in Florida, imported some European nightingales to enrich the beautiful music from his tower. They soon pleased audiences with their best efforts. But soon the nightingales' songs were heard throughout the surrounding areas, being sung by local mockingbirds, even being improved upon. Upon hearing the mockingbirds' renditions, the caged nightingales were shamed into silence.

Evidence shows this remarkable singing ability is not restricted to a few talented individuals, but is shared among all mockingbirds.

Since first found in South Carolina, it has extended its range into New England, and west to our Southwest, Nevada and California. It is even seen rarely in the northern tier of states out to the Northwest.

A Gentleman But A Drunkard

In the cedar waxwing's scientific name, *Bombycilla cedrorum*, the *Bombycilla* is from the Latin *bombycinus* meaning silky, which is derived from the Latin word *bombycis* for silkworm. The *cilla* suffix is Latin for tail. I don't see how the tail can be considered any more silky than the rest of the plumage, for the entire plumage presents the appearance of being silky or velvety. Such a texture is consistent with the dress of a dignified gentleman, standing with an upright posture and an air of authority that commands respect. That is the impression given by this cedar waxwing as it is perched on the branch of a tree. It also has a long crest evincing authority, like the tall headdress that makes a military officer look taller.

In addition to its trim cinnamon-brown body, this bird is blessed with a white-bordered black mask that extends from the base of its bill, widening through the eye, to taper off on the side of the head. That gives the bird a bright, smart, shrewd look.

This gentleman of authority has another virtue, that of high moral altruism, as it appears to a watcher of birds. Where a cluster of its favorite berries is far out on a limb, accessible to only one waxwing at a time, that lone bird has stretched to pluck one berry at a time, turned to give it to its neighbor behind it, who then passes it bill by bill to the flock down the line, giving each bird a berry to eat.

They have often been noted when lined up on a limb to pass a berry beak to beak down the line, then return it up the line again. This goes on back and forth until the berry gets worn out, whereupon one bird finally eats it. This reminds me of the witticism where the mother who gave the animal cracker to her little boy to play with notices it is missing, and asks him where it is. The little boy says it got too dirty to play with, so he ate it.

The scientific name *cedrorum* is from the Greek word *hadros* for cedar tree, for this bird's favorite fruit is the berry

The side of a building is an unusual choice for a cedar waxwing's nest.
Photograph by Dallas Quamme

from the red cedar, or juniper. So the species name *cedrorum* literally means of the cedar trees.

One ungentlemanly characteristic of the cedar waxwing, however, is its voracious appetite. Sometimes it may continue eating so much that its stomach and throat and bill are packed with berries, and it becomes unable to fly, and falls to the ground helpless. One expert thinks that the mass of berries pushes against blood vessels, including its carotid artery, so the blood supply to the brain is interrupted to cause the bird to blackout.

Sometimes berries are over-aged and become fermented. Both robins and waxwings injudiciously eat them anyway, and continue to imbibe to the point of becoming drunk. They fall to the ground, staggering helplessly. Once a waxwing I saw thus inebriated became the prey of a house cat. Only a pile of waxwing's feathers remained.

Most of our exposure to cedar waxwings is from seeing a flock of twenty or hundreds appear from nowhere to descend on a fruit tree. They frantically eat, each bird moving restlessly from cluster to cluster, until in a moment the berries are gone. Then they arise as one flock to go rest nearby to digest what they have engorged, or fly off to find another feast if they weren't stuffed already.

During their brief banquet at the fruit tree, they all continued trilling a faint soft high pitched whistle. Their vocalization is the highest pitched of all bird songs, being at eight kilo Hertz. A person beginning to get hard of hearing will not be able to hear the cedar waxwing's song while he still can enjoy the songs of other birds.

Waxwing is an odd name for a bird. The secondary feathers of the wings each end as a drop sized piece of red pigment that looks like sealing wax, hence its name. This protects the secondary feathers from wear, but I don't see why these feathers need any special protection.

When stuffing themselves with berries, they may return to their nests to regurgitate the berries one by one into the young ones' eager maws. The fruit the adults eat is digested and the seeds defecated to sew where dropped to produce new fruit trees.

Cedar waxwings don't migrate like other migratory birds do, for some are with us all year. But I see more of them in the winter when a visiting flock adds to the excitement of winter birding.

When a Warbler Perched Motionless

Warblers are the most restless of birds, always in motion, darting around foliage, picking at tiny insects, flitting from spot to spot. Birders are frustrated trying to identify them. They rarely come out from behind the leaves to show themselves. They are all small look-alikes. Most are here only a couple days before moving on in their migration. Identifying marks are seen only when the bird perches at a certain angle, and in good light. And they never pose.

So it is a once-in-a-lifetime experience to see one close at hand and immobile. This happened to us once in Theodore Roosevelt National Park's Cottonwood Campground. I was sitting in our car when I heard a loud thump and looked toward the source of the sound in time to see this bird fly away from the car door to land on a branch in a juniper tree only eight feet away, in plain sight.

There it sat. But it didn't fly away. It didn't move. It was motionless. It remained still as a statue, minute after minute, for some 30 or 40 minutes. Its eyes were open, but as the minutes went by its eyelids closed half way. Then it vanished. I got out of the car and looked on the ground where it would have fallen, but could not find it. So it had recovered enough from its cerebral concussion to have flown off.

What was it? This was late enough in the spring for red-eyed vireo, always the last species of birds to arrive. They were common now, singing their monotonous repetitive ditty.

The red-eyed vireo has a dark crown, a white streak above the eye, a dark streak running through the eye, and a dark smudge below and behind the eye. This bird lacked the smudge. The eye here was not red.

The red-eyed vireo has a back and tail that are brown with a strong tinge of green; this bird had green with a tinge of brown on its back and tail. This was a Tennessee warbler. A final difference is that this warbler's bill is smaller than the vireo's bill.

Why do birds crash into something? Skill in flying must

be learned; in the process there must be bumps and bruises and crash landings. This bird had a definitely greenish cast to the color of its back and tail, which makes it a young first year adult, according to the *Sibley Guide to Birds*. So it was young and inexperienced.

Windows present a double hazard. At one angle a window is transparent, so the bird sees through it and aims to fly into what it sees on the other side of the invisible barrier. At another angle the window is reflective, showing a mirror image of the landscape behind the bird, so the bird blissfully continues flying into the illusion. Any flat shiny surface might act as a mirror.

Especially at night, as in during migration, the speeding bird rams into wires and transmission towers it cannot see in time. Looking on the ground around them at the dead birds thus killed shows how big a problem this is.

In the daytime, when a songbird is chased by a raptor it is flying so fast and so desperately that it cannot exercise proper caution in avoiding obstacles.

So which was the reason this Tennessee warbler crashed into the door of our car?

Forest Fires Sustain This Warbler

There is a species of warbler that would die out if there were no forest fires!

It lives mostly in only three counties, Oscoda, Crawford and Rosecommon, in the Lower Peninsula of Michigan. It nests only among jack pines, and only if they are six to eighteen feet tall. It takes about ten years for jack pine to get tall enough to satisfy this bird, and about ten years later the trees are too tall for them. A bird that persnickety in its breeding requirements would never be common, and indeed this bird is on the endangered list. Locals call that bird the jack pine warbler, others name it Kirtland's warbler.

A. C. Bent in his *Life Histories of North American Wood Warblers* says that in 1851 a man collected a specimen of a new unknown bird in northern Ohio and gave it to his father-in-law naturalist, J. P. Kirtland, who gave it to the ornithologist S. F. Baird. Baird wrote it up in the scientific literature and named it Kirtland's warbler.

This bird's breeding ground was discovered in 1903 in Michigan's Oscoda County by a trout fisherman who knew a new bird when he heard it. He collected that specimen and took it to the University of Michigan's curator of birds, N. A. Wood, who immediately took a train there for an eight day search of the area. Wood finally found the first nest on the ground in a stand of jack pine three to eight feet high, in an area that had been burned by a forest fire a few years earlier. The nest of grass and fibers was on the ground, covered by a roof of grass, with an entrance on one side, like the domed nest which gives the oven bird its name.

The precarious future of Kirtland's warbler was worsened when settlers moved into the region cleared by logging the white and Norway pines, and started farming. This inadvertently introduced the cowbird, which moved in to lay its eggs in the warblers' nests, to cause the warblers to become much rarer. This alarmed the public, who formed a unique alliance of state and federal governments with the Audubon

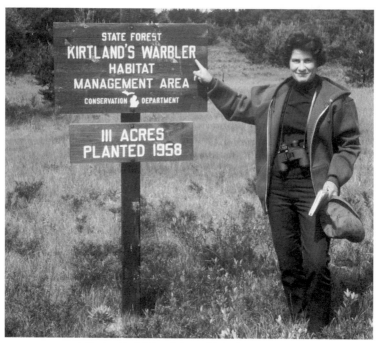
Author's wife, Adele pointing to Kirtland's warbler sign.
Photograph by Kenneth J. Johnson

Society to start a cowbird trapping campaign in 1972. The warbler population leveled off to 200 singing males, and by 2003 had increased to the goal of a minimum of 1000 singing males annually.

Foresters and Nature lovers in the 1920s regarded forest fires as evil destroyers of Nature which must be prevented or fought whenever discovered. But now it was realized that in order to secure the future of this warbler the heresy of deliberately starting forest fires was mandatory! So a series of controlled burns now is part of the program to preserve Kirtland's warbler. This also secures the future of the jack pine, for its small pine cones are tightly sealed and can open only by the intense heat of a forest fire. Then they explode with a popping noise to spray a shower of seeds far and wide, aided by the wind caused by air heated by the fire. These controlled burns are timed now so there always are areas of young jack pine growing which satisfy this fastidious bird.

Kirtland's warbler large portrait sculpture in Mio, Michigan.
Photograph by Kenneth J. Johnson

When we added the Kirtland's warbler to our life list on July 6, 1969 west of Rose City, Michigan we were the only humans around. Nobody was supervising. It was easy to see the singing male. Today bird watching there is different. Nesting areas are posted and off limits. Camping is only in designated campgrounds. The visitor must stay with the guide on tours and follow his instructions. Vehicles must stay on auto tour routes. A permit is required for entry to their habitat, obtainable at Mio.

Visitors' headquarters are in the town of Mio, Michigan, which has a museum for this warbler, and where there is located a unique four-foot tall sculpture of this Kirtland's warbler.

This warbler is almost six inches long, four inches smaller than a robin and a half inch shorter that a house sparrow. Its blue-gray back is heavily streaked with black; its yellow breast has black streaks only on the sides. White color is only on the eye ring and the two inconspicuous wing bars. The male is tame and conspicuous when singing, which it does maybe 200 times per hour. Its loud musical song, said to be the most

THE KIRTLAND'S WARBLER, ONE OF THE WORLD'S RARE BIRDS.
IT IS ESTIMATED THAT LESS THAN ONE THOUSAND EXIST.
THEY NEST ONLY IN THIS PORTION OF MICHIGAN AND WINTER
IN THE BAHAMA ISLANDS.
IN OSCODA COUNTY, THE U.S. FOREST SERVICE,
MICHIGAN DEPARTMENT OF CONSERVATION, MICHIGAN AUDUBON
SOCIETY, CONSERVATION CLUBS, FOREST INDUSTRIES AND
CITIZENS ARE COOPERATING IN EFFORTS TO PRESERVE THIS
WARBLER BY IMPROVING THE NESTING RANGE.

ERECTED JULY, 1963
BY CITIZENS OF OSCODA COUNTY

Kirtland's warbler sign. Photograph by Kenneth J. Johnson

beautiful song of any warbler, is low pitched for a warbler, so it can be heard over a half mile away.

That has been a remarkable history of cooperation between government, business, organizations and the public to protect and preserve an endangered species of bird.

Prothonotary Warbler Convicts Red Spy

This is a true story. It must be true, because nobody could have dreamed up such a tale, made out of whole cloth. How a brilliant State Department official, powerful and influential, was proven to be a traitorous spy giving Communist Soviet Russia our precious state secrets. And a guilty verdict because he was a bird watcher!

Whittaker Chambers was a senior editor of *Time* magazine who renounced Communism in 1938 after years of secretly being a Communist. In August of 1948 he appeared before a House Un-American Activities Committee in the U.S. Congress claiming that Alger Hiss was a Communist who had worked with him in the Communist underground. That was unthinkable, for Hiss was president of the venerated Carnegie Endowment for International Peace after a long career as a lawyer in a high and trusted position in the U.S. State Department.

So Hiss sued Chambers for libel in September, 1948. In 1938 Hiss had given him a packet of documents, copies of classified secret State Department papers. Chambers had hidden them instead of delivering them to the Communists, I deduce, because he had had a change of convictions. During the 1948 proceedings he retrieved them together with photographs of them. When Chambers was served with a subpoena, officials went to Chambers' farm where he retrieved them from their hiding place – a hollowed out pumpkin. They became known as the famous Pumpkin Papers. This trial ended in a disagreement and deadlock, so a second trial was set. It began on November 17, 1949.

The case of Alger Hiss was on the front page of every newspaper, day after day. It was called the most important trial of the century. Hiss was a brilliant lawyer, slick with an articulate mastery of convincing arguments. His strategy was to uncover Chambers' entire past life, stressing any antisocial behavior, even questioning his sanity.

Hiss denied he was a Communist. Hiss denied that he

ever met Chambers, he ever knew Chambers, or that he ever heard if him. Chambers recited a plethora of details about his many meetings with Hiss, plus descriptions of Hiss' various homes when he was visiting Alger Hiss there, and of his periodically receiving from Hiss Communist Party dues. Clearly, somebody was lying under oath.

As for appearances, a jury would tend to favor Hiss. He was tall, thin, handsome, neat, well-dressed. Chambers was short, fat, scruffy, obtuse. Hiss was the better, more convincing speaker.

The second trial displayed much the same techniques – show the other side as deceitful. But this time Chambers testified that they shared the same hobby; they were "ornithologists," or bird watchers. The two were birding together, had seen a prothonotary warbler, a rare bird, a once-in-a-lifetime sighting.

The prosecutor set a trap. During an intermission, he extracted from Hiss the statement that he indeed was an "ornithologist." Hiss went on to say he saw a prothonotary warbler on the Potomac, and described its identifying characteristics. When another prosecutor and Hiss were alone, Hiss confirmed the sighting, same place, same time as Chambers saw the bird.

This was the clinching testimony. In less than twenty-four hours, on January 21, 1950 the jury returned a verdict of guilty of perjury. (The statute of limitations had prevented Hiss from being tried for treason.) Hiss was sentenced to five

Prothonotary warbler declares a Guilty verdict.

years in prison. A Court of Appeals dismissed Hiss' case on December 7. 1950. The U.S. Supreme Court refused to review the case on March 12, 1951.

Of course, it's against the law to harm a wild bird (unless it's a house sparrow or a starling), but just looking at a lovely song bird (a prothonotary warbler, no less), when that act topped a pile of evidence of perjury, sent this man to prison!

Kentucky Warbler

Kentucky Warbler, addled from repeatedly flinging itself against a window pane.
Photograph by Norton R. Johnson

When a building with a window invades a virgin woodlands for the first time in history, that new phenomenon, the window, that reflective but transparent barrier, is a challenge. The woodland bird has no preexistent instinct to cope with it, and probably lacks enough intelligence to know how to learn from the window.

So it was that this Kentucky warbler would fly against this window. It either wanted to fly at the reflection because of the mirror effect, thinking his own reflection was a rival male that was challenging him. Or it had a stubborn insistence of wanting to fly through that transparency to whatever the inside of the building could hold that was so enticing.

Whichever the reason was, the warbler lacked the ability to learn from experience. Slamming one's head against a hard unyielding surface must damage the brain, and the more this trauma is repeated the more the brain is damaged. If cerebral concussion is repeated enough the resulting damage is permanent and irreversible.

If that warbler belonged to the *Corvidae*, the smartest of the birds (except for parrots), would it have known better? No, for I think of that crow that fought its reflection in the glass door of that barber shop at Bismarck's Arrowhead Plaza. It kept banging its head until it left its blood on the glass.

Back in happier halcyon days a warbler could live its entire life without encountering a window. It spent its entire summer breeding range living in the lowest three feet of deep dense deciduous forests. It foraged for insects among leaves on the forest floor, only occasionally flying up less than a yard above the ground to catch a moth. There on the forest floor it built its nest.

Today its habitat is unchanged, for it is one of the birds unable to change its ways. Today there are far fewer Kentucky warblers. Four main reasons are responsible.

Since the buffalo were killed off and cattle put in their place, the buffalo birds became cowbirds, who spread eastward from the prairie to the new cattle pastures that replaced much of the eastern forest. These cowbirds then invaded the forest margins to find warblers' nests. The latter birds, poor to adapt to new things, were helpless in avoiding feeding the young parasite cowbirds that hatched instead of their own.

The lumber industry and the increased populations of new settlers, both in its North American summer range and in its winter range of lowland forests of Central America, have caused a severe decrease in the woodlands that these birds must have in which to live.

The exploding population of white-tailed deer in the United States devours the vegetation of the forest floor, robbing this bird of its security and its food.

Our civilization brought with it pet house cats. They run wild, night or day, to kill birds for food and for sport. Some don't return home, and become wild. Unwanted cats and kittens are bagged, carried far enough away from home so that they never show up at home again, and are dumped. If they don't die, they survive by becoming wild. These feral cats survive by killing birds for food, not sport.

One factor in the future of a migratory bird is whether it has to cross the Gulf of Mexico, that endurance contest obstacle course into which many migrants crash into and drown. Some Kentucky warblers fly across that water hazard, but more follow the land route through eastern Mexico and along the Coastal Bend of Texas.

The bird in the picture was photographed on the ledge of a window in eastern Kentucky, at the center of its summer range, which is the southeastern quadrant of the United States. This species was first seen in 1832 in Kentucky, so the pioneer ornithologist Alexander Wilson who found it named it the Kentucky warbler, which is where he also found it to be most abundant.

Its scientific name, *Oporornis formosus*, is Greek for the autumn bird that is beautiful. I wouldn't argue over whether it is beautiful, but why more so in the fall I do not understand. The male, the female, and the first winter bird all have very similar plumages consisting of greenish-olive back, yellow under-parts plus the line above the eye, and black from under the eye down the side to the bend of the wing.

There are many birds with this problem with windows, such as that cardinal pictured in the chapter There is Humor in Birding.

Contrast In Conforming

Skip this chapter, unless you are analytic, curious, and of a scientific bent.

The genus *Geothlypis*, to which the yellowthroat belongs, responds to environmental influences more readily than does the genus *Oporornis* of other warblers. That means that when the area gets crowded and younger birds get squeezed out they are better able to adapt to new land they must invade. These immigrants produce descendants, and as the years go by their characteristics change from those of the early forebears that are or were back in the ancestral homeland.

The yellowthroat is the extreme example of this process, for thirteen subspecies have been identified on this North American continent. I will number them when I list them.

By contrast, there is only one race of Kentucky warbler, a homogeneous population that is incapable of change, so is endangered, as mentioned in the previous chapter.

Those thirteen subspecies identified by early ornithologists have been separated from each other by characteristics such as body size, size of bill, details of plumage, intensity of color, habitat preference.

(That shows the discovery mind-set of naturalists in those days, for Bent in his life histories series on sparrows also describes 16 savannah sparrow subspecies, 21 song sparrow subspecies, and 27 towhee subspecies.)

1. The type subspecies, *G. trichas trichas*, the first one to be named, was the northern or Maryland yellowthroat.

2. The Florida yellowthroat has a longer leg, tail and bill; a deeper yellow belly; a browner back and sides; and a wider black mask – a more brightly colored bird, as befits the peninsula of Florida. And it is a permanent resident, not migrating.

3. The Athens yellowthroat, named after the city of Athens, is a central and southern Georgia resident. It has a much smaller bill, and brown, not olive green, on its back. As a resident, it is leap-frogged by the northern and Maryland

races during migration.

4. The western yellowthroat is larger, with grayer back and stronger yellow throat, that lives in Oregon, south Idaho, California, and Baja California, and winters in the valleys of southern California.

5. The northern Great Plains yellowthroat lives in Washington, British Columbia, north Idaho, east to North Dakota, and has a grayer back, flanks and belly. It migrates through Colorado and Arizona into Mexico and south.

6. Salt-marsh yellowthroat is a local race living year-round near San Francisco.

7. Golden yellowthroat in Sonora, Mexico and adjacent Arizona is much more yellow to fit its yellow desert environment, and lives in the uplands, not in marshes.

8. Tule yellowthroat lives in marshes of tule, a southwestern species of large bulrush. It has a longer tail, is brighter and larger than the western race. Its range is split. Some live along the Pacific slope from Lower California north to Santa Barbara, CA. The others live from the mouth of the Colorado River, along the river, up to the Virgin River as far north as Nevada and Arizona.

9. Pacific yellowthroat, smaller, is along the Pacific from British Columbia to Mexico. In winter it stays along that portion of the mainland coast of Mexico that is straight east of the south tip of Baja California.

10. Brownsville yellowthroat is in the lower Rio Grande Valley below Brownsville, Texas, but nevertheless migrates south.

11 San Blas, 12 Belding's peninsular, and 13 Goldman's peninsular yellowthroats are all resident in their own areas in Mexico.

Be amazed at how over the centuries a species with the ability to adapt can and has spread over a continent, and adjust to a life different from its distant ancestors, but not yet evolve into new distinct species. Originally a marsh dweller living a few inches above water, some of these birds have moved to meadows and prairies, and even to uplands.

Its scientific name gives no clue to this unusual ability. But of course, the naturalist studying the bird specimen in his hand could see only the bird and remember the events involved in securing it. *Geothlypis trichas* is Greek. The Greek word *ge* translates as earth, or ground. The word *thlupis* means a small bird that is a kind of thrush. Yet in spite of all its evolving, the yellowthroat still lives close to the ground, whether in the marsh, the upland, or along a desert arroyo.

It is important for survival for all species of life to be adaptable, and the yellowthroat has done so.

Chat With The Chat

People always raised their eyebrows and looked suspiciously at that one child who looked very different from his siblings. Likewise, birders looked twice at the yellow-breasted chat, which has been placed in all the bird books with the wood warblers. It didn't seem to belong there. It is too big to fit there, being seven and a half inches long, while all the warblers are only about five inches in length. It is obvious it doesn't act like the other family members. They are all so fidgety and shy, while the chat is so noisy, and attracts attention to itself. Furthermore, its bill is larger, and more curved.

But taxonomists, experts in their field, have decided the chat has anatomy closer to a warbler than to other birds. So be it. They have DNA studies to prove it.

The chat, like its family members, is secretive, but in being shy and hiding from view it is contradictory with its loud repertoire of musical sounds, catcalls, versatile bird sounds and whistles. During all that prolonged singing the chat is not sitting still, but is hopping about and flitting from bush to bush, always keeping out of sight except to expose its head here and there for a second.

Chat, the name of this bird, is a contraction of the word chatter, which is a good description of the songs and noises that it makes. Its scientific generic name *Icteria* is Greek for yellow jaundice; the scientific species name *virens* is Latin for green. So the ornithologist who named it was impressed by this bird's yellow breast and olive green back.

Another prominent color feature of the chat is the conspicuous white broken circle around each eye, connected by a white bar over the nose, and offset by a bright white malar line. This qualifies the

Newly banded yellow-breasted chat, about to be released by the bird bander, is chatting loudly. All other birds were mute when banded.
Photograph by
Kenneth J. Johnson

chat as one of the three birds with a plumage that displays eyewear. The spectacled eider wears goggles of a broad white circle around the eye. The black-capped vireo's black head is accentuated by its bright white circle around each eye, connected by white lores. So it mimics a pair of white plastic frames. The chat's glasses can be called partial frames.

While mentioning colors, we note that the male's mouth lining is black, and the female's mouth lining is pinkish red. Since both parents feed the young, I do not see any reason why this sex difference occurs.

Another puzzle is why the chat uses its foot to hold its food, since they eat all varieties of insects, and when other birds eat those same kinds of bugs they don't seem to hold them with their feet.

Eric Kinsey in *Condor* 36:235- 237 studied a chat all day, and found it had a strict itinerary. This male wakes up on a certain perch on a certain dead cottonwood tree, sings, then flies down to one spot in this meadow. There it feeds and returns to the same perch to sing a while. Next it flies down to a certain elderberry bush, then to a particular nettle, then to where its mate is brooding eggs on her nest, feeds his mate, and returns to his original dead cottonwood. Then he flies to the irrigation ditch for a bath, and back to the cottonwood to preen. Next down to the same meadow for more insects, back to the cottonwood, again to the elderberry, and to the nest. And so on, all morning.

In the afternoon he would go from that cottonwood to another elderberry patch and another meadow and the same nest, again and again. The morning routine was on the east side of the cottonwood, towards the morning sun; the afternoon was on the west side of the cottonwood, towards the afternoon sun. A creature of habit!

My closest chat neighbor spends his summers in Sibley Nature Park, south of Bismarck, N. D. To chat with him, park your car, walk west bearing to the left on the loop path. As you approach the Missouri River, listen for his chatter in the thick bottomland forest underbrush.

An easier view of the chat is among the scattered bushes, which provide no good hiding place for it, on the slope toward the Little Missouri River in Little Missouri State Primitive Park, and Theodore Roosevelt National Park in western North Dakota.

Cardinal: Beautiful Body, Homely Face

Since the cardinal was first discovered its range has been spreading. The first check list for birds, made in 1885, listed its range as south of the Ohio River; it was a true Southern bird. Each successive list found it with a larger area, first New England, next the Mississippi Valley, then the prairie states and Texas. In the 1920s all our neighbors in St. Paul, Minnesota were thrilled to see this beautiful new bird appear, with its pleasing song, to join our local birds.

Three reasons may be offered for this steady expansion. The climate has been getting warmer, extending the warmth of the Deep South northward. It adapts easily to humans, coming into towns and nesting in bushes and gardens and parks. And people have been feeding birds with seeds which are the cardinals' favorite food. As the winter proceeds, when bird feeders remain stocked the cardinals stay instead of migrating south.

A fourth reason may be added, for they have an unusual characteristic of raising three broods a year, not just one or two.

This robin-sized bird lives around houses all day. Its brilliant color screaming for attention, accompanied by its repetitious wheat, wheat, wheat, chew-chew-chew-chew accounts for its popularity. So it was no surprise when in 1982 the United States Postal Service issued a series of fifty commemorative postage stamps, one for each state's favorite bird, as determined by the people in that state. In seven states, Illinois, Indiana, Kentucky, North Carolina, Ohio, Virginia and West Virginia, the cardinal was selected to be pictured on that state's stamp.

During courtship the male stretches his neck and his crest raises high, so that he looks long and slender. It reminds me of the man who pulls in his abdomen to look more slender when an attractive woman comes into the room.

The cardinal's crest is an indicator of its emotions and attitudes. Some individuals, male or female, are pugnacious, fighting any other cardinal that comes to the feeder or approaches its nesting site. When attacking its crest is raised. Often the attack is directed to its own reflection in a window or mirror. When the attacks on this phantom are repeated it is like shadow-boxing. In the chapter "There is humor in birding," a cardinal is described as an extremely persistent fighter.

This beautiful bird is homely, in my opinion. It has a massive beak that qualifies as a schnozzle. (Remember the comedian Jimmy Durante?) It is the typical finch bill, but grosser. This triangular shaped bill of the cardinal is almost as huge as that of the evening grosbeak bill, which occupies two fifths of the distance from front to back of the head. Why is it so massive? It is designed to crack hard-shelled seeds. But much smaller finch bills can crack the same nuts.

In the bird's scientific name, *Cardinalis cardinalis*, the Latin *cardinalis* is translated as a chief, the chief being that Roman Catholic important church official who wears a red robe. (There is another bird that is also named after a Roman Catholic church official; that important clerk is dressed in a yellow garment. That bird is named the prothonotary warbler.)

Lazuli Bunting Or Eastern Bluebird?

While our little group of birders were picnicking in south Bismarck's Sibley Park, we continued to enjoy sighting an occasional eastern bluebird, and to hear its distinctive song, three conjoined notes at a low pitch, lower pitch, and intermediate pitch, at a cadence that simulates the word Juliet.

Much of the time the bird would perch on a low branch, fly down to the ground to pick up an insect, then fly back to its perch. Sibley calls this unique behavior "ground sallying." A flycatcher would leave its perch to catch an insect in midair instead, then return to the same perch.

Our picnic meal finished, we strolled looking for whatever bird came to view. At the edge of the brushy woods harboring the park's campsites, up high on a bare branch, was a bird I considered to be another bluebird. It also had the red and white breast and bluish head and back as well as could be recognized, as it was silhouetted against the sky. Being a repeat bluebird sighting, I didn't mention it to my companions.

But in 20/20 hindsight, I'm sure it was a lazuli bunting, which would have been a prized addition to the group's bird list. Did that bird have a blue throat or a red throat? I didn't pay attention because I hadn't done my preliminary homework to remember the importance of this distinction. Shame on me. In trying to recall, I think its throat was blue, making it a lazuli bunting.

Studying my bird guides back home revealed a curious comparison. Robbins-Zim Golden Guide has the eastern bluebird breast 2/5 red and 3/5 white. National Geographic guide shows the breast as 2/3 red and 1/3 white. In Sibley's book the breast looks 1/2 red and 1/2 white. In Zim's book the bird has a white chin, in the other two books the chin is red.

With the lazuli bunting the underside is two sevenths lazuli (sky) blue, one seventh red, and four sevenths white in Zim's book. National Geographic shows the underside one part lazuli, one part red, 1-1/2 parts white. The Sibley lazuli bunting shows the underside one part deep blue (not sky blue), one part red,

three parts white. Because
of the uneven demarcation
between the two upper
breast colors, the red band
appears to be narrower than
the blue.

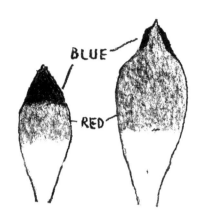

Underside of lazuli bunting on left
and eastern bluebird on right.

Three explanations for
these inconsistencies among
bird guides comes to mind.
Birds do vary between
individuals in details
of coloration. Different
printings have shown they
vary in the exact shades of
colors. Most importantly,
publishers must avoid showing a bird exactly like a rival
publisher does, in order to avoid a lawsuit for plagiarism.

I believe I must have made the common mistake of after
seeing a certain bird species repeatedly, assuming that the next
bird look-alike is another example of that same common species.
B. J. Rose, arguably Bismarck's most astute birder, then later an
international professional birding tour guide, told me once that
when he saw a number of birds of a certain species he always
double-checked every individual for an occasional interloper
from another species.

The eastern bluebird is America's most lovable songbird.
Our literature is familiar with it. Noone has said a negative word
about this "bluebird of happiness."

This insect eater is prized for this beneficial contribution.
The lazuli bunting, as a Western bird, is not familiar to the
public, so does not share the affection shown to the eastern
bluebird.

The bluebird has the thinner bill of an insect eater. The
lazuli bunting, eater of both large insects and seeds, has the
thicker bill of the seed eater.

So where the ranges of these two overlap, keep both birds in
mind when afield.

Divergent Dickcissel

Bird-banding has shown that birds which migrate return the next year to the place where they were hatched. That is the norm. But one bird, the dickcissel, doesn't abide by that rule.

Each year presents a dilemma as to where to find a colony of dickcissels. They will be present one year, then be gone the next year, even though the feeding and breeding conditions seem to be the same there. This writer can recall three times he has seen the bird. Once driving in eastern Nebraska, for mile after mile we heard the dick, dick, siss-siss-sill song with 1-3-567 timing. Once they were present on the outskirts of Bismarck, North Dakota north of Burleigh Avenue (which today is a housing development), adjacent to where the ancient cottonwood tree grows in the middle of the road. We found a colony in the fields on the south side of the entry road which runs from North Dakota highway 22 heading eastward into the Little Missouri State Primitive Park. In other years they were absent there.

After years of absence or scarcity in North Dakota, 2006 was a banner year. They have been reported in a number of places in North Dakota, as well as in Montana and South Dakota. These birds seemed to be especially numerous around Bismarck and south of Valley City. For Bismarckers, the easiest place to find dickcissels was in alfalfa fields from where highway 1804 descends to the Missouri River bottoms, north to Double Ditch. But before this column could be published in the *Bismarck Tribune*, the farmer cut and baled the alfalfa, destroying the dickcissels' nests and their contents. It is questionable if the young were raised successfully.

Why this erratic behavior of not showing up certain years? History indicates that they have always been that mysteriously unpredictable. In the 1800s they were common in Pennsylvania, New York, and east of the Allegheny Mountains. Then from 1900 to 1925 they were gone. Then they were present again from 1925 to 1955, but in small numbers since then. Today they are rare east of the

Alleghenies. As human development and agriculture moved into the Midwest the 1900s found dickcissels adapting to that region. But wherever they are found their numbers vary greatly from year to year. The National Audubon Society has its Blue List of birds with serious losses of populations. The dickcissel is on that list. And in South America, their winter home, they are "persecuted" (Sibley says) because they strip entire fields bare of grain. As human population explodes, this clash can only exacerbate.

Where to find them? Their favorite habitat is a clover field, or alfalfa; second best is a hay field; third best is tall grass prairie. Their worst enemy is a mowing machine, since it destroys nests.

The males arrive a fortnight before the polygynous females, who choose the male that claims the field with the best food sources and nesting sites. The female constructs the nest and incubates the eggs and feeds the young. During this time all the male does is sing, especially during the heat of the day. When the female completes the raising of the young the male quits singing.

Bent (on page 171 in his book *Life Histories of North American Cardinals, Grosbeaks, Buntings, Towhees, Finches, Sparrows, and Allies*) relates an incident where a sharp-shinned hawk swooped down and carried off a female dickcissel as she was carrying food to her young in the nest. The singing male saw this but did nothing except continue singing. During the next two days as the young slowly starved to death he continued singing. It seems our child support laws didn't touch him!

A clue to their abundance may be their food. In studies, the stomach of young birds yielded 1/4 seeds and 3/4 insects, while the stomachs of adults yielded 3/4 seeds and 1/4 insects.

After the young leave the nest dickcissels engage in communal roosting, and assemble in foraging flocks numbering up to a thousand birds.

What does the dickcissel look like? Imagine a nine inch meadowlark shrunk down to a six inch finch. In his breeding

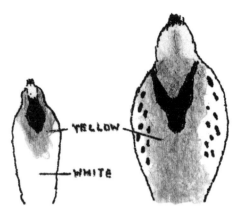

Underside of dickcissel on left and western meadowlark on right.

plumage the male is beautiful. He has a gray back, brown side, white belly, yellow breast, and black bib. The dickcissel's scientific name, *Spiza americana*, is Greek for American finch.

Should you ever be lucky enough to find a field of dickcissels, or a flock of them foraging, share your good news with your birding friends.

Avian Automobile Adaptation

The canyon towhee is about the size of a robin, and often runs along the ground for a few feet, then pauses, reminiscent of the robin; but this large towhee is a bit plumper with a slightly longer tail. But more noteworthy, it looks like someone had cut off its bill, for the towhee has a stubby bill like a parakeet's but without the overhang of its upper mandible.

This bird has taken advantage of modern man's intrusion into its desert habitat. Whenever an automobile parks in its neighborhood, it soon investigates. Its innate preference for dark recesses finds expression in its liking to explore under the car. It is astute enough to harvest the insects collected by the car in its travels on highways. We have observed this, for example, around newly parked passenger cars south of Alpine, Texas.

But the most memorable meeting with this bird was in Chaco Canyon National Monument, in northwestern New Mexico. It was a hot day, so when we parked we left the windows wide open on our station wagon. The canyon towhee in whose territory we had parked came over and looked under and around our car, as expected. But then, unexpectedly, it landed on the left front window sill, paused, and moved inside the car to perch on the back of the driver's seat, as it carefully looked over the inside of the car.

Then, as we watched by our car, it completely surprised us as it picked up a fairly long hair that our daughter had shed, and flew off with it to add it as the final touches to the nest it was building!

But would this bird be interested in an object as inconspicuous as a human hair? I cite Bent, page 624 in his *Life Histories of North American Cardinals, Grosbeaks, Buntings, Towhees, Finches, Sparrows and Allies.* Its nest, against the trunk of a tall bush, well shaded and hidden, is made from twigs, stems and leaves, then lined with fine strips of bark, fine stems of grasses and animal hairs.

Consistent with the nature of this bird to seek out dark recesses behind thick foliage, canyon towhees never fight among themselves. It is said they are too shy and unobtrusive. The formerly conspecific California towhees are always

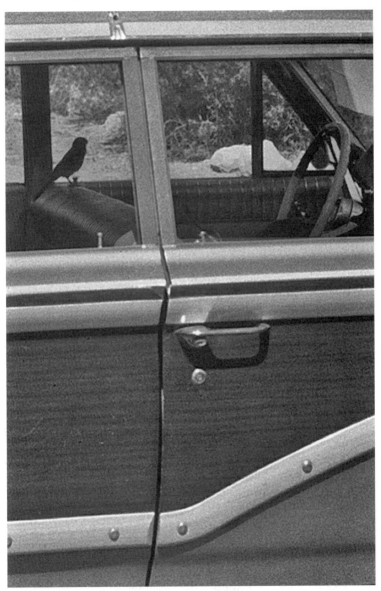

Canyon towhee inspecting inside of car. Photograph by Kenneth J. Johnson

fighting, whether it is an intruder or a reflection in a window or a shiny hub cap. The canyon towhee males don't sing to defend their territory, but do sing briefly in early morning to greet the rising sun. As winter merges into spring, the male sings constantly until he finds a mate. After he finds her, he quits singing. After mating he is silent unless an unmated male comes too close to his neighborhood. Then, upon hearing that stranger's song, he mounts a tree to sing his brief warning, whereupon the unmated one promptly moves away without a challenge.

Because of their shy nature and silence after mating, canyon towhees are often overlooked, even though they are not rare. So, park your car and wait for it to come to inspect your car if you wish to see one.

The scientific name of the canyon towhee fits this bird. *Pipilo fuscus* is named from the Latin *pipilo* meaning chirp; *fuscus* is also Latin, meaning dark or dusky or tawny – darker and browner towards the south of its range, paler and grayer in the drier north of its range. Perhaps in some distant future it will split into a dark southern species and a pale northern species. The similar California towhee used to be the same species, but now the two are separate species because their ranges do not overlap and their voices are different, and these birds do not migrate. The canyon towhee lives in New Mexico, old Mexico, and southeastern Colorado.

Living in a desert, the canyon towhee wouldn't have available the sources of water enjoyed by birds in moister habitats. So it sips dew drops found everywhere on plants in the early morning, before the sun comes up to evaporate the dew. Humans in the Sahara Desert do the same thing, and collect the early morning heavy dew off tents and objects to store in receptacles for drinking the rest of the day. By hiding in the shade and avoiding the sweating that comes from flying, they conserve water.

Could this bird be showing us the avian version of the peaceful society that nations today are desperately seeking?

A Bird For Non-birders

The chipping sparrow's scientific name, *Spizella passerina*, is of mixed origin, for *spiza* is Greek for finch, but *ella* is Latin for small. The Latin word *passer* means sparrow, *passerina* means like a sparrow.

This is a bird for a person not interested in birds. It is inconspicuous, has a rather drab appearance, doesn't make loud noises as it flies around human habitations, and has no reasons to be disliked. The non-birders will see it every day, for it is very common around him, and he will be content to dismiss it as one of those little brown birds, and mistake it as another one of those pesky house sparrows.

It is the chipping sparrow's misfortune to be confused with that alien bully, the house sparrow. The chippies' diet consists entirely of the seeds of pesky weeds and harmful insects. Ragweed, amaranth, lambsquarters, purslane, knotweed are all gardeners' enemies, favored in this bird's menu. Caterpillars, grasshoppers, leafhoppers, ants, spiders, bugs are farmers' enemies, which the chipping sparrow chooses to eat. During the breeding season in May to July they concentrate entirely on

Chipping sparrow. Photograph by Richard Hinton, *Bismarck Tribune*

insects, and later when the weeds go to seed they concentrate on weed seeds, such as ragweed, the chief cause of air-borne allergy. So the chippie is the hay fever victim's best friend.

It is our good fortune that the chipping sparrows, the most domestic of all sparrows, have chosen to live in the suburbs of our cities. There they like to nest in ornamental evergreens and other trees and even around our doorsteps.

Before European settlers came to America, before there were any cities or hamlets or farms, the chipping sparrow lived and nested in areas that resembled contemporary farmyards and lawns and plantings. These areas were forest openings, shores along streams and lakes, and stands of pines, spruce bogs, and aspen groves. The sparrows' descendents still live in those same habitats, wherever they may still exist. So they adapted well to civilization, much better than most other bird species have done.

As to what chippies look like, they're slighter of build and smaller than house sparrows. Their breast is a dirty plain grey, and never has the black bib of the house sparrow. The crown of their head in both sexes is plain brownish red, with white band (bright in the male, dull in the female) between the red crown and the thin black line running through the eye.

Being slimmer, it flies more quickly with faster wing beats and less direct flight than the more plodding move of the house sparrow.

The house sparrow's voice repertoire consists of the monotony of only one harsh grating cheep. Sounding off outside the open church window as the collection plate is being passed around, it may be a reprimand for the parsimonious donor.

The chipping sparrow's voice repertoire consists of only a trill of rapid chips, but at least that varies in being fast or slow, and in the number of notes in each song. If the observer pays attention and can count fast, he may discover that the number of notes in a trill is eight, or a multiple thereof—8 or 16, or 24. If so, that makes this bird compatible with poets and hymn writers using eight beats to a measure.

A most remarkable fact about the chipping sparrow is that the favorite component of the nest is horsehairs. They even remove horsehairs from old nests to use again. Deep in Minnesota's Itasca State Park, far away from any horses, an experimenter once begged some horsehairs from a horse breeding friend and took them to where these sparrows were nest building. Upon seeing the horsehairs, the females immediately abandoned other materials and eagerly wove the horsehairs into the nests.

When automobiles replaced horses the chipping sparrow started using hair of cattle, deer, dogs and fur, and even humans. Once when we were camping our teenage daughter was sitting at the picnic table brushing her hair. One of her hairs floated down to the ground to land at her feet. Promptly a female chipping sparrow startled her by landing at her feet, picked up the hair, and carried it up to her nearby nest being built, and wove it into the nest! Chipping sparrows have rightly been called hair birds, back in horse and buggy days.

As the female builds her nest, the male defends the site by singing and by chasing intruders. As she broods, he brings her food. After hatching, the young birds are fed by both parents.

So, welcome this hair bird that trills for us as it patrols our yards and gardens for noxious weeds and bugs.

White-crowned Sparrow

This Inland Alaskan native prized a black and white striped sea shell which he acquired from the Bering Sea coast by trading with other natives. He always wore it on top of his head. In his old age when it was time to die he traveled to a high spot of land where he could look over his beloved valley. There he died. In death he was transformed into a songbird, and rose up into the sky and flew away. Today he lives on as the bird with its black and white crown, the white-crowned sparrow.

To land credence to that legend, we consulted a field guide to Pacific Coast shells, and deduced that Alaskan native likely was treasuring a species of scallop.

That legend indicates how conspicuous the white crown is for humans recognizing this species of bird. Scientists studying the behavior of these birds have discovered that the white crown is the key to how these birds react to each other, too. The bird with the brightest black and white crown stripes is the dominant individual. That is the adult male. The adult female, with stripes less bright, is subservient. The juvenile female is at the bottom of the pecking order, since it has the dullest black and white stripes.

Because of its head coloring it is the easiest migrating dickeybird to identify.

Several other species of birds have similar stripes in their plumage, whether as camouflage or as an attention-getting device. Smith's longspur has bright black and white on the side of its head. The long-billed dowitcher has zebra-striped armpits. The chukar has black and white stripes on the side of its body. The back of the snipe is striped. The belly of the stilt sandpiper has alternate vertical black and white lines. But of all these, the white-crowned sparrow's crown is the most flamboyant.

How influential that feature is, is shown by instances where the male

FIG. 163. White-crowned Sparrow. (Natural size.)

Picture from page 536 of *Birds of Eastern North America*, by Frank M. Chapman.

has been successful in having two wives, and two families, both at the same time. Bent in part three of his book on sparrows documents this polygamy. Two females built their nests in territories next to each other, where the male could easily service both. Each female defended her area against the other female by loud singing and fighting. If one female followed the male when she went into her rival's territory, a fight ensued. The females locked feet and jabbed each other on the breast. Bent did not mention whether the male was up to the task later of helping feed both families of young ones, both at the same time. Nest building and incubation had been no problem for him, for with white-crowned sparrows the female dos both exclusively, with no help from the male.

Except for a race that is resident on the West Coast, the white-crowned sparrow is a migrant we see only when it stops to grab a quick bite to eat, then hurries on. It breeds in the Far North. Its home is subarctic or alpine, but south of the tundra, in the open stunted tree and brush taiga, the Hudsonian Life Zone, where black spruce and dwarf birch grow.

Besides those in Alaska and Canada, other white-crowned sparrows live in Montana, Colorado, and California, and migrate up and down the mountainside according to the season.

Another group of white-crowned sparrows nests in Puget Sound, Washington and winters in Berkeley, California where a resident race lives. The two groups live together in winter quite amicably. When in Puget Sound, one observer found, one female was very busy feeding her young and building a new nest for a second brood, both at the same time. Holding down two jobs at the same time, she got overworked and brought nesting material to her young and laid it at its feet as it continued crying for food! Six days after the first brood left the first nest, that female laid the first egg of her second clutch in her completed second nest. The observer did not say what that bird did in her spare time.

So this dweller in the high altitudes or high latitudes is unmistakable as we are thrilled to see it visit us, even if it is only passing through.

What Was Your Greatest Thrill In Birding?

What was your greatest thrill in birding? That one adventure or bird sighting that you will always treasure in your memories above all others? In my lifetime of birding all over North America, in all fifty states and in all ten Canadian provinces, that one memory that stands out more than all the others, happened right here in North Dakota in Burleigh County at the Long Lake National Wildlife Refuge.

It happened on April 28, 1974. There on the top strand of the barbed wire fence at the southwest corner of the refuge area was sitting a songbird much different from any I had ever seen before, and have never seen since. It was sparrow sized. Its back was similar to a sparrow's. But its throat and breast and abdomen were the most beautiful pure golden caramel color. On the side of its head were striking horizontal jet black and snow white stripes. It acted as though it wasn't acquainted with civilization, for it perched on the fence wire for a long time, looking at me as it changed poses as I stared at it.

Studying thoroughly Peterson's *Field Guide* and the Golden Guide of *Birds of North America* I finally found it partially hidden in Peterson and in a tiny picture in the Golden Guide. The full breeding plumage my bird displayed would normally be seen only on its breeding range in the Northwest Territories of Canada in the Arctic Barren Lands along the shore of the Arctic Ocean. It was a male Smith's longspur, *Calcarius pictus*. The scientific binomial is from the Latin *calx* meaning spur or heel, and the Latin *pictus* meaning paint. So the ornithologist who gave it its scientific name regarded it as the bird who is pretty as a picture (I agree!), who has a long spur! An obsolete name of it is the painted bunting, which was a poor choice because there turned out to be a different species of bird, a painted bunting (*Passerina ciris*), which summers mostly in Texas and Louisiana, and winters somewhere far south of the Mexican border. In 1844 John James Audubon named Smith's longspur after his friend, Dr. Gideon B. Smith, who lived in Baltimore.

Lapland longspur on breeding grounds. Photograph by Torgeir Nygaard

Perhaps the field guides displayed the male's breeding plumage almost as an afterthought because the editors thought no one would ever be up in the northern limits of the tundra to see the bird anyway. The non-breeding winter plumaged bird stays in northeast Texas on airport landing fields, which are off-limits in this age of terrorism.

Of the four species of longspurs, Smith's longspur has the smallest population and occupies the smallest range. The chestnut-collared longspur breeds in North Dakota, and is hard to find now in its diminished native prairie habitat. McCown's longspur breeds in North Dakota only in the southwest corner on barren fields, and is quite rare. Lapland longspur comes here in flocks in winter only at inopportune times, it seems to me, such as in a driving snowstorm. So, to find any longspur is a feat, but to see a Smith's longspur is the greatest feat.

How The Cowbird Got That Way

Early Europeans visiting the Great Plains found huge herds of bison, walking slowly as they grazed. As they grazed their hooves cut the prairie sod to expose insects, and they disturbed insects in the grass which flew up, all of which were eaten by certain birds which the people named buffalo birds. As the prairie was eaten down the herd moved on and didn't return until the grass grew up again. Since the herds kept moving, the female buffalo birds couldn't establish a stationary nest and still follow the herd. Being opportunists they adapted by laying their eggs in nests of other birds.

With the buffalo gone, these birds maintained their niche by finding the settlers' cattle and by staying around close by them. So now they're called cowbirds. But having lost their nest-building know-how, they're constrained to continue to lay their eggs in other birds' nests. The male birds are black with brown heads; the females are a dull gray-brown. The birds easily adapted to cows, and spread to the eastern United States as they found farmers' cattle east of the Great Plains. So cowbirds have extended their range to the eastern United States.

So now, while other birds are busy building nests and getting food to feed their young, we often see a group of several greenish-black birds with dark brown heads with time on their hands (I should say toes!) singing a gurgling song and lazing around, freed of the chore of feeding young cowbirds.

If the light is wrong it is hard to see the brown on the head of the male, but the cowbird's bill is thicker than that of the other blackbirds'. When ground feeding the cowbird tips its tail up more than the other blackbirds do.

Concerned scientists, following population trends, have good reason to be concerned about the cowbird's brood parasitism. The populations of species of songbirds being victimized have decreased over the years. Kirtland's warbler, living only in a small area in Lower Michigan, was so endangered that wildlife officials have been conducting a campaign of eradicating cowbirds.

What factors increase or decrease the population of cowbirds? Scientists find that a cowbird has only about a 3% success rate for one of its hatchlings to reach maturity. Many of their eggs are laid in nests of inappropriate hosts who are poor foster parents, such as ducks, killdeers and terns. To fool the host bird who can count, the cowbird often removes one egg before laying her own egg. In a new territory where hosts haven't met cowbirds they are more vulnerable until they eventually learn to remove the strange egg. If the host isn't strong enough to lift the strange egg the victimized birds either raise the young cowbird, or build a new layer of nest on top of all the eggs, or abandon their nest. The fledgling cowbird has a more rapid development, grows faster and crowds out its nest mates, and grows to maturity being fed by the foster parents. And the cowbird has a unique advantage in that the duration of its egg-laying ability is much longer than that of any other song bird – the cowbird can lay forty eggs a year over a two month period, as it searches out nest after nest all summer long.

Bottom line: Brood parasitism seems to be a very successful way for preservation of the species – but not if everyone tries it!

Towhee And Oriole Look-alikes

We were confronted with a puzzle recently. Out in the wide open mid-Dakota prairie with no trees in sight was this lone tipped over skeleton of a tree, devoid of leaves or twigs or bark. On one naked branch were two robin sized songbirds with black backs and heads. They were perched so that a peek of their sides showed a deep chestnut red color. No prairie bird has plumage with that combination of colors. These were out of place, perhaps migrants briefly passing through. What were they?

After considerable reflection, two possibilities came to mind: towhee or orchard oriole. Of the two towhees with that color scheme, the eastern towhee lives east of the prairies, and the spotted towhee lives west of the prairie. But birds have wings, and use them to travel great distances, so quite often they are found outside of their traditional ranges. Avid bird life-listers delight in traveling great distances to add to their list a casual, or an accidental, or an irregular.

Then these two strangers posing for us turned for us to see all of their undersides, to display a solid deep chestnut red color to the entire sides, flanks, and belly. Both towhees have a white belly. So that rules out the towhees and leaves the orchard oriole, whose range covers all of the Dakotas. In the prairie it favors timber belts along streams, and tree claims around farms and ranches, and shelter belts. That explains why these two were hovering around that lone relic of a tree out on the treeless prairie.

We have three degrees of white marks on the backs of these three birds. The spotted towhee, living up to its name, has numerous white spots on its back, while the eastern towhee has only one white spot, which is on its wing. The eastern bird hunts near the ground, in thick woods and dense thickets, shaded from the sun, where in the shade much white would make it

Eastern towhee on left, male orchard oriole in middle, spotted towhee on right.

conspicuous. The spotted towhee lives in the West, where the more open chaparral lets spots of sunshine fall on the bird, helping the white spots to intermingle with the sunny spots to act as camouflage.

The orchard oriole has a degree of white dorsally that is intermediate between that of the two towhees, to reflect the intermediate amount of sunlight it probably enjoys among the trees which it prefers.

When we look at scientific names, we are shocked at the orchard oriole's specific name, *spurius*, in *Icterus spurius*. The ornithologist who named it thought that the female Baltimore oriole, more brightly colored than the duller female orchard oriole, was a male orchard oriole. The first year male orchard oriole is also yellow green. So when he saw that black and chestnut colored bird (which is a genuine second year male orchard oriole) consorting with the female orchard oriole he blundered by considering it to be spurious. The English word spurious means false, counterfeit, illegitimate, or bastard.

Both Baltimore and orchard orioles have the same generic name, *Icterus*, which is from the Greek *ikteros* meaning a yellow green bird. So when the female orchard oriole, which is yellow green, was conforming to its scientific name *Icterus*, how could its mate be all black and chestnut? Maybe that explains how in this case the ornithologist who did the naming was more amazing and incredible than the bird.

The towhee scientific names are more straightforward. Both species are in the genus *Pipilo*, where the name is from the Latin for a bird that chirps or pipes. The spotted towhee is *P. maculatus*, where the species name is from the Latin *macula* which means a spot, plus the Latin adjective *latus*, meaning rather extensive. The sketch conforms that this towhee has a goodly number of spots.

The eastern towhee is *P. erythrophthalmus*. The Greek *erythros* means red, the Greek *ophthalmos* stands for the eye. Here the northern birds, which were the ones the bird namer saw, have a red eye, but the southern ones have a white eye.

Birding is as amazing and incredible as the birds!

Overlooked Red-winged Blackbird

Female red-winged blackbird. Photograph by Norton R. Johnson

This mystery bird was photographed in the Red Rock Canyon parking lot of Glacier National Park in Montana. After thorough study of all possible perching birds, it was concluded that the only identification possible is that of the most common species – a female red-winged blackbird.

Human nature wants us to think we have discovered some rare exotic, when practically we should consider first the commonest most likely bird.

When the females flock together (the males migrate north earlier, each to stake out a spot for a nest site) many birders regard them as sparrows, and can't identify them. But the harsh grating rattle they utter is unlike the more pleasant sound any true sparrow will make.

One male will have several females as mates in the cattail marsh. But as he vigorously and unceasingly defends his little territory from rivals he unwittingly is defending some of his little flock of females who are really incubating eggs that were fertilized by neighboring males!

In *Agelius phoenicus*, the scientific name of the red-winged blackbird, the genus name is from the Greek *agelaios* for gregarious, correct since they breed socially in groups in cattail marshes, and migrate in sky-blackening myriads that wipe out farmers' corn and wheat harvests. The species name also is from the Greek *phoenix* for crimson, referring to the male's red epaulet, at its brightest as the male flaunts it in courtship and in defense of his chosen bit of marsh for the nest. But the subservient female, in her drab brown plumage, has no such epaulet, nor even a trace of one, yet must share that specific name with her mate.

Being our most abundant species, the red-winged blackbird has broken down its massive numbers by dividing springtime northern migration into seven distinct stages. Each stage consists of a distinct sex and age of bird.

A. C. Bent in his *Life Histories of North American Blackbirds, Orioles, Tanagers, and Allies* lists these seven consecutive migrations in pages 125- 127. Bent quotes Arthur A. Allen who in 1910- 1914 gave time sequences when the seven migrations arrived in Ithaca, New York. It is presumed the time sequences are similar in more western regions at comparable latitude.

1. The earliest migratory wave arrives February 25 to March 4, consisting of vagrants. These are adult males who rest rriefly, then move on to Canada, 300 miles into Quebec, Ontario and Manitoba, and even into the Northwest Territories. They wintered farther north than the others.

2. Migrant adult males arrive March 13 to April 21. These males stay in flocks that fly away when approached.

3. Resident adult males arrive March 25 to April 10. These males do not stay in flocks that fly away when approached, but break up to stay in their chosen marsh, each individual in his little spot, to raise young and leave in the autumn.

4. The first females and immature males come March 29 to April 24. At this time the reproductive organs of the resident males (group 3) increase in size, and they show slight

interest in these newly arrived females, but these females shun the males, who drive them off.

5. In the third week of April, April 10 to May 1, the resident adult females arrive. These flocks also break up, and each female picks a spot near the water surface and near one or more males. Now when they attempt to fly away they are chased by one or more males. If a female from group 4 is chased this way, she flies away, never to return, but a female from group 5 returns to her chosen spot again.

6. Resident immature males appear May 6 to June 1 and continue to arrive in small groups.

7. Resident immature females arrive from May 10 to June 11. By June they far outnumber the resident immature males.

So it takes two years for a redwing to grow up. How to tell an immature from a mature? The mature male is shiny jet black with red and yellow shoulder patches, the size of which he can control by muscles at the bases of those colored feathers. The immature male has a duller black color interspersed by brown spots and lines, and its shoulder patches are duller, smaller, and barely visible. The immature and mature females look quite the same.

Europeans traditionally have eaten songbirds, so when homesteaders in America, never far from hunger, were in dire need for food, they did so too. Vern Sylvester was born in 1914 in his parents' pioneer frame house in the town of Palermo just east of Stanley, North Dakota. He recalls his father with his shotgun shooting migrating red-winged blackbirds along the railroad tracks in the fall. Vern then plucked their feathers and removed the internal organs. Then his mother cooked them as a stew. The meat was picked off the tiny bones by finger. What shot there was fell away by its own weight. He also remembers his grandfather in his sod house homesteading in Willow City having eaten snow buntings.

So give the overlooked redwing, the female without the red wing, her proper respect and recognition.

What Is Vesper About The Evening Grosbeak?

What is vesper about the evening grosbeak? Why was this species of bird identified so closely with that particular time of day? Even its scientific name, *Hesperiphona vespertina*, is preoccupied with the evening. The genus name *Hesperiphona* is Greek, referring to Hesperides, the Daughters of Night who lived on the western edge of the world, where the sun went down; and the species name *vespertina* obviously was derived from the word vesper.

A. C. Bent in his book, *Life Histories of North American Cardinals, Grosbeaks, Buntings, Towhees, Finches, Sparrows and Allies, Part One*, provides insight. U.S. Major Delafield in August, 1823 described this bird that he noted sang only at twilight. The flock hovered about camp at arm's length. The ornithologist Forbush felt that the black in its plumage represented the night as it encompassed the gold of sunset, while the white foretold the dawn that follows the night. This grosbeak's primaries are black, its back and sides and belly are yellow, and its secondaries are white.

The only evening grosbeak I ever encountered that could be associated with evening was one that definitely was in the twilight of its life. It arrived at our bird feeder with a flock of these grosbeaks each evening, but quickly distinguished itself from the others. Instead of actively devouring the seeds, it passively picked at them, more weakly at each visit. Then it listlessly sat looking at them helplessly. Its bill was broken, each mandible bent askew at a different angle, rigid, the result of some terrible accident. It weakened more each day, as it stayed at the feeder after its mates flew on. Then it, too, was gone, and that was the last we saw of it.

When Major Delafield, working on international boundaries for the government, encountered the evening grosbeak in 1823, it was in the swamp of the Savannah River. He was on the early frontiersmen's canoe route from Lake Superior on the portage which led to the Mississippi River Drainage Basin. Since then its range has spread eastward along the international border and our border states. It appeared in Toronto in 1854, in Indiana in 1878, in Kentucky in 1887, and in Massachusetts in 1890, Bent says.

So it was that on August 4, 1965 we found breeding birds in New Brunswick in towns and on lawns, even in much greater numbers than robins on our lawns back home in North Dakota!

Now its breeding range is extraordinary, stretching from British Columbia to southern Manitoba eastward to roughly straddle the International Boundary, well into the Maritime Provinces of Canada. In that strip their nests are mostly hidden in dense evergreens in swamps.

The Chippewa Indians living in that Canadian-Boreal Life Zone named it paushkydamo, which in their language meant berry-breaker, a reference to the remarkable strength of its bill.

Grosbeak, meaning big bill, is well named, for the yellow cone-shaped bill of the evening grosbeak, larger than all other North American grosbeaks' bill, is extremely heavy and acts as a powerful shears. The observant Chippewas watched them as they discarded the flesh from wild cherries; then the cherry pit, the hard seed, they cut in half with one bite, causing a sound like a very loud pop. The heart of the seed was eaten and the hard shell rejected. Their favorite food, experts agree, is the winged seed of the box elder. They snip the winged pod from the branch, then skillfully massage the seed out of the winged pod with their two mandibles, swallow the seed and allow the winged pod to twirl to the ground.

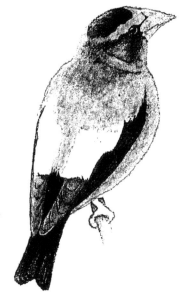

This bird is not a loner; it always appears in flocks, where they continually call to each other. One such flock caused us to have a misadventure once. We were in northern Alberta, driving up to Northwest Territories. The road through the boggy spruce land was covered by a thick layer of gravel in an attempt to keep the road surface dry. I heard a flock of evening grosbeaks nearby, so I stopped our car to listen. But we quickly sank down in the loose gravel; any attempt to move dug the wheels down deeper. Hopelessly stuck, no habitations for miles, there was no traffic coming along in this wilderness. But after a while our guardian angel brought a road grader along. It pressed its blade against our rear bumper, and easily pushed our car out to resume our trip to Yellowknife.

House Finch And House Sparrow

One thing house finches and house sparrows have in common is that they both are newcomers to North Dakota. But each bird's story of how they got here and from where is very different.

Roger Tory Peterson's 1947 edition of his *A Field Guide to the Birds Giving Field Marks of All Species Found East of the Rockies* doesn't even mention the house finch. Yet his 1980 edition says it was introduced to northeastern U.S. in 1940 and reached Illinois by 1980.

The house finch was endemic in the Western United States, reaching east as far as Wyoming, South Dakota's Black Hills, and west Texas. Pet stores in New York City illegally sold wild birds as Hollywood Finches, until in 1940 these dealers released them to avoid prosecution. From there they spread into New England and southward and westward. Bob Randall, an early founder of the Bismarck-Mandan Bird Club, was the first one to record the presence of the house finch in North Dakota, when he saw the bird in his back yard in 1979. It was seen in Fargo also. It has been a regular member

House sparrows. Photograph by Torgeir Krokan

of our fauna ever since. In Aberdeen, S. D., it was first noted in 1985, yet its population didn't start increasing until 1991, according to banding records there. Today in Bismarck the house finches nest in our spruce trees about as abundantly as the common grackle.

The house sparrow originated in the Middle East, but starting about 7,000 years ago it spread into Europe along with the movement of agriculture northward. Then in the 19th Century as European colonists moved into other parts of the world, house sparrows went along uninvited as stowaways on their ships. The house sparrow is now in the Middle East, North Africa, Australasia, Europe, South-east Asia, New Zealand, South America, Hawaii. Today it is the most widely distributed of all land species of birds.

In North America a few birds were introduced in 1850 to Brooklyn, New York, to combat canker worms (native birds being incompetent?). By 1875 they had spread to occupy the continent as far as San Francisco, and now as far south as Panama and as far north as Hudson Bay.

The house finch and house sparrow both live preferably around humans, in cities, breeding in roofs and crevices of structures. The house finch is well liked, but everyone is unanimous in condemning the house sparrow. It is extremely prolific, aggressive, builds messy nests, replaces native birds by taking over their nests, damages crops and gardens, eats poultry's food, kills other birds' nestlings. The U.S. Migratory Bird Treaty, which forbids people harming wild birds, exempts house sparrows. So I didn't and don't feel any remorse for my boyhood practice of filing a notch on the barrel of my B-B gun (air rifle) for every house sparrow I shot. That sparrow that Jesus said God knew about that falls on the ground (Matthew 10:29) was the exact same species, *Passer domesticus*, that I shot; but note that He didn't frown on the incident, He only was aware of it.

The house sparrow is resident, often spending its entire life within a two mile width of city. The house finch is also a resident, although the Midwest and Eastern populations seem to migrate a short distance now. So summer's group might be replaced in winter by more northerly relatives.

Whereas the house sparrow male is distinguished only by a black bib, the house finch male has a red crown, breast and rump. But sometimes the red is really orange or yellow, depending on how much carotene the bird gets in its diet. (A lot produces red, a little yields yellow.) Years ago on a piece of Connecticut land owned by the National Audubon Society we saw in an enclosure a white horse that was of a uniform orange color; the sign warned against feeding it because it was on a diet restricted to carrots! A human eating excessive amounts of carotene develops carotenemia, a condition where the skin turns yellow. Why the horse and the human develop this color uniformly, but only in the crown, breast and rump in the house finch, escapes me.

For those people for whom house sparrows are a pain, there is happy news. Evidence shows their numbers have decreased. Credit is taken for this by the abundance of domestic cats and feral cats, the use of pesticides and the replacement of the horse by the automobile to decrease their food supply, and the ability of the newcomer, the house finch, to hold its own and to stand up to the house sparrow. I now see and hear two or three times as many urban house finches as I do house sparrows!

But this is partially offset by bad news. The house finch has been afflicted by an epidemic of a virus disease of the eye which causes blindness and death. Let us hope this will not cause a decrease in their numbers.

Thistle Finch Is Well Named

The American goldfinch's scientific name is *Carduelis tristis. Carduelis* is from the Latin *cardualis*, meaning the thistle finch, which was derived from the Latin carduus, for wild thistle. This is fitting, since goldfinches are especially attracted to thistles. Thistle seed is a favorite for them in bird feeders. The species name, *tristis*, is from the Latin *tristis* meaning sad or melancholy. This seems odd, for the goldfinch is regarded

Flower of thistle, a plant four feet tall, which made the goldfinch the thistle finch.

as always cheerful. Yet the person who named it regarded its note as plaintive, so he condemned the bird with this dismal negative name. Perhaps he was thinking of the plaintive, loud, prolonged with rising inflection, ch-e-e-p note. Certainly not the cheerful, well-known per-chick-a-ree flight song.

The nesting season is very late – July to September – since that is the season for seeds to be available, and raising young must be done when there will be enough food. The nest is always less than 300 yards away from the thistles going to seed. No thistles means no nests, it has been noted.

As a lad I was tramping over the hills near my boyhood home in St. Paul when I noticed this strange bird feeding on the seeds on this large thistle plant. It allowed my close approach to a mere yard away. Its striking yellow and black beauty enthralled me. I studied it intently, so I could copy its details onto paper to show it to Dr. T. S. Roberts, *The Birds of Minnesota* author. Taking the streetcar to the museum at the University of Minnesota, there I found him in his office, a very kindly elderly man who showed me the museum's drawers of bird skins, each mounted on a sturdy wire for handling. It was my introduction to our American goldfinch.

While incubating, the female stays on the nest while the male feeds her. As he approaches the nest with food, he sings his flight song. The female answers with her warbling call for food. He takes her bill and regurgitates the milky viscid mass down her gullet as she quivers eagerly with partially spread wings. After the young hatch she also gathers food, so they both feed the young by regurgitation.

The nest is so well constructed that it may last several years. Strips of fiber torn from tree trunks and woven around the nest help make the nest so solid that a rain may flood the nest and the water seep out very slowly, so young birds have been known to drown in the nest.

As an adult in Bismarck, I was mowing our lawn once when I noticed this young bird just out of its nest flutter down awkwardly and crash against the trunk of an elm tree. There it clung, about to fall to the ground. I walked over to inspect it, but the parent bird rushed over and fluttered noisily between me and her baby, preventing my approach. In a moment that young goldfinch gained enough strength to fly away, escorted by the adult goldfinch.

I saw a goldfinch that was a glutton once. Usually when a bird is at a bird feeder there are other birds there or nearby, and the one at the feeder is given only a few seconds before it is chased off or frightened away by some perceived danger in the vicinity. But this goldfinch I found eating its favorite seeds at this feeder. All was quiet around there. No other birds were within sight or sound as it leisurely kept eating seed after seed after seed. When it finally paused, it turned to fly away. Now goldfinches have a distinctive flight pattern, a bounding flight, a series of undulations. But this bird now had excess baggage, so on takeoff it swerved to the ground, and had to strain mightily to fly up to the lowest branch of a tree, until its feast was digested.

It was in an overgrown weedy field south of Bismarck, on a clear March day. A sizeable flock of goldfinches were feasting on the seeds of thistles and other weeds in this snow-covered field. But what was remarkable was that in this flock of goldfinches were individuals in their somber winter plumage, others in their brilliant summer breeding plumage, and others in all mottled intergrading stages in between the two extremes! What other species of bird can show such a spectacle at one spot, at one time?

IV. POTPOURRI PEARLS

How To Hypnotize A Bird

A bird can be hypnotized – if that is the right word for it. It can be caused to fall into a trance, wherein it lies or sits motionless for a moment, without harm to the bird.

Bird banders have noticed that after a bird has been disentangled from the mist net and banded, if it is held gently in the hand upside down, and the hand is then opened slowly, the bird may lie motionless on the palm for a moment. The spell is broken by noise or by slight motion of the hand, and the bird flies away unharmed.

Newly-banded goldfinch, still in hypnotic trance as it lays on the bander's palm.
Photograph by Judith Ekberg Johnson

A small bird may be held gently in the hand and rocked to and fro by swinging the lowered arm forward and backward a few times, or by raising the arm above the head and waving it in a circle, leisurely. Then one can open the palm slowly as the bird lies upside down. It will lie on the palm motionless for a moment before it flies away.

A pigeon or a chicken can be caused to sit upright motionless after one's finger has waved in a circle before or around its head a few times. I have also held my hand directly in front of the chicken or pigeon and pointed my index finger at the bird, then gently held my finger tip against the tip of the bird's beak for a moment. With either technique the spell is broken by a sudden loud noise or by some movement the bird can see.

The Internet describes two other methods, with which I have had no personal experience. One is to lay a chicken on its side, the other is to hold the chicken on its back.

To lay a chicken on its side, the wings are folded as the chicken is held down gently with its head flat against the table. Then move the free hand's finger in a line parallel to the length of the beak, from a point almost touching the tip of the beak to a point some four inches distant from the beak. Move the finger back and forth a few times along that line.

With holding the chicken on its back, place a book or a block against each side of it to keep the bird on its back. Then with two digits of the free hand, gently rub the breast.

It is said that a wild bird is easier to hypnotize than a domestic chicken, perhaps because its survival skills in playing 'possum are still fully functional. Some birds "play 'possum" as a means of escaping harm from a predator that is enticed only by motion on the part of its prey. See chapter *Opossum of the Bird World*.

It seems that what these different techniques have in common is a repetitive stimulation of the vestibular system that controls balance, as the body is held immobilized. That is a bit similar to a child on a swing or a merry-go-round or in a rocking boat on water, not tolerating the motion.

An expert was demonstrating hypnosis of birds at a county fair once, but was stopped by a spokesman from the SPCA (Society for the Prevention of Cruelty to Animals). So to protect myself and my feathered friends, I hereby state that the above data is for information only, and not intended to be imitated or duplicated.

Owl Pellets, Fecal Sacs And Guano

Pellets, feces, excrement, droppings, guano, emesis, scat, vomitus all are names of something vital to life functions but not mentioned in polite society. Yet people are interested in the taboo subjects of scatology and emeticology.

One of the best ways to find an owl is to look on the ground! Most owls swallow mice and rats whole, then fly to their favorite roost for the eight hour long process of digestion. The undigestible parts, such as the bones and fur, are rolled up into a little compact oblong rounded mass. This so-called pellet is then regurgitated and falls to the ground. These pellets accumulate below the roosting site, a tell-tale clue as to where the owl is resting.

An Elderhostel is a non-profit organization, based in a college or university, for people over 55 years of age. It provides a week long course of classroom lectures and field trips on many different subjects. One Elderhostel, run by a branch of the University of Texas, has been held on Mustang Island on the Gulf Coast. One of its classes has the elders examining and dissecting owl pellets. Scientists doing this can identify which species of mammals are prey for the owls. The size of the pellet

Note broken bones of mouse wrapped up in its fur in this owl pellet.
Photograph by Ravn David Saeter

is determined by the size of the owl. One five inches long is produced by the great horned owl. A pellet an inch long is from the saw-whet owl. An intermediate sized pellet may be from a long-eared owl or a screech owl.

Cormorants also regurgitate undigestible parts of fish they have eaten, which form oval shaped pellets.

It is claimed that some young birds of certain species, such as great blue heron, use a defensive tactic of regurgitating or defecating onto a predator who is climbing up toward the nest.

A good method of finding the active nest of an eagle or a falcon is to look for white streaks on the cliff wall below the crevice used by the raptor. The young birds lean over the edge to defecate. Similarly, finding a cluster of bird droppings on the ground under a tree points to a bird roost directly above.

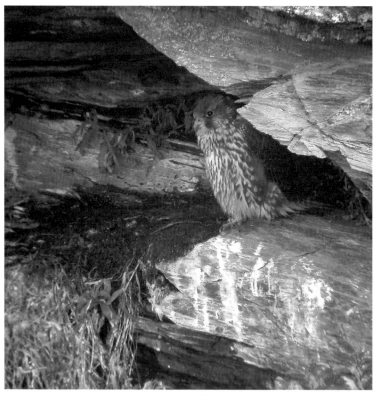

Young gyrfalcon by nest. Note streaks on cliff. Photograph by Jan Ove Gjershaug

Some people eat what is disgorged by a bird! Fishermen in East Asia train cormorants. They place a ring around the lower neck so the bird can't swallow. The tethered bird dives overboard, catches a fish and returns to the boat. Since the ring prevents the fish from entering the bird's stomach it regurgitates the fish into the boat, where it is salvaged by the fisherman.

Water bird and grouse newborn chicks are precocial, in that they can run around as soon as they are hatched. By defecating elsewhere they avoid the problem of disposal of feces. Songbird newborn chicks are altricial, in that they not only cannot move about but can barely lift their heads up. So instead of waste matter fouling up the nest, their feces is like a gel wrapped up in a mucous membrane. This bill-sized fecal sac is easily carried away or swallowed by the parent bird. In contrast the adult bird produces a more liquid stool of a thick watery consistency. Water, which, being heavy, would make flying more difficult if in the body of the bird, is reduced to a minimum by defecating frequently to increase the ease of flight.

Bats and cave-dwelling birds drop their feces to the floor of the cave, which scat accumulates to form a deposit called guano. Colonies of sea birds on islands off the coast of Peru have accumulated so much guano that it has been harvested as fertilizer by the Peruvians.

Dangerous Birding

Birders have exciting adventures – some even dangerous.

SEA BIRDS AND RUSSIAN SHIP: We boarded a chartered fishing boat out of Westport, Washington. Only birders, not deep sea fishermen, were on board for the nine hour trip to go far out to sea, far beyond the littoral zone along the coast. Out on the open ocean we left the gulls behind to observe the pelagic species instead, such as shearwatwer, fulmar, petrel, kittiwake, albatross.

To attract the ocean birds up for close observation we dumped overboard small portions of "chum." This consisted of a smelly mixture of fish oil and popcorn.

But then we were distracted by the appearance of a large ship. This Russian "fish factory" spends months at sea. Its giant net scrapes the ocean bottom, dragging up everything, leaving the sea floor as destroyed as the path of a tornado through a city.

Our captain said, "Now watch this." The instant he radioed the Coast Guard to report them, the eavesdropping Russians then immediately pulled up their net and took off. Our captain maneuvered our little boat right up alongside, causing the curious sailors to line the railing. But to prevent any desertions the Communist overseer chased them all below deck. Then the ship brought out hoses and tried to squirt us. But we stayed just out of range.

This happened Sunday, July 23, 1972; see photograph on page 472.

FIVE-STRIPED SPARROW: For those lifers – birders whose ambition is to add many species to their list of North American birds – the five-striped sparrow is a prize. Its small range in Mexico barely reaches into southern Arizona, into a portion of the border that is barely accessible.

So it was with great anticipation that we joined this birding tour. We had been warned about the antisocial inhabitants of the village of Ruby in that mountainous area, but had passed through there uneventfully. The two rut trail through Coronado National Forest was washed out as it went down a steep hill, so we decided to take another route back home. We did find the five-striped sparrow, alongside our van, just a stone's throw from Mexico.

But on returning home on this alternate trail we came upon an encampment of drug runners on their illegal inholding. A scowling man came out holding a huge chain, accompanied by a vicious German shepherd dog, and forbad us to pass. So we had to go back, by our original route. To get up that bad hill everyone had to get out as all the men pushing were barely able to get the van out.

We arrived at our base hotel in Patagonia long after dark. Next day at breakfast in the local hotel, we told our story to a uniformed officer who sat at the next table. His face turned red as he stiffened and sat motionless. They probably were drug runners.

PRIBILOF MURRE: On the east side of St. Paul Island, one of the Bering Sea's Pribilof Islands, there is a colony of thick-billed murre. They are confined to a steep rocky cliff with numerous narrow ledges. Each crowded ledge is occupied by a pair of these birds. They don't seem to need a nest, for their egg is shaped so it won't roll off into the sea far below.

MURRE

30. *Uria troille.* 16 inches.

In summer the throat is brownish black, but in winter the throat and sides of head are white; feet blackish bill, long and stout, 1.7 in. long, while that of Brunnich Murre (Uria lomvia—No. 31), is shorter (1.25 in.) and more swollen. The ranges and habits of the two species are the same. Murres are very gregarious, nesting in large colonies on northern cliffs. In summer every ledge available at their nesting resort is lined with these birds, sitting upright on their single eggs.

Notes.—A hoarse imitation of their name "murre."

Nest.—Their single eggs are laid upon the bare ledges of cliffs. They are pear-shaped to prevent their rolling off when the bird leaves; greenish, gray or white in color, handsomely blotched or lined with blackish (3.40 x 2.00). Their eggs present a greater diversity of coloration and marking than those of any other bird.

Range.—Breeds from the Magdalen Is. northward; winters south to Long Island.

Reproduction of the murre page from the *Bird Guide: Water Birds, Game Birds and Birds of Prey East of the Rockies*, 1906.

This writer was with a birding tour, but one day I wanted to get a closer look at the thick-billed murre so I went alone across the treeless plateau over to the edge. There I crawled down to lay prone so close to the nearest thick-billed murre that I was eyeball to eyeball with it. But I didn't reach out to touch it because I needed all four limbs to clutch tightly the crumbly rock ledge.

Why didn't I slip off to fall into the surf far below? My guardian angel was hanging on to my shirt tail.

PHANTOM GREAT-TAILED GRACKLE: Below Falcon Dam on the Rio Grande in Texas one can stand along the cinder block fence and look at the large concrete spillway far below.

My wife and I were standing there enjoying the view and looking for birds, when we heard one of the songs – or noises – from the great-tailed grackle's large repertoire of squeals, rattles, chucks, and harsh rustling sounds. This last sound reminds me of the noise made by shaking a large sheet of stiff plastic. I looked down below, up above, all around, but could not see the grackle anywhere, even though there was no shrubbery in which it could hide.

Then I looked down by my feet. There, almost stepped on, was a rattlesnake, coiled and vibrating its tail, poised to strike! The grackle I thought I heard was that rattlesnake!

I grabbed my wife and jumped back. With an adrenalin rush, we vented our fright by arguing as to how big it was. Then it uncoiled and crawled along the base of the fence to escape. By figuring its length by counting the cinder blocks it stretched along, we determined that it was a good six feet long.

What Do Birds Do All Day?

A person sees but a fleeting glimpse of a bird, and that likely is only because the bird permits it, for a bird typically is aware of the birder first. So what happens to it the rest of the day? We'll investigate these birds.

They look for food. Like most animals, the search for food occupies most of their efforts. The Clark's nutcracker in the picture is lingering about the observation stop for tourists in Rocky Mountain National Park, having learned that they will toss it tidbits of food.

Clark's nutcracker.
Photograph by Kenneth J. Johnson

They eat. Having found food, they may store it for future consumption, but mostly eat it immediately for sustenance, then look for more. See the picture in the chapter titled "How Birds Got Their Names."

This peregrine falcon was so hungry and eager to eat that it snacked on the prey it was carrying in its talons while in flight before it arrived at its destination.

They do their toilet. Many times during the day they pause to rearrange their feathers, obtain oil from their oil gland to lubricate their feathers, and probably seize and reject any parasites from their plumage. That's what the Canada goose is doing in the picture in the chapter "Do Angels Really Have Wings, Like Birds?"

They sleep. Whether they're diurnal or nocturnal. they all need their sleep. When those who are awake during the day migrate at night, they need to catch up on their sleep during the daylight hours. That's why this greater scaup is napping in the photo in chapter "What Diurnal Birds Do At Night."

They court a mate. A whole book can be written on what

White-tailed ptarmigan. Photograph submitted by Kenneth J. Johnson

males (and the female spotted sandpiper–see chapter "North Dakota's Loyal Peep") do to attract a mate. Their courtship antics may be beautiful, spectacular, comical, ridiculous or tender. No two species employ the exact same technique. In the photo in the chapter "Humor In Birding" the common goldeneye is craning his head backwards, to impress the female.

They defend their territory. The immediate area of their nest is guarded from encroachment by enemies, especially by members of their own species. Singing by the male is sufficient most of the time, but fighting and chasing works if singing fails. The sparrow pictured in the chapter "Scientific Names" is guarding his domain. The rooster pictured in chapter "How Did That Avian Expression Originate" relies on action more often than words. See chapter "Barnyard Chickens Have Fifteen Different Voices."

They build nests. Some nests take days to build, and are used, with needed repairs, for years. Other nests are completed in only a couple of days, yet are marvels of construction, and serve their purpose admirably. A cliff swallow's nest, built of mud, is shown in the chapter "Cliff Swallow."

They incubate their eggs. We'll never solve the riddle of which came first–the chicken or the egg–but we will always marvel at the egg with its embryo hatching out the nestling,

Common loon in winter plumage. Photograph by Patricia Burke

especially if the egg is only as large as a navy bean, as with the hummingbird pictured with the chapter "Black-chinned Hummingbird."

They feed their young. This is the time in their life when they must work the hardest. Besides finding food for themselves, the parents must find food for their two to several young which have voracious appetites and bottomless stomachs. This period of nesting and nurturing must and does coincide with when the most food with the most nourishing calories is available. We chose the rock pigeon pictured in the chapter "Water In The Life Of A Bird" to epitomize this activity.

They hide. All birds have enemies. Most live on borrowed time, living from moment to moment. To us they seem nonchalant, such as singing unconcernedly right after escaping the talons of a raptor. Different species have different techniques for hiding. For many it is to rely on protective coloration. The camouflage of this white-tailed ptarmigan shown here makes it look just like one of the rocks among which it is crouched.

They travel. The prairie chickens roost in grass fields, fly several miles to feed, then fly back to roost again. A few lone great American egrets fly north each fall after nesting season, then fly south for the winter. Flocks of cedar waxwings fly far and wide after raising their young, before moving south for the winter. The dunlins pictured in chapter "People Who Bond With Birds" are on the move.

They migrate south in the fall to escape the winter cold and because their food supply is gone, and fly north in the spring to raise a family. How they find their way to their winter haven, then north again to last year's same nesting site, was a great mystery. Recently scientists seem to have solved this, as described in the chapter "When Migratory Birds Can No Longer Migrate." The bright nuptial plumage is no longer needed in autumn, so when feather-renewing molt occurs after reproduction is consummated, winter plumage is drab, as shown in this common loon that was photographed in the waters of the Gulf of Mexico.

So, birds are busy all day long, and they live close to death and danger.

What Diurnal Birds Do At Night

Other than burrowing owls and short-eared owls and snowy owls, our North American owls are, well, night owls. So they are active at night. But what about other birds; do they all sleep at night? Not quite, it appears. In the Deep South the mockingbird often is heard singing in the dark. They must catch up on their sleep during the day by taking catnaps. (But how can a bird have anything in common with its archenemy, a cat?) The black-crowned night heron is nocturnal but during nesting season is seen in daytime, too. Night or day, if you hear a dog barking out in a wetland, that's more likely this night heron.

Black-crowned night-heron. Photograph by Jan Ove Gjershaug

Anyone looking at ducks during springtime has noticed so often some of them are floating out on the water with their heads tucked in, sound asleep. By nightfall they must be all slept out. The so-called moon watch may give insight into what is happening here.

Lovers may be noted for looking at the moon romantically, but when birders are looking at a full moon on a clear night they have something else in mind. One technique for counting birds in migration on such a night is to use a telescope, or what birders call a spotting scope, to count how many birds' silhouettes are seen flying across the moon's image per unit of time. This data is of value scientifically.

Compare the size of the moon with the wide expanse of the sky, and realize that those you can see with the full moon as a background are but a tiny fraction of the hordes that are flying all over the rest of the sky. And this continues all night long, all

Duck napping in daytime, on its nocturnal migration journey. Photograph by Jon Arne Saeter

going in the same direction, northward in the spring, and southward in the fall. Try to grasp how many millions of nocturnal travelers pass overhead during migration – big birds, little birds, some beating their wings faster than others.

These are the diurnal birds, flying with utmost energy, all night long. Their flight must be nonstop until daybreak. To try to land in the dark would end up in a fatal crash. And if over the Gulf of Mexico they must keep flying in daytime until land is reached.

I was on a pelagic birding tour once with a group of fellow birders, on the Gulf of Mexico far out miles from the shore, when my friend was thrilled and ecstatic to see a new addition to his life list – a blackburnian warbler! It had seen this boat and landed on it, exhausted and desperate. It seems such an event is not rare, to see a small land bird on an ocean-going ship, for the weaker long-distance migrants never make it and crash-land into the ocean surface when no ship is in sight. Survival of the fittest is at work.

Dry Tortugas, the westernmost of the Florida keys, each year is host to individuals of various species. Having landed there in a weakened condition, they find no food to replenish their stores of energy. Such was the dilemma of the egret I saw there once, which had interrupted its fall post-breeding dispersal migration across the Gulf of Mexico. That poor bird is pictured in the chapter, "World Explorer".

Nighttime migration also avoids hawks, updrafts, and enervating solar heat.

Water In The Life Of A Bird

As with all other life forms, water is crucial in the life of a bird. When altricial birds hatch they are helpless and require days of special attention by their parents before they can leave the nest. So how do these hatchlings get their water? The food their parents bring supplies it. This is utilized and saved from the digestive tract by defecating the fecal sac, which contains concentrated dehydrated waste matter enclosed in a membrane. The parent bird can carry that fecal sac away from the nest for sanitation and to prevent predators from discovering the nest. To be able to transport this sac easily the adult voids its own waste matter in the form of very liquid droppings. This arrangement also results in a dry bodily weight with no watery excess baggage, so as to permit most efficient flight.

Pigeons, with their strong neck muscles, pump pigeon milk (liquid predigested food from the parent's crop) into the fledgling's gullet. So squabs defecate liquid droppings, not fecal sacs. Pigeons have another distinction. Their strong throat muscles enable them to swallow water with their head held down and their bill submerged. Other families of birds must dip their bill in the water, hold a drop or two in their bill, then elevate their head for gravity to assist the water down to the stomach. They have to repeat this process to

Homing pigeon feeding. Photograph by Jon Arne Saeter

Common black-headed gull drinking salt-free water. Photograph by Jon Arne Saeter

quench their thirst, watching for enemies between each sip.

Of course, much of the water they need is extracted from the food they eat, as is true with the baby songbird.

All land birds must keep in mind where sources of water are, whether ponds, puddles, or bird baths, and must drink there regularly. Where water sources are few, such as in deserts, each spring or oasis is a life saver. Since birds from nearby and from miles away must visit there, a prime viewing spot for seeing birds is where the water is, so the birder is best rewarded by patiently waiting close by the oasis.

The sound of dripping water attracts birds to a bird bath. The bird bath that backyard bird watchers set out is aptly named, for the birds bathe in it as much as they drink water from it. A very special bird bath comes to mind. The Coleto Nature Center near Boerne, Texas has a remarkable feature. A few years ago a severe flood in the nearby Coleto Creek washed away the topsoil to expose bedrock which contained elephant-sized footprints of a certain species of dinosaur. Now before we visited this nature center in mid-February a heavy rain had filled the footprints with water. So here was a Winter Texan robin taking a bath in the inch-deep water in one of the footprints of a far distant ancestor! But the robin showed no evidence of veneration or respect for this priceless specimen of paleontology.

The typical bather such as a robin crouches in the water,

The dinosaur footprint (described on previous page) used as birdbath by camera-shy robin. Photograph by Kenneth J. Johnson

fluffs out its feathers to expose the skin between each feather, and rapidly flicks its wings in and out of the water. This splashes drops of water down between each feather onto the skin. Then as it flattens its feathers down the water squeezes out, carrying along debris such as excess oil and flakes of skin. As the bird bath gets dirty it must be cleaned regularly.

A swallow dips into the water as it flies, and flips up its tail to spray its back as it vibrates its feathers. A flicker bathes by sitting quietly with feathers raised during a drizzling rain.

A water bird may open its feathers and wings while floating. After the bath the birds shake themselves to throw off the water.

Barn and cliff swallows use water in building their nests. They pick up a beak-full of mud from a shore, fly to a chosen wall, and plaster each bit of mud onto the wall to form a shelf. As the black skimmer flies along the surface of calm water, scooping up food with its jutting lower bill, it also scoops up water.

Ocean water is too salty to drink. So how do pelagic species manage to stay out far away from fresh water and thrive? Tubenoses have the answer. They have a life-saving adaptation to a diet of salty food in salt water. The shearwaters and petrels are called tubenoses because they have large nostrils to excrete the large amounts of salt they must ingest in their diet. They have salt glands above the bill which remove the excess salt from the blood. They don't mind having a runny nose!

Songbirds do not have this adaptation enjoyed by the tubenoses. So if you feed birds take care that you do not offer them humans' food such as potato chips, crackers, salted nuts, etc. Too much salt can kill. Our city water is chlorinated, so I wonder if it wouldn't be justified to fill the bird bath with distilled or salt-free water. In nature a puddle – nature's original bird bath – contains rain water, which is salt-free.

Pros And Cons Of Having Feathers

A creature without feathers isn't a bird. A bird cannot live without feathers, so pros must outweigh cons in evaluating their functions.

When a bird isn't busy finding food, it spends much time preening. If done leisurely it must be taking oil from its oil gland located above its tail to spread around on its feathers, keeping each feather in place with its bill. When preening frantically, it must be attacking the lice which live on its dandruff, or on the mites, which suck its blood. Both parasites cause itching, which is very annoying. A young purple martin fell to the ground once from our martin colony, which action always causes the parents to abandon the fledgling. When I picked up the unfortunate young one, my forearm began to itch as I saw dozens of dark pin-point sized mites racing around in circles on my bare skin.

Feathers provide wonderful insulation. In cold weather a bird fluffs up its feathers to create a thin layer of air between each feather to help preserve body temperature. Fluffing feathers also increases body size, since a large foe is more intimidating than a small foe. Insulation from the cold explains why the legs of the snowy owl living in the Arctic are feathered. In a step further, the ptarmigan's toes, as well as its legs, are also feathered. Feathered toes also help the ptarmigan to walk on snow without sinking.

But on the other hand, if a body part is bare does that imply an attempt to cool off? Hardly – for the featherless head of a vulture has a better explanation. Sticking its head inside a cadaver would dirty up any feathers if they were present.

Then why does a turkey have a naked head, for it isn't a carrion eater like a vulture? With a bright blue head and a bright red throat, such vivid colors must be a fetish or stimulant to mating. Examples of brightly colored plumage for sexual attraction are too numerous to mention – almost universal. Color can also be useful as camouflage.

A number of birds line their nests with soft down feathers,

Eider down being harvested. Photograph by Jon Arne Saeter

the prime example of this being the eider duck, whose nest consists of copious amounts of down plucked by the female from her breast. Men have harvested this down to make eider down quilts and bedrolls, unequalled for soft comfort and warmth.

Feathers present some problems, though. They don't last forever. The edges wear off. Experts have figured out what month a feather was moulted by determining how much of the original edge is missing. They fall out in sequence so they can continue to insulate and so the bird can fly. But ducks, after they breed, lose so many flight feathers that for a while they cannot fly and must go into hiding, explaining why they're so hard to find then until the new sturdy primaries are ready for the southward migration. This eclipse plumage is well named because its colors are drab compared to the brilliant colors of the nuptial plumage which attracts females in early spring.

Birds have an extreme dislike of having their feathers ruffled. The wind is the prime culprit for doing that. Therefore, when birds are perched side by side on a wire, notice that they all face the same direction – into the wind. Side winds are a problem, most obvious with a great-tailed grackle. I've seen a strong side wind from the north bend its great tail to turn the grackle around from its intended westward walk.

Feathers aren't placed equidistant on the skin, but in tracts separated by bare skin. A brood patch is a bare patch of skin on the abdomen, allowing the bird's temperature to keep the eggs warm during incubation. A primary or flight feather is on the forward part of the wing, used for flying.

Tail feathers, used as a rudder, may be modified as spikes to prop against a tree trunk, as on a woodpecker or brown creeper. The short body feathers form the contour of the bird's shape. The flight, tail, and body feathers are used for

Great-tailed grackle.
Photograph by Jan Ove Gjershaug

combat, courtship, or camouflage. Down is fluffy, closest to the skin. Semiplumes are more fluffy and larger, providing more insulation. Bristles around a poorwill's mouth funnel insects into its maw. The ear opening of birds is protected by filamentous feathers called ear coverts, which allow sound waves to pass clearly.

A feather is a symbol of lightness; nevertheless, a pound of feathers (which contains 16 ounces) weighs more than a pound of gold (which contains only 12 ounces).

A feather is made up of keratin, an insoluble protein, same as in fingernails.

A hundred years ago stylish women's mania for huge hats with large plumes threatened to decimate the population of egrets. Then legislation outlawed taking of feathers. But there is no restriction on feathers of our two greatest pests, the house sparrow and the starling.

And finally, feathers can be used again. Many birds in nest building pick up shed feathers off the ground to use

Little blue heron scratching itself. Photograph by Patricia Burke

as lining in their nest that is under construction. "Goldie" Goldmann, the Mandan builder and weekly inspector of hundreds of his bluebird boxes, recalls that he would procure white down chicken feathers and hold them up near the nest box. The bluebird on a fly-by would snatch that feather from his fingers and add it to its nest.

Yes, feathers are here to stay.

Color In Courtship And Eating

In the realm of birds, the male's plumage is brightly colored, but the plumage of the female is subdued and dull. Her primary role is to set on her eggs in a nest hidden from enemies, so she must blend into the background, even be camouflaged. The male, brightly colored, is to divert attention from the nest, after attracting a mate with his bright colors.

That is the common assumption. Recently researchers have been finding evidence that proves that this widespread concept is correct.

Scientists studied sixty male barn swallows. Half of them, the test group, had their naturally orange breasts colored a darker red, using a lipstick type red color marker that is sold in stationery stores. The other half, the control group, were left unaltered with their paler more bland breasts. The researchers found that the test birds that had the red makeup applied were more attractive to female barn swallows, and mated more often. This also caused a rise in the level of the males' testosterone, the sex hormone that increases virility.

The European robin flaunts his red breast to intimidate other males. This has been demonstrated by scientists by waving a red ball of similar size. The male defending his territory and enticing a mate attacked the ball. Waving a similar ball of another color did not induce an attack response. It follows that this is evidence that shows that its red breast is the thing that allures the female robin.

Our most prolific perching bird, the red-winged blackbird, owes its success largely to its red epaulets. These shoulder patches of bright red and yellow can be enlarged by raising the colored feathers, and the male spreads his wings slightly for greater effect, so its display before the female becomes impressive indeed. The role of color is proven by noting that the red patch is small and duller outside of the breeding season.

The American redstart is adorned by a large patch of red on each side of the base of the tail, plus two patches of red on each wing. In courtship the male spreads his tail and wings widely, producing a flashy display that can't help but impress his female.

All birds don't use red as a sex attractor. The blue-footed booby, which comes up to the Salton Sea from the Gulf of California, stomps his bright blue feet in front of the female to arouse her interest.

The peacock's huge tail has much bright blue in it. When fanned out it produces a very impressive display.

The eastern (rufous-sided) towhee spreads out its tail to show its white spots distinctly, and his white-marked wings also are spread and folded in the courtship display, as explained in Bent's book.

The courtship of the hooded merganser involves the male's body rising up in the water with depressed crest on the top of his head, then coming down to the water again with neck stretched forward, as the crest is fully erected. When its crest is depressed the white stripe on the side of the head is narrow; when the crest is expanded the brilliant white area widens to cover most of the side of the head. The female cannot miss seeing it. Even halfway across a lake that white spot stands out like a beacon.

There are many more examples of how the colors of the plumages of male birds act as a stimulant to courtship.

But aside from its place in courtship, color is vital in fledglings' survival. These young ones must grow rapidly in the short time they have to mature, so they must eat ravenously. Appreciate the ways Nature has met this challenge with the following examples.

Most gulls have a spot of contrasting color, such as red, on the tip of the bill. The young one, prone to pecking at conspicuous spots of a different color, pecks at the tip of the parent's bill. This stimulates what we call the gag reflex, which induces the parent to regurgitate food for the hungry one to eat.

At the tip of the spout on the hummingbird feeder is a plastic flower with red petals. The red attracts these birds, so they place their bills at the opening for their tongue to get the sugar water in the feeder. Women have told me a printed shirt with red on it attracts hummingbirds that are looking for red flowers.

Many fledglings have a red or yellow or white spot or nubbin in their throat. When they open their mouth wide at the approach of the parent bird, this bright color induces the bird to place the piece of food it brings accurately into the maw of the young one.

So color does have an important part in the sex and sustenance of birds.

Do Angels Really Have Wings, Like Birds?

A Nineteenth Century humorist once reminded his readers that insects have six appendages, and inasmuch as today's pictures of angels unanimously consider them to have a pair of wings, they must have six appendages; therefore angels are insects.

However, wings are always feathered. All birds have feathers. No creatures have feathers except birds. Therefore, angels must be birds. But how can an angel be both an insect and a bird?

Browsing the Internet we find that every civilization from mankind's early beginnings has envied and adored creatures that fly. They have pictured a man, or a divine spirit in human form, with a pair of wings, whether on sculpture or hieroglyphics or cliff-wall paintings. So, being consistent, people today imagine angels as having wings.

The *Bible* must be the ultimate authority on angels. Could it resolve this dilemma of an insect-bird?

An Internet web site says Old Testament people believed the world was flat, and covered by a huge dome, above which God resided. His angels went back and forth carrying messages between certain men and God up in heaven. (Our English word "angel" comes from the Greek word angelos, which means messenger.) In order to fly with the messages they must have wings, just as birds use wings to travel through the air. (Recall contemporary homing pigeons, used by men to carry messages in our time, in war time and in peace time.)

But what does the Old Testament actually say about angels? Genesis 18:1-8 recounts how three men appeared by the door to Abraham's tent. While these three (same number as the Trinity) were indistinguishable from ordinary men, it soon became evident they weren't ordinary men. Normally men couldn't be traveling in the heat of the day – siesta time – in this hot desert. Their demeanor had an air of authority when they announced to old Abraham that his elderly wife, long in her menopause, would become pregnant and bear him a son. These were angels without wings, appearing as men.

Likewise in Genesis 19 two angels in the form of men, who had no wings, came to Lot, who was living in Sodom. He welcomed them into

If angels have wings, how do they preen their feathers – like this Canada goose?
Photograph by Jon Arne Saeter

his house. But the depraved men of the town demanded the two come out so they could commit sodomy on them. When they almost broke the door down in their determination, the two men struck the mob with blindness so they could not find the door. Further evidence that these two were angels was when they forcefully insisted Lot and his family leave the town because the Lord was about to destroy it. These two angels in the form of men had no wings. (The practice of sodomy got its name from Sodom, the city's name.)

In Genesis 28:12 in his dream Jacob's ladder reached from earth to heaven, and angels were climbing up and down the ladder. They had no wings, and resembled men, and didn't fly.

In Joshua 5:13 a man with drawn sword but without wings appeared to Joshua as a good omen before he and his men of war conquered the city of Jericho.

In Judges 6:11-21 an angel in the form of a man came to Gideon with the message that Gideon was to lead the Israelites to victory against their enemy. When Gideon asked for a sign to prove that message, the man (men don't have wings) ordered him to place food on a rock. The man-angel struck it with his staff, incinerating the food, convincing Gideon that this was the Lord's angel.

When King Nebuchadnezzar had Shadrach, Meshach, an Abednego thrown into the fiery furnace (Daniel 3:1-25) the king saw a fourth man with them in the furnace. That fourth man had no wings that the king could see, yet the king identified that fourth man as the Son of God.

As the Apostles watched Jesus ascending up to heaven, two men stood by them in white robes (Acts 1:10): but they had no wings, yet were angels.

Paul admonished Christians to show hospitality to strangers (Hebrews 13:2), since thereby some have entertained angels unawares. Strangers don't have wings.

There are many other Bible passages depicting angels appearing as men, never with any suggestion they had wings. The common theme in these appearances was that it was only after the man gave his message or performed some supernatural feat that they were recognized as an angel sent from God.

Through the centuries men have envisioned numerous variations of an angel. A most dainty picture was originated by some artist in the 1600s, it is said. It is a chubby cherub floating in the air, with stubby wings inadequate to enable flight. This appears on today's greeting cards and Valentine cards, a figment of an artist's imagination with no Biblical evidence to support this fantasy.

If an artist, trying to portray an angel, doesn't furnish it with wings, how else can the artist display it as an angel, not just a man? Wings show that the creature can levitate and travel through the air and appear and disappear, like an angel does.

Yet present day people who affirm they've seen their guardian angel don't recall that it was adorned with a pair of wings.

Actually, humans' proneness to attach wings to angels is testimony to how much people adore birds.

Miracle Of The Bird's Egg

An ostrich's egg is so large it can produce a dozen omelets, for it has the mass of thirty chicken eggs. Bedouins in the Sahara Desert can subsist for days in a land of no water by carrying an ostrich egg which has been emptied to carry water in it. A hummingbird's egg is no bigger than a navy bean.

An egg must be turned frequently to keep the embryo from settling against the shell. The nesting parent bird does this by turning it with her bill. The nighthawk does it by her weight pushing against it as she lands on it. The penguin does it with his feet as the egg rests between his body and his feet, insulated from the subzero Antarctic weather. Egg factories do it by mechanically moving the tray periodically, just far enough each time to keep the yolk (for egg eating humans) or embryo (for hatcheries) in the middle of the shell.

The domestic chicken shouts, "Cut-cut-cudaw'-cut" after she lays an egg. Is she bragging, or expressing awe and surprise at what came out of her, or reminding the farmer that if he killed her for meat he wouldn't be getting any more eggs?

When a cuckoo lays its egg in another bird's nest, the host bird either doesn't realize it and raises a young cuckoo, or picks up the egg with her bill to discard, or builds another nest on top of it, or abandons the nest.

Altricial birds, who must live in the nest until strong enough to fly away, remain undetected by predators because the parent bird picks up the tell-tale egg shell and flies off with it.

By laying an egg, the female bird isn't impeded in flight by having to carry the weight of developing young in her body.

The egg has effectively entered into our culture; for example, we are walking on egg shells if we start talking about a sensitive subject. If we make a mistake we may have laid an egg, or gotten egg on our face. To urge one to continue, we egg them on. A likeable fellow is a good egg, but he should not put all his eggs in one basket by not diversifying his savings. One's monetary savings is their nest egg. A bad egg is a villainous person.

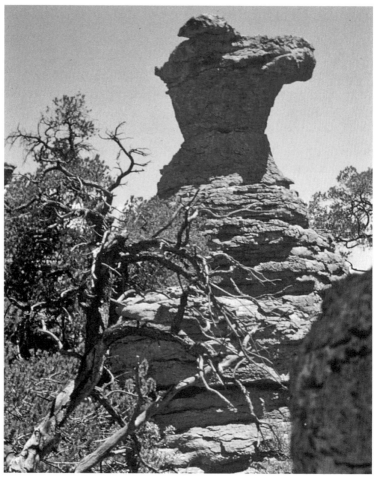

This natural formation in Arizona's Chiricahua Mountains is the world's largest bird, incubating its eggs on its nest atop a rock pedestal. Photograph by Kenneth J. Johnson

The wonderful boon to our economy, the chemical DDT, turned out to be a disaster that had to be banned when it was discovered to be the cause of thinning of egg shells in birds higher up in the food chain. Calcium in the shell is what gives strength to the egg. The larger the egg, the thicker the shell, needing more calcium for strength to protect against cracking and breakage.

The baby bird inside the egg has a little nubbin near the end of its upper bill with which it files back and forth on the inside of its egg shell, to crack it open so the bird can hatch.

Making a large collection of eggs from many species of birds used to be a hobby of bird watchers until it was banned, for it had become one cause of some species becoming threatened. Some eggs, such as an eagle's, were worth hundreds of dollars...

Candling an egg – looking through an egg at a light source such as a lit candle – can tell if the egg is good.

Air must go through the shell for the embryo to survive. An egg shell won't sink; as a boy I would eat a hard boiled egg by removing some of the side shell (not the end), scoop out the egg, and float the empty shell, pretending it was a boat.

In the *Bible*, in Luke 11:12 it says inasmuch as a father won't give his son a scorpion if he asks his father for an egg, so our Heavenly Father knows even better how to give to us when we ask him.

The early Israelites were taught preservation of our environment in *Deuteronomy* 27:6. When they came upon a bird's nest they were allowed to take the eggs but not the mother bird, since she can produce more eggs.

In conclusion, the profound mystery of the egg is still the answer to the philosophical question, "Which came first, the chicken or the egg?"

Making A Dinosaur From A Bird's Egg

Dinosaurs have caught the fancy of the public. Dinosaur movies have been box office hits. There are dinosaur theme parks that attract crowds. Dinosaur toys are popular. Archeological digs yield dinosaur skeletons that become featured attractions in museums. The public is captivated and enthralled with the fantasy of seeing a live dinosaur.

Scientists have demonstrated ample evidence that dinosaurs are ancestors of birds, so imagine a bird that is a throwback to its dinosaur ancestors. A dream of seeing a live dinosaur may become a reality for some young reader of this column before he dies; modern science is developing the technology of how to breed a dinosaur! There are even two methods being researched today for how to accomplish this. One is to extract enough samples of DNA from archeologically recovered specimens to reconstruct the complete sequence of a dinosaur's DNA, then implant them into a closely related relative's egg.

On the other path of research, it studies in great detail the embryo in a bird's egg, and finds the stages of development that are analogous to those of a dinosaur. Today the chicken egg is most easily available and has been the species of choice for study. Here are some examples of what has been accomplished:

A dinosaur has a number of vertebrae in its tail. The hatched chicken has only four vertebrae in its tail. But in the chick embryo sixteen vertebrae are present! What happened to the other twelve? As the embryo developed a control gene turned off the growth of those twelve.

There are one thousand control genes present, each programmed to turn on or turn off the development of a certain part of the growing embryo at a certain stage in its development.

The dinosaur has a hand on each forelimb, seemingly capable of gripping. The bird's wing has three vestigial fingers. As the embryo develops today, phalanges fuse or fail to develop into a functional hand like that of the dinosaur, because they were turned off by a certain control gene. Instead, they provide support for the flight feathers of the bird's wing. In a South American bird, the hoatzin, the young bird has a modified first and second phalanx which act as two claws on each wing, used to help climb about. The claws disappear as the bird matures.

The dinosaur's mouth is similar to a bird's bill, but has teeth. But a typical bird's bill has no teeth. However, careful study of the chick's bill in the embryo shows a row of little projections, embryonic teeth, on the edge of its bill at one stage of its development. Then they disappear as the embryo develops. But the present day merganser has tooth-like serrations on the edge of its mandible, justifying the name of sawbill for this species of duck. So a bird with teeth may not be too far-fetched. Refer to the snow goose's grin patch in chapter "Superabundant Snow Goose" in section "I. Parlor Guide to Water Birds and Game Birds."

Some species of dinosaurs had feathers, in various stages of development. It seems that a scale is a precursor to a feather, and if a scale is turned on by its particular control gene it will develop into a feather. Indeed, I have seen in county fairs a breed of chicken whose legs and toes are covered with feathers, some even three inches long! Ptarmigans and snowy owls have feathered feet.

Both dinosaurs and birds have hollow bones. Both dinosaurs and birds have oblong eggs, both laid in a nest, the complexity of the nest varying greatly with the species. A round egg, such as a turtle's which the turtle buries so it can't roll, will roll if on an exposed slanted surface. An oblong egg, narrower at one end, will oscillate instead of rolling away. Bipedal locomotion, using only the hind limbs for walking on the ground, is common to both dinosaurs and birds.

New species have been created by control genes. New species have also been created by a mutation – the sudden appearance of an individual which differs from the rest of the population and transmits that difference to its descendants. To create a dinosaur from a bird, a number of mutations would be necessary, which would be extremely unlikely in nature or in the laboratory, and the mutations could produce something similar to a dinosaur, but not a duplicate of a known dinosaur. To use control genes, many of them would have to be used, and as of this writing it is becoming theoretically possible.

For many years scientists have been aware that ontogeny repeats phylogeny – that the stages through which an embryo goes in its development in womb or egg mirror the stages that life has gone through for millions of years in the distant past. Now we are able to anticipate how we can reproduce some of those stages of development by turning on and turning off control genes.

V. BIRDS HAVE A ROUGH TIME

Cats Versus Birds

Is there a birder – or anyone – who has never seen a domestic cat carrying a bird in its mouth, or seen a cat catch a bird, or heard alarmed birds scolding and sounding distress calls, then looked to find that the object of their fear was a skulking cat? How can this be – one moment dear Tabby is affectionately brushing against our leg while purring, then later viciously attacking a poor little bird? A split personality, a feline Dr. Jekyl and Mr. Hyde, a creature of extremes.

Mankind's attitude toward cats has also gone to extremes. Ancient Egyptians actually worshipped the domestic cat as a god; if anyone killed a cat he was given a death sentence. Then in the Middle Ages Pope Gregory IX, in agreement with the times, declared the cat to be a diabolical creature; if someone had one as a pet that person, together with their cat,

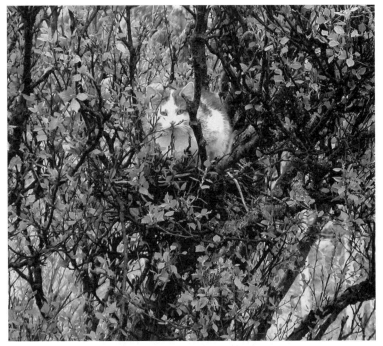

Cat in a crow's nest. Photograph by Georg Bangjord

were both put to death. Black cats and witches today are part of the lore of Halloween (that "hallowed evening" before All Saints Day). Although we say so with tongue in cheek, we still say it is bad luck to see a black cat cross the road in front of us.

Dr. T. S. Roberts, author of the two volume *The Birds of Minnesota*, the most comprehensive state book on birds ever written, I believe, says that after man, the domestic cat is the greatest destroyer of birds. He advises that all stray cats should be put to death.

Cats come by their dual personality naturally, for their distant ancestors were wild animals that lived by preying on birds and small animals. So even a well-fed cat on an ample diet when exposed to a tempting target will revert to instinct and attack it, like it does with a ball of yarn or a rubber ball.

According to the U.S. Census Bureau there were 30 million cats owned as pets in 1970, and 60 million in 1990; today I presume, keeping pace with human population, there are more. As to semi-wild farm cats and feral cats, who knows – there are probably over 100 million of those plus tame cats, it is estimated. Roberts says one ornithologist (Dr. F. M. Chapman) in 1902 figured there were over 25,000,000 feral cats. Roberts also calculated that one of those free-roaming cats kills 50 birds a year. Contemporary specialists estimate that rural cats are now killing hundreds of millions of birds each year in this nation. A house cat kills for sport, a feral cat kills to survive.

I'm informed that a National Geographic television special says in a survey of felines that the most dangerous predator is not the lion, tiger, leopard, bobcat or puma, but the domestic house cat, the most prodigious successful killer.

In 1936 Roberts said, "Cats have no legal standing." In 1983 M. L. Boddicker of the University of Nebraska in his publication on *House Cats* (feral) declared that a cat wearing a collar is considered personal property. As to the North Dakota Attorney General's office regarding the legal status of a free-roaming domestic cat not wearing a collar, they refer me to the police department of my city, or to my county sheriff if I am outside city limits. Our Bismarck Police Department says if the cat is not at its home they should be called and would impound it and take it to the humane society. Or if on my property I may trap it but may not harm it, lest I be fined. Outside of Bismarck in Burleigh County if such a cat is found one is free to dispose of it as long as the sheriff doesn't know about it. My sense is that any law enforcement agency, wary of animal rights groups, regards the subject as a hot potato.

Of course, I may be prejudiced, since when I was a boy I had let out my pet pigeons from their coop for exercise that winter day. I had earlier built an igloo and the mild weather had then collapsed it. A stray cat had hidden behind a block of snow from the igloo. When a pigeon had wandered close by, the cat sprang out, pounced on it, bit a large chunk of flesh out of its breast, and left my pigeon for dead.

So what can one do? Keep your pet indoors. The ritual of "put the cat out" at bedtime frees the cat for a night of revelry and reproduction and predation. Imagine what Tabby did the night before to necessitate those extensive cat naps it enjoys the next day. Neuter your cat. To bell the cat or de-claw it is ineffective in saving birds.

Locate bird feeders away from cover which can be used by cats in which to lie in wait to ambush birds. If a tree is used by birds for nests, put an animal guard around the trunk.

Outdoor pet food dishes and garbage cans attract stray cats; don't feed stray cats.

People often get tired of a cat, or trap one and plan to get rid of it, so they carry the unwanted feline out into the country and dump it. This terrible act is cruel since it moves the bird-killer to another location where it starves or kills more birds and small animals, and breeds more of its kind. Oftentimes a whole colony of up to twenty cats is formed, whose members become wild and live independent of man, subsisting on wildlife, also displacing the wildlife the colony doesn't eat.

Constant Enemies: Snakes And Birds

Between the snake and the cat, the song bird is between a rock and a hard place.

Some scientists have conjectured about the anatomical relationship between reptiles and birds, but upon considering the appearance and behavior of any species of bird, the one that is most reminiscent of a snake is the anhinga. Living in swamps and marshy lakes of Florida and southern states along the Gulf of Mexico, its long neck is extremely serpentine and sinuous. As the anhinga swims through the water, it bends and arches and curves its neck to remind one of a snake in motion. For good reason it is called the snake bird. And part of its diet is water-snakes.

This writer has found no instance where a snake and a bird have lived in harmony with each other. It seems usually they avoid each other. If not, the large bird, if it is a carnivore, eats the snake; if the bird is small the snake eats the bird.

In the New Testament's Matthew 10:16, Jesus contrasts snake and bird when He says, "Be wise as serpents, and harmless as doves," inferring that snakes are wise and cautious, while birds are gentle, innocent and guileless.

The desert Southwest's roadrunner has an exceptional trait. A good part of its menu consists of snakes. It will jerk a snake off the ground, flip it in the air, catch it by its neck, crush its head, and swallow the snake head first. Its reputation for killing and eating rattlesnakes has been well substantiated.

The roadrunner is not the only bird to kill a snake. The golden eagle shares that distinction. Bent in his remarkable 26 volume series of books on North American birds states that this bird kills many snakes. The golden eagle was observed once feinting at a coiled rattlesnake several times until it uncoiled. Then the eagle quickly seized it by its neck, cut off its head, and flew off with the decapitated snake.

The red-tailed hawk has eaten rattlesnakes, bull snakes and smaller snakes. Swainson's hawk was observed to swallow an entire rattlesnake, Bent records, while the broad-winged hawk first skins a snake before it is eaten.

"Goldie" Goldmann, the Mandan citizen who has built and mounted hundreds of bluebird houses, then inspected them weekly, related an interesting observation to me. When he opened the lid of one on his bird boxes, he found a young bull snake inside. This snake had crawled up the fence post on which Goldie had mounted his box, and had entered through the round entry hole. Once inside it had devoured the eggs or baby birds. But on attempting to exit found that his meals had increased his girth so much that the lumps thus formed didn't fit through the entry. So the bull snake was trapped inside!

The Wednesday, July 21, 2004 *Bird Column* in the *Bismarck Tribune* recalls an amazing incident involving some thirty mountain plovers and a large bull snake. The plovers formed a line on each side of the snake, impelling it to proceed in a straight line out of the plovers' foraging area until it entered the stubble of an adjoining field.

The red-cockaded woodpecker, an inhabitant of our southeastern states, drills its nest hole only in a diseased large living pine. Then it drills little holes around the nest opening. The pine pitch that oozes out of these holes dribbles down the trunk of the tree to cover the bark with the stickiness which snakes abhor, thus protecting this woodpecker's nest from the snakes.

T. S. Roberts in his *Birds of Minnesota* speculates about why the great crested flycatcher so often includes the cast-off skin of a snake in his nest. It logically could be to repel live snakes and to intimidate intruders. But Roberts questions this theory, since often the snake skin is buried in the nesting material or is in broken pieces, which he presumes would be overlooked by invaders.

Be aware of the annual contest going on each summer in the grass of our prairies. The meadowlarks create their nests as cleverly as possible, bending blades of grass and building a canopy to roof over the spot to hide their eggs and young. Then the snakes (and other predators) exercise their detective skills to their utmost to try to find the nest. That the meadowlarks are so abundant is evidence of the birds' expertise.

The songbirds that nest in trees produce nests that are easier to find. When the snake crawls out on the branch that holds the nest, it seems that the best the birds can do is swoop down and pick at the snake with their bills. The songbirds' defense is aided when the neighbor birds, hearing the commotion, come over to attack the snake, too.

Turtles And Birds

The *St. Paul* (Minn.) *Daily News* for July 8, 1934 had a prominent illustrated article in its third section on page 8, columns 4- 5 about a snapping turtle with a tenacious grip on the foot and leg of a struggling mallard duck. Attracted by the thrashing in the water, this man rescued the duck by grasping the tail of the snapping turtle, which still refused to relax its jaws. The picture in the newspaper was too fuzzy to be acceptable for today's publications, so my sketch of that photo is illustrated instead.

The documentary proof of such an action is rare and worthy of a news article, but it turns out that snapping turtles are routinely pulling waterfowl below water to eat as part of their regular diet.

In another encounter, a snapping turtle grasped the leg of a gosling, who struggled to prevent being pulled under water. The Canada goose parents were agitated but helpless to save it.

In this book in the chapter "Birds Never To Be Forgotten", in the paragraph "The Silenced Merganser", the hapless merganser in Michigan had its leg seized by a snapping turtle. After being pulled under water it was torn apart and eaten.

The Internet also reports a similar attack on a black duck in North Carolina. This time the duck escaped from the jaws of the snapping turtle. But the escape would have been of little avail, since being crippled by an amputated foot or a broken leg, the duck would not have lived long before it would be eaten by a predator.

In Texas a common moorhen and a laughing gull were also seized by snapping turtles. Indeed, can anyone refer to any species of waterfowl that has never been a victim of this fate?

But birds are not always the victims. The Internet relates watching a great blue heron picking up a turtle, placing it on a rock, and trying to stab it with its bill. Repeated attempts to split the turtle's shell were futile. The heron couldn't swallow the turtle, either. Finally one of the turtles present bit the heron's tongue, causing much bleeding. The heron eventually gave up and waded away.

In an article in that same *St. Paul Daily News* for March 24, 1935 a conservationist proposed that all snapping turtles should be eradicated, because snapping turtles are the greatest destroyers of waterfowl. Authorities today have a more mature knowledgeable attitude. Turtles have a place in the scheme of things. When some vandal killed a snapping turtle in the demonstration plot on the grounds of the North Dakota Game and Fish Department headquarters in Bismarck, ND, that destruction was strongly condemned by everyone.

Sketch of newspaper photo of man holding tail of snapping turtle
with its jaws still locked onto foot and leg of mallard duck.

Nature's Poisons That Harm Birds

A world wide problem for waterfowl is botulism. This disease causes paralysis, causing the victim to stagger and contort. Flight is impossible. Death results.

It seems the water birds eat rotting plants or fish which are contaminated by botulinum toxin produced by the bacterium named *Clostridium botulinum.* This "bug" is anaerobic, living on decaying plant and animal matter in the absence of oxygen. North Dakota with its alkaline lakes is especially deadly when hot weather and drought come. When these conditions prevail, people are disturbed to find the dead birds that result.

Being an inland mid-continental state, North Dakota escapes the phenomenon in the ocean called the Red Tide, more accurately known as HAB (harmful algal bloom). Plankton, microscopic algae on which all higher forms of life depend in life's food chain, consists of diatoms, containing silica, and dinoflagellates. The latter are tiny cellulose-covered balls, each with a pair of little whips for locomotion. They make sugar from carbon dioxide and light. In size, a dinoflagellate has a diameter of the width of five human red blood cells placed side by side.

Unfortunately, some of these species of algae produce neurotoxins, such as saxitoxin from dinoflagellates and domoic acid from diatoms. When phytoplankton is eaten and passes up through the food chain they sicken and kill birds and other victims who feed on them. Brown pelicans and cormorants have died in large numbers from eating anchovies tainted from toxic algae.

When the red tide reaches the surface to color the water red, as the algae are multiplying by cell division, they emit a toxic cloud of gas into the air. When close to these fumes,

One egg in this peregrine falcon nest did not hatch, probably due to high contents of poison.
Photograph by Torgeir Nygaard

or when a breeze blows the fumes over the beach, creatures inhaling them develop itchy eyes and throat and cough. The air-borne brevetoxin has produced paralysis, gasping, and loss of control of bladder and bowels, in loons, gannets, cormorants and white pelicans.

Now here is an interesting side observation. Many dinoflagellates are bioluminescent. They react when jostled (such as in breaking surf or by swimmers and waders) to give off flashes of light at night. I am reminded of standing along the railing of my troop ship during World War II at night. Because of wartime blackout it was pitch dark. Looking down at the water pushed aside by the ship, in the wave thus created were bright flashes of light. These surely were caused by jostling of forms of sea life such as this plankton.

Aflatoxin, produced by the fungus *Aspergillus flavus*, damages the immune system. Deer corn, set out by hunters as bait, has been found to be contaminated by this fungus in half the samples tested by the Texas Department of Agriculture. When wild turkeys eat this deer corn containing at least 20 ppb (parts per billion) of aflatoxin they get sick or die.

In Nature mercury is found in cinnabar ore and other rocks and soil, coal, oil and natural gas. When rocks erode, soil decomposes, or petroleum products burn, mercury is released into the air. When airborne it is carried by the wind and falls to the earth with snow or rain. There it is absorbed by certain bacteria in wet areas, which turn it into methylmercury, which is taken up by other microorganisms which feed successive larger organisms. At each step the mercury becomes more concentrated. By the time wading birds eat the fish it may be toxic. Mercury lodged in the muscles and brains of herons, mergansers, gulls, rails, sandpipers explain their symptoms of mercury poisoning – crippling, seizures, kidney failure, brain and nerve damage, blindness.

So birds do lead a hazardous life.

The Snare Of The Fowler

Bird banding is a method of determining the travels of birds. The bird is trapped in a net, and its species and age and sex recorded. An inscribed aluminum band is placed on its leg, and the bird is released. Hopefully the bird is later caught in the same or another net, or found dead or shot by a hunter. If the finder of the bird reports to the address on the band valuable information is obtained.

Catching birds in a net has an interesting history and an ancient origin. A fowler is a professional bird catcher. Ancient Egyptian paintings show fowlers using their techniques to harvest birds in the marshes of the Nile Delta thousands of years B. C. (Before Christ). The profession is mentioned in the *Bible*. To quote Jeremiah 5:26: "For among My people are found wicked men; they watch, as fowlers lie in wait they set a trap, they catch men." And in Psalms 91:3: "For He will deliver thee from the snare of the fowler, and from the deadly pestilence."

The Internet (www.bibletools.org) tells us that beyond the use of snares and nets, fowlers have used other ways to capture birds, all of which would be frowned upon by a Humane Society today. The fowler would take young birds from their nest, raise them, and hide them in hidden cages. Their calls would attract other birds of that species, who were then shot by bow and arrow by hunters lying in wait. Or the hunter would throw an 18 inch long stick at the legs of a quail-sized bird. Sewing shut the eyes of a captured bird, its calls would entice others of its kind, which were then harvested.

Then what would be done with the birds after they were caught? Some were sold to become a cage bird, to be looked at and listened to. They were good eating; in Southern Europe small birds are still caught in nets and eaten as gourmet snacks. (Remember the old English nursery rhyme, "Four and twenty blackbirds baked in a pie.") For more on this, see chapter "Incredible Edible Birds." The net would be put up at night or early in the morning, then inspected later in the morning. Wild pigeons and doves were caught in nets to be used by Jews to follow their religious customs, using them as sacrifice to the Lord. In Jesus' time the Jews purchased the doves from merchants in the Temple, but the system had degenerated into a practice of overcharging, it seems, and cheating the people who had to exchange their currency for what was acceptable in the Temple. Seeing this dishonest practice of taking advantage of worshipers, Jesus was outraged and threw the money-changers out of the Temple, according to John 2:13-16.

In accordance with Jewish law, Joseph and Mary brought baby Jesus to the Temple along with a pair of turtle-doves or two young pigeons, the birds to be sacrificed (Luke 2:22-24), as the baby was dedicated. These birds either had been caught in a fowler's snare, or were descended from birds that had been caught in such a net.

Birds are still caught in nets today, but for a new purpose – to advance scientific knowledge. The Inland Bird Banding Association's members set up mist nets woven of fine inconspicuous strong threads. The songbirds don't see them in time and get tangled. It is extremely important that the net be inspected frequently, before the struggling bird becomes crippled. Untangling the bird is a delicate maneuver to prevent damage to the net or the bird. My clumsy fingers are not adequate, so I don't band birds. Avoiding damage to the bird's leg is another hazard in placing the band on the leg.

Jacket patch of the
Inland Bird Banding Association

Bird banding and monitoring nets can be dangerous. I accompanied a refuge worker once in his visit to the mist net he was watching in Kodiak National Wildlife Refuge in Alaska. He was carrying a rifle. Asked why he needed a rifle to check a mist net, he replied that Kodiak bears had been damaging his nets. It seems that this Big Brown Bear, the largest of all bears, weighing up to 1500 pounds, wasn't to be inhibited by a flimsy mist net, so it plows right through or brushes it aside when it is in his way. I did see considerable damage done to that refuge worker's net because of bears.

cormorant

Succulent Song Birds?

In the chapter labeled "How did that avian expression originate?" it describes the expression, "to go for a lark." In that situation the people intent on capturing songbirds to eat harvest them from nets set out to ensnare them.

It seems hard to believe that a person would think of a pretty little songbird as something to eat, especially something so tiny with hardly one mouthful of flesh. It is said that it takes a dozen small birds to constitute an adequate dinner for one person. So I consulted the Internet. The information found there was a surprise.

For hundreds of years southern Europeans have captured songbirds to supplement their meager diet, and were able and content to secure few enough so as to not upset the balance of nature. But in the last decades new techniques have been developed and old methods used more intensively, so now the population of migratory passerines is declining drastically, even to the point of a few species being threatened with extinction.

Double-barreled shot-guns that needed reloading after two shots have been replaced by semi-automatics, fired by lines of hunters posted along flight routes, who don't quit when they secure a bountiful number of birds to eat, but who continue shooting just for the fun of killing. Superfluous birds are left on the ground.

In Cyprus, I am told, lime sticks have been used for hundreds of years to supplement the natives' scanty food. But now lime sticks are much more common.

A lime stick is a small twig, or a branch of two or three feet length, which is smeared with very sticky lime, the result of boiling plums from the Syrian plum tree. These sticks are placed among the branches of bushes and small trees. When birds land on the sticks they cannot escape from the gluey concoction.

Mist nets are also used, but in addition new-fangled tape recorders are placed at the site, which continuously play the song of the bird all night long. Next morning hundreds and thousands of migrants are yielded from the battery of mist nets.

What used to be a needed addition to a scanty menu has changed to become a luxury added to a hearty diet of ample or excessive calories.

By counting the number of shot-gun cartridges sold annually, it has been estimated that 500,000,000 birds have been shot every year.

What is being done about this? Laws have been passed in many countries to protect the birds. The European Union has the EU Bird Directive on its books to prohibit spring migration hunting, mist nets, traps, lime sticks, and tape recorders when used with them.

In Malta especially, the 20,000 hunters in a population of a third of a million residents flaunt the law protecting birds. The hunters are such a powerful group that the police are afraid of them.

The Maltese hunters have a custom of ringing chaffinches. This involves sticking a ring the size of a common key-ring through the breast and blinding the bird by puncturing its eyes. Then this decoy is placed on a branch at a trap. A long string is attached to the ring. Since the bird is blind, it

Ringed chaffinch

calls often. When a flock comes by the string is jerked by the hunter lying in wait, making the decoy flap its wings to maintain its balance. The motion and the calls entice birds from the passing flock to be captured. In parts of Spain the baracca hunt is practiced. A group arrangement of evergreen trees is constructed. In this so-called baracca are placed a number of lime sticks. During the night a tape recorder, which plays bird songs all night long, is set in the baracca. Migrating flocks of songbirds are attracted, and up to a thousand birds are caught nightly. The fact that this is illegal hasn't stopped the baracca hunt.

How the fowler prepares the songbird for eating is not clear to me. I cannot imagine anyone eating feathers or entrails. In preparing a chicken or a quail, it is customary to pluck the feathers and singe the little hairs and gut the organs. If the gall bladder, especially, spills or touches anything it will ruin the bird for eating. Mourning dove eaters remove the breast for eating and discard the rest of the bird, so I am told. The same is said for squabs (young rock pigeons). I have seen a carnivore, such as a house cat, bite into the breast of a rock pigeon it has caught, and eat the breast, then abandon the rest of the corpse.

Now let us fantasize a moment. A TV evangelist claims proof from the *Bible* that our pets will meet us in heaven. In Acts 11:1- 10 in Paul's vision a sheet holding animals and reptiles and birds of the air was lowered to him, and Paul was told to kill and eat. Then the sheet was drawn up again into heaven. So birds will be up in heaven to greet us! And those poor trapped tortured birds we cited shall get their reward in heaven?!

So the songbirds migrating between northern or central Europe and Africa must run an obstacle course. If they escape the mist nets, tape recorders, lime sticks, baraccas, shot guns, decoys, raptors, poles, wires, and storms, they still must cross the wide Mediterranean Sea. Those that arrive in Africa are heroes.

When European immigrants came to the American

Midwest in the early and middle nineteenth century, it was a hard struggle for them to establish a farm and raise crops and eat. These homesteaders' survival required living off the land. Though not well-known, this involved shooting songbirds as well as wild game.

For example, Vern Sylvester, raised in Palermo, North Dakota (which is near Stanley, N. D.) recalls going out with his father to shoot blackbirds along the nearby railroad tracks. Then Vern would pluck feathers and remove the entrails and legs. The birds were cooked in a stew. Any shot, being heavy, would sink to the bottom of the kettle.

Vern's grandfather, who homesteaded in Willow City, North Dakota would shoot and eat snow buntings to help survive in the Dakota winter.

Whooping Cranes That Were Shot

Who would shoot a whooping crane? For those who did, different fates resulted, and all were amazing and incredible. Read on.

In the 19th and early 20th Centuries homesteaders and farmers came west to the prairies to settle a new land, to transform a wilderness into a plowed land for crops and fenced grassland for pastures. Native animals and birds were tolerated only if they did not interfere with the introduced animals and birds. Wild game and waterfowl were so abundant that today the early accounts of their incomprehensible numbers seem unreal.

So the settlers had no concept of conservation nor concern for preserving for future people. They also had to live off the land, and shoot game to survive. One such instance was mentioned in *North Dakota Outdoors* for June, 1947, page 7. Harry C. Jones in 1891 at age 6 recalls his father shot a whooping crane and brought it home for food. They lived three miles south of Garrison, N. D. But hunters often degenerated into killers who shot anything that moved, to see how many they could kill.

Most shocking are the incidents where a whooping crane was shot and hung up with head turned and wings spread out, to be photographed with a man holding a rifle and standing beside the body. One such picture, taken at Stump Lake in 1889, was on the cover of the *North Dakota Outdoors* magazine for August, 1964. Another such picture, of Elmer T. Judd and his two boys, was taken in Towner County, N. D. in 1894. He stood with his rifle beside the whooping crane hanging by its neck; each boy was holding a wing out for display. Nevertheless, Judd later became the N. D. State Game and Fish Commissioner!

The most amazing incredible story of a whooping crane that was shot, yet became a barnyard pet, was written up in North Dakota Outdoors for April, 1967, pages 3- 5 (vol. XXIX, no. 10). The following is adapted from that information.

In about 1882 S. W. Oliver was a young boy who lived on his father's homestead in central Dakota Territory. Wild fowl were still plentiful, so the youth shot at this family of three whooping cranes (mother, father, and young one) among the other southward migrating waterfowl. He killed the father(?) and wounded the young whooping crane in the wing. Oliver's dog ran it down, and the boy tied their legs together. They ate the adult bird, but placed the young one in the hen house. The uninjured parent hung around the area calling for three days before giving up and flying south to Arkansas.

Later, when released from the hen house, the crane walked about foraging, and calling to passing whooping cranes, but not joining them. I doubt its wing had healed enough yet to enable it to fly. He (they named it Bill) spent the winter in the hen house.

The farmers learned never to tease Bill, for once Oliver's older brother jerked back a piece of bread from Bill, who promptly raised his feathers and attacked him with a loud throaty noise, beating with its wings and striking with its bill. The family had to pull the crane off the brother.

When spring came, Bill could hear and see the northbound whooping cranes long before any humans could; the cranes have these senses far superior to our senses.

Bill would walk to ponds and sloughs, being gone all day, and sometimes stay out there overnight. When he came back to the house he would make a guttural noise.

One wild goose they captured in the fall became Bill's companion. Next spring when geese came north this goose left the farm to join the north bound migrants. But once when their hired hand brought home a sandhill crane he captured they put it in the hen house. Bill, who had learned by observing the humans how to pull the string that opened the hen house door, entered and attacked the sandhill crane. He was in the process of killing the supine crane by fighting with beak, wing and foot. Oliver rescued the beaten crane, which left the farmyard as quickly as possible.

As time went on, Bill was now gone from the farm for

days at a time, then eventually flying home, making whooping sounds.

Three years after Bill and his father were shot, Bill's life came to an end when a young Easterner shot him because that dude had never seen a big white crane, didn't know what it was, so therefore shot it. Even today there are farmers who shoot any creature with which they are not familiar.

Bent in his book, *Life Histories of North American Marsh Birds*, page 227, avers that many hunters have been severely wounded by the powerful strikes of the sharp bill of a whooping crane they had shot. Thus in 1879 a young Indian from Portage la Prairie, Manitoba never returned from his shooting trip. After a long anxious search his young wife found him. He had approached this large white whooping crane he had shot, who then had stabbed him in his eye so forcefully that its bill had entered deep into the Indian's brain. He fell forward onto the crane, dead. There she found the two dead bodies.

So it is extremely dangerous to approach a wounded adult whooping crane. Today public opinion and federal laws also make it very bad to harm one of these large white birds.

VI. BIRD CURIOSITIES

The Feelings Birds Have

Birds certainly do have feelings. We can't realize how true that is since we see only a fleeting glimpse of birds now and then. But where a gregarious cage bird such as a parakeet is under observation all day long day after day, then can some insight be gained. Listen to this true story:

This lone parakeet had been purchased from a pet store. Removed from the company of the pet shop's other parakeets and other cage song birds, it was taken home and placed in a small cage out of sight and hearing of other birds. After the novelty wore off the new owner gradually lost interest in the bird. Cleaning the cage became a nuisance, and little attention was given to the bird. This long period of solitary confinement produced a bedraggled appearance of the inmate. The bird in sheer boredom took to pulling out its feathers. The neglected small dirty cage matched the forlorn bird. The owner finally wanted to discard the cage and kill the bird that inconvenienced her, but lacked the courage to kill the bird, so she asked her neighbor to do so. Instead of killing it he gave it to a friend who raised parakeets.

This bird breeder gave it to my daughter, whom, he had observed, treated her healthy parakeets with tender care and plenty of affectionate attention. Their cage was always open; each bird's option was to fly about the room, land on their own high perch in the corner of the room, or perch on a family member's hand or shoulder.

The newcomer presented a stark contrast to my daughter's birds. That new bird had pulled out all her reachable feathers! She was thin and weak. Although she couldn't fly, she enjoyed this new life. As the months went by, down appeared in her bare spots, and new feathers started to grow out. In time, her ability to fly returned slowly, although she could not keep up with the others.

(How do we know she was a female? The little nubbin at

the base of the upper beak was brown, as is true in females. Males have a bright blue nubbin there.)

This newcomer's place was at the bottom of the pecking order, which status she accepted with joy since she was so pleased to be among others of her kind. Her happiness was evident when she sang. This exuberance earned her her name, Sparky. Sparky revealed a repertoire of over ten songs, which she sang frequently, which is unusual for female birds.

Goldie, also yellow in color, often fed Sparky. When the two were on the perch, Sparky would gradually edge toward Goldie until she would nibble on Goldie's bill to beg for food. Often Goldie would then feed her by regurgitating.

But after two years of living with friendly parakeets, Sparky had never fully regained her health. Then one fatal day she was found sprawled on the bottom of the cage, breathing heavily. When she took her last breath and lay motionless, Goldie preened Sparky's ruffled feathers so that they were smooth in death. Goldie wouldn't eat for two days. But let my daughter relate the end of the story:

"One of my birds just died this morning. (The one that had been mistreated before she came to us and had pulled out all her feathers.) She had not been up to par for some time now. It is still sad, especially seeing the other bird go through the discovery process of her friend's death.

"First she called to her, hopping nearer and nearer to where her motionless friend lay on the cage floor. Then she carefully approached her and touched her with her beak. After no response, she began to carefully clean her feathers, (tail feathers especially, as these were the dirtiest), something I never witnessed when they were both alive. After that, she began to gently pull on her feet, an attempt to get her up, I suppose. She continued to clean Sparky's feathers, and she lay next to her for a long time. She would return again and again, to check up on her.

"Who says animals can't feel? I will miss that bird because she really loved to be with us, and to sit on our shoulders for periods of time.

"She was an unusual female as she could also sing many different bird calls and songs, so I assume she had lived a long time in a pet store before ending up in that home that neglected her."

Song birds, considered delicate, tender, dainty by all of us, might be expected to be deep-feeling and emotional and demonstrative. But how about raptors, those ferocious killers of defenseless songbirds and other weaker creatures? Could these "tough guys" of the bird world ever have tender feelings?

If in doubt, consider the peregrine falcon, the indisputably fiercest, most deadly, most capable predator of all the birds of prey. Hear what my Norwegian son-in-law translated from his local newspaper: "The (male) peregrine falcon which nested nearby Trondheim broke its leg early this summer. It was healed in an animal hospital in Oslo. Yesterday (mid-August) it was released at Oysanden. From its wife, who still sat waiting for him at the nest place in the steep mountain wall, the people releasing the bird could hear a 'shrie' of happiness when she saw her husband. The two birds immediately joined together. Soon they are expected to emigrate south for the winter."

Female peregrine falcon. Photograph by Anders Lamberg

Diving Birds' Amazing Underwater Vision

When one of us humans tries to open our eyes to look when we are underwater, our eyes burn and everything looks rather fuzzy, not needle-sharp. So how does a diving bird manage to stay under comfortably long enough to find and catch its prey?

G. Katzir and H. C. Howland, Israeli and New York scientists, did some meticulous research to reveal the amazing secret of how these birds do it. (I found Katzir and Howland on the Internet by asking for cormorant+underwater+vision.) They studied cormorants, but the mechanism apparently is similar in other diving birds. Their report was copyrighted in 2003 by The Company of Biologists Limited.

But to appreciate how these birds' vision is superior to ours, we first review the nature of humans' vision. When at rest, the human eye is adapted to parallel rays of light – light that's coming from more than twenty feet away. For light rays coming from an object closer than twenty feet away, the eye lens must thicken to focus those rays onto the retina, not behind it, so that the image can be seen in sharp focus. Then the closer to the eye the object, the harder the eye must strain to focus on it. The most accommodation for looking at close objects that the lens in the human eye can do is to thicken only slightly. As a human being ages he must hold a printed page farther and farther from his eye to read, and when arm's length doesn't suffice, he is forced to get bifocals.

Even an elderly cormorant's senile eye is far stronger than that, for it can focus sharply on a fish only 3-1/2 inches in front of its eyes, at the tip of its bill! To accomplish that feat its lens can change shape from lenticular to spherical by bulging forward against the iris, even to protrude into the pupil! For this the lens must be very malleable and the ciliary muscles very strong.

In the human eye the cornea and both anterior surface and posterior surface of the lens refract light to bring light rays which are from an object closer than twenty feet to sharp focus on the retina. That is true with the cormorant's eye, too, but with it the material within the lens can also further refract the rays, too.

With the lens bulging through the iris the pupil can't constrict, but doesn't need to. In air the curved cornea helps focus; in water, which is denser than air, the water has the same density as the aqueous humor which is behind the cornea, so the cornea can't focus the light rays. So in all diving birds the lens must do all the job of focusing, but it can do it because it is now spherical.

The iris is able to be firm so the lens when pressed against it can become spherical, which the lens couldn't do well if the iris were limp and flaccid.

The loon, that Great Northern Diver, is the underwater swimmer without equal. It not only has the advantages of the cormorant's eyes, but another one, too. It has red eyes. The red pigment in the retina filters light and further sharpens underwater vision.

A different added bonus held by the hooded merganser when submerged is that its third eyelid, the nictating membrane, is transparent, so while protecting the eye underwater (humans lack this advantage) they can continue to see. Land birds have this membrane opaque, not transparent. Watch one of them blink, and note the white film come over the eye briefly.

The red-headed duck has been shown also to have the same lens-rounding capacity of the above.

The dipper, a songbird living along mountain streams in the Black Hills of South Dakota, is amazing to have adapted this same accommodation apparatus to use for preying on submerged little invertebrates found on the bottom of these streams.

Scientists have concluded that these birds associated with water have developed their skills by bobbing their head up and down to learn about how the air-water boundaries cause distortion by reflection and refraction.

Birds That Use Their Sense Of Smell

The only things humans can taste are salt, bitter, sour and sweet. All other foods that taste so good and can be identified by their taste are actually smelled, not tasted. To confirm this, pinch your nose together with thumb and index finger as you eat your favorite tasty food and see what it tastes like. The sense of smell does not get the credit that it deserves.

Birds, too, smell their food. Some birds' sense of smell is far more sensitive than that of other birds. But all birds have olfactory nerves in their nasal passages. Scientists have concluded that different substances are able to be smelled by different birds. Sparrows, chickens, pigeons, ducks have been shown to have prominent olfactory nerves which do transmit electrical impulses.

Some species have body odors strong enough to be detectable by humans. The crested auklet smells like tangerines. The kakapa, a New Zealand parrot, has a sweet musky scent. All smells are strongest during the breeding season, it appears, implying they are a form of sexual attraction.

The tubenoses – shearwaters and fulmars – can smell their food from great distances. Birders on pelagic birding tours far out on the ocean dump chum – popcorn soaked in fish oil – on the water when there are few or no birds in sight. Soon the tubenoses show up to eagerly devour the smelly chum. How did they know? They smelled the fish oil from far away. These sea birds can smell a pheromone that fish give off when stressed, which may be part of the attraction of the chum. These birds also are attracted by the smell of citrus fruit.

The kiwi of New Zealand finds earth worms by probing in the mud with its long bill, at the end of which its nostrils smell the worm.

Some stormy petrels that nest on land find their burrows by smell. They land downwind and follow the scent to their own specific burrow among others.

In the so-called ruff-sniff display auklets bury their bills in the neck feathers of their mates, in the region from which their tangerine odor emanates. Many other bird species also nibble their mate's neck feathers, using, it turns out, their sense of smell.

Leach's storm-petrel, showing the nostril that secretes salt and also smells food from miles away.
Photograph by Torgier Nygaard

One of Nature's official remover of dead animals is the turkey vulture. This large dark bird with its wide motionless wings set in a flattened V tetrahedral as it teeters in the wind is unmistakable – and unforgettable. As we watch this bird soaring overhead soon others appear from somewhere and together they wheel about, not aimlessly, but apparently seeking a shared goal. Eventually they descend gracefully to a certain spot. In the course of their wheeling about they are choosing air currents of rising hot air, or updrafts which are carrying odors from the ground below. If the odors are of no interest, they may choose to continue being borne higher in the sky or find another updraft to sniff. If they detect any odor associated with carrion they descend on that air current following that odor to its source.

Experts that scoffed at the idea of smelling an odor from carrion on the ground while the vulture was high in the air should have known that when a strong horizontal wind wasn't blowing, hot air rises. So updrafts from areas of sun-heated ground are carrying odors from the ground with them high into the sky. When a strong horizontal wind is blowing there are no updrafts, so the vultures aren't wheeling about then.

The vulture's large nostrils, larger than other birds', are a clue as to how they find their carrion food. Their acute sense of smell is incredible. A scientist once placed a dead chicken on the floor of a tropical rain forest, and watched. Soon after, a vulture maneuvered through many feet of dense foliage from the sky above, and landed at the dead chicken, its goal achieved.

There is a recess in a small cliff west of Mandan, North Dakota where a pair of turkey vultures have nested year after year. It can be visited with very little effort, but, like all nests, should not be approached lest the birds be disturbed to the point of abandoning the nest.

In recent years ornithologists have gotten interested in the importance of the roles of the olfactory nerves of birds. Research is revealing new knowledge on this which is amazing and incredible. Stay tuned.

teal

How Birds Use Their Saliva

We were in the beach park along the Gulf of Mexico at Rockport, Texas where picnickers like to feed the laughing gulls by tossing them crackers and pieces of bread. Holding a piece high in the air was fun to have a gull snatch it from your hand. I held up a piece of bread partly hidden between my thumb and forefinger. A gull attempting to get at it pulled hard on my thumb. The gull was unable to remove my thumb and couldn't even break my skin, but in its effort left my thumb dripping wet. The colorless liquid left on my thumb was its saliva.

Surprisingly, all birds have saliva, but some have their salivary glands much more highly developed than do other bird species.

The typical woodpecker pecks a hole in a tree trunk, the little wood chips flying as the tunnel goes down to the wood-boring worm. The path of the burrow goes to the sound of the gnawing grub which the woodpecker locates by ear each time it pauses to listen between pecks. When it gets to its goal it touches the worm with its tongue, which sticks to the worm so well that the woodpecker is able to pull the worm out to eat it.

One can watch a flicker sitting on the ground where some ants are crawling about, and see it touch each ant with its tongue as fast as it can. The ants always stick to the flicker's tongue and are eaten; the saliva of the flicker keeps the tongue moist. The ants cannot escape because of the adhesive quality of the saliva.

All birds that regurgitate food to feed their young must involve their saliva to facilitate and lubricate this type of feeding.

The chimney swift uses its sticky saliva not to pick up pieces of food to eat, but to use as a glue to hold its nest together. The twigs, which are used exclusively for the nest material, are held together and to the vertical surface by the adhesive quality of the chimney swift's copious saliva. The vertical wall used for the nest used to be the inside of a hollow tree, but since dead trees are cut down by humans, this bird has cleverly adjusted to using chimneys instead, hence its name. A disadvantage of this change to a chimney instead of a hollow tree is that in a heavy rain the raindrops falling down the chimney dissolve the glue, causing the twigs to come apart, allowing the eggs or young swifts to fall down the chimney. But the young birds, with their strong claws, and propped up by their tough spiny tail feathers, climb up the chimney wall again to a hurriedly rebuilt second nest built by the parent birds.

But the extreme example of use of saliva is the bird nest that is made of saliva exclusively! For some 1500 years the Chinese have made these nests into soup, and have considered them to be a great delicacy.

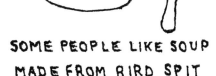

SOME PEOPLE LIKE SOUP MADE FROM BIRD SPIT

Today there is an active industry in Thailand for harvesting these swifts' bird nests. Nests are located high up on temple walls near the ceiling. To reach the nests, Thais must climb rickety ladders and stretch to reach the nests, which helps explain why they are so expensive. To meet the great demand, entrepreneurs in Thailand, Vietnam and Indonesia have been constructing small buildings to entice wild swiftlets to build their nests inside them, where the nests can be easily harvested. If a nest doesn't meet the expectations of the merchants, the nest and the eggs are destroyed. In this way a race of swiftlets is being bred which produces a colony of so-called house nests more suitable to the trade.

The nest is a small shallow cup placed as a narrow ledge, and consisting of a translucent off-white lump of jelled bird saliva.

The first nest, built in March, is white and free of contaminants, so is harvested before any eggs can be laid in it. This is the most expensive. The second nest, built by the persistent birds, appears in April. This one is also harvested.

The third nest is built but is left for the swiftlets in which to raise their brood. After the young have grown and have flown the nest, this used nest is harvested in August. This one is of poorest quality, and may appear a reddish brown color, thought to be tinged with blood from the birds' overworked salivary glands. But chemical analysis showed the color was due to rust, since third nests contain contaminants.

Analysis has also shown the saliva from the nest contains mostly protein. Human saliva contains ptyalin, a digestive enzyme that breaks down starch into sugar as the food, such as bread, is being chewed. No one has studied whether the swiftlet's saliva has similar properties. Believers have attributed amazing health benefits to the drinking of birds' nest soup.

The species of swift that constructs the highest quality nest is the so-called edible-nest swiftlet, *Collocalia fuciphaga*. The genus name is derived from the Greek *kolla*, meaning glue, plus the Greek *kalia*, meaning a bird's nest. The species name seems to be from the Latin word *fuco*, meaning to color or embellish, plus the Latin *phago*, a glutton; or maybe the Latin *fucus*, devour, plus the Greek *phagaina*, ravenous hunger, or the Greek *phagain*, to eat.

In any event, the ornithologist labeling the edible-nest swiftlet with that scientific name was swayed by the idea that certain specific people craved its nest as a gourmet delicacy.

Other small swifts also construct edible nests. Thus the white-bellied swiftlet, *Collicalia esculenta*, has its species name from the Latin *esculentus*, which translates as good to eat. The black-nest swiftlet's nest is that color because this bird mixes feathers from its black plumage into its nest, making it inferior quality for soup.

Any swiftlet's nest is labor-intensive, for all impurities must be tediously picked out by hand, and the nest must be soaked and washed several times.

So that is how birds use their saliva!

How Hawks Hunt

What techniques do hawks use in hunting? Let's find out.

An expert falconer tells me that the gyrfalcon stands for a few minutes on a high promontory, not upright but leaning horizontally like a tern. Its superb eyesight can see its prey for miles away. Then when it spots a victim it makes a bee-line for it by flying just skimming above the ground until it arrives. Then it rises and plunges down on the prey from behind before the hapless bird can react. Like other birds that live north of where trees grow, it never lands on trees.

My life list gyrfalcon was seen on Attu, the westernmost Aleutian Island, where it was on a direct straight course, on some urgent business.

The prairie falcon sits upright on dead trees and other conspicuous places where it commands a wide view. Bent in his *Life Histories of North American Birds of Prey, Part Two* (page 36) says, "usually they catch their food by dashing, lightning like swoops that are the very essence of grace and wildness," delivering so powerful a blow that the prey is killed instantly.

The peregrine falcon is the swiftest bird of prey, easily overtaking any other bird, and feeds almost exclusively on birds—unless they are too big and heavy for it to carry. It rises higher than its prey, then folds its wings and swoops down with high velocity on the doomed birds, similar to some other falcons. But the peregrine falcon also approaches the targeted bird from the side. Or it turns upside down to seize the bird with its talons from below. This foils the instinct many birds and other creatures have to escape by dropping down.

As part of their training the young just out of the nest may be fed by their catching the dead bird in midair after being dropped by the parent bird.

A male has been observed near the nest transferring a small bird from his talons to the talons of his mate that flew out from her nest to fly upside down under him to catch her food.

The peregrine plucks feathers from the bird before eating it. However, a shot bird that was dissected revealed entire wing bones and leg bones and entire newly hatched terns in its stomach, making one suspect that feather removal may not be thorough.

But it can't eat grouse because it can't zigzag and twist among the dense branches of thick woods. It seems the long pointed wings of this falcon are not adapted for the brush as well as are the short wide rounded wings of a grouse such as the ruffed grouse.

Audubon records seeing a peregrine enter a pigeon coop through a hole, seize one of the tame birds, and leave with the pigeon through another hole in the coop.

The merlin is also a bird eater, but it does not descend perpendicularly on its avian prey like the peregrine falcon. Instead it pursues its prey from behind. It easily overtakes its intended bird, but cannot turn abruptly to catch up with its outmaneuvering, unless the chased is sick or wounded.

One merlin caught tame pigeons in their home, as the peregrine falcon recorded above did, but entered each exposed nest box, not the enclosed shack-like pigeon coop.

Once a merlin was observed flying with a mouse as it bent its head down to tear off and swallow a piece of flesh from the prey it was holding in its talons.

Another birder watched a merlin fly into a flock of blackbirds, huddled together for mutual protection, and emerge with a blackbird in each talon.

Once a merlin attacked a blue jay, which escaped into a tree top. The merlin did not follow; a sharp-shinned hawk would have dashed in after the blue jay.

The sharp-shinned hawk, being smaller, adds insects, frogs and mice to its diet of birds. This hawk sits watching on an inconspicuous perch, or gliding low over meadow or under branches, then striking quickly before the dickeybird is aware. Or it spies a small bird, races towards it, and engages in a high speed chase to catch it on the wing.

One was noted to alight on the ground next to a rail fence, reach under the rail with its foot, and drag out a small pullet and fly off with it.

The sharp-shinned hawk is an expert in speeding through dense tangles of trees and underbrush.

Cooper's hawk, like a larger edition of the sharp-shinned hawk, is very similar in flight and hunting strategy to its fellow *Accipiter.*

The red-tailed hawk eats a few birds and insects, but its main food is mammals. It has three techniques for getting them. First, in soars high in the sky, keenly scanning the terrain far below, then plunging down. Second, slowly flapping along over fields. Third, perching on a tree or post, ready to pounce.

When a red-tail is on the ground with its talons on the little animal, it fans its tail out, creating a shadow. The prey seeks to hide in the dark shadow. This makes it easier for the hawk to control its prey.

An astonishingly clever hunting maneuver of a Swainson's hawk is described in the chapter, Birds Never To Be Forgotten. That particular hawk caught a blackbird, but their diet is mostly rodents.

The marsh hawk or harrier has a leisurely gliding flight, with upturned wings, ten to thirty feet high over meadow or marsh. Then it stops suddenly to drop onto a rodent or small bird. It is eaten on the spot, or carried over to its nest elsewhere on meadow or marsh. The harrier is unique among raptors in that it also eats carrion.

The turkey vulture, living exclusively on dead corpses, won't eat it until convinced after close examination that the body does not move.

The Harris hawk of southwest Texas hunts in a group. One hawk walks through the arid chaparral until it flushes its prey, such as a scaled quail. Then that hawk's partners, who have been watching from high perches nearby, chase and catch the quail. All the hawks share in eating the quarry.

So each species of flesh eater has a different technique for securing its food. Consequently, each species fills its own niche, so they dove-tail each other and minimize competition and conflict.

Using Birds To Test Your Hearing

A North Dakota birder is at a disadvantage insofar that the smaller prairie birds sing faintly and in high frequencies. Firstly, high pitched sounds do not travel far without scattering and bouncing off objects, thereby confusing a predator or a birder trying to locate the bird. And secondly, the high frequency sound is the first to go as the birder gets older. When he travels in Minnesota woods, he hears woodland birds with louder lower pitched sounds easier to hear.

In a hearing test the audiologist uses an audiometer in a sound-insulated room, playing notes into each ear, varying the pitch and loudness. The patient's responses are marked on a graph which records degrees of loudness measured in decibels, and frequency of sound waves measured in Hertz. (A Hertz is one sound wave, or one pulsation of air molecules.) As people age, sounds higher than 1000 Hertz, or 1 kiloHertz (kHz) become harder to hear. The higher the pitch the greater is the hearing loss. The audiometer tests as far as 8 kHz. Most bird songs are about 4 kHz.

The late Dr. Robert Gammel, the former general practitioner in Kenmare, North Dakota, told me once that he first realized his hearing was going when he watched a nearby cedar waxwing move its mandibles but couldn't hear its song. Dr. Gammel was an expert birder. He even hosted the newly formed American Birding Association at its first ever convention when it met in Kenmare. His astuteness was manifest by his observation, for the cedar waxwing sings at the highest register of any songbird, at 8 kHz.

So if your cedar waxwing acts like it is singing but you can't hear it, check with a bird whose song registers at 6 kHz, such as the black-and-white warbler. That warbler that climbs tree trunks isn't common, though, and is heard only briefly in June. Or try the western kingbird's song about 6 kHz, higher than the eastern kingbird's around 5 kHz. Then try the house wren, which ranges from 4 to 6 kHz. It's common around houses and sings loudly and frequently.

A male brambling listening to a rival he can not see. Photograph by Jon Arne Saeter

Everybody knows a robin, seen and heard everywhere in town. Its song is around 3 kHz, the same pitch as the warbling vireo which stays in trees.

At 2 kHz the unobtrusive white-breasted nuthatch and the repetitious red-eyed vireo make their presences known. The crow at 1500 Hertz and the mourning dove at 1000 Hertz sound off low enough that their calls don't qualify for the high pitches that fade in presbyacusis, the hearing loss of aging.

Not many birds sing in a monotone. The song of most birds includes notes that range up and down the musical scale. So the singer may be identified even though the higher notes are missed. Or hearing the lower notes only may not be enough to identify the bird.

The ruby-crowned kinglet is of interest because of its two part song in two different pitches. The beginning is high and weak at near 8 kHz; the main song has loud ascending triplets at 3 kHz. So you hear the triplets, but did you hear the preceding monotone prelude?

But at what distance from the bird should one be in order to conduct the avian hearing test? A stone's throw away. And if you are at that distance, how do know when or if the bird is singing? Have a fellow birder with good hearing accompany you, to signal when the bird sounds off. If no birder is available, a young child could do the signaling. Unfortunately, a teen-ager or a young adult may not be competent, since they likely are auditorily challenged (read hard of hearing) from listening to rock concerts and overuse of ear phones!

There is no sharp division between hearing and not hearing. A sound could be loud, soft, faint or barely audible. Hearing loss is relative. The listener must decide how much hearing loss is tolerable for his enjoyment of the quality of life.

One type of hearing aid amplifies sounds. The worth of making the highest pitched songs louder may depend on whether the listener's ability is completely lost or only decreased. Another type of hearing aid lowers the frequency of high-pitched songs down to a lower frequency and into a range where the birder has normal hearing.

A *Bible* verse that is relevant here is Ecclesiastes 12:4b: "When men rise up at the sound of birds, but all their songs grow faint." The elderly person wakes up early in the morning, when birds start singing; but with the decreased hearing of old age he can barely hear them.

Auditory Afterthoughts

In birds, where the trachea splits into two bronchi, one going to each lung, there is a specialized area of the trachea which is surrounded by muscle. This syrinx widens and narrows the passage-way for air. As the bird breathes, the constriction of the syrinx produces sound, the narrower the opening the higher the pitch of the sound. A two-toned voice is heard if the opening to one bronchial tube is narrowed more than that to the other tube. The volume of the sound depends on the length of the trachea, the longer length causing the louder sound.

In the average bird the trachea or windpipe is short, and only a few sound waves go bouncing up the walls of the windpipe before they scatter to the outside of the bird. With a longer windpipe more sound waves have time to be formed, and the sound waves are bounced more and thus reinforced louder before escaping into the atmosphere. In the whooping cranes and sandhill cranes another factor increases the volume, for the ridiculously long trachea in these birds expands into the breast, out to the keel of the sternum. This large area acts as a sounding board. Physics scientists call this phenomenon "resonance."

Dr. T. S. Roberts in his book *The Birds of Minnesota*. states that he has dissected all the stages of sandhill cranes from the fully formed embryo to the adult. The baby crane starts out with an ordinary trachea, but then it keeps elongating, until by adulthood it is a ridiculous length of two feet. In the whooping crane that windpipe becomes six feet

Consider the volume of sound from this classic army-type trumpet's few inches of tubing with that from the whooping crane's six feet of windpipe.

Fɪɢ. 148. Above, sternum and shoulder girdle of adult Sandhill Crane, showing the trachea, or windpipe, coiled in the front of the keel; below, same of adult Whooping Crane, showing the entire keel occupied by the trachea. Drawings by W. J. Breckenridge from specimens in the University of Minnesota Museum.

Picture from page 431 of *The Birds of Minnesota*, by T.S. Roberts

long! For comparison, consider the volume of noise from a trumpet, which has only a few inches of tubing to embellish its noise.

A. C. Bent in his book *Life Histories of North American Marsh Birds* says the whooping crane can be heard at a distance of three miles. In my Breeding Bird Surveys out of Hudson Bay, Saskatchewan I had to be careful not to count a sandhill crane more than once, when I could hear the same bird at three consecutive stops, each stop a half mile apart.

Each spring migration in North Dakota it is a thrill to hear the tremulous calls of the vibratoes from a flock of sandhill cranes. I look all over for them, then finally find them far up in the sky, a long string of cranes one behind the other, barely visible at that great height. Aviators have reported seeing flocks of sandhill cranes a mile or more above the earth!

Why would they fly that high? If they were going a short distance, it would be out of their way to attain that altitude. While on Attu, the westernmost of the Aleutian Islands, I saw in June a sandhill crane flying in a northwesterly direction, headed for Siberia, where it breeds. It must have wintered in Texas, the closest place in North America Sibley (*The Sibley Guide to Birds*) says they winter.

coot

Birds That Make Sounds With Wing Or Tail

A North Dakotan may have a special treat if they are on the open prairie on a summer evening. A common nighthawk may interrupt its erratic choppy flight in the sky to suddenly dive. As it swoops down a few feet overhead, a low pitched whoosh is heard as it swerves past the observer's head. This loud humming sound is made as air rushes between the primary feathers of the wings. The nighthawk is warning the intruder; but if the dive is some distance away, it would be a mating display.

That North Dakotan may have another special treat if they are up early on a sunny June morning, such as at Bismarck's Sibley Park, south of the trees. There a common snipe will fly up high over the marsh to dive, making a tremulous whistling sound. This "winnowing" is possible because the snipe has more tail feathers than any other shore bird, and puts them to good use by fanning them out to vibrate as the air rushes through them when the bird plunges downward.

Common snipe's flight display making a low, throbbing whistle.
Photograph by Tore Wuttudal

The woodcock's range, covering the Eastern United States, barely touches the northeast corner of North Dakota, the Sheyenne National Grasslands, the Missouri River bottomlands, and the Turtle Mountains. The closest place this writer has found to observe the woodcock's amazing song-flight is Minnesota's Maplewood State Park. It was on the grassy knoll at the south end of the campground, where the entry road joins the park road. The sun had gone down, and it was dark on this clear night of June 9. Suddenly the bird shot straight up perfectly vertically in a tightly spiraling flight, with a continuous high-pitched twittering sound made by its wings. High in the sky, almost out of hearing, it abruptly turned and spiraled down singing what author Bent calls its love song: chickaree, chickaree, chickaree. As the bird came to land at the same take-off spot, it uttered a nasal peent sound, similar to that of a nighthawk. This whole procedure was repeated at brief intervals.

So the woodcock display sounds come from the wings as the bird is flying up and the voice as the bird is flying down.

In North Dakota look for the ruffed grouse in the Turtle Mountains. In the spring its drumming is heard or felt as a low pitched muffled thumping. We saw this grouse perform once from a distance of less than twenty feet! While standing on a small log its wings whipped rapidly up and down in an arc from above its head to down below its body, so fast the wings were a blur. The sound came from the wing feathers vibrating in the air. We saw this performance from the side. In A. C. Bent's book he shows a series of photographs taken from the rear to prove his observation that the wings went forward and upward in a blur, requiring the tail to be propped against the log to maintain his posture to counteract the backward movement of his body created by the forward thrust of the wings. This is consistent with what we saw. The wings hit nothing but air in making the sustained so-called drumming.

A male mourning dove noisily flaps his wings together above his back in his nuptial flight. Any mourning dove taking off leisurely does so quietly, but if startled or frantic it claps its wings together above its back, the degree of loudness apparently depending on the degree of desperation. Domestic pigeons (rock pigeons) do the same.

Hummingbirds are named because their wings beat so rapidly that they create a humming sound.

Any large bird with each downstroke of its wings creates a soft swishing sound, audible only when the bird flies past just a few feet away from the birder. But an owl's flight is noiseless, which is necessary if it is to catch rodents. Their silent flight is possible because the forward edge of the first primary feather on each wing is serrated instead of smooth. Thus the vortex noise from airflow over a smooth surface is avoided.

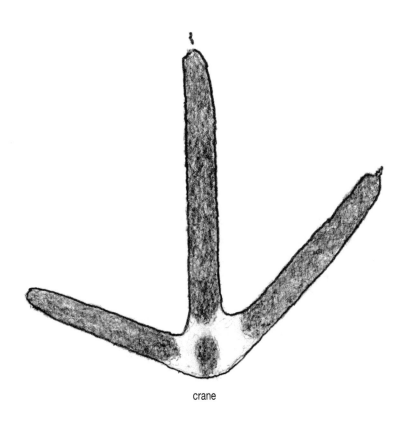

crane

Left-handed Birds

Left-handed people are in a small minority and they have been the object of disapproval, discrimination and denigration. To be right-handed is to be dextrous, which means expert and skillful, and to have dexterity. To be left-handed is to be sinistral, a word whose Latin origin is the same as that of our word sinister.

In grade school my penmanship teacher was a bombastic character who sprayed spittle when she taught the Palmer Method of Penmanship. She forbad me to write with my left hand, so I had to use my right hand for pen and ink exercises in her writing class. Then afterwards in other classes, using a pencil, I surreptitiously wrote with my left hand.

In the animal world, it's been noted that some dogs, raccoons, horses and others prefer to use one certain forelimb when reaching or pawing at something, so mammals may be right-handed or left-handed. The Internet, though, says all polar bears are left-handed.

Now go to birds. We should know most about those species that we can see most of, such as cage parrots. While eating they hold their food in one foot, so it's easy to note which foot. Here, it seems, at least two species are unanimous in all individuals being persistent with a preferred foot. The Amazon parrot always uses its right foot, the African Grey its left foot. But I suspect each species has its exceptions.

Right-handed parakeet.
Photograph by Jon Arne Saeter

Internet's www.bbc.co.uk/nature/animals/pets/testyourpet proposes that you test your bird to determine its handedness. That website has devised an experiment to accomplish this: Secure a cardboard tube wide enough to accommodate the bird's claw (that website pictures a parrot), but too small to allow the bird's head to enter. Place its favorite food inside the tube where it can reach into it with its claw but not its head. Watch to see which claw it uses. Repeat this experiment to determine if the bird's preference, right or left, is consistent or haphazard.

Doesn't a raptor hold its prey on a firm surface with one talon as it tears the flesh with its hooked beak? Or doesn't a raven, or a magpie, do the same with its foot? The Dakota Zoo in Bismarck, North Dakota conducted an experiment. Director Terry Lincoln's staff conducted observations daily from November 29, 2005 through December 22, 2005. They placed the meat at exactly the same spot in the separate enclosure of each of four red-tailed hawks, and watched closely.

Left-handed gyrfalcon, painted in 1911. Photo submitted by Jon Arne Saeter

Each hawk would swoop down from its perch, land, and hold the meat with one talon as it tore pieces off with its beak. Occasionally it would stand on its prey with both feet as it fed.

Bird # 1 used its left foot 15 times, its right foot 8 times, and both feet once.

Bird # 2 used its left foot 10 times, its right foot 9 times, and both feet 5 times.

Bird # 3 used its left foot all 24 times. It had no injury to either leg, nor any indication that it couldn't use its right foot.

Bird # 4 never used its left foot alone, but used both feet 19 times and its right foot 5 times.

I am impressed by how different individual red-tailed hawks are from one another in their behavior. Birds # 1 and # 2 had no marked preference for either foot. Bird # 3 was consistently left-handed, whereas Bird # 4 never used its left leg alone, yet had no discernible reason why it couldn't.

The zoo's bald eagle refused to eat as long as anybody was watching.

The author wishes to thank the zookeeper staff for their faithful observations.

Be on the alert to watch for handedness in other species of birds, such as a titmouse when it holds a seed against a tree limb with one foot as it chisels on it.

plover

Birds That Walk On Water

Every birder should go out to Long Lake near Moffit, or Lake Harriet just south of Arena, North Dakota to see western grebes walk on water. In their courtship dance suddenly a pair will leap out of the water to assume a vertical posture and patter with their feet along the surface, side by side, then drop down into the water again. If that seems impossible, when you're out on the swimming beach raise your arm high above your head, open your palm, and slap your hand down on the water as hard as you can. The stinging pain will convince you that water can be quite firm. Or stand on shore and throw a flat rock to see it skip along the surface instead of sinking like a round rock would.

In South Texas the jacana is called the Jesus bird by Mexicans because it walks on water. This bird has extremely long toes and nails, enabling it to spread its light weight over a much bigger area than any other bird can. But actually the jacana is mostly walking on lily pads.

Diving ducks, grebes and coots run on the water when taking off into flight, but to become airborne they must run, not walk. Flapping their wings gets them speeding fast enough to avoid sinking back into the water.

In the days of sailing ships the sailors were much closer to the water than they are on today's huge vessels. So they were closer to the little sparrow-sized birds which flitted over the surface of the ocean. They hovered near the ships and followed them closely, especially in winter before and during storms, which gave them their name, stormy petrels. The name petrel is derived from Peter, whom, the *Bible* says, walked on water when he saw Jesus doing the same. Wilson's storm-petrel patters its long legs along the surface of the water while fluttering its wings. So this walking on the water reminded the sailors of Peter.

If water were thick enough could a bird walk on it? As the concentration of saline gets high enough water gets like a thick soup or "molasses in January." The thickest body of water in the world, the Dead Sea in the Holy Land, 1300 feet below sea level, is so thick that swimmers in it find it impossible to sink. But the Dead Sea is lifeless, with no bird food there, so birds stay away.

In conclusion: Birds can walk on water if they don't allow each foot enough time to sink below the surface.

sandpiper

Why Does The Bird Do That?

There are two types of perching birds, the walkers, such as pigeons, crows and pipits, and the hoppers, such as sparrows. Why the difference, and what is the advantage in each method for covering the ground?

In walking, putting each foot forward alternately, the bird moves its head forwards and backwards as it walks. In doing so the bird determines the distance of each surrounding object. To illustrate, stand next to a line of telephone poles and look down the line. Then move a little to one side, and note that the closest pole seems to have moved the farthest from its first position, and each adjacent pole farther away moved less, until the furthest pole didn't seem to have moved at all. So each step the walking bird takes tells it how far away each object is, and so how much of a danger each object presents.

Smaller birds who spend much time in trees, hop. By hopping they go farther using less energy. The walkers, who are mostly larger, can take longer strides, and so use less energy moving one leg at a time. The pipit, a small bird that walks, doesn't have trees in which to perch in its native tundra or prairie, and by walking can forage more efficiently.

An owl moves its head up and down as well as to the right or left when concentrating on an object. One ear is higher in its head than the other ear, so by moving its head it can determine the exact location of the object, since the ear closer to it receives a louder sound. When the owl's head is turned so the sound is of the same intensity in each ear, the object is dead ahead.

Watching shore birds move along the edge of the water we note how each species has its own way of proceeding. Most distinctive and conspicuous is the sanderling with its racing along like a clockwork toy. This smooth incessant pace was adapted to its niche of chasing along the beach just out of reach of the surf, looking for tidbits dislodged for a brief second between each wave. The sanderling is expert in just avoiding being splashed by each wave, before its tiny prey settles back out of its reach. This technique was used during its winter sojourn on the shore of the Gulf of Mexico. So the sanderling is habituated to move the same way even around calm water.

Why does the phalarope on a shallow pond spin around in a tight circle like a top? Such eccentric behavior serves a very useful purpose. Its toes are lobed to produce a greater roiling effect than unwebbed toes would as it circles in water shallow enough for its toes to almost touch bottom. The currents thus produced carry insect larvae and tiny

WILSON'S PHALAROPE: "I swim in circles to stir up food to eat"

crustaceans towards the surface where the phalarope rapidly picks them off.

What was that terrible noise, a loud staccato, like a machine gun firing? It's amazing that the little downy woodpecker can make such a loud noise by drumming on a tin roof. It must know banging on a sheet of metal will yield no food, but pecking with a slow tempo on wood is what yields wood-gnawing grubs. This rapid tempo drumming is either a call for a mate or a warning to other woodpeckers to stay out of his territory. So once again birds show they are opportunistic. The sound of drumming on a dead hollow tree is nothing like the loud noise from the rain gutter or tin roof which civilization has provided.

Astute birders have noted that the alarm note is virtually identical among all perching birds – a sharp staccato split-second high pitched note. Surely this is of advantage to all other birds, for a danger to one is a menace to others, and a short note is faster to deliver where speed is of the essence.

Sexual Intercourse Is For The Birds

In the *Bible*, Genesis 1:22 says, "Be fruitful and multiply and fill the waters in the seas, and let birds multiply on the earth." So God likes sex, since it is libido that stimulates sexual intercourse that causes each new generation to be produced to carry out His directive to multiply.

But how can birds accomplish this, since there is no visible adaptation for this on the outside of the body of either sex? The goal of this chapter is to analyze how the business of making baby birds is done, with all its modifications and adaptations by various species of birds.

In copulation the male mounts the female from behind, they hold their tails back out of the way, each turns away their feathers from around their cloaca to ensure a secure fit. Each cloaca, swollen by a sex hormone surges to make a larger area for contact, and presses against the other in the cloacal kiss, so the sperm can't leak out as it rushes into the female's cloaca and oviduct. In some males during breeding season the cloaca may swell to the degree that it may protrude and become visible.

Does the male approach the female toward the right rear or to her left rear? The sex opening to the oviduct lies to the left in the female cloaca, as in the sketch. In a series of illustrations of coitus of various species, in six species the male was on the right side of the female's tail, but only one species showed the male on the left side. That is logical, for by aiming from the right a direct straight trajectory to the oviduct would be the most successful for fertilization.

Nature's purpose for coitus is to perpetuate the species,

View of female reproductive organs

so to ensure that this happens sexual intercourse is made pleasurable. The barnyard chicken utters a distinctive voice, a soft trill of delight, when the rooster presses down on her, and their swollen cloacae meet.

Suppose the copulation was a case of rape. Aggressive forced copulation is common only in ducks and geese, I read. Here the female has recourse. The section of the cloaca receiving sperm has a lining of digestive epithelium plus powerful cloacal musculature which ejects the contents, both feces and sperm.

Different species prefer different sites for their sexual intercourse. Most land birds copulate on the ground, or on a tree limb or other perch. White-throated swifts and black swifts copulate in flight. Cliff swallows do it while landed at the mud puddle that is providing mud for their nests. Barn swallows do it there while hovering. Phalaropes and ducks copulate in the water. Some female ducks get submerged and seem to almost drown in the process.

The buffalo weaver (*Bubolornis*) has a false penis, made of solid connective tissue, lying next to the cloaca on the side toward the head. It produces an orgasm, prolonging copulation.

Small birds, without penises, are successful in transposing sperm from male to female. Being small, it would be efficient to not be encumbered with any extra baggage to impede flight. Big birds do have penises. Being big, it may be more difficult and more awkward with too much juggling to hold the two cloacae together without leakage. So a structure that would narrow the stream of sperm and increase its speed would make the fertilization more successful. Such a structure also prevents water from washing away the sperm in birds (ducks) who copulate under water.

The penis is a tube. Its thick walls, called corpus callosum, are made of collagen fibers between which is an anastomosing network of spaces. These interconnecting spaces become filled with a liquid under pressure during erection of the penis in copulation. In waterfowl this liquid is lymph;

in ostriches and related birds it is still unknown whether it is lymph or blood.

Only 3% of bird species have a phallus or penis.

The male cassowary has a phallus. It looks like a penis but is a roll of tissue with an opening at its tip, but is separate from the testis and spermatic and ejaculatory ducts. It retracts into the cloaca by turning inside out, then everts when the birds are mating, to act as an erect phallus as the sperm bypasses it. The female has an identical phallus that is much smaller.

The Australian lake duck, *Oxyura vittata*, has a penis eighteen inches long, corkscrew shaped, with a brush on its tip.

Much of this information was provided by the Internet, under a search for "structure of bird's penis."

So humans say sexual intercourse is for the birds when they have coitus for pleasureful self-gratification but don't want pregnancy because of its obligations and the responsibilities of parenthood.

Working Birds

Birds are pretty to look at and we are pleased to listen to their songs, but there have been times when they have been put to good use working for men, then having done their job they live to enjoy another day.

The classic example of this was the miner. When he descended underground to work he carried a caged canary along, and kept a close eye on it. When the canary took sick and started to die, all the miners beat a hasty retreat up above ground. The canary was sensitive to poisonous gases and a lack of oxygen. Canaries have saved many a miner's life.

In the culture of Southeastern Asian fishermen they use captive cormorants to fish for them. The tethered birds are placed in the water with a ring around their neck tight enough to restrict them from swallowing the fish. Then they are reeled in again back into the boat to regurgitate the fish onto the bottom of the boat, from where the fish is harvested by the fisherman.

Domestic geese and chickens provide us with meat and eggs, of course, but we shall mention their value as guards warning us of imposters and thieves invading the farmyard. In the early days of television's Grand Ole Opry the artists appearing on the show were genuine Hill Billies (not gussied up actors singing their own composed copyrighted love songs), playing tunes handed down by mountaineers for generations, mostly by authors unknown. The words of this following song tells us of the value of farmyard fowl as very raucous alarm-sounders: "Behind the hen-house late one night/ I fumbled around 'cuz I had no light./ By some mistake got hold of a goose;/ The white folks say, 'You better turn him a-loose!'" So being raucous pays. Rural people's best guards were their geese because of their ear-splitting alarms, more valuable than watchdogs.

Today the most important damage to commerce by birds is done by airplanes hitting birds – "bird strikes" – during takeoff and landing. Yet it is other birds that are the most effective solutions to this serious problem.

The International Bird Strike Committee says over 400 aircraft have been destroyed and nearly 400 people were killed in these collisions. The greatest damage is from birds being sucked into the engines.

The Federal Aviation Administration's National Wildlife Strike Database has compiled a list of those bird species involved most frequently in bird strikes. Gulls by far are the biggest hazard, 2-1/2 times more so than the second place blackbirds/starlings. (When mangled inside the engine it takes an ornithologist to differentiate them.) A lot of geese, ducks, hawks, rock pigeons and sparrows were victims, too.

The amount of damage done to plane and bird depends by far on how fast the plane was going, although a still important factor is the larger the bird the worse the wreck. (Refer to Internet; ask Google to search airport+falcons+chase+starlings.)

So who are the birds that will help this problem? Falcons. Falconry, the use of trained falcons, has this raptor come out to the airport on the forearm of its trainer, the falconer. With gulls or other offending birds in view, the falconer removes the blind from the falcon's head. If the raptor is hungry it will chase the birds, who immediately cry out in alarm and flee in panic, thus clearing the field for airplanes to take off or land. So this working bird merits the prime care that it receives and the owner the compensation that he is paid. Sometimes a hawk is used for this patrol duty.

Homing pigeons (a gifted strain of rock pigeons) have worked for man by carrying messages. They are most effective at this when the bird has a nest or eggs or young at home, so its motivation to return home is greatest. Its return is best assured if in its training it first was removed only a few yards, then removed to progressively longer distances from home for each flight home. The bird's use to man occurs when at the point of its release in the field its leg is fitted with a message, whether valuable market information or wartime message from military site to headquarters. As soon as the

Homing pigeon. Photograph by Jon Arne Saeter

bird enters its home loft the message is removed from its leg.

The homing pigeon has a tiny kernel of the iron compound, magnetite, in its brain and on its bill, which responds to the earth's magnetic field, which field consists of parallel lines of magnetic force running between the north magnetic pole and the south magnetic pole in the earth. We assume the pigeon is aware whether it crosses a magnetic line of force or stays between two adjacent ones. This awareness plus memorizing roads, tree, buildings and all other landscape features combine to get it to its destination. Surely, all birds likewise find their way by these methods, but man hasn't learned how to take advantage of any other birds in this manner.

The jungle fowl has been bred into today's living "egg factory" to lay an egg a day, providing an important part of our food, yet without harm to the hen.

A twist to this concept of the bird working for man is the bee bird of Africa. It induces man to work for it, for mutual benefit to both man and bird. This bird finds a small party of men, attracts their attention, and entices them to a hive. There they relish that discovery and raid the hive for its honey. The bird benefits by eating the injured bees which were damaged or killed and smeared by honey during the raid.

roadrunner

Birds Predict Natural Disasters

For thousands of years humans the world over have noticed unusual behavior of birds and animals before an earthquake, tsunami, hurricane, thunderstorm or volcanic eruption.

Such episodes have been noted so many times, in so many cultures, for so many years that they cannot be dismissed as old wives' tales, but must have some basis in truth. Here are some examples of such incidents.

The flamingoes on the southern coast of India flew inland shortly before the coastland was flooded by a tsunami.

Southward migrating songbirds "backed up" in the Carolinas and Georgia until after hurricane season.

Fresh water sharks hurried out to sea from Florida rivers with other sharks from shallow water near shore hours before the hurricane hit land.

Fishermen find that fish bite much better before a storm.

An hour before a tsunami hit Thailand, elephants used for giving rides to tourists became so agitated and restless they broke their chains and fled inland. Dogs also howled and ran to higher ground.

Ocean birds, pigeons, chickens show unusual behavior before an earthquake.

Caged birds may exhibit strange behavior when thunderstorms come.

A rain crow is another name for a yellow-billed or a black-billed cuckoo because it sings so much before a rain.

Sparrows flocked and fled before a volcanic eruption.

Scientists worldwide have investigated these phenomena, and have theorized and have found convincing explanations for why they all behave the way they do.

Birds have hollow bones, of much lighter weight than other creatures have, which enables their ability to fly so well. Many little pockets of air are trapped inside the bone surface. The pressure of the air therein is the same as outside the bone. But before and during a storm the barometric pressure falls as the air cools and expands. The air pressure inside the bird's bones tries to expand to equalize the atmospheric pressure but can't, causing pressure against the bone in which it is trapped, causing pain, causing change in their behavior. The same situation causes joints to ache in humans, since the synovial fluid inside the joints' membranes cannot equalize the pressure outside as the barometer falls. So our elders can tell when it's going to rain, too, and complain more of arthritic aches then.

The barometric pressure also falls with a hurricane, with the same results in birds.

Before an earthquake or tsunami (a tidal wave started by an earthquake deep below the surface of the ocean), or a volcanic eruption, the earth quivers and shakes. Humans can't detect these slight vibrations, but birds and animals do. They can feel that through their feet. The nerves in the avian tibia and fibula can detect these tremors. These are part of the so-called vibratory sensory system. Herbst corpuscle is a sensory end-organ in the bill and tongue of a duck. Recently it has been found also between the tibia and tarsus of many bird legs. This corpuscle is sensitive to vibrations. Certain nerves in the lumbosacral spinal cord and in the sciatic nerve also are sensitive to vibration, so much so that they all pick up tremors of the earth when the bird is not flying.

A line of dots running along the side can be seen on many fish; this is a row of nerve receptors that detect vibration or pressure changes in the water. This has been credited to explain why fish bite before a storm, since they crave food before they migrate, and then move to safer waters.

Infrasound is sound waves that are coming much slower than the human ear can detect. They have a frequency lower than 100 Hertz. Some birds, many animals, and all elephants can detect ultra-low frequencies of vibration from tsunami-causing earthquakes under the ocean. The same applies to earthquakes occurring on earth whose surface is above water.

So those birds and others become agitated when they can sense either the shaking of the earth or the ultra-slow pulsation of air molecules we call ultrasound.

The sense of smell is another factor. In thunderstorms the lightning heats up the air to thousands of degrees of temperature to cause formation of ozone, whose chemical formula is O_3. The penetrating odor of ozone can become so strong that humans can also smell it. So strange behavior may also be caused by storms, when ozone is smelled.

Electromagnetic changes also precede an earthquake, which is why creatures become frightened then, or when a thunderstorm approaches.

Domestic animals and birds are inconsistent in their ability to detect impending disasters. This may be due to their loss of sensitivity due to domestication, or the complication of other similar confusing sensory stimuli that civilization creates.

A bird can predict a natural disaster by detecting one or more of these eight physical entities: sound, touch, temperature, vibrations, electrostatic activity, chemical compounds, magnetic field, barometric pressure.

A fair amount of this information is from copyrighted material which is permitted to be used here because it qualifies for "fair use" for educational purposes to advance understanding of environmental issues.

VII. HUMOR IN BIRDING

There Is Humor In Birding

Birding is fun, and interesting, and fascinating, and educational. But funny ha-ha? Yes, it can be mirthful, amusing and a cause for a good chuckle.

POORWILL AND THE GIRLS: David got a summer job out at the Theodore Roosevelt National Park working as one of the college students which the Medora Foundation hires. In consistency with his preference for working in the Medora zoo, he liked to drive out on the paved loop road in the South Unit of the Park at night to see the poorwill. There on the pavement in the darkness his car's headlights would be reflected from the eyes of the bird, to reveal its presence before it flew up.

Being at the extreme edge of this western nightjar's range, it is a prize to find this bird in North Dakota. So, wanting to share his rare find with somebody, he invited one of the pretty girls, a coworker at Medora, to come along in his convertible to see the poorwill. Now I reckon she was very intrigued, but wasn't quite sure what his intentions were, so she got permission from him to take along another girl for company. The word got around. Then when he drove to her dormitory to pick her up, a swarm of girls piled into his car. So an overflowing car full of girls got to see a poorwill, even if nothing else happened!

ELUSIVE MOUNTAIN CHICKADEE: We were on a birding expedition in the Chiricahua Mountains in Arizona. The group of birders left the bus in the parking lot and took off, intent on finding a mountain chickadee. But wifey, being less foolhardy, stayed behind with an elderly heart patient, and birded in the parking lot. After an interminable time of tramping up and down rough country the exhausted bunch returned frustrated, not having found a trace of the bird. There in the parking lot we learned that mountain chickadees had flitted around by the bus in our absence, but were finally found there in the parking lot by the group for their life lists.

WHY, THOSE ARE DUCKS!: A group consisting of game warden, ornithologist, scientist, expert birder, forest and park ranger, were on a field trip researching the avifauna. They were a rough looking bunch, wearing beat up clothing suited for grubbing in the brush. So when their car was parked on this back road and they were all looking at this pond, they aroused the suspicions of the local sheriff as he was cruising his area.

The sheriff got out of his squad car and approached them cautiously and demanded they explain what they were doing. They said they were trying to determine the identity of those birds down on the pond. The sheriff looked down there, looked back at them, and in a disgusted tone of voice said, "Why, those are ducks!"

THE CONFUSED PTARMIGAN: Ptarmigan live high in the mountains or far out on the Arctic tundra, but in either case they are very inaccessible to birders. Of the three North American species the closest one lives in Colorado. The most convenient site to visit to add it to a life list is south of Georgetown, Colorado, up high (11,669 feet elevation) in Guanella Pass. In the winter this species, the white-tailed ptarmigan, is pure white. But in the summer when the road through the pass is open the birds are molting, so various degrees in mottled brown plumage may be encountered.

The bird we found was some yards off the road where the ground was almost bare of snow. As it saw us it hurried over to a snow bank and crouched down on the edge of the snow. Its front half was mottled brown while its rear half was still snow white. But it blundered. It placed its body so that the dark front was on the snow, while its white rear was on the dark brown soil, and the demarcation between its two colors continued the line of distinction between the snow and the soil. Instead of blending into the scenery it now stood out conspicuously!

THE LADY AND THE HUMMINGBIRDS: What is there about a hummingbird that is so enchanting? It is dainty, tiny, elusive, and shows flashes of brilliant colors as it hovers or flies up, down, forward or backward.

It was up the Madera Canyon in Arizona, when a restaurant still nestled among some rental cabins. We had chosen a table by a window. Just a foot or two outside the window a hummingbird feeder was poised, hovering in the air. Several species of hummingbirds were coming and going actively. A little old lady in tennis shoes saw them, and got so excited she climbed up on our table and pressed her face against the glass as she talked baby talk to them in a loud voice.

FOGGY BREATH: In the winter it is often cold enough to see your breath, but have you ever seen a bird's breath? I have. In the summer time, in June, yet. In North Dakota. It was in a chilly early morning after a rain. As I was looking at the eastern horizon where the sun was about to come up, this western meadowlark in front of me sang. As it sang, I laughed to see that its breath was visible as a tiny cloud issuing from its bill! My breath formed a cloud many, many times larger.

LONG-TOED STINT: It was near the Aleut village of Gambel on St. Lawrence Island off the coast of western Alaska. A discussion arose among a group of expert birders as to the identity of a certain shorebird. The matter was resolved when

Topographic map of Gambel, domain of the long-toed stint. June 1979. From the Photo Mart, Lansing, Michigan.

they noted where it walked in the mud, then went over there to measure its footprints, and agreed that yes, it was indeed a long-toed stint!

THE DECOYS: We were overnighting in a private campground. There was a small pond on the property, so as usual my binoculars were put to good use identifying the three ducks floating there. But these didn't look right. Some of their colors were wrong. As they rode the waves they tipped back and forth oddly instead of riding the waves smoothly. And after a while they still stayed in the same positions instead of swimming about. It finally dawned on me. These were decoys someone had anchored in place!

COMBATIVE CARDINAL: It was just starting to get light in this Texas campground. Though it was far too early to get up, the persistent dull thump...thump prodded us to investigate. This male cardinal had found his reflection in the rear view mirror of our camper. Since we had parked in his personal territory it was unacceptable to this cardinal for this phantom imposter to be here. Each thump turned out to be

CARDINAL: "I CAN KEEP FIGHTING THIS INTRUDER AS LONG AS HE CAN"

his futile crash against our mirror as he attacked his perceived rival. Only after we placed a paper bag over our mirror were we able to go back to sleep in peace and quiet. But later when we got up and dressed, we found that same cardinal fighting his reflection in the rear view mirror of the pickup truck parked ahead of us!

Love Makes Males Do Strange Things

So you think men do strange things when they're in love? Well, "You ain't seen the half of it yet!" Consider what male birds do in the breeding season.

The Eastern Pacific's blue-footed booby stomps his bright blue feet in front of the female to get her attention.

The Australian bower bird builds a bower of twigs, and adorns its entryway with shells and pebbles and brightly colored objects.

The sandhill crane waves its wings and jumps up and down to impress its female of choice.

The great horned owl may catch a rabbit and lay it before a female.

The male hooded merganser has a crest which he raises when aroused, which changes from a white slit into a brilliant wide white triangle on the side of his head.

The ruffed grouse bends upward, bracing his tail against the drumming log for balance, then by rapidly beating his wings in the air makes a low pitched thumping or booming sound; when the female appears he leans forward, fans his tail upwards and erects his ruff.

The male red-winged blackbird's epaulets are hard to see when he is immature, but when breeding season comes the lesser coverts on the wings turn bright red and the median coverts yellow. Then when the male displays before a female he stretches his wings to widen the epaulets and raises the red feathers to flash a flaming red wide shoulder patch.

Our sharp-tailed grouse acts as usual most of the time, but on the lek, the communal displaying grounds, he changes. He dances, opens his wings, raises his tail, and tips his body forward with head lowered. Then he inflates his esophageal air sacs to expose a large patch of purple skin on each side of the head.

The wild turkey, 46 inches in length, is a huge bird, so when he performs its nuptial display it is impressive indeed. He struts around before the female as he erects his tail feathers and spreads them out into a semicircle, showing off beautiful bands of brown and black. I am told the wild turkey has a tan outer edge to the ends of the tail feathers, while the domestic turkey's tail ends in a white band.

The pigeon, or rock dove, or rock pigeon struts about his mate as he coos and bows up and down, inflating his breast to show off the green and blue and purple iridescence of the breast feathers.

In the male western kingbird's courtship display he flies up into the air some fifty feet then tumbles down to earth closely to land near the female, who is very impressed by this wild performance.

The American redstart impresses his female by flashing his tail and wings in front of her. Spreading the tail widens out the two bright orange-red quadrants of color on the proximal part of the black tail; and opening each wing enlarges the bright orange-red band running along the middle length of the black wing.

The nuptial flight of Sprague's pipit takes it up into the sky as high as the height of North Dakota's 16 story state capitol building. The entire display may last as long as forty minutes. If your hearing is sharp, you can hear his song while high in the air—repeated series of sweet faint notes descending in pitch. When finished it folds its wings and plummets to earth, braking before hitting the earth to land close to its adoring female.

With common grackles, two males may face each other in a bill-up display and stretch themselves higher and higher, until finally one of them blinks.

Two male brown thrashers in adjoining territories sing as many songs as they can conjure up. The female then mates with the suitor who has the larger repertoire.

A male robin may chase its would-be mate interminably, as the haggard female continues trying to escape.

A rooster repeatedly pecks a hen on the back of her head, until the subdued hen submits to his mounting her.

In breeding season the white pelican lifts up its head to show his pouch and inflates it with air. He also has a fibrous epidermal plate on top of the bill near the tip, which knob enlarges during breeding season.

Common goldeneye. Photograph by Torgeir Nygaard

In their courtship dance a pair of western grebes suddenly rise up out of the water, their bodies tilted upward, and with their feet on the surface, patter across the lake side by side.

A male tern holds a minnow in his bill and offers it to a receptive female tern.

The "eight-hooter," the barred owl, sounds its eight hoots in the woods at night. Then from a distance its mate repeats the call in a slightly different pitch.

The non-breeding plumage of the male wood duck consists of a somber grayish head, neck and body with off-white bridle. But in spring time his bridle turns whiter and he sports a green crown and drooping crest, black cheek and neck, red chest, yellow flank, and white belly and side—truly a gaudy bird.

As for humans, I trust young women already are familiar with what males do to impress "the weaker sex." Look back at the above examples, gals; are you reminded of any man?

What Did That Bird Say?

People are prone to translate birds' songs into English words. The listener may have a wild imagination, but the interpretation does help a lot in remembering and recognizing who is singing.

Instead of speaking in a monotone, most people's speech is in a voice going up and down in pitch from syllable to syllable. And birds who sing that same way produce songs which are most prone to be verbalized. And a song with several notes in it is easier to verbalize than a brief song.

The interpretations of some songs require a greater stretch of the imagination than others.

To my mind the bird that vocalizes most clearly and obviously is Gambel's quail when it says, "Chicago." In another case, a person's background influences him, too. It must be so for our neighbors to the north when they hear "Pure sweet Canada, Canada, Canada!" which the white-throated sparrow sings in its homeland, Canada.

Although birds spend a lot more of their time looking for food than do humans, people have thought of eating and drinking when they heard these five birds: The white-winged dove asks, "Who cooks for you?" But the wild turkey with its "gobble gobble" is more interested in just gulping food down. After the meal comes the beverage amenities. So the Carolina wren calls for the "teakettle, teakettle." Then the eastern race of the rufous-sided towhee admonishes, "Drink your tea." The western birds, being less fastidious, garble this message. However, the boorish olive-sided flycatcher upsets the tea party by shouting, "Quick, three beers!"

Being now in an after-meal sociable mood, the chestnut-sided warbler chortles, "Pleased, pleased, pleased to meetcha," as the robin chimes in with "cheerily cheer up!"

Meeting others at our fanciful party, the tufted titmouse shouts, "Peter! Peter!" while the dickcissel introduces himself as "Dick, Dick, dickcissel," and the bobwhite cries its name. The bobolink embellishes its name as it sings, "Bobolink,

bobolink, spink spank spink!"

Sensing things are getting out of hand, the ovenbird tries to restore order as it calls for the "teacher, teacher." But the common yellowthroat considers that to do so is being a spoilsport, so it objects by crying "witchity witch."

The party over, our jungle fowl/domestic rooster crows, "Cock-a-doodle-do," so our rock dove/domestic pigeon coos, "Look-at-the-coon-wuk-wuk."

Finally, to restore a sense of propriety and respect, the greater pewee reverently carols, "Ho-say, Maria."

swallow

Pete, The Pet Magpie

Sheila Robinson was raised on a stock farm near Coleharbor in North Dakota. One day as she and her two sisters were riding their horses on her father's spread, they came upon the huge ball of twigs in a tree that is the typical magpie's nest. Inside the nest were four young, only at the pin feather stage with bare skin still exposed. The girls selected one and rode back to the ranch house with it. An empty four foot by three foot cage became its home. Feeding it hamburger, milk and eggs wasn't adequate, so it became sickly until a week of spoon feeding of vitamin A enabled it to walk and thrive. They named it Pete.

When it had developed a glossy sheen to its plumage Pete liked to ride on a child's shoulder.

Grandma lived in her own little house adjacent to the ranch house. She would open her window whenever she saw Pete, who was always happy to come inside to visit. He spent his time there after Sheila held him by his feet once to take him into the living room to show the visiting ladies, the curious members of the Homemakers Club, for by now Pete was famous.

Out free in the yard it would fly in the window to eat at the table at meal time. More often Pete ate with the dogs from their dish outside. The dogs didn't seem to mind, but often had altercations with each other about the food. In one of these scraps Pete got in the way and lost one eye.

The pet magpie was known to pull off the lid of the peanut jar at Grandma's house. Filling its beak with the unsalted peanuts, Pete would fly outside to cache them, each covered carefully under a different leaf in the yard. Then he would go back to the window for another beak full.

The ranch had three dogs. The youngest one, a black Labrador, was the only one that would tolerate Pete to ride on its back. So Pete would perch on the back of the neck next to the dog's collar, but not touching it, and wobble while gripping the loose skin as they traveled about the ranch.

Pete developed a vocabulary, mimicking the words he heard, such as "OK" and "Whatcha doing?" He specialized in repeating laughter, mimicking each person's voice very accurately. His favorite was one man's especially loud guffaw.

Once a stray dog came to the ranch. Since three dogs were plenty, the stray was not welcome, so was not fed. While sitting forlornly off to the side, Pete up in a nearby tree called out, "Come here!" Eagerly the stray dog went to the tree from where it heard the invitation. Again Pete called, "Come here!" But the stray was confused and puzzled when it could not find the person supposedly calling him.

The pet magpie survived the winter, living in the cow barn perched near the top.

Next year Pete collected sticks and carried them up to the eave of the ranch house. There he left them in disarray, so they were blown off the ledge by the wind. Since the male magpie collects sticks and the female magpie arranges them into a sturdy nest, it seems the girls named Pete correctly by giving him a male's name. That year a female magpie showed up at the ranch, but nothing came of it. She did not like humans.

When human visitors drove their car into the yard to visit, they were startled by Pete's landing on the hood of the car to look through the windshield for a close inspection of the strangers.

Ranchers do not like magpies. One reason, Sheila informs me, is that there is a so-called heel fly that lays its egg on the skin above the hoof of a cow. (If you see a cow running for no apparent reason, it may be she is being tormented by a heel fly.) There on the heel the egg hatches into a worm that burrows under the skin, to emerge later on the back of the cow. There the grub opens a hole in the hide and leaves its host. A magpie may find it before it escapes, and eats it. But the magpie then continues to peck at the worm hole to enlarge it and eat the flesh of the cow. Pete, the pet magpie, must not have been guilty of this, for it had bonded with humans and hung around the ranch house and yard instead.

A pair of glidng Cooper's hawks align themselves above the soaring turkey vulture for God's way of saying, "Have a nice day, you watchers of birds!". Submitted Photograph.

W. A. Riley on page 68 of his *Introduction to the Study of Animal Parasites and Parasitism* names this hairy fly the warble fly, and the swelling it causes on the cow's back is called a warble.

The antics of Pete, especially his calling the stray dog, merits his inclusion in the humor section of this book.

This European alpine chough seems to be showing us who her favorite is! Photograph source Internet

Spouse Of A Birder (S.O.B.)

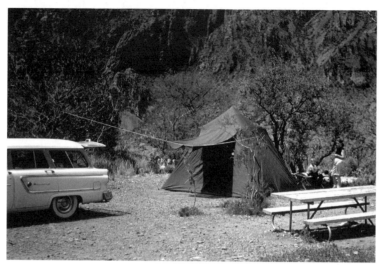

The author's wife, Adele G. Johnson, together with son Bruce camping in Big Bend National Park, Texas, in 1957. Photograph by Kenneth J. Johnson

Although I, Adele G. Johnson, had been an outdoor girl all my life, little did I know when I married handsome Dr. Kenneth J. Johnson in 1944 what I was getting into. After his Army combat duty we were able to spend the last nine months of service in Hawaii together, where I got a job in a children's hospital as a nurse. Ken was at Schofield Barracks. It was there I discovered he was an avid bird watcher all his life. So after that, all travels and destinations involved national parks, national monuments, state parks, country-sides, neighborhoods, back yards and ends of the road, looking for birds and certain species to add to his life list.

So whenever he had an outing or trip planned I was ready. By this time it was four kids and a tent. My interest in birding was growing. Going to bird club every month we found some good friends, many of the men professional wildlife workers. Our Audubon Bird Club sponsored the Audubon Screen Tours – in the days before television. So we had the opportunity to have some of the speakers for coffee and dessert after the evening show on birds and travel. One of the most notable was Roger Tory Peterson. This was in the 1950s and '60s. When TV came into being the interest in screen tours diminished.

It was in 1956 when the screen tours started that Ken had to "come out of the closet" to let his medical colleagues know he was a birder so he could sell tickets to the tours. At that time people as a whole considered bird watching a rather off-beat weird hobby, done by little old ladies in tennis shoes.

Then our bird and camping buddy and wife started us in the breeding bird censuses in 1968 and we ran five different routes in North Dakota for 26 years. Later, in 1976, we added two in Saskatchewan and two in Manitoba way up north, which we did for eleven years. Using up vacation time and cold wet snowy weather soon cooled the adventure of the north Canadian routes.

By this time Ken was getting ready to retire and was nearing his 700 mark for his ABA list (American Bird Association life list),.

So we were doing ABA meetings and tours, plus all of Canada's provinces and all the states; then wintering in Arizona and Texas helped add to this list.

Today Elderhostels and birding festivals are conducting many wonderful birding trips all over America and the world. As the years go by more people are taking up bird watching after retirement. As a hobby it is exceeding golfing in popularity.

It was at an Elderhostel in Edinburg, Texas that I found out what an S.O.B. was, and figured out that was what I am – Spouse of a Birder! After all these years helping my spouse achieve some of his goals I joined him in his hobby after he promised to keep my life list up to date.

– Adele G. Johnson, spouse of a birder.

VIII. FAR AWAY ADVENTURES

Discovering New Birds With Lewis And Clark

Lewis and Clark's expedition was a phenomenal success. The great distances they could travel in a day were amazing, in spite of bad weather, wild animals, intolerable mosquitoes and prickly pear spines. The many Indian tribes they encountered required superb tact and negotiating skills, and they were up to the challenge.

President Thomas Jefferson chose Meriwether Lewis to be in command. Lewis chose William Clark as second in command. The president admonished Lewis not to waste time on familiar species of birds, but to obtain a comprehensive knowledge of all birds, plants and mammals in the entire area from St. Louis in what is now Missouri to the Pacific coast. That stupendous assignment was fulfilled. Fifty three species of birds were mentioned in the report, in such sufficiently accurate detail that later scientists are able to identify them.

To honor these two leaders, two birds they discovered, new to the civilized world, have been named after them: Lewis' woodpecker and Clark's nutcracker. Lewis' woodpecker, eleven inches long with greenish black back, white nape and red face, perches prominently in western Montana and Idaho trees. Clark's nutcracker is a jay found in mountain coniferous forests. It is twelve inches long, white with black

Clark's nutcracker. Photograph by Per Gustav Thingstad

wings. Its range is also in western Montana and Idaho, yet it occasionally wanders into North Dakota.

Since the expedition's longest stay was in Fort Mandan near present day Washburn, it is not surprising that they recorded several new birds in North Dakota During their stay in the late fall, winter and spring in the land of the Three Affiliated Tribes (Mandan, Arikara and Hidatsa) they recorded the wood duck and the white pelican along the Missouri River. Near their Fort Mandan encampment they mentioned snow goose, sharp-tailed grouse, golden eagle, flicker and cedar waxwing. As they passed the mouth of the Little Missouri River they noted the great horned owl. Also in North Dakota they described the black-

Golden eagle. Photograph by Dag Roettereng

bellied plover and the poor-will. By Fort Berthold they didn't overlook the whooping crane. Before leaving what is now North Dakota, at the mouth of the Yellowstone River they found the bald eagle and magpie.

Four magpies were obtained from the Mandan Indians and caged and shipped east with a consignment of materials from Fort Mandan in April, 1805. President Jefferson was delighted to have one of the magpies as a pet at his Monticello home. He later gave it to a museum where it lived out its full life. Lewis and Clark's journals related how the magpie boldly raided camps to seize food, and typically seized scraps of meat when hunters were preparing skins from the bison they shot.

Other birds new to science they described were western grebe, western tanager, McCown's longspur, and grouse. These latter included sharp-tailed grouse on the prairie, blue grouse in fir or pine forests, spruce grouse in spruce woods, ruffed grouse in mixed woods and sage grouse on sagebrush plains.

The food they carried in their gear couldn't be enough, so they continually had to hunt. So they paid especial attention to game birds as well as bison, deer and elk. However, they never shot anything for "sport"—only for food and for study for reporting back to Washington, D. C.

The indispensable member of the expedition turned out to be the Shoshone Indian woman Sakakawea, kidnapped as a child, brought to the Hidatsa village, now hired by the expedition as a guide. She lived at what is now called Knife River Indian Village near Stanton. Her knowledge of the country and her presence as a woman in each scouting party of explorers reassured each new tribe they met that they were not meeting a war party. Miraculously, one such party turned out to be Shoshone, led by its chief, her long lost brother! What better way to create cordial relations with the Indians, and secure needed horses to cross the Rocky Mountains!

She saved the expedition from starvation with her expertise in finding edible plants and prescribing medicinal herbs. She showed them which direction to take. Sakakawea's name translates from the Hidatsa language as Birdwoman. Indians believed that birds held sacred powers, so Birdwoman is a name of respect. Lewis and Clark valued her so highly that after they capsized in a bad wind storm and she rescued their invaluable gear, they named a river, Birdwoman's River, after her.

Birding While On Army Active Duty

It is possible to continue to be a birder while on active duty in the armed services, yet not be detracting from one's line of duty. Here is one serviceman's record.

During World War II this writer was stationed briefly in Georgia while awaiting overseas orders. On a day with free time three of us lieutenants decided to explore the countryside. We were walking down a dirt road after a recent rain. Sitting by one of the puddles was a huge bullfrog, a good half foot in length. As we stood nearby looking at it, a common ground dove flew down for a drink of water and landed directly in front of the bullfrog. Quick as a flash, the bullfrog swallowed the dove in one gulp.

Later in this war, going overseas, this writer was on a troop ship sailing from Seattle to Honolulu. We were in a convoy. Because of Japanese submarines every ship had to sail in unison, zigzagging together so as to elude enemy torpedoes. Our ship's faithful guardian was this large gray bird, a black-footed albatross with a white ring around the base of its bill. Its long narrow wings, of eighty inch wing span, were held almost motionless as it floated on wind currents alongside the bridge of the ship.

During the age of sail an albatross alongside was considered a good omen, and it was a very bad omen for a sailor to kill an albatross. If the luckless man did so the dead bird was hung around his wretched neck for punishment. We arrived in Honolulu safely.

Now in Schofield Barracks there followed days of waiting for assignment to the Western Pacific. The birding was better in the city of Honolulu than it was on Schofield Barracks. All identification had been removed from the telephone building in downtown Honolulu, and sandbags had been placed along its walls, but the alien house sparrows weren't fooled by this wartime camouflage – they still nested in its crannies.

In the Western Pacific my troop ship anchored in Ulithi harbor along with thousands of other U.S. ships. On my turn for shore leave I found this island had endured a bitter battle,. Some palm trees were badly damaged. But on one palm tree leaning precariously, high above the ground, was a tiny egg. Why it didn't fall off was a mystery. And attending to it was the most beautiful dainty little snow-white bird with a black ring of feathers around its black eye. This love tern, or fairy tern, is considered by many people to be their favorite bird. How incongruous, and inspirational, to see this little bit of beauty after such devastation!

During combat there were no birds. In the Battle of Okinawa America had suffered the heaviest losses in the Pacific. But now all was quiet. It was after the fighting was over in the south end of Okinawa that, having time off, and upon hearing a rumor of a cache of silk in the city of Naha, being a captain now I commandeered a jeep to take me there, in spite of the reticence of the driver. We were not prepared for what we saw. Naha was completely destroyed. There was no life, no plants, insects, animals or birds. The dead silence was eerie. Nothing stirred. No birds. The silk cache had lost its allure. We turned around and hurried out of there. Imagine what life would be without birds!

Now the war was over. I was back on Oahu. When I was back out west on Okinawa with the unit to which I had been assigned, they had often talked about how idyllic the area was where they had been stationed near Kilauea on the Big Island of Hawaii. So when I qualified for R & R (rest and relaxation) it was amazing to discover that R & R was at that same place! After arriving I soon agreed with their opinion about its beauty and serenity. Here was a tropical mountain forest in its pristine state. Here was the undisturbed home of endemic Hawaiian birds, unique in a shrinking native forest.

The apapane, crimson with black wings and tail, flitted among the tops of ohia trees, feeding on the nectar of its flowers, called lehua. The iiwi, bright vermilion with black and white wings and a long down-curved pink bill, fed on lehua nectar and insects. The amakihi, green above and yellow below, fed on insects on the same ohia trees. The

The iiwi hovers around the only tree I know of which has one name for itself (ohia), and another name for its flower (lehua). Submitted photo

akepa, reddish-orange male and green and yellow female, moved about in flocks.

But the best part is that the R & R trip was with all expenses paid by the Army, for both me and my wife Adele, who had come to Honolulu to work as a registered nurse.The R & R area is now part of Hawaii Volcanoes National Park.

Private Boat Charter To Dry Tortugas

Some people have a yen to collect things, whether it be stamps, coins, dolls, antique cars or rifles. This writer had the obsession to visit all the units of the National Park System. So it was that he felt the urge to visit Dry Tortugas, one of the most difficult units to visit.

Dry Tortugas is 75 miles west of Key West, Florida. This key was named after a sea turtle, and had no potable water, so was "dry." When we were there in June 2, 3 and 4, 1961, the lone National Park Service boat took no passengers. The only access was by chartering a fishing boat. We found one, the 38 foot Lark II, owned by Captain Arthur C. Pegg, for the large sum of $700 plus food for Pegg and his helper!

Our transportation, Lark II, at the Fort dock. Photograph by Kenneth J. Johnson

Looking at pelagic birds on the trip out there was difficult because of the motion of the boat, which caused seasickness which made birding even harder. One of our sons made a mad dash for the railing to vomit and almost fell overboard.

The park ranger at Dry Tortugas was amazed to see visitors tie up at his dock, a very rare event.

The hexagonal brick Fort Jefferson completely covered the island, even up to the water's edge. Inside the two story

Ramp to Fort Jefferson. Photograph by Kenneth J. Johnson

structure was a large courtyard of grass, cocoanut palms and tropical plants such as sea grape and pandanus.

Several listless cattle egrets were wandering around on the grass. We were told they had migrated here only to find no food and were starving, too weak to fly to the mainland.

The park ranger gave my family (wife and me, boys age 15, 13, 12, and girl age 10) and Capt. Pegg a tour of the fort, explaining the roof where the turrets and a few remaining cannons lay between the corner bastions.

The expression, "Your name is mud," came from the sad fate of Dr. Mudd, who treated the injured foot and ankle of John Wilkes Booth. After shooting President Abe Lincoln in the back of the head, Booth leaped from Lincoln's box down onto the stage of Ford's Theatre and limped away. Outraged authorities banished Dr. Mudd to Fort Jefferson as a prisoner. Before his death Dr. Mudd distinguished himself by eliminating yellow fever from the key. We saw the tiny cemetery in the courtyard housing yellow fever's victims. Today's contemporary Roger Mudd, television newscaster, worked for Dr. Mudd's redeemed name and pardon.

Having gained the trust of the park ranger, he took one of my sons and me in his little rowboat across the narrow

Colony nesters on Bush Key Refuge. Photograph by Kenneth J. Johnson

channel to Bush Key, the off-limits bird sanctuary. There by crouching down and moving very slowly, I was able to take pictures of the two species of ocean breeding birds, sooty tern and brown noddy.

The sooty tern was abundant. Large flocks filled the air, while many terns rested on the ground where each incubated its egg when it was not exposed to the sun. Some eggs were on bare ground, others were among the ground-hugging plants.

Just as two species of birds dominated the tiny island, so only two species of plants were apparent – one small one carpeted the sandy ground, the other was scattered in clumps the height of a man.

The sooty tern's scientific name is *Sterna fuscata*, where the generic name *sterna* is from the Danish *terne*; the specific name *fuscata* is from the Latin *fuscus* meaning dusky. Its old species name used to be *fuliginosa*, from the Latin *fuliginosus*, meaning having the color of soot. I don't see any advantage in changing the name to *fuscata*, except for the scientist by getting his name in print in a scientific journal, which assures prestige in his profession.

The other bird breeding on Bush Key was the brown

Brown noddies, nests and young, Bush Key, Dry Tortugas, June 4, 1961.
Photograph by Kenneth J. Johnson

noddy, a tern whose scientific name is *Anous stolidus*. *Anous* is Greek from the Greek *an-*, not, plus *ous*, ear. Without ear referred to their tameness, assuming that tameness was due to deafness. The species name is from the Latin *stolidus*, meaning dull or stupid. Noddy means a stupid bird. I presume it was so named by sailors because it wasn't afraid of humans. The noddies I saw allowed me to approach to arm's length. I didn't try to get closer. The birds I saw on their nest or roosting probably had never seen a human before.

While sooty terns were abundant, noddies were rare, and seen only on the bushes or stunted trees, not in the air or

Sooty terns on nests on ground, Bush Key, Dry Tortugas, June 4, 1961.
Photograph by Kenneth J. Johnson

on the ground. Both birds are pictured on their nests on the previous page.

The sooty tern is white below, sooty above, with dark forked tail with white outer edge. The noddy is uniformly dark but with white crown. Its tail is not forked.

While this author was birding, what were the fishing guides doing? After tutelage by the captain our youngest boy was thrilled to catch a yellowtail off the side of the boat, and the captain's assistant caught a record breaking permit on a 23 pound line, as my wife and daughter studied tropical fish and other life in the moat in front of the fort.

As we departed Dry Tortugas to return to Key West we passed the old pier used for refueling U.S. Navy ships with coal. There we saw the great cormorant, the masked (blue-faced) booby, and the brown booby.

The Thousand Mile War Revisited

The Aleutian Islands extend from the south shore of mainland Alaska far across the northern Pacific as a chain of volcanic islands pointing at Siberia and Japan. So it was understandable for Japan in World War II to invade and occupy the westernmost islands, since they are closest to Japan.

Attu, the farthest west island, and Kiska were the two sites of the only military campaign against Japan fought on American soil. But what about birds? In Dutch Harbor rats had become such a problem that the armed services published regulations that protected eagles, hawks and owls in what was called the Rat Campaign, to quote Brian Garfield in his book, *The Thousand Mile War.*

A rare touch of humor in that account of that miserable war was when a nervous GI on Attu shot at a flock of geese, mistaking them for some Japanese airplanes!

Now go fast forward to 1979. A group of birders under the leadership of a group called Attour negotiated a charter flight with the only airline (now bankrupt) from Anchorage to fly over the chain of Aleutians Islands to the little airfield on Attu. The only human life in the island was the "U.S. Coast Guard's Loran Station Attu Islands" (now replaced for navigation by global satellite positioning). We group of birders slept in a Quonset Hut left over from World War II but now abandoned by the Army. We went out each day looking for birds. Attu is unique in that during spring migration a storm with a strong west wind would divert birds aiming for eastern Siberia. When they landed fatigued on Attu they were eligible for listing on a North American life list, a prize since they would be expected nowhere else in America.

This writer obtained a jacket patch from the U.S. Coast Guard's little building. The patch shows AK (Alaska) with the Aleutian Islands dotted across the bottom of the patch, ending with Attu housing its Loran beacon. In the center of the patch is a caricature of the horned puffin above the legend, "Home

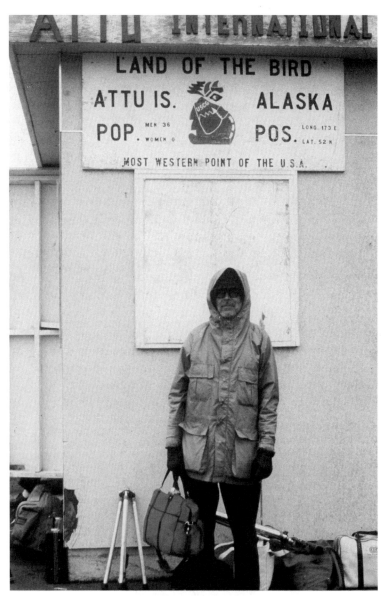

ATTU INTERNATIONAL

LAND OF THE BIRD

ATTU IS.   ALASKA
POP. MEN 36   POS. LONG. 173 E
· WOMEN 0   LAT. 52 N

MOST WESTERN POINT OF THE U.S.A.

Author standing by Attu Air Station shack. Submitted photo

Photograph by Jon Arne Saeter of the U.S. Coast Guard's six-inch sized jacket patch, showing their caricature of the horned puffin.

of the Horny Bird." I guess the Coast Guardsmen identified with the horned puffin because they lived with it there and felt horny (macho and virile).

Attu, the Aleutian Island closest to Japan, being the only piece of American soil the U.S. Army had to retake after the Japanese army had invaded and occupied it, still had war materiel left over from the conflict, abandoned because it was not feasible to ship it back home.

One day this writer strayed off alone to explore, to find what the strong west wind had delivered. The grassy tundra yielded only a snowy owl, who hissed menacingly. Then some acrobatic ravens appeared, rolling and tumbling in the sky. They completed their act as one turned upside down, grasped

Jacket patch of Attour, the tour group that visited Attu Island, showing the white tailed eagle. Photograph by Jon Arne Saeter

Avid birders on Attu, the westernmost part of the U.S., where 40° F rain falls horizontally, May, 1979. Photograph submitted by Kenneth J. Johnson

the talons of another raven, and the pair flew in tandem.

But the climax of the day came when I saw a small sign stuck in the ground, made from a board from a wooden crate. I walked up and went around it to see what was printed on the front side. It said, "Danger. Keep Out. Mine Field." My guardian angel was on the job flying alongside me, once again!

Lieutenant Colonel Al Hartl, Commanding Officer of the 17th Infantry Regiment, who fought in the Battle of Attu, lived in my condominium here in Bismarck until his death. He told me there were no minefields on Attu. Nevertheless, that's what that sign said!

But this is certain: Because our soldiers fought and suffered and died in the Battle of Attu, the white-tailed eagle, an Attu birding specialty, (featured on Attour's jacket patch), when that bird flies over American soil it will never see Japan's white flag with red ball. When a flag flies over there now the eagle will see the Stars and Stripes.

Hudson Bay Bird Run

HUDSON BAY BIRD RUN (028SASK, BREEDING BIRD CENSUS ROUTE)

I was frustrated wanting to hear the spring songs of thrushes and warblers who come through North Dakota on their way to breeding in Canada. So, having gotten to know Chandler Robbins, senior author of *Birds of North America*, from meetings and field trips of the American Birding Association, (he was chief instigator of the Breeding Bird Censuses in North America), I volunteered to conduct some of those in Manitoba and Saskatchewan. All the lati-longs in both countries had been mapped out in Washington and Ottawa, but a number had never been claimed in northern Canada–Canadians qualified and interested were in short supply. (A lati-long is the area between two degrees of latitude and two degrees of longitude.)

Danny Bystra of the Migratory Bird and Habitat Research Laboratory, Laurel, Maryland, to whom I was referred, was delighted. He provided maps and forms to be returned with my data. (When my annual summary sheets returned to headquarters including over 25 species listed which I had to add, they revised their form to conform better to the rich fauna in that area of Canada.)

Of the eleven routes in North Dakota and Canada we had run,

when we finally retired from doing them, we found we had run them a total of 82 times, and my all-time favorite was the Hudson Bay bird run. This route had the greatest variety of habitats, the largest number of bird species, and the most interesting travel experiences. It is located by the edge of the so-called parklands and the boreal forest. We had counted it for eleven years, 1977 through 1987.

Hudson Bay is a town in eastern Saskatchewan 425 km. (263 mi.) north of the Canadian border. It used to be called Hudson Bay Crossing because the railroad forked there. One rail goes east into Manitoba, then south-southeast to Winnipeg. The other rail goes northeast to The Pas, Manitoba, then northeast to Churchill, a town on the shore of Hudson Bay on the Arctic Ocean.

Each year we would arrive in Hudson Bay the night before, to camp in the Hudson Bay Provincial Park south of town. The camp had electricity and pit toilets. In a jack pine forest, it was on a high bank of the Red Deer River. We had to start a half hour before sunrise, at 4:58 a.m. Central Daylight Saving Time, unless it was raining or a strong wind was blowing. The most noteworthy birds in our first ten stops we had seen or heard included nighthawk, yellow-bellied sapsucker, barn swallow, crow, house wren, robin, hermit thrush, ruby-crowned kinglet, red-eyed vireo, yellow warbler, house sparrow, red-winged blackbird, grackle, chipping sparrow, white-throated sparrow, song sparrow, myrtle warbler, redstart, Swainson's (olive-backed) thrush, belted kingfisher, veery, orange-crowned warbler, cedar waxwing, goldfinch, yellow-shafted flicker, black-capped chickadee, starling.

A remarkable total of 75 species just for the first ten stops was accumulated from all eleven years. A few of them were seen only once that first five miles of the route. (We stopped every half mile to observe for three minutes.) These ten stops included the river bank camp, jack pine forest, very noisy saw-mill (the main industry in town), the city, and a spruce bog.

In the city one specified stop was alongside an apartment abutting the sidewalk. One year it was cold, and my wife/recorder couldn't hear me reciting my finds through the closed car window. My loud voice caused the apartment dweller to call the sheriff, who caught up with me at the bog. This young fellow, out of uniform, never heard of a breeding bird census, nor even of his government being concerned about birds! My Canadian Wildlife Service forms enlightened and pacified him.

In the next fifteen stops the highlight was some years hearing a wolf or two in the spruce bog. The further end of the bog harbored the city dump, which was a mecca for black bears. Its gulls couldn't be seen or heard from the route's specified birding stop. Care had to be taken not to over-count ravens in the spruce bog, nor sandhill cranes in the mixture of forest and plowed fields, for both had such loud voices they could be heard easily from over a mile away in the deep silence.

Notable sightings at sites 11 through 25 were loon, snipe, ring-billed gull, killdeer, blue-winged teal, ruffed grouse, bufflehead, sora, great horned owl, solitary sandpiper, bittern, gadwall, pintail, wigeon, red-tailed hawk, marsh hawk (harrier), brown-headed cowbird, purple finch, Canada jay, tree swallow, mourning dove, downy woodpecker, yellow-bellied flycatcher, least flycatcher, alder flycatcher, eastern phoebe, black-billed magpie, Tennessee warbler, mourning warbler, ovenbird, yellowthroat, clay-colored sparrow, Lincoln's sparrow, Baltimore oriole, blue jay, Brewer's blackbird, eastern kingbird, solitary vireo, purple martin, brown creeper.

We often saw moose along the south side of this stretch of the highway. I have a red hunting cap that says, "Hudson Bay Moose Capital of the World."

At Elwood, a group of scattered farms, we turned right at site 25 and left the pavement to turn south onto a fine gravel road through meadows past ponds. On this road our specialties included: mallard, shoveler, coot, kestrel, common goldeneye, Virginia rail, least bittern, lesser scaup, ruddy duck, willet, Philadelphia vireo, palm warbler, black-and-white warbler, Connecticut warbler, Wilson's warbler, savannah sparrow, chimney swift, hairy woodpecker, vesper sparrow, Sprague's pipit, solitary vireo, olive-sided flycatcher, bobolink, Cape May warbler, swamp sparrow, green-winged teal, black-billed cuckoo, warbling vireo, Le Conte's sparrow, western meadowlark.

There is one large barn here that always has a large colony of cliff swallows, not barn swallows, on its side. Why so is a mystery.

Now at site 38 we turned left onto a narrow dirt road through poplar woods, past Smoking Tent Creek and a long marsh to end in Porcupine Hills. One year the marsh's huge colony of yellow-headed blackbirds all sounded off their rarely heard descending trill call at once, quite a concert hearing hundreds of birds in chorus! Or so I thought at the time, but in hindsight I realize now that what I heard actually was the whinnying of many soras, hidden in the cattails below the blackbirds' nests! Distracted by the spectacle of yellow-headed blackbirds, I had completely overlooked soras.

This was a dangerous road, for lumber trucks came racing with not enough space for two way traffic. In later years they were absent. We heard that the Cree Indians in Porcupine Hills got fed up with the lumbering and kicked them out. This stretch was the menagerie, with bear, moose, deer, elk and wolf, all with young, and smaller mammals.

Many warblers and more species were found, such as eared grebe, black tern, ring-necked duck, lesser yellowlegs, black-crowned night heron, broad-winged hawk, horned grebe, pied-billed grebe, gadwall, goshawk, great crested flycatcher, marsh wren, northern waterthrush, golden-crowned kinglet, bay-breasted warbler, chestnut-sided warbler, swamp sparrow, rough-winged swallow, magnolia warbler, pine siskin, olive-sided flycatcher, brown thrasher, redstart, ovenbird, blackburnian warbler, evening grosbeak, Nashville warbler, black-poll warbler, sedge wren, red crossbill, rusty blackbird.

This makes a total of 132 birds! But I never did find the gray-cheeked thrush; it nested farther north. Later, on the way to The Pas, we passed a huge wetlands with too many Nelson's sharp-tailed sparrows to count.

What a wonderful 4-1/2 hour of birding, plus all wild animal displays and a variety of habitats, the result when civilization meets wilderness.

Odd Incidents That Happen On Birding Tours

In the course of traveling on many birding tours, it is inevitable that interesting incidents will happen. So let's share those happenings with the reader.

This birding tour van was speeding along this California highway in a procession of vehicles. I was sitting on the rear seat enjoying the scenery. Then an odd site caught my attention: on our left was a closely parallel strip of pavement, separated from the highway by a row of trees. A patrol car was parked there, but as we came by it started up and paced us for quite a distance. Sensing we were being timed, I shouted a warning, but was ignored over the chatter of the other birders. At the end of that long strip of pavement the law turned onto the highway with siren wailing and lights flashing and forced our driver to stop. Out of pity for our driver, we all chipped in to pay for his fine.

That was indeed a most elaborate speed trap!

B. K. was a clever tour leader. Once I found him hiking alone, with spotting scope and tripod over his shoulder, and water canteen and a huge hunk of cheese along for snacks. Asked what he was doing out alone while the group he was in charge of was sitting back in camp, he said he was out scouting and staking out birds. Could it be that he was using his group to subsidize his travels so he could find interesting birds for his own pleasure? Yet his clients all found the prize birds he sought for them and they seemed to be satisfied. To show a bird to others you must first find it yourself.

The Greyhound-sized bus chartered for this American Birding Association tour was directed to visit the garbage dump. But to be politically correct I must call it a land fill. The site was very productive, especially for gulls. However, while there the bus got stuck. Only after it was completely emptied, and with considerable struggle by a large tow truck and other help, was the bus able to get out so as to haul its passengers back to the convention hotel in time for supper.

At another A.B.A. convention there were so many birders signed up for tours that more buses were urgently called. The only available transportation turned out to be some buses driven by non-union drivers. Upon seeing this, the union drivers refused to drive the already contracted buses, and went on strike. Chaos resulted. In the emergency, a barely adequate number of private vehicles volunteered. So we secured a ride with a gracious couple from the Eastern United States and were able to see and hear the francolin in Louisiana. During the ride in their car I mentioned that the eastern meadowlark had a squeaky song in contrast to the beautiful song of the western meadowlark. Identifying with the bird back home, the Easterners took offense at my remark!

In our birding tour in Northern Minnesota one of the members of the group had brought along her parents. Her father, it turned out, had difficulty seeing this certain bird, a veery, that the others readily identified. The tour leader, K. E., very patiently was helping him. But the other birders became impatient and intolerant and started making insulting remarks. That elderly man eventually discerned the veery, resulting in a happy fiftieth wedding anniversary for him and his wife.

On this westernmost Aleutian island, Attu, three of us birders were resting on the tundra inspecting the steep cliff before us. My companions were enthusing over the eye-browed thrush perched near the top of the cliff. I couldn't see it, even though it was in plain sight. Finally I made it out as I saw it defecate, and extrapolated its camouflaged body upward from the source of the droppings.

We were members of the first birding tour group in the early 1960s V. E. ever conducted. He drove a European model Mercedes-Benz passenger van which ran only on diesel fuel. In the long distances in Texas he discovered that local filling stations did not handle diesel fuel in those days. So he drove alone to a distant metropolis for fuel while our group of birders stood around in a field waiting for our breakfast and our leader to show up. Finally he arrived, hours late, to serve us lox and bagels draped out on the fender of another car. He learned by mistakes, and now has become one of the very best world tour leaders in the birding field.

Somewhere in Texas on another tour everyone in the group got excited over finding a shoveler. I thought how pitiful, since back in

North Dakota I see hundreds of them. We had occasion to cross over a fence, and I had the poor judgment to put my weight on one of the barbed wires, causing it to come loose, pulling its staple out of the partly rotted wooden fence post. The tour leader scolded me, and rightly so. My manners needed mending.

Out in California we rented a Volkswagon to go birding. We drove farther than the rental agency intended, I deduce, for we encountered a road block which was stopping and inspecting every vehicle for emission control standards. Our rented car failed the test, even though it bore a tag on its windshield stating that the car was inspected and found safe. Luckily I didn't have to pay the fine, since I was renting the car.

In the U.S. Virgin Islands we rented the only available car, a Volkswagon. It didn't have the standard manual gearshift I had learned on as a youth. Someone had torn off the metal tag which showed the position of each gear for operating that strange gearshift. And everyone drives on the left side in the Virgin Islands! I sweated trying to drive the car. So I earned my sighting of that bananaquit.

Back home the tour leader had arranged in advance for this local resident in Nome to secure a school bus ready to take us into the Alaskan back country. After landing from our air flight, we found that the young driver had forgotten to fill up the gas tank. After some delay, he finally was able to rouse some gasoline on this Sunday. Now all the roads leaving Nome fizzle out some distance out in the wilderness. After a long drive it became imperative for the group to visit what Nova Scotians call the necessary house. Away from civilization, the bus stopped for the men to go into the brush on the right side of the bus as the women went into the brush on the left side of the bus. But when the bristle-thighed curlew voiced what *The Sibley Guide to Birds* calls its "human attention whistle," I don't think it was impressed by what it might have seen as we all relieved ourselves.

Birds Never To Be Forgotten

At sometime in everyone's life I expect that they have had an encounter with a bird that left a lasting impression, an event not easily forgotten. Here are some of my experiences; may they jar your memories to recall your examples.

COMMON LOON: One can observe a bird and other wild life closer from a car than when on foot. That's why it's illegal to shoot deer when sitting in a vehicle. Similarly, a canoe doesn't alarm wildlife easily if the canoeist moves slowly and quietly. So it was that while canoeing on a lake in Northern Minnesota we ventured into an inlet which looked interesting. There we saw a pile of reeds floating on the water, on which was sitting a loon. We drifted up to it. It crouched down. As we crept up to less than a canoe length away, it slipped off its nest and slid into the water without a sound or a ripple, and swam away underwater.

Don't try this, for loon nesting areas are off limits now, lest the loon abandon its nest when it is disturbed.

LOON AND MAGPIES: Near Tobin Lake in Saskatchewan we saw a drama take place. A loon had landed on a plowed field and was unable to take off. Now, its feet are located far to the rear of its body, so its breast was scraping along the dirt in a futile attempt of its legs to gather momentum for flight. Such a body construction is superb for underwater chase, for no fish big or small can escape a loon. But on land they are helpless. As we watched, a pair of magpies noticed its dilemma, and flew down to harass the loon. Finally, as it came to a slight elevation in the field, it was able to get enough momentum to take off.

Chandler Robbins, the bird guide author, said that where in the Far North settlers have cleared and plowed new land, the field looks like a body of water when seen by water birds from overhead. So that poor loon must have mistaken that new field for a lake.

FRIGATE BIRD: Yours truly was attending a convention in Miami Beach, Florida. The hotel room to which I was assigned was on an upper floor, at the outermost corner of the building. As I looked out the window, here was a magnificent frigate bird hovering steadily, taking advantage of the strong steady wind coursing around the corner of the building. It was so close we could have carried on a conversation without shouting – if it were able to talk. We did look at each other, however. After a while it must have become bored of me and drifted off with no obvious movement of its outstretched wings, as is typical of this bird.

THE FIGHTING GANDER OF BENTSEN: Bentsen Rio Grande Valley State Park in Texas is world famous as a place to see rare and exotic wild birds. But no one anticipated that one bird there would gain notoriety.

A resaca (ox-bow lake) forms the northwest boundary of the park. The primitive campground on the shore of this former river channel has a boat ramp. On the other side of the water is a human habitation, the home of a small flock of domestic geese. They swim across and march up the ramp for handouts from park visitors. The gander who heads the flock isn't satisfied with the speed with which the people feed him, so he ends up biting and pinching them with his bill.

When my wife was feeding the gander on one of our recent trips there she cried in pain and surprise as she became his latest victim. This writer dashed over there to protect her. The chase that followed as the gander ran away ended only when the gander, flapping its wings for speed, ran around a picnic table. This author, attempting the sharp turn around the table, slipped on the moist ground running after it.

The geese don't come over to visit the park any more.

THE SILENCED MERGANSER: We were camping in a screened shelter in Isle Royale National Park on Lake Superior. Early in the morning as it was beginning to get light I heard the quack-quacking of a common merganser on the inlet outside our shelter, so I crawled out of my bedroll and crept out very quietly. There was a big moose wading slowly, eating water lilies and mumbling contentedly in accompaniment to its borborygmi (stomach rumblings). It was so close it would have completely filled the viewfinder of my camera.

Then suddenly the serene quacking of the merganser changed into a higher pitched squawking, together with violent splashing and thrashing about in the water, followed by silence. What pulled the merganser below the surface of the water to its death? A huge snapping turtle, or a muskellunge, or what?

VULTURE: This young woman we met told us she was on a solo birding trip along the Rio Grande Valley in south Texas. She was driving her minivan at a rather fast speed, I gather, when she suddenly came upon a road-kill. Before she hit it, a large dark bird rose up from it, and smashed her windshield to land on the hood of her car. It was a vulture. She was uninjured, but too shook up to tell whether her kill was a black vulture or a turkey vulture.

HAWK STRATEGY: Never underestimate the intelligence of a bird. This was demonstrated once when a group of birders met for lunch in one of their vans parked in an abandoned farmyard south of Long Lake National Wildlife Refuge. The car was parked next to a small corn crib, where some of the corn had spilled out of the west side onto the ground. A red-winged blackbird was feeding quietly on the spilled corn. A Swainson's hawk flew eastward past our car, noticed the blackbird facing north, then flew past the corn crib. We thought the hawk had gone, but it circled around the crib, came around the southwest corner and pounced on the redwing from behind before the prey was able to react.

THE LAUNDRY ROOM ROADRUNNER: The roadrunner is the best known bird of the American Southwest, now that it has starred in movie and television cartoons as the wacky character that matches wits with the wily coyote in races across the desert. Before television it was most familiar to people traveling along dusty roads because of its habit of running along with the car or horse before turning aside into a cactus thicket. That gave this bird its local name of chaparral cock.

Roadrunner, uninvited guest in the laundry room. Photograph by Kenneth J. Johnson

Our most interesting encounter with a roadrunner was at a recreational vehicle park at San Ygnatio, Texas. Here a roadrunner had taken advantage of the RV park's laundry room door always being open. This bird had taken up residence on a shelf up near the ceiling. There it perched quietly as it looked down at us.

SPRUCE GROUSE: It was a memorable day in Minnesota's North Country when this writer was trudging along a primitive road in a spruce bog. Suddenly a hen spruce grouse reared up in front of me, wings spread, feathers raised, scolding anxiously, threatening to attack. Then appeared her little chicks at my feet, peeping as they avoided being stepped on. They looked like little pieces of bog, small enough to fit in my palm. They were so perfectly camouflaged that by the time they ran two feet to the side they became invisible. As they hurried as best they could mother followed them and also became invisible. Protective coloration was superb.

RING-NECKED PHEASANT: Driving down a North Dakota highway, a ring-necked pheasant flew across in front of my car. I thought I hit it, since looking in my rear-view mirror I saw no sight of it. But when I stopped the car I found no trace of the bird nor damage to the car. Days later at a full service filling station the attendant found the pheasant hidden between the grill and the radiator, and he dumped the bird into a trash can. So my car had become an avian hearse!

CAVE HILLS ROCK PIGEONS: The domestic pigeon, called rock dove by birders because its ancestors lived on cliffs in Spain, is an immigrant largely ignored and often not counted on bird lists. These rock pigeons, their new name by 2006 decree of the American Ornithologists' Union, living under bridges or nesting on buildings for generations fail to qualify for membership in our fauna by some because they are fed by people, I suspect.

But there are some rock pigeons who cannot be ignored. These have been free-living and independent for generations. It took that long for their droppings to be inches deep in this certain cave in the Cave Hills, north of the Black Hills of South Dakota. The walls of this cave are covered with mineral growth, a coating of fuzz—patina—deposited by evaporation over many years of mineral-laden water seeping out of the rock. On the wall of this cave is engraved the signature of a soldier who was with General Custer's expedition. This patina also covers the soldier's graffiti, proving its age and authenticity.

SCREECH OWL: When I was a little boy I slept on a cot against the windows of our upstairs back porch. It was like living up in the trees, for a large oak tree extended its branches to almost touch the windows. One night a very loud screech sounded right outside the window by my cot. It was so terrifying I froze with fright, even unable to run to my parents for protection. The cause was an eastern screech owl perched in the oak tree not more than six feet away!

MURDERED BOREAL OWL: Boreal owls live in Canada's far north evergreen forest and muskeg, and are rare in Northern Minnesota's Arrowhead back woods. There it is found best at night in bitter winter by walking through deep snow.

So when one went south to the outskirts of Duluth, and chose to linger in someone's back yard in plain sight, the word got around by the birding hot line and by word of mouth.

Soon it became a major attraction as people flocked to this spot to see this rare hard-to-see bird.

The landowner was somewhat of a recluse who preferred quiet and solitude, so he resented the traffic and publicity that boreal owl brought him. Finally he felt he had suffered enough, so he shot the bird, so I am told.

CHIMNEY SWIFTS, NOT: Unless the bird is a chimney swift, it seems chimneys are bad luck for birds. We heard some strange faint noises coming from our fireplace. A brief look revealed nothing amiss. But finally in a check farther up the chimney by the damper I extracted a robin! It had fallen down the chimney and had gotten stuck. On releasing it outdoors it flew away unscathed. It is too bad it wasn't as adept as Santa Claus.

Another encounter with chimneys didn't turn out as well. This man I met at a campground told me he took his recreational vehicle out of storage and went camping with it. After lighting his propane stove his RV caught on fire because he didn't realize that house sparrows had built their messy straw nest in the stove flue, plugging it up to allow the hot exhaust fumes to ignite the nest!

TUFTED TITMOUSE: In the campground of the South Llano River State Park near Junction, Texas the tufted titmouse called from the live oak tree. Then it flew down to

TUFTED TITMOUSE: "THAT HUMAN DOWN THERE THINKS HE'S SO SMART—HE SURE CAN'T HOLD A SEED WITH ONE TOE WHILE HIS SNOUT SPLITS IT OPEN!"

a branch just out of reach of me to sound off again. Then it moved to another branch just as close and repeated itself. Campers there are enthusiastic feeders of birds. Figuring it was asking for food, I tossed out a cupful of bird seed onto the pavement of the campsite. Promptly the titmouse flew down, picked up a seed, and returned to the small branch. There it placed the seed on the branch and held it in place with its toes, and pounded the seed repeatedly with its bill. Splitting open the hull, it ate the meat of the seed.

HOUSEHUNTING BARN SWALLOWS: How often has a birder stopped on a roadside, motor turned off and windows open, to look and listen for birds? In no time barn swallows appear, circling around in an inspection visit, about to fly in the car window. Their curiosity isn't idle, for I'm sure they are looking for a nesting site.

The limiting factor to a bird species' abundance isn't primarily food supply or climate or predators, I am told, but a place to nest. So realize how important it is for us to make our world favorable for birds, so they can reproduce and stay with us.

A PICNIC WITH PINYON JAY: The Canada jay, or gray jay, is called the camp robber by North Country outdoorsmen, and with good reason. That bird is notorious for invading a wilderness camp to make off with food, even being so bold as to steal off a camper's plate.

But that bird must share that reputation with its cousin, the pinyon jay. My wife and I were lunching at the picnic area in Jewel Cave National Monument in the Black Hills of South Dakota. I was sitting at the picnic table eating. Suddenly without warning this pinyon jay came from nowhere, snatched some food off my paper plate in a split second, and flew off with it! To say I was startled is correct.

CONNIVING CONNECTICUT WARBLER: Bismarck is fortunate in being situated on the western edge of a major flyway, a route migratory birds travel between Canada and points far south. Each year a few eastern warblers show themselves here to observant and persistent birders.

So it was one spring that this Connecticut warbler announced itself in Sibley Park, at Bismarck's south end of Washington street. Its song is unique and unmistakable, a cadence like the chuga chuga of an engine. That immediately alerted this group of birders, who hurried toward the source of the call. The chase became a hide-and-seek game. Then as the group was intently looking up in the trees in the campground loop, the warbler came out of a bush near the ground and, true to its habit of staying close to the ground, flew literally right between their legs, unnoticed!

Finally, when it sang again in the nearby woods, one of the group finally saw it, confirming its identity for doubters. So, it seems, birds can easily outwit humans.

BROWN-CAPPED ROSY FINCH: The lumpers put them all in one species, rosy finch. The splitters divide them into brown-capped rosy finch, black rosy finch, and the gray-crowned rosy finch, which they further split into Bering sea, coastal and interior rosy finches. These all vary from each other in small differences in plumage , and each resides in its own distinct range.

All live up in the high mountains; the most convenient bird to see is the brown-capped rosy finch. We got our lifer by stopping at Pass Lake in Loveland Pass in Colorado, then climbing up the steep mountain at 12,000 feet elevation. The National Park Foundation's book, *The Complete Guide to America's National Parks*, says, "Even healthy persons are normally winded by the slightest exertion at these levels." I found myself crawling up foot by foot, finally sprawled motionless gasping for breath.

Meanwhile the brown-capped rosy finches flit about me effortlessly. I felt embarrassed as it seemed to me like they were laughing at my helplessness and inadequacy!

THE ADOPTED ORPHAN: Near the headquarters of the Grand Canyon National Monument on the north side of the Grand Canyon we saw a most remarkable sight. A tiny bird was feeding a baby bird that was much, much bigger than itself. Intrigued, I set up my tripod to record such a phenomenon with my camera.

The ranger's wife, peering out her window and overcome with curiosity, finally came out to investigate. The mystery was solved when the woman recalled that a recent severe rainstorm had completely destroyed a finch's nest near their window, and both parents and babies had vanished. So here was a lone survivor being adopted and fed by a stranger, a 4-1/2 long bushtit feeding a fledgling 6-1/2 long Cassin's finch!

EVENING GROSBEAK: Our bird feeder hung outside our kitchen window, for easy access and close viewing. This particular year a flock of evening grosbeaks visited daily. But one looked different. Its two mandibles pointed in different directions. It soon became apparent that it acted differently. While others ate rapidly, this poor bird made a feeble pass at the seeds, unable to pick up any. Each day it was less active, and sat looking at the food listlessly. It no longer kept up with the flock, and sat alone, hunched down forlornly. I waited until dusk and crept out to pick it up, hopeful that if we got it to a veterinary he could be of help. But just as my hand slowly reached toward the bird, it roused itself and flew away, never to return. What had been the cause of this tragedy; had it flown into a window, or had someone shot at it?

IX. PEOPLE WHO ARE BIRDERS

How People Become Bird-Watchers

With the number of bird-watchers growing rapidly, it would be of interest to find out the reasons and the happenings that cause this phenomenon. So we investigated. Our findings are surprising. Here are some examples of those persons, arranged in chronological order.

1. Some are born that way. Albert recalls having had an interest in birds all his life, even from his earliest memories. He provides no specific details, but after high school he chose a college major in biology, forestry and ornithology. He became an employee of the federal government in the Fish and Wildlife Service.

Ben's lifelong interest in birds is recalled by his early fascination of watching blue jays as they called, and seeing robins cocking their head, then jabbing an earthworm and pulling it out of the ground, and listening to white-throated sparrows singing in an autumn rain. Birds always intrigued him. In college he found no opportunity to make ornithology his career, but his profession allowed him to continue bird-watching as his hobby throughout his life.

2. With some their interest was fostered by childhood experiences. Carol's best friend in grade school was the daughter of a game warden. They would go camping together enjoying the outdoors. She also delighted in collecting the little cards in each box of Arm & Hammer's baking soda. Each card pictured a certain bird, with a brief explanation of that bird. As an adult she continued her interest in birds.

Doris was born and raised on a North Dakota farm. Her early memories were of listening to the western meadowlarks. They were all over the countryside, in plain sight, singing their loud cheerful song which carried long distances across the prairie. This led to an interest in other less common and less obvious birds, with no one's help or encouragement.

A certain man from Brownsville, Texas was an

entrepreneur who ran a small business driving tourists in his station wagon across the border to see the sights in Matamoros, Mexico. He had befriended poor Mexicans, and would bring a small gift for one of them on every trip. On one trip he carried a cage with a green parakeet and gave it to a little girl. On the next visit he found that Estella had two parakeets in the cage. What happened? The little girl said she left the cage door open, and a wild green parakeet flew in! Estella became an eager bird-watcher. We didn't see her cage, but we added the green parakeet to our North American life list when we heard and saw the daily flock fly in from Mexico at exactly 4:30 p.m. to roost in Brownsville's Fort Brown, and bite holes in the trunk of a palm tree – I suppose to chew out a hole for a nest.

3. Others started birding as a teenager. Freda was in her terrible teens, a time when all old people such as her middle-aged parents were out of it, old fogies, not hip – each younger generation, it seems, has its own name for the older generation. So when she was dragged along on this camping trip she was sitting at this picnic table, bored as she brushed her long hair. One of her hairs floated down to land at her feet. Then a little dickeybird startled her as it flew down, picked up the hair, and carried it up to add to the nest it was building. Her boredom was cured then as she took an interest in birds.

Upon graduating from college, a classmate and I joined a group of young inner city boys on a canoe-portage-camping trip over the Boundary Waters of Northern Minnesota. They were tough and macho. An interest in loons and mergansers was met with suspicion. Then one day I arbitrarily wore my letter sweater earned by long distance running on the college track team. This one stocky blond in particular stared. Gus's jaw dropped, his eyes widened, as he admired my sweater. An athlete who birded deserved great respect, so bird watching must be an in-thing.

4. As a young adult: Helen's friend Irene was a confirmed birder, who urged Helen to come along on birding trips. After the third invitation she finally accepted. That convinced her. Now both Helen and her husband are enthusiastic birders.

Jane went with my wife and me on a field trip with the Bismarck-Mandan Bird Club, where people were listening to birds singing in the wild. She was surprised to know of such people, since she was aware only of those who sat behind their windows watching birds at bird feeders. She was taking biology at the state university, but this experience led her to a Master of Science degree in Wild Life. She is now employed at a National Wildlife Refuge.

5. As a person of middle-age: Katie and her husband enjoyed their backyard with its garden, small swimming pool, and bird bath. After a hard day, they would like to relax in the pool as the sun set, and savor the sights and sounds of the world going to sleep. But then appeared at the bird bath a screech owl! It looked around cautiously, climbed in and splashed. Its mate then replaced it, followed by their baby. After the baths, they would fly into a nearby pine tree to dry before leaving for their nightly adventures. The owls' home was in a hole in a nearby elm tree. Fascinated, the onlookers became engaged in watching the other birds coming to their yard.

LaVerne tells me he found an egg on the ground in a field once. Fascinated, he took it home and placed it in a robin's nest. The robin incubated it. When it hatched it grew to become a meadowlark. This stimulated him to increase his interest in birds.

6. Retired people: At the Elderhostel near Smith Point, Texas were several recent retirees, looking for some hobby to pursue. They chose bird-watching. Many retirees are doing this and enjoying it.

So how do people become bird-watchers? The examples above are just a sampling of the many. The number of reasons are almost as many as the numbers of birders.

If you are not already watching birds, try it, and see what you've been missing. The local newspaper may have a Calendar of Events that lists a bird club to visit. The local library or book store should have books to aid you.

Did You Know That God Is A Bird Watcher?

Raven: "This flotsam and jetsam sure beats staying in Noah's stuffy old ark."
(Genesis 8:7)

Did you know that God is a bird watcher? The *Bible* says so;. In Matthew 10:29-31 it says that God knows when a sparrow falls. Doesn't that make Him a bird watcher? God is extremely intelligent, so it must be acceptable and a smart thing to be a birder.

Birders logically progress to taking an interest, then being involved in, the protection of birds. So we deduce that He also is concerned about the welfare of birds. Accordingly, in Deuteronomy 22:6 God admonishes the Israelites when they raid a bird's nest that they may take the young or the eggs but to spare the mother bird. The adult bird can produce more offspring for the future, so it should be preserved. To be like the man who killed the goose that laid the golden eggs would be counter productive.

But to go back to the beginning, in Genesis 1:21 God created "every winged bird;" in Genesis 1:31 He saw that that was very good.

God had the best interests of both man and bird in mind when in Leviticus 19:9-10 He told the Israelites to leave a strip of vegetation untouched along the edge of the cultivated field. That provided cover for birds to live and nest and forage in for insects which would damage the crop and the adjacent field.

God the bird watcher is also like the feeder watcher, who sets up a bird feeder then provides it with bird food. Evidence for this is Matthew 6:26, which says your Heavenly Father feeds the birds. So is it fair to say that people who feed birds may be blessed?

We must not underestimate the ability of a bird to analyze the object of its attention. Proverbs 1:17 claims that a net spread out in the sight of any bird is done so in vain, for the bird will catch on and avoid the net so of what use is the net? The bird at hand at the erection of the net can't or doesn't warn other, later birds.

Birds, however, may act as informers. The *Bible* says so. Ecclesiastes 10:20 claims that even in the privacy of one's home and in the absence of electronic listening devices one's voice may be caught by a bird who will "make the matter known". So when a gossiper is asked where they got their information, they reply, "A little bird told me!"

Noah certainly was a bird watcher. After forty days cooped up in his ark, he opened up a window and sent forth a raven. It flew around looking for some dry land. Being a wilderness bird, it had no motivation to return to the ark. It probably landed on flotsam and jetsam, which provided sustenance for this eater of carrion. Noah then sent out a dove, who could not find a place to land, so, being adapted to civilization, returned to Noah who put out his hand and returned her into his ark. A week later he sent her out again. That evening she returned carrying an olive leaf in her bill. Another week passed and he sent her out, never to return. One reason God chose Noah to build and fill the ark must have been because He knew Noah was an excellent bird watcher!

Native Indians And Birds

When Columbus in 1492 was approaching America he saw a flock of birds flying south. His sailors, on the verge of mutiny, were so desperate for the sight of land that it was decided to turn and follow the birds, since these migrants would lead them to land. But landing on a Caribbean island instead of the mainland didn't change him from naming the native Americans he found there Indians, since Columbus thought he landed in India. And just as big a misunderstanding was the later European settlers of the original North American culture. While the settlers' attitude was to invade, occupy and transform, and destroy whatever interfered, the Indians' culture was to respect, revere and coexist with Nature. They apologized to an animal when they killed it for food. The whites killed for sport. Recall photos of hunter with rifle surrounded by many dozens of corpses of game birds he shot. Indians had reverence for life, which included birds. They, like all early cultures, had a reverence

Indian feather dancer. Photograph by Jon Arne Saeter

for birds and their ability to fly, and therefore had direct access to the heavens, symbolic of achievement and hope. Migrating birds returning in spring signified rebirth and renewal.

An Indian brave often took the name of a raptor, such as Black Hawk or Little Eagle, out of admiration and respect for it. Some Indian women took the name of a bird, such as the Arikara tribe member Doreen Yellowbird.

Since Indians for centuries had lived with Nature, one would expect they would have become acquainted with birds, and they were indeed.

Purple martins originally nested in cavities in trees and cliffs, and also in bird houses set up by Indians. They would trim adjacent saplings or set up poles next to their tepees, and hang hollowed-out gourds to prongs of one or two foot-lengths on these poles and saplings. The grateful purple martins nested in those gourds as they kept the area quite free of mosquitoes.

Little boys used small bows and arrows to shoot song birds. This trained them for later life in using larger stronger bows and arrows for warfare and hunting.

The front end of the shaft of an arrow holds the flint arrowhead, and the rear end holds the bird feathers; this so-called fletching of feathers had two purposes. One is to provide weight to balance the weight of the flint point so the arrow won't fly end over end in flight. The other is to make the arrow fly straight, because the feathers are arranged so the arrow moves in a spiral motion, just as rifling inside the barrel of a rifle makes the bullet fly in a tight spiral straight trajectory for greater accuracy in hitting the target. Each feather is mounted very carefully to accomplish this. In front of and behind the uncut feathers on the rear end of the shaft, other feathers may be glued or sewn which had some of the barbs of the vane removed from the quill. The placing and angling of each feather shows how great was the knowledge and skill of the native who designed and constructed the arrow!

The feathers of the turkey were the favorite of the arrow

Platform for scaring blackbirds away from the corn. Jamestown National Historic Site, Virginia. Photograph by Kenneth J. Johnson

makers, but they also used feathers of the eagle, goose, crow and hawk.

Turkeys were domesticated by aborigines that lived in what is now Mexico. The Anasazi in what is now our desert Southwest wore robes of turkey feathers, savored turkey meat, and bred turkeys to keep grasshoppers and other pests away from their crops. Archaeologists there have discovered burials containing remains of turkeys buried with the person for companions of the dead, with remains of humans wrapped in turkey-feather robes. The feathers on the robes were from turkeys bred in separate flocks for different colors!

A birder friend of mine went out to a Burleigh County farmer to buy some sunflower seeds for his bird feeders. The farmer was receptive until he asked my friend for what he would use the seeds. Then he became irate and flatly refused to sell the seeds since they would feed those (censored) blackbirds that come in flocks to destroy his crops! The Plains Indians before us had the same problem as that farmer. Their solution was to erect scaffolds in their corn fields to use as watchtowers. The women and children kept off the Brewer's blackbirds and red-winged blackbirds. When a flock appeared an alarm was shouted and all the watchers joined in until the blackbirds withdrew.

People Who Are Birders • *405*

Nevertheless those North Dakota Indians in the early days often had to eat their corn while it was still green, or not have it at all.

Being in daily contact with birds, Native American Indians inevitably were bird watchers. Cherokee Indians, displaced to Oklahoma from the southeastern United States, had names for most of the species they met. This writer found information on the Internet. Many of the names of the birds, such as that for the robin, were untranslatable. Little sparrows we often would similarly brush off as "little brown birds" were called by them as "the principal bird" because they were everywhere.

Many birds were named to imitate their call, such as the screech owl, great horned owl, whip-poor-will, crow, bobwhite, Carolina chickadee, Canada goose. The Cherokees' name for acorn sounded like the mourning dove's call, so they called that dove "it cries for acorns." The eastern meadowlark was named "star" because its spread tail in flight suggested a star to them. The white-breasted nuthatch was called "deaf" because they figured that was why it came so close to humans.

If a wing or tail feather of an owl is soaked in water, that water bathing the eyes of a child renders that child with the ability to stay awake at night. Water in which a blue jay's feather is soaked then used as an eye wash makes a child an early riser, the Cherokees also believed.

The goshawk was recognized as the raptor which would strike and kill a bird in flight. The common moorhen was given the name "crippled" since it flew only for a very short distance. For some obscure reason the little blue heron was called "sun-gazer." Feathers of the American (great) egret were worn by ball players. But feathers of the turkey vulture were never worn, lest the wearer would become bald, since the vulture ate carrion (which is taboo), and since its head is bald.

Both greater and lesser yellowlegs were given the same name. Scissor-tailed flycatcher was named "fork." Because the ruffed grouse has a large brood but loses most of it before they mature, pregnant women were forbidden to eat its meat.

The Carolina chickadee was the teller of the truth, but the tufted titmouse was a liar.

(Reference: www.earthbow.com/native/cherokee/birdtribes)

It is probable that many other Indian tribes were equally astute at recognizing the many species of birds and studying their behavior, more so than most whites today.

pipit

War Bonnets

War bonnet quilt showing circle of eagle feathers, made by Tillie Little Soldier, wife of August Little Soldier, Arikara member of Three Affiliated Tribes. Photograph 2005 by Kenneth J. Johnson

Early Native Indians were very cognizant of birds, but eagles, golden and bald, were in a class by themselves in meriting respect and awe.

The largest, strongest, bravest bird that could soar and fly so high up in the air that it can rise out of sight surely deserved the reverence it was accorded. So it is logical that its most impressive part, its tail feathers, were so highly prized – one horse in exchange – for use for decorative and ceremonial purposes.

The tail feathers were made into a headdress. In early days each feather represented a certain feat in battle, so the headdress deserved its name, the war bonnet. Each magnificent feather was white with a black tip. Its origin was either from an immature golden eagle or a sub-mature bald eagle. The war bonnet could be worn only by a few men who had earned the honor to do so in warfare. But if the war bonnet consisted of say, twenty feathers, that didn't mean 20 enemies were killed. The Plains Indians had a tradition that the brave who killed the enemy didn't receive the greatest honor. That was merited by the first four warriors who touched the victim, whether he was already dead or dying. (The first one deserved that honor, but the council couldn't tell which it was among the rush to the body, so they chose the four most plausible.) Their logic was that it took more bravery to kill the person face to face, such as with a knife, than to kill him from a distance, such as with bow and arrow or gun. So one person killed could have merited five feathers in the headdress.

Today every eagle feather you see worn at a powwow doesn't represent a man killed. They are also worn on the head now for decoration and for ceremonies. Eagle feathers from the wing have been made into a fan, when waved before a person to waft the regal qualities from the eagle onto the person being fanned. Smaller eagle feathers are sewn onto war costumes and fixed onto shields. A buck-skin shirt often was adorned with these feathers as ornaments. They are mostly for religious and cultural purposes, such as for healing, marriage and naming ceremonies.

Where did the Indians get those feathers? A certain highly qualified man was sent out to kill an eagle. Or an eagle's nest was robbed and the young eaglet was raised to maturity in captivity. Or a trap was devised by some tribes. This consisted of a pit dug in the ground on some high open plain, covered with branches, and topped with bait. A man hid in the pit and patiently waited. When an eagle landed to seize the bait the man reached up to grab its legs and jerk a few feathers out of its tail. Such a pit was pointed out to me once. It was about four feet wide, but over the years had become partly filled in with soil, yet was still clearly recognizable. No method yielded many feathers, so there was always a shortage for something that was in such great demand.

The shortage intensified when Congress in 1940 passed the Bald Eagle Protection Act, and in 1962 included the golden eagle in it. It ended the collection of eagles and eagle parts.

Then in the 1970s the U.S. Fish and Wildlife Service came to the Indians' rescue by establishing the National Eagle Repository.

State and federal wildlife people salvage all dead eagles from unlawful shooting or trapping, vehicle collisions, electrocutions, or natural causes. They are then sent to the National Eagle Repository near Denver, Colorado, where each specimen is inspected, cataloged, and refrigerated.

Enrolled members of a federally recognized Indian tribe can register a request for an eagle or its part (wing, tail, feather or talon), promising it will be used for religious purposes by Indians only. These requests are placed on a waiting list and filled on a first-come first-served basis.

Each year about a thousand people apply for only eight or nine hundred available birds. Because of the large imbalance between supply and demand the N. E. R. has several red tape forms, hard to obtain and hard to fill out satisfactorily. As a consequence, this service is not advertised and is de-emphasized. Even so after he applies it may take some five years for an Indian to receive his request for a full body, or about seven months for a few parts.

Ernest Thompson Seton

In my formative years I became absorbed in the books by Ernest Thompson Seton about wild animals. His facts were correct, based on his observations, about actual mammals and birds that were notorious or distinguished or famous. One of Seton's birds that he wrote about which I cited is in this book's chapter, "When A Crow Calls, Each Caw Means Something." What irritated professional scientists was his style of writing that portrayed the animals with human attributes; but this style of writing endeared him to the general public, and popularized his many books. An innovation was the liberal sprinkling of his drawings in the margins of his books. He was a fascinating lecturer. He did appease scientists, though, with articles in scientific journals and with volumes of scientific books on wild animals. He was interested in the welfare of American youth, and wrote the first handbook of the Boy Scouts of America.

This illustration, from page 83 of Seton's *Animal Tracks and Hunter Signs*, is typical of his illustrations, but is of particular interest to people who are especially interested in birds.

Here Seton recorded a woodland tragedy exactly as it happened, except to condense it to fit on one page. At point A a 5 by 9 inch round place in the snow was found, where a cottontail rabbit had bedded down. Because something had alarmed him, he leaped out and landed at B. The dimple in the snow behind the hind leg prints showed he was sitting up looking around for danger.

C and D show sharp maneuvers where the rabbit's hind feet prints are in front of the fore feet prints, indicating great speed. D, E and F show leaps and dodges in a desperate attempt to escape an enemy. What enemy?

At G drops of blood appeared; more at H. The cause of all this must be air-borne, and at point I there were the marks of a pair of broad strong wings. What bird, which raptor, would that be?

Sketch by Ernest Thompson Seton, explained in the text.

The end of the trail was at J, where there lay the remains of a partly eaten cottontail. If the bird had been an eagle, it would have carried its prey away, not left it there. So was that hunter a hawk or an owl?

That raptor told us which it was when it stepped in the snow. Seton's sketch at K shows that a hawk's footprint has three toes pointing forwards and one toe pointing backwards. An owl has two toes pointing forwards, two backwards. So this was an owl; but which species of owl?

Careful search by Seton found a downy feather stuck on a small sapling at the site of the kill. It bore three broad bars, which told Seton that a barred owl was the slayer of the cottontail.

That masterpiece of detective work shows how expert Seton was in reading faint clues in Nature. This knowledge was gained by years of watching the sights and listening to the sounds during hours spent in the woods and fields of Canada, North Dakota, and the West. Much of his expertise was absorbed by befriending and listening to the native Indians of his day. He lived from 1860 to 1946.

In recognition of E.T. Seton's many writings that reflect his tracking expertise, refer to the legend on page 283.

X. HISTORY

People Who Bond With Birds

There is an occasional person who seems to have a special relationship or rapport with a certain bird or with any bird. Remember the pirate who nurtured a parrot that perched on his shoulder. Or the elderly person in the city square surrounded by pigeons which he was feeding. And the person on whose head the wild songbird perched, seemingly in preference to other people.

There's a true story, preserved in a movie, of some people who had tamed some geese and a sandhill crane in Canada. They housed them in a small trailer for transportation. When it was time to come back to the United States, they were stopped at the border and told by the border patrol they could not transport these birds into the States. So they had to shoo their birds away and drive their car and trailer across the border without them. But after stopping a short distance into the States, they saw their birds fly across the border and join them, as the agents stood by helplessly!

Some people have a rapport with mammals, too. I know of one young man who worked in a zoo, who was able to hold a wild wolverine in his lap, while other zoo workers would be attacked if they ventured into the wolverines' cage. There is a horse trainer who is able to take any wild stallion and talk to it for an hour or two, calm it down, place a bridle and saddle on it, and ride it. He understood what the horse was thinking by watching its ears, its head and tail, and general posture and actions, and gained its complete confidence and trust.

St. Francis of Assisi lived in a town in central Italy in the late 12th Century and early 13th Century, but was no ordinary Catholic saint. He had an amazing rapport with animals, especially birds, and a great love and appreciation of nature. Legend recalls he tamed a man-eating wolf and induced it to live docilely among the people of a nearby town, who fed it. It is told that at a place where a large number of crows, rooks, magpies, wood pigeons and bullfinches were present they did not fly away when he approached them but listened to his sermon to them. The birds allegedly spread their wings, stretched their necks, opened their bills, and looked at him. This sounds like the actions of baby birds when begging food from their parents.

Once he met a boy taking to market some wild turtle-doves he had caught and persuaded the boy

Statue of St. Francis of Assisi, the lover of birds, in a private garden in Bismarck, North Dakota.
Photograph by Kenneth J. Johnson

to give them to him. St. Francis then took the rescued birds (*Streptopelia turtur*) to his friary, made nests for them and tamed them. Once when swallows (*Hirundo rustica*) were shrieking and chirping so loudly the audience couldn't hear him talk, he asked the swallows to be quiet, which they did until he finished his sermon.

What do these people have in common? What is their secret? For what it's worth, this writer feels the person must be sincere; creatures seem to be able to sense if one is faking it. Some of our body language should be to move slowly, speak softly and make yourself seem small so you will not appear threatening. Study the creature and learn what its body language means, so you will speak its language. ("When in Rome do as the Romans do.") Try to think like the creature thinks. What are its fears, its cravings, its desires, its needs, its instincts? Then accommodate yourself to those. ("Do unto others what you would have them do unto you.") I would say love them, but that word has been abused and twisted to mean other things. But the thought occurs, isn't all this quite what the Holy Scriptures teaches about what our interactions with other humans should be?

Nature photographer picturing a flock of dunlins. Photograph by Terje O. Nordvik

Birds On U.S. Postage Stamps

In 1982 the U.S. Postal Service issued fifty commemorative postage stamps, one for each state bird. These birds were chosen by non-birders as their favorite, and were picked since they were the most conspicuous and most familiar and cherished.

In the Deep South the mockingbird was the obvious choice for Arkansas, Florida, Mississippi, Tennessee and Texas. To the north the cardinal was chosen by Illinois, Indiana, Kentucky, North Carolina, Ohio, Virginia and West Virginia. To the west the western meadowlark won with Kansas, Montana, Nebraska, North Dakota, Oregon and Wyoming.

These states went for imported birds: South Dakota voted for the ring-necked pheasant because of its popularity with hunters; Delaware and Rhode Island, with their scarcity of wild life, went for chickens – "blue hen" for the former and Rhode Island Red for the latter. American robin won with Connecticut, Michigan and Wisconsin. American goldfinch was favored by Iowa, New Jersey and Washington. Massachusetts and Maine chose black-capped chickadee; Missouri and New York both picked eastern bluebird; and Idaho and Nevada the mountain bluebird.

Other birds, chosen by lone states, include yellow-shafted flicker, Alabama; willow ptarmigan, Alaska; cactus wren, Arizona; California quail, California; lark bunting, Colorado; brown thrasher, Georgia; nene, Hawaii; brown pelican. Louisiana; Baltimore oriole, Maryland; common loon, Minnesota; purple finch, New Hampshire; road runner, New Mexico; scissor-tailed flycatcher, Oklahoma; ruffed grouse, Pennsylvania; Carolina wren, South Carolina; hermit thrush, Vermont. After the Mormon settlers' harvest was being ruined by grasshoppers California gulls saved the crops, so Utah's choice was inevitable for the California gull to be its state bird. A famous statue of these gulls in Salt Lake City is in honor of this bird.

These choices all testify to what a discerning job each state's committee has done. It seems the general public has a feel for birds in general, and especially for that bird which is the essence of that particular state.

In the twenty-five years since the USPS printed those fifty state bird stamps, by my count it has issued bird stamps an amazing seventy-six times! The USPS-appointed committee for choosing subjects picks things which the public has requested and which people will buy, since most of those stamps will be saved and mounted in stamp albums, yielding a profit for the postal service.

The bald eagle, our national symbol, is the most popular choice, being on stamps twenty times since 1982, from the 22 cents denomination up to the $14 face value one.

The white dove, the symbol of love and peace, has been on stamps with a love theme several times. American folk art was honored by four decoys: redhead, mallard, canvasback and "broadbill" (scaup?). Audubon's paintings are portrayed twice, with scarlet tanager and western tanager. Five lovable hummingbirds made their debut: ruby-throated, broad-billed, Costa's, rufous and calliope.

The USPS went outside North America to give avian philatelic status to eight: Antillean Euchoria, green-throated carib, crested honeycreeper, cardinal honeyeater, iiwi, king penguin, black-necked crane and parakeet. The birds of prey that made the list include kestrel, snowy owl, elf owl and bald eagle. Water birds are represented by mallard (not the decoy), wood duck, mute swan, Canada goose, great blue heron, snowy egret, whooping crane, flamingo, roseate spoonbill and common loon.

To complete the long list, land birds include:: bobwhite, Gambel's quail, ring-necked pheasant, common domestic rooster, white-winged dove, red-bellied woodpecker, Gila woodpecker, red-headed woodpecker, barn swallow, blue jay, brown-headed nuthatch, cactus wren, cardinal, mockingbird, rose-breasted grosbeak, eastern bluebird, mountain bluebird, eastern towhee and Bachman's sparrow.

On March 14, 2003 the U.S. Postal Service issued a commemorative postage stamp picturing a brown pelican. This marked the 100th anniversary of the establishment of the Pelican Island National Wildlife Refuge, the first unit in today's system of over 500 refuges.

While there were 76 bird species featured in the 21 years from the 1982 state birds to 2007, there were only 17 species pictured in the 36 years from 1946 to 1982. Of these seventeen, all were duplicated after 1982 except six (great gray owl, barred owl, great horned owl, California condor, light Brahma rooster and great white heron. Doesn't this indicate that interest in birds is indeed increasing?

Bird Watching One Hundred Years Ago

Wouldn't it be interesting to know what it was like to be interested in birds one hundred years ago? Chester Reed first copyrighted in 1906 his books, "Bird Guide: Land Birds East of the Rockies" and "Bird Guide: Water Birds, Game Birds and Birds of Prey East of the Rockies." They offer a fascinating insight into that area in time. Both books are shaped to fit into one's pocket, being 5-1/2 inches long, 3-1/4 inches high, and 1/2 inch thick.

Each bird occupies one page, with its picture in color on the outer edge of the page. Most of the page consists of the text for that bird, which occupies the part of the page next to the binding. Now for the surprise. Chester Reed, author and curator in ornithology in Massachusetts, innovated a system of assigning each bird its own number! In the water birds book number one was awarded to the western grebe, considered the most primitive bird east of the Rockies. The loon was number seven.

The least primitive bird in Reed's sequence, the last bird in the land birds book, was the bluebird as number 766. Now the second edition of the American Birding Association Checklist listed 838 species, but that list included the many

CAROLINA PAROQUET

382. *Conuropsis carolinensis.* 12½ inches

Adults have the fore part of the head orange, while young birds have the head entirely green, with only a trifle orange on the forehead.

With the exception of the Thick-Billed Parrot, which is very rarely found in southern Arizona, these are the only members of the Parrot family in the United States. They were once abundant throughout the southern states, but are now nearly extinct. They are found in heavily timbered regions, usually along the banks of streams, where they feed upon seeds and berries.

Note.—A sharp, rolling "kr-r-r-r." (Chapman.)

Nest.—Supposed to be in hollow trees, where they lay from three to five white eggs (1.31 x 1.06).

Range.—Formerly the southern states, but now confined to the interior of Florida and, possibly, Indian Territory.

17

Reproduction of the Carolina paroquet page from the
Bird Guide: Land Birds East of the-Rockies, 1906

birds west of the 100th meridian, plus all the accidentals and vagrants and exotics and flukes and imports observed in 100 years of intensive searching since 1906.

When you learn what happened in the 20th Century you are in for a jolt. Using Reed's numbering system, number 32, the razor-billed auk, is gone. No. 33, the great auk, is extinct. Only seventy were still alive on date of publication. No. 156, the Labrador duck, is no more. Reed's book says no. 266, Eskimo curlew, is "very rare now anywhere;" today it is gone forever. No. 306, heath hen, has been extirpated. No. 315, passenger pigeon, has been slaughtered to extinction. Our Southern U.S.' own native parrot, the Carolina paroquet, no. 382, is no longer with us. Ivory-billed woodpecker, no. 392, is a thing of the past. I trust the lone newly discovered Arkansas bird is unable to prolong the species. No. 551, dusky seaside sparrow, is now only a memory. No. 640, Bachman's warbler, is no longer found. So ten native species have become extinct since Reed's book was written!

That numbering system is no longer used, for one reason because one bird species may split into two or more, or two may be lumped together into one species. The eastern meadowlark, no. 501, was found to be different from its

IVORY-BILLED WOODPECKER

392. *Campephilus principalis.* 20 inches

Male with a scarlet crest, female with a black one.

These are the largest and most rare of the Woodpeckers found within our borders. Their decline in numbers is due, to a certain extent, to the killing of them because of their size and beauty, but chiefly on account of cutting off of a great deal of the heavy timber where they nest. They are very powerful birds and often scale the bark off the greater portion of a tree in search for insects and grubs, while they will bore into the heart of a living tree to make their home.

Note.—A shrill two-syllabled shriek or whistle.

Nest.—In holes of large trees in impenetrable swamps. On the chips at the bottom of the cavity, they lay from three to six glossy, pure white eggs (1.45 x 1.00).

Range.—Formerly the South Atlantic States and west to Texas and Indian Territory, but now confined to a few isolated portions of Florida and, possibly, Indian Territory.

23

Reproduction of the ivory-billed woodpecker page from the
Bird Guide: Land Birds East of the-Rockies, 1906

Reproduction of the Bachman warbler page from the *Bird Guide: Land Birds East of the-Rockies*, 1906

western counterpart after the numbering system was put into practice, so the western meadowlark had to become no. 501.1, awkward at best. Introduced birds, such as the ring-necked pheasant and English sparrow, received no number, but both were given three asterisks (***) instead, even more awkward. But the starling, also introduced, got no. 493. Why? It seems the starling was living in Greenland, which was then considered to be part of North America.

In Reed's day his books were popular enough to justify two more editions, but bird watching was regarded as being practiced only by little old ladies in tennis shoes, and birders were self-conscious enough to hide their hobby from the public so people wouldn't make fun of them. Next, Roger Tory Peterson enters the scene in 1934 with his *"Field Guide to the Birds Giving Field Marks of all Species Found East of the Rockies."* Peterson discerned one or more distinguishing characters of each bird which could be seen from a distance, and made an arrow on his picture pointing to that feature. Thus the birder knew what to look for as soon as the bird was spotted in the field, and could thereby identify the species instead of holding the bird in the hand after shooting it, as the pioneer ornithologists had to do. That revolutionary idea of pointing out each bird's unique field marks, which he said he learned from Ernest Thompson Seton the Canadian naturalist, transformed the hobby into an endeavor which was welcomed by the general public. Birding has become acceptable.

As years went by, more and more people took up the hobby, especially as several bird guides were published that were great improvements over Peterson's. His field guide showed the bird's picture on one page, the text for that bird on another page, and in later editions when a range map was added, that was on a third page. Such fumbling around for information, which cooled off many birders' ardor, was eliminated when later authors put the picture, text, and range map all on one page. Now there are several newer field guides, and they keep getting better all the time.

Today there are more birders than hunters, and more birders than golfers. And many birding magazines, newspaper columns for birders, bird clubs, parks' and states' and regional bird check lists, special birding equipment, birding tours and field guides are all in great demand, in addition to seminars and conventions.

Goldie's Bluebird Houses

Florian Goldmann, a retired car dealership service manager, lives in Mandan, North Dakota. His original concern over bluebirds' shortage of nesting sites started him on a hobby of building bird houses for them. Goldie – everyone calls him Goldie – since has become noteworthy for his famous hobby of building nest boxes for bluebirds, then placing them and monitoring the birds' welfare weekly.

He has done that for 32 years, mounting them beginning in April on roadside fence posts over a large area. Then he retraced these routes every weekend, inspecting each box carefully, recording which birds occupied them and noting their progress in nest building, egg laying, and success in raising their broods.

One route went southeast as far as Huff, another reached west to New Salem, another south along Highway 6, and a fourth reached north into Oliver County. Each route had about 35 bluebird houses on it! He has built a total of 303 boxes, recorded their data in two large books, and reported his findings each year to the North Dakota State Game and Fish Department.

WHAT'S WRONG WITH THIS PICTURE?

Goldie found landowners unanimously to be receptive and cooperative, although he has found over those 32 years a total of twenty boxes that have been destroyed by shot gun blasts. Occasionally some stranger will steal a box.

He always faced the box to the east or south, for protection from wind and rain. One of Goldie's boxes can last for 30 years.

Each box is made from nine inch pieces of one inch white pine. The front is six inches wide. The top slants forward, and has a tar-paper roof. The front lifts up by means of a nail midway into each side at each edge of that piece of wood, to act as a hinge, for a look at the inside. Another nail is loosely slanted into each side at the bottom of the front so as to remove the nail by hand for weekly inspection and for ease in cleaning out the box at season's end. With this maneuver the upper part of the front pushes into the box as the lower part moves outward towards the viewer. When Goldie approached the nest box first he covered the 1-1/2 inch diameter round hole with his left hand, then he opened the front with his right hand to reach up into the box to trap for digital inspection of whatever was inside.

What Goldie has found inside is often a surprise. The occupant is not always a bluebird! If the nest builder is away, he could tell which species of bird built the nest. Wrens like these bird boxes, and they use twigs as nesting material. Bluebirds use grass. House sparrows use grass, straw, paper and miscellaneous things to build a huge pile to fill the box with a mess. Tree swallows create a neat little nest of grass which they delight to adorn with feathers, especially white feathers. Goldie had fun bringing along downy white chicken feathers, and he has trained the tree swallows to pluck them from his fingers from midair!

But about three times a year he surprised a young bull snake in one of his boxes. It had climbed up the fence post, was small enough to enter the entry hole, and crawled inside. There it ate the bluebird or its eggs or young. But after swallowing them, each formed a lump in its body, a swelling so thick that its girth was wider than the entry hole. So the bull snake was trapped inside the nest box!

Every time I see where some neophyte has placed a peg below the entry hole of his self-made bird box to serve as a perch, I cringe. Goldie has learned not to provide a perch there, for if it is present a house sparrow will use it to reach inside to viciously peck the head of the bluebird until it kills the bird, whether it be a young or an adult.

He knows about the harmful effects of paint on birds, so he never painted his bird houses. In consideration of the young birds ready to fly, he roughened the wood in the box below the exit hole so the young can climb up to the hole more easily. He usually used an assembly line technique to cut out several pieces of each part of the house before proceeding to the next piece.

Goldie has witnessed the struggle between bluebirds and tree swallows for occupancy of a bird box. The first bird to claim the site in springtime is hard to evacuate. The bluebird's earliest arrival date is March 21, and its length is 7 inches, the tree swallow's April 4, and length 5-3/4 inches, so the former should have the advantage. But the tree swallow often is the better fighter. Goldie has helped stop this fighting by placing another bird box 30 feet away.

The New Kids On The Block
In The World Of Birds

It has been said that our world is entrusted to us, and we are responsible to those who come after us for its condition when we bequeath it to them. So, in respect to birds, we are obliged to influence appropriately which or whether a certain species should be introduced. Alien birds have had a tremendous effect on our native birds.

The state of North Dakota has been impinged in this way. We can learn by noting what happened in the state which has experienced the greatest effect from avian immigration. That state is Hawaii.

Before Captain Cook discovered the Hawaiian Islands they contained only the native birds and animals and plants. Since he opened it up (he was killed by the Hawaiians in 1799) ever since then there has been a steady invasion of foreigners: humans, animals and plants, and the slogan the Paradise of the Pacific to some extent has become a euphemism. For instance, rats jumped ships and invaded homes and damaged sugar and pineapple plantations. Someone recalled that in India mongooses killed rats, so they imported mongooses. But then it turned out that mongooses were active in the daytime, while rats foraged at night. So the two got along famously and each went their separate way, creating two pests.

Now there are two groups of birds in the Hawaiian Islands, the endemic species now relegated to the mountains, and the immigrants living on the plantations and in the cities.

The newcomer humans felt compelled to "improve" (change and conform) the land by bringing in exotic flowers, shrubs, trees, birds and domestic animals. These new people missed birds they left behind when they moved, so for years they brought in foreign birds. They even formed a society, the Hui Manu, who scoured the world searching for beautiful songbirds to introduce, without a thought as to the impact that would result.

So now look for
barred dove from
Malaysia, very tame,
now common around
residents. Mynah from
India walks around
lawns in groups and
roosts in large very noisy
colonies. White-eye
from Japan flits quickly
from bush to bush,

Common myna.
Photograph by Jan Ove Gjershaug

behaving like our mainland chickadee. Strawberry finch, near
Pearl Harbor, flocks along edges of sugar cane fields. Rice
bird from Malaysia is in large flocks which rise in unison
from open grassy fields. It has brown back and head, black
and white scalloped breast. Brazilian cardinal, from South
America, with gray back, white breast, flaming red head,
is around residences. House finch from California roosts
on telephone wires and favors bird feeders, along with our
cardinal from our Eastern states. And, of course, the house
sparrow which arrived uninvited and unwanted as stowaways
on ships, and does not stay in one niche.

Today one of the best places to still look for the native
Hawaiian birds, which still cling to the original tropical forest
habitat, is in the Hawaii Volcanoes National Park, on the
Big Island of Hawaii. There look for the apapane, crimson
with black wings and tail, which flits among the tops of ohia
trees, feeding on the nectar of its flowers, called lehua. The
iiwi, bright vermilion with black and white wings and a long
down-curved bill, feeds on lehua nectar and on insects. The
amakihi, green above and yellow below, feeds on insects on
the same ohia trees. The akepa, reddish orange male and
green and yellow female, moves about in flocks.

It seems that the native species weren't able to adjust
to large fields of one crop, nor to buildings, nor to asphalt
pavements, so they left an area devoid of birds when they
retreated along with their forest habitat. The void this left

was filled by those exotics which found it compatible. Then everyone lived happily forever after; or perhaps I am missing something?

When North Dakota was changed from native prairie to pasture and cropland, the new niche this created was filled by the introduced Mongolian pheasant, as our native game birds found it hard to adapt. In theory, if a new niche is created to which the natives can't adjust, a compatible alien is acceptable. In practice, can we forecast whether that newcomer will go on to adjust beyond that niche and even go so far as to compete with and threaten the natives? I am reminded of the horrible example in plant life where the Georgia State Highway Department imported the kudzu vine to stop erosion on highway embankments. This it did. But now I saw a parking lot and entire buildings completely covered by kudzu, rendering that area unusable in spite of desperate but vain efforts to eradicate the kudzu.

Like the new kid on the block, that new bird is probably here to stay, for better or for worse.

How European Birds Got To America

Upon inquiring into how American birds got here, it seems there were almost as many ways as there are families of birds.

Early ornithologists considered American pelicans and European pelicans to be identical, so they called them both the same species. Therefore the two populations of today must have had a common ancestor, with a continuity of range. That continuity of range would have been, ornithologist Dr. F. M. Chapman postulated, in the late Tertiary Period of geologic time, when there was a warm temperate circumpolar climate. So those ancient pelicans lived in what is now the Arctic. Then as the climate changed toward the cold Ice Age, the pelicans were forced south from the chilling mild Arctic, some to America, some to Europe. I quote Bent in page 292 of his book, *Life Histories of North American Petrels and Pelicans and Their Allies.*

The magpie in America is a different species from the magpie in Europe, but the two used to be considered the same species. So America's magpie arrived here as a matter of decree by scientists!

The cattle egret arrived here on its own. A native of southern Europe and northwest Africa, it repeatedly got caught up in the trade winds that continually blow westward close to the equator. They ended up in the area of the Caribbean Islands. Since the land in French Guiana, on the northeast coast of South America, had been cleared of forest to provide pasture land for cattle, the egrets survived and multiplied there. This South American environment matched their Old World homeland where they lived by catching insects stirred up by grazing cattle. From Guiana they migrated north, finding pasture land along the way. In the United States they spread rapidly and widely, always associating with cattle.

The English sparrow, or house sparrow, was introduced by someone figuring American birds were inadequate in curbing insect pests. They proved to be of no help; their beak is that of a seed-eater. Instead, the house sparrow has become the great pest that drives away native birds, kills their young, usurps bird houses, and adapts to cities and buildings as did their Old World ancestors. Most house sparrows also got to America – and all over the world – by being stowaways on ships traveling from the Old World to the New World and worldwide.

The starling used to be listed as a *bona fide* American because it lived in Greenland, which was considered to be part of North America When geologists and politicians decreed otherwise, that bird became an imposter, so the starlings in the U. S, and Canada are now considered as having been introduced, since there is no evidence that the Greenland birds moved to mainland North America. Why are they here now, then? Someone got the inspiration to introduce here every species of bird mentioned by Shakespeare in his plays! Shakespeare mentioned 57 species of birds. Fortunately that starry eyed visionary died long before he achieved his goal.

Colorful cage birds such as parakeets came as captives from their native lands to the Southern United States, primarily Florida. There they escaped their cages and adapted to subtropical American life. The American Ornithological Union and American Birding Association agree that to be accepted into our fauna a species must survive here for fifteen generations. Several species have done so, such as some parakeets.

The Eurasian collared-dove has the most spectacular story of its invasion. Its homeland was southeastern Europe and Asia and Japan. Then in the 1900s it spread to western Europe and the British Isles. From there humans transported it to the Bahama Islands in the mid 1970s. Then by itself it emigrated to Florida by the 1980s. The next thirty years witnessed a dramatic spread like wildfire over the South, the Atlantic Coastal States, and especially the Midwest, state by state.

This population explosion in the United States is an

example of a new bird species finding an unoccupied niche in the new civilization established by the growth of this country. This Eurasian collared-dove found is own niche between the respective realms of the rock pigeon and the mourning dove. It gets along fine with other birds.

The barnyard chicken is a domesticated bird from Europe. Since it doesn't live wild in North America it can't be considered a member of the North American birds. But the jungle fowl of Kokee, Kauai is the same species as the domesticated chicken. The jungle fowl has lived in a completely wild state in Kokee for many generations, thus qualifying it as a recognized member of Hawaiian fauna, having escaped from the Polynesians who migrated to the Hawaiian Islands in 400 A. D. Hawaii is one of the 50 United States, which nation is considered to be North American. So by a stretch of semantics this author includes the jungle fowl here!

Many thousands of years ago there was a land bridge between Eurasia and North America, which bridge today is submerged by the shallow Bering Strait. That land bridge allowed the ancestors of today's American Indians to migrate across from Siberia to Alaska, and provided opportunistic birds also a chance to move across. Bluethroat and northern wheatear now breed in Alaska and winter in Eurasia. These American and European birds are exactly the same species.

Several wide-ranging Atlantic Ocean birds, such as the Manx shearwater and Wilson's storm-petrel, are listed in both American and European field guides because they live in both areas, intermittently and interchangeably.

So it is that most birds, being able to fly and move around, always have had and do have the ability to change their ranges, abetted by changing climate and food supplies and nesting sites.

Incredible Edible Birds

Here are some examples of incredible edible birds.

The French have placed a goose on a board and nailed it onto the board by using broad-headed nails on the webs between the goose's toes. With the goose unable to move away, the person then grabbed its neck, forced open its bill, and crammed food down its maw. After it became abnormally fat, the goose was killed and its flesh and liver eaten as gourmet food.

Modern day chicken farms and turkey farms have huge buildings holding thousands of birds jammed together and fed daily. This mass production is so large a man is hired to walk daily through the shed picking up any dead birds. In Asia the chicken farms are similar, but less hygienic. The crowded flocks are prone to harbor chickens sick with bird flu. The workers there are in much closer contact with the birds than in American farms, so they have caught bird flu from the birds. Epidemiologists worry that the sick chickens may transmit the virus to other birds that migrate to Alaska. They also worry the virus may mutate enough to spread from infected chicken farm workers to other humans. As of this writing, that calamity has not happened.

With the understanding that an egg is a form of a bird because it is delivered from a bird and develops into a form of life with wings and feathers that is called a bird, we place a chicken's egg in this essay. People prone to allergies are often allergic to eggs.

Provocative food testing is done by an allergist when certain symptoms come after eating eggs. To prove this suspicion, the patient completely refrains from eating anything that contains eggs or has been made from eggs, then abstains long enough so all traces of egg which had been eaten before the test are gone. The persistence or absence of symptoms are then noted.

Next, when free of symptoms the eggs are again eaten freely. If symptoms promptly reappear they are blamed on the eggs. Such symptoms could be asthma, eczema, itching, nausea, vomiting, or diarrhea.

If a person is allergic to eggs he should not get one of the vaccines that was made from eggs, such as the influenza vaccine or the yellow fever vaccine. Tissue from a chicken embryo is used to culture mumps and measles vaccines and is supposed to be safe, but if it were my allergic child getting vaccinated I would consult my pediatrician first.

Raising squabs for eating is a small industry for breeders of rock pigeons. I ate one of these young rock pigeons, called squabs, in a Chinese restaurant once. It was jet black, not appetizing to look at, but it was edible–for me an adventure in eating. I'm sure there are more conventional methods of preparing a squab.

When I was a boy I had a pigeon coop, and my bird notebook for 1931 has this entry for Sunday, August 2: "We had 5 young ones killed some time ago and we ate them. Net profit 60¢ (15¢ each). (Mine didn't count.) Russ [neighbor young man] broke their necks. Then recently we gave 4 others to Olson's. [the other next door neighbors] Net profit $.60. Now I have 4 young ones left." There is no record of how they were prepared, and no mention of how we enjoyed the meal of those squabs.

Consider this nursery rhyme:

> Sing a song of sixpence a pocket full of rye.
> Four and twenty blackbirds baked in a pie.
> When the pie was opened the birds began to sing.
> O wasn't that a dainty dish to set before a king!
> The king was in his counting house counting out his money,
> The queen was in the parlor eating bread and honey.
> The maid was in the garden hanging out the clothes,
> When down came a blackbird and pecked off the nose!

Is it hard to make sense out of that nursery rhyme? Consider this interpretation:

It is a happy occasion when the harvest is so good that one can fill one's pockets with rye grains. In Europe, including England, in medieval times it was common practice to catch

"When the pie was opened, the birds began to sing."

songbirds to cook or bake or stew and eat. So the court jester caught some, but while they were still alive placed them in a deep dish pie plate, covered it with a baked pie crust, and presented it to the king as a blackbird pie. The crust was thick and hard enough to use as a scoop. When the king broke open the crust the blackbirds cried out.

The peasants' conception of how the king and queen and maid spent their time is shown in the rhyme. One of the blackbirds that were imprisoned wreaked its revenge on the only castle dweller available that was not indoors, by pecking off her nose.

There is evidence in legends and old literature that that same joke would be played on a wealthy knight, after which a valid pie would be served him.

Dr. Alan Van Norman, a widely traveled birder, reports that on Madagascar the people have converted much of the island to rice fields, and continuously use for food all the mammals and birds they can catch on the rest of the land.

Norwegian chickens taste like fish because they are fed fish meal.

Coots will eat anything, so they function as scavengers of the marshland and potholes. That affects the taste of its flesh, so hunters don't harvest them. Canvasbacks are the favorite duck of the epicure because its principal food is the roots of the water plant valisneria. Alaskan mallards eat dead salmon and salmon eggs, prairie mallards eat grain from stubble fields, Southern mallards eat rice. So what the mallard tastes like depends on where it was shot. Mergansers are fish eaters, so are not considered good table birds. The hooded merganser, however, is better eating because it eats more insects than it eats fish.

For generations people have survived by eating birds, the culture determining which bird. Hunters today still like to add birds to their larder. Today various birds are considered as a gourmet food to experience

Ibises

Three birds have held prominent positions in the folk lore of civilizations. The raven, as discussed in the chapter on Ravens, holds this position in contemporary cultures.

The eagle held the grand position among birds in Biblical times. We cite Psalms 103:5; Isaiah 40:31; Deuteronomy 28:49.

In ancient times, in early and middle Egyptian culture, the sacred ibis was venerated as a god! This ibis-god's name was Thoth. It was regarded by the Egyptians as the scribe for all the other gods.

Thoth the ibis invented writing, the ancient Egyptians divined, and was the creator of hieroglyphics, those mysterious (to us) figures portrayed on the walls of the ancient Egyptian tombs and edifices. When archeologists study those burial places today they find that a large mummy wraps up a royal human, such as a king, and a small mummy envelops a sacred ibis.

The four facsimiles of this sacred ibis along the margin of this page are accurate tracings of effigies on the walls of those structures. These show how various scribes rendered their artistic version of the sacred ibis – each different, yet all recognizable as that bird.

It is said the sacred ibis no longer lives in the valley of the Nile River in Egypt, but does live now in Ethiopia and southward, and in southern Asia. The bird feeds on insects, frogs, and water invertebrates. But it also visits garbage dumps! It seems that garbage dumps are inappropriate for a sacred bird, a small god, to honor with its venerable presence.

Why must humans be so perverse? For here is another example of people introducing a species into a foreign environment, not anticipating how that will disturb the balance of nature and create problems. When the sacred ibis was introduced into southern Europe it multiplied rapidly and now devastates breeding colonies of terns and displaces egrets from their nest sites. In winter, when egrets and terns migrate, the sacred ibis, which lacks an inherited instinct to travel south, survives by eating at garbage dumps.

Americans have been as irrational as Europeans, for they have introduced the sacred ibis in Florida. But before this foreigner becomes the cause of a catastrophe, the Internet quotes the *South Florida Sun-Sentinel* of Fort Lauderdale, Florida as saying on November 14, 2007 the Audubon Society is helping county and state and federal officials to eradicate the sacred ibis. This bird, being the same species as the ancient Egyptian, has the same bad behavior of preying on chicks and eggs of nesting colony water birds, including other species of ibises such as the white ibis.

The white ibis lives in Florida and along the Gulf Coast and rarely ventures farther inland beyond northern borders of the Gulf states. There are thousands of nests made of sticks and twigs in this bird's huge colony. The ibises form a vee as

White ibis in adult plumage. Photograph by Patricia Burke

they fly out to feed on wetlands which provide bugs, small crabs and crawfish, snails and snakes. Each morning the procession leaves the colony, and each evening it returns; how far the distance traveled depends on how far they must go for food.

With long legs and long bills their forage area is larger than a bird's that has short legs and a short bill. Any food that they stir up that moves out of their reach is seized by the larger great egret, which follows the white ibis closely as an opportunistic freeloader.

That is true for food that is on the surface. But for eating crawfish a surprising technique has been observed. The crawfish burrows a hole down through the mud to where there is water. The mud excavated to form the hole was used to create a chimney extending the hollow tube-hole higher than the surface of the mud. The white ibis breaks off pieces of mud from the chimney wall to drop down the hole. This causes the crawfish to push the mud chunks up out of the hole to reopen the hole. As the crawfish reaches the top of the bore hole doing this the white ibis seizes it and eats it! Is that instinct or learned behavior?

Crawfish eat fish spawn. When ibises eat crawfish they permit fish to multiply. Fish eat mosquito larvae. So fishermen have reason to like ibis, since they keep the mosquitoes down and boost the fish population to improve fishing. Ibises also eat young poisonous water moccasin snakes.

The scientific name of the sacred ibis is *Threskiornis aethiopicus*, derived from the Greek word *threshos* which means religious, plus the Greek *ornithos* meaning a bird; the species name *aethiopicus* means belonging to Ethiopia. Contemporary scientists find the sacred ibis in Ethiopia but no longer in Egypt.

The white ibis has the scientific genus name *Eudocimus*, from the Greek word for being very well known and greatly respected. The species name, *albus*, is Latin for white.

Carolina Paroquet

The coming of the white man produced tremendous changes in the bird life of America. Few species increased in numbers, such as the robin and the grackle. Many more species decreased in numbers, such as ducks and shorebirds. For some it was a calamity, as with the famous instance of the passenger pigeon.

The least known example of a species that was incompatible with humans is that of the Carolina paroquet. Early naturalists spoke of it as abundant in the South, which doesn't sound possible to us today. But as soon as civilization touched an area, it seems, the Carolina paroquet disappeared. In the chapter "Bird-watching One Hundred Years Ago," under section X History, the illustration from a little field guide dated 1906 says the Carolina paroquet still lives on in isolated portions of Florida. Frank M. Chapman, in his *Birds of Eastern North America*, in 1932, states there are four reasons for its extinction.

They liked fruit, and any farmer with fruit trees found that they descended on his orchard and ate all the fruit, or damaged and destroyed what they didn't eat. Of course, the only recourse for the farmer was to destroy those birds.

Professional bird-catchers, encouraged by those whose commercial interest was hurt by these birds, or who wanted them removed because of their raucous discordant screechy squawks, trapped and bagged them in enormous numbers.

Being typical of members of the parrot family, their plumage was gorgeous if not gaudy. The head and bill were bright yellow with a flaming orange face. The body and long tail were brilliant green, plus a touch of sky blue on the outer edge of the wing. Such an array of colors is always attractive to humans, as ornaments to wear, or display to decorate, or admire in a bird cage.

Sportsmen in early days before conservation was a concept slaughtered them wantonly because they were conspicuous targets, and because it was heroic to demonstrate how many they could kill.

Even Chapman states he saw thirteen and killed four near

Lake Okeechobee, Florida, in 1904. Those were the last ever seen in the wild.

Before we condemn Chapman, though, we must be reminded that in those early days the pioneer naturalists discovered, studied, described and preserved all the new species of birds by first shooting them. I shudder to think of how many birds James J. Audubon killed in his lifetime of wandering over North America painting all the species of birds he could sight down the barrel of his rifle. Have you ever wondered why Audubon painted his birds in such awkward unlikely postures? A dead bird does not have a life-like posture, so he laid out the corpse to show certain features he wished to emphasize. We must believe the birds died for a worthy cause.

The thing that is amazing about this bird is that the illustration shows how the hooked bill was powerful enough to cut a hole in soft wood for its nest; the short legs with two toes forward and two toes backward made for poor walking. Being a good climber and a strong flier made up for that.

FIG. 49. Carolina Paroquet.
Picture from page 131 of
Birds of Eastern North America,
by Frank M. Chapman.

XI. WHAT'S IN A NAME?

How Birds Got Their Names

In Genesis 2:19-20 God assigned to Adam the happy project of naming all the birds. (This isn't male chauvinism; at the time God hadn't yet removed one of Adam's ribs for creating the first woman, the *Bible* says.) So, as people spread over the world and encountered new species, it was natural that they gave names to each new bird seen and heard.

With over 700 species in North America alone, how were all those names determined? The birds themselves provided clues – how they looked, what sounds they made, where they lived, what unique action distinguished each.

Some birds get their names from the sounds they make. Most people who listened felt these birds were very happy, for they named them warbling vireo, whistling duck, laughing gull and whooping crane. And the chipping sparrow and clapper rail and trumpeter swan were in a good mood. How the screech owl felt is uncertain. Maybe the mourning dove felt sad because of what happened to the following bird. The old-squaw, being garrulous like an elderly Indian woman, violated political correctness, so now it must be called long-tailed duck. The saw-whet owl is all business, making a sound like a carpenter sharpening his saw.

A lot of birds announce themselves, for they verbalize their names. At a prairie pothole hear the killdeer, godwit and willet. In our woods listen for the bobwhite, cuckoo, flicker, pewee, phoebe, jay, chickadee, veery and towhee. Out on the prairie hear the pipit and dickcissel. South of here at night chuck-will's-

Chachalaca in Bentsen.
Photograph by Kenneth J. Johnson

widow, whip-poor-will and poor-will will verbalize. Along the Rio Grande will be the noisy kiskadee and chachalaca. The murre is an ocean bird that announces its name.

Some birds get their names because of what they do. The shearwater and the skimmer fly along the surface of the ocean, the shearwater almost touching the water as each wave moves up or down, while the skimmer's lower bill, being longer, scrapes the surface of the water to pick up food. The turnstone gets its food by turning over pebbles on the beach. The oyster-catcher's bill is flattened laterally to stab open mollusk bivalves.

The woodpecker digs holes into old trees to get at worms, while the sapsucker digs into the bark, then later returns to drink the sap oozing out of each hole, and eat insects caught in the sap. The brown creeper doesn't pierce the bark, but eats insects hiding in crevices in the bark. In creeks in South Dakota's Black Hills, a songbird, the dipper, flies along the water then dives in and walks along the creek bottom. A wagtail move its tail up and down, not from side to side like a dog. Of course, a warbler warbles, a nutcracker cracks nuts, a seed-eater eats seeds, a gnat-catcher catches gnats and a flycatcher catches flies. The mockingbird is aptly named because its songs mimic the songs of so many other species of birds.

In the process of being named, some birds were given adjectives so unfamiliar that a dictionary is needed to understand. So to relieve the reader of some time and effort to look it up in an unabridged dictionary, the writer offers these elucidations for the reader.

The pied-billed grebe has a bill with spots of different colors (pied). A falcated teal is adorned with long sickle-shaped (falcated) feathers which overhang the tail. The ferruginous hawk is a rusty iron color (ferruginous), while the peregrine falcon is noted for traveling (peregrine). The pomarine jaeger is named for a peculiar scale-like (pomarine) covering over its nostrils. Ruffed grouse is named for its high prominent collar (ruff). Pectoral sandpiper sports a heavily

The peregrine falcon got the name because of its traveling.
Photograph by Anders Lamberg

streaked breast (pectoral), and the semipalmated sandpiper
walks on partly webbed (semipalmated) feet. The glaucous-
winged gull wears a mantle that is sea-green colored with a
gray-blue cast (glaucous). A flammulated owl is so named
because it is ruddy (flammulated). Pileated woodpecker sports
a crest (a pileus, or cap) extending from its bill to its nape.

How the loggerhead shrike got its name is obscure; it has
a large head for its body size, but loggerhead means blockhead
or dunce. The plumbeous vireo is lead colored; the chemical
symbol for lead, or plumbium, is Pb. Pechora pipit, which
visits Attu, the westernmost island in Alaska, is named after
a river in northern Russia. Bohemian waxwing is a wandering
visitor in flocks from the north in winter; Bohemian is a
synonym for roving.

The blackburnian warbler name dates back to the 1700s
when someone named the bird after a bird-watching English
woman whose brother collected birds in North America. The
prothonotary warbler is colored like a chief clerk. Black poll

warbler's name makes more sense, for poll means top of the head, which really is black in this bird. Finally, the familiar cardinal is named after a chief Roman Catholic official dressed in deep red clothing.

sparrow

Scientific Names

With each bird's description in your bird guide is a pair of foreign words. This binomial nomenclature is that bird's unique Latin or Greek name. Why?

When the average person sees a bird they call it by the name of a known bird it resembles, so the new bird is misnamed. When European immigrants saw a red-breasted songbird in America it reminded them of their European robin back home, so they called the new bird a robin. Many people use the terms grouse and partridge and prairie chicken interchangeably. Any little brown bird is a sparrow. A buzzard could be a vulture or a Buteo hawk or a carrion crow. A teal or a merganser or a gadwall is still a duck to many people. A bird often has a name used locally, which name is unknown in another part of the country.

Such confusion and disorganization was unacceptable in any science. Two hundred fifty years ago Carl von Linne, a Swede, devised a brilliant system of classification of all plants and animals. In his honor scientists Latinized his name to Linnaeus.

A species is a group of plants or animals whose members differ among themselves only in minor details and who can interbreed fertilely. A genus is a group of similar plants or animals composed of one or more species. Linnaeus gave each species a name consisting of two Latin words. The first word was capitalized and is the name of the genus to which he assigned that species. The second word was not capitalized and is the Latinized name given to that species. That binomial is permanent and universally accepted by all scientists. (Except in later years occasionally more knowledgeable experts felt that new discoveries justified adjusting the binomial to recognize more accurate interrelationships.)

Since each species of bird has a binomial name using either Latin or Greek words, or English words with Latin endings, these identify, classify or describe the bird. Learning the meaning of these two words gives an understanding of the bird, and an insight into why the scientist named it so. Editors of any publication using the English language print a foreign word or phrase in italics, so the bird's Linnaeaan name is always italicized. In creating a Latin name for a bird, it is the custom to use a Latin name which describes some distinctive characteristic of that bird. Or sometimes the namer honors the name of the discoverer of that bird. For instance, Couch's kingbird is named *Tyrannus couchii* because it belongs to the genus of kingbirds which act as tyrants to other birds, and a man by the name of Couch first described it in the scientific literature. Our familiar robin is *Turdus migratorius*. *Turdus* is the Latin name for thrush; the robin is one of our thrushes. It migrates every year, so *migratorius* is very appropriate. Our ever-present house sparrow is *Passer domesticus*. *Passer* is the Latin name for sparrow. The English word "domestic" means "belonging to the house or household." The house sparrow hangs around houses and buildings.

Noisy birds impressed ornithologists. The vociferous killdeer is *Charadrius vociferous*. The long-tailed duck is *Clangula hyemalis*. "Clangus" is a now-obsolete word which meant making a clanging shrill harsh sound. This duck, formerly called old-squaw, was so-called by frontiersmen, but certain sensitivities rendered that name taboo. Fortunately, scientific Latin names are immutable, so *Clangula hyemalis* remains its scientific name.

The American crow is *Corvus brachyrhynchos*. *Corvus*, the generic name, is Latin for crow. The specific name is Greek for short beaked, because the crow's beak is shorter than the raven's.

Our black-capped chickadee, close relative of titmice, used to be called *Parus atricapillus*. *Parus* for titmouse, *atri* for black, *capillus* for hair—a titmouse with black hair on its head. (Maybe the man did not know the Latin or Greek name for feather?) But then some later scientist changed its generic name to *Poecile*, which means many-colored. Do you think that is an improvement?

Our local starling is *Sturnus* (Latin for starling) *vulgaris* (Latin for common). Brown thrasher is *Toxostoma rufum*. All thrashers with down-curved bills – bow-shaped in profile – are in this genus. *Toxo* means bill, *stoma* means mouth. *Rufus* is Latin for red. So this is the bird with the bow-shaped bill that has red-brown plumage.

With *Ardea herodias*, the great blue heron, *Ardea* is Latin for heron, and *erodias* is Greek for heron. When I first saw *herodias* I whimsically thought of the Bible story (Mark 6:14- 29) in which Herodias was King Herod's brother's wife. Because Herod married her John the Baptist reprimanded Herod for this. So Herodias wanted to kill John. She got her chance when her daughter's dancing induced the intoxicated Herod to offer her anything, and Herodias told her to request John's head on a platter.

White pelican is *Pelecanus erythrorhynchos*. *Pelecan* is Greek for pelican. The specific name is Greek for red snout. Hmm; I always thought the pelican's bill is yellow, not red!

Great horned owl is *Bubo virginianus*, since *bubo* is Latin for owl and *virgin* is Latin for pure. The great horned owl, therefore, must be the pure essence of owlness. North Dakota's favorite bird, the western meadowlark, is *Sturnella neglecta*. *Sturnus* is Latin for starling, *alla* is Greek for light. *Sturnella* should mean a bird looking like a light colored starling. *Neglecta* is Latin for not gather. It may refer to early scientists neglecting to distinguish this bird from the eastern meadowlark.

Pied-billed grebe is *Podilymbus podiceps*. *Pod* is Greek for foot. *Limbus* is Latin for edge. The grebe has unique lobes on its toes. *Cephalicus* is Latin for head. If *ceps* refers to head, am I missing something here in the specific term *podiceps*?

Columba livia is the feral pigeon, the birders' rock dove. Its generic name is Latin for dove. Its specific name is from the Latin meaning livid, or black and blue, the coloration of this bird. ·

The white-breasted nuthatch is *Sitta* (Greek for

woodpecker!) *carolinensis*. The specific name refers to the life zone of the Eastern United States, where this nuthatch lives.

Yellow warbler is *Dendroica petechia*. *Dendroica* is Latin meaning eating worms or grubs. *Petechia* means little spot or patch. So the yellow warbler is a worm and grub eater who has little spots – referring to the reddish rows of spots on its yellow breast.

With ducks familiar to North Dakotans the largest genus consists of eight species, all placed in the genus *Anas*, which is Latin for a duck.

The mallard, *Anas platyrhynchos*, is from the Greek *platy* meaning broad or flat, and *rhynchos* meaning snout. Flat bills are uncommon among birds, for most are laterally compressed or rounded in cross-section.

Anas strepers is the gadwall, where *strepers* is from the Latin *strepo* to make a loud noise, as in the English "streperous," meaning loud.

Anas acuta is our pintail, where the Latin *acutus* meaning sharp must refer to this duck's most obvious feature, its pin-shaped tail.

Our wigeon, called American wigeon in contrast to the European wigeon, is *Anas americana* since it is the one that lives in North America.

Northern shoveler, *Anas clypeata*, comes from the Latin word *clypeus*, or shield. Ancient soldiers carried a round convex bronze shield, apparently called to mind by the huge bill of the shoveler.

The cinnamon teal, *Anas cyanoptera*, got its name from its blue speculum, as *cyano* is Greek for dark blue, and *ptera* is Greek for wing. This precluded the blue-winged teal from using that moniker, so it had to settle for *Anas discors*. The Latin *dis* implies deprive, and *cor* for heart; *discoras* means disagree or clash. I reckon that's how the frustrated name-giver got his revenge for having the blue-wing stolen from the blue-winged teal.

The goldeneye is *Bucephala clangula*, where the Greek

stands for *bu*, the idea of greatness, and the Greek *cephalis* for cephalus, or head. The specific name *clangula* is the Latin *clango* for resound. So the one who named this bird was impressed by its large head, and by the loud whistle in the male's mating voice, plus the loud whistling the male's wings always made in flight. The bufflehead is *Bucephala albeola*. The specific name *albeola* is from the Latin *albeo* for white. This bird's most striking field mark is the prominent white side of its large head.

Lophodytes cucullatus is the hooded merganser. *Lophodytes* is a combination of two Greek words, *lophus* meaning crest and *dytikos* meaning fond of diving. The Latin word *cucullatus* means hood. So this bird's name is an excellent description of a duck who likes to dive, and of the male for having feathers on his head which can be raised to form a huge crest with a brilliant white side and jet black frontal ridge.

Common merganser and red-breasted merganser share the generic name *Mergus*, which could be either from the Latin *mergo* for immerse or plunge or from *mergus* meaning a diver. The common merganser's species Latin name is *merganser*. The red-breasted merganser, the so-called sawbill, has the specific name *serrator* from the Latin term *serratus* meaning saw-shaped or serrated because of the saw-like edges to its bill.

Our ruddy duck was given the name *Oxyura jamaicensis*, where the generic name is a combination of Latin names *oxys* for sharp and *ura* for tail. Its upturned sharp stiff tail is distinctive. The specific name fits the three Latin words *jam* for now, or present time, plus *aio* for to affirm, plus *ensis* for sword, which fits this duck's tail.

Five ducks seen in North Dakota belong to the genus *Aythys*, which is Latin, derived from the Greek *aithuia*, meaning a gull or diving bird.

The canvasback's specific name *vallisneria* is named after the Italian naturalist Vallisneria. The favorite food of the canvasback is the water plant *Vallisneria spiralis*, named after that naturalist.

The greater scaup, *A.* (same genus) *marila*, has its specific name derived from the Latin *marinus*, or belonging to the sea. In the winter in Texas this scaup stays in the Gulf waters near the shore, while the lesser scaup stays inland near the Gulf coast. The lesser scaup is known as *A. affinis*. This species name is derived from the Latin *affinis* meaning nearby, or related to. The redhead is *A. americana*, so named because it resembles its European look-alike, the pochard. The ring-necked duck is *A. collaris*, named for its collar, which is barely visible.

Now let's translate names of sparrows. Our only winter visitor from the sparrow family is *Spizella arborea*. *Spiza* is Greek for finch, *ella* is Latin for small, for the genus name; *arbor* is Latin for tree, for the species name. So this American tree sparrow is called a small finch in a tree, although it breeds on the treeless tundra.

The field sparrow is *S. pusilla*, where *pusillus* is Latin for very little. Of the 19 sparrows listed here, nine are bigger and seven are smaller.

The clay-colored sparrow befits its name, *S. pallida*, for *pallidus* is Latin for pale, and clay is pale colored. *S. passerine* is fitting for the Bismarck's and other cities' breeding sparrow, the chipping sparrow, for the Latin *passer* means sparrow, so *passerina* would be a small sparrow.

Four of North Dakota's sparrows belong to the genus *Ammodramus*. It is Greek for sand (*ammo*) and drama (*dramus*). These four species all have beautiful dramatic songs. Baird's sparrow (*A. bairdii*) got its name from Spencer F. Baird, the American naturalist. Grasshopper sparrow (*A. savannarum*) lives on a treeless plain, so its specific name is from the Latin word *sabanum* for savanna. LeConte's sparrow (*A. lecontii*) was named for John E. Le Conte, naturalist and U.S. Army engineer. Nelson's sharp-tailed sparrow (*A. nelsonii*) is named for the first man who described the bird in the scientific literature, as was the custom in the 1800s.

Savannah sparrow, *Passerculus sandwichensis*, has the binomial as cryptic as its taxonomy, for its seventeen races could be seventeen species if there weren't so much intergradation among them. *Passerculus* means *passer* for sparrow and *culus* for of a curling form, or the posteriors, or to sit; *sandwichensis* means a piece of meat between two slices of bread, plus *ensis*, a sword or a brand. I'm mystified.

With vesper sparrow, *Pooecetes*, the genetic name, is a Latin combination of *po* (post, or possession) and *ecere* (the exclamation, there!). The specific name *gramineus* from the Latin *gramin* means grass.

The lark bunting is *Calamospiza melanocorys*. In Greek *calamos* means reed; *spiza* is Latin for finch. With *melanocorys*, *melano* is Greek for black and *korys* is Greek for crest. Certainly the lark bunting has the blackest head in the sparrow group.

Chondestes grammacus is the lark sparrow; *chondros* is Greek for cartilage, *estete* is French for decapitate, *gramma* is Greek for grammar. What went wrong here?

Harris' sparrow is *Zonotrichia* (Greek *zone* means girdle, Greek *thrix* means hair) *querula* (Latin *querulous* means complaining). When this bird's black face doesn't hide it, the necklace of black spots across the neck is distinctive. Feathers have been called hair by these people, sometimes. Presumably the scientist who named it thought its song was whining.

White-throated sparrow's name, *Z. albicollis*, is straightforward, with Latin words *albus* meaning white and *collum* meaning neck. White-crowned sparrow is *Z. leucophrys*, with Greek *leukos* meaning white and Greek *phren* meaning wind(?!).

The fox sparrow's name is *Passerella iliaca*. *Passer* is Latin for sparrow, with *ella* being Latin for small. That is odd, because this sparrow, being seven inches long, is one of the largest sparrows. And is its specific name *iliaca* from the Latin *ileum* meaning the large upper part of the hip bone, or from the Latin *iliac* meaning "belonging to that party"?

The one who named the song sparrow *Melospiza melodia* was really impressed by its beautiful singing. *Melos* is Greek for song, *spiza* is Greek for finch, and *melodia* is Latin for melody. Lincoln's sparrow is *M. lincolnii*, another example of a bird named after its discoverer. *M. georgiana* is the swamp sparrow, the third of this genus who all sing very pretty melodies. The Greek *ge* means earth, the Greek *ergon* means work. The Latin *georgicus* means husbandry or agricultural. I do not know which language was used here.

So some binomials make sense and are informational. But with many it is hard to figure out what was on the mind of the namer, what he was thinking.

The Lumpers And The Splitters

In naming birds a dilemma has surfaced, as to whether two individual birds may be the same – belong to the same species or represent two different species.

A species is a group of birds whose members differ among themselves only in minor details and who can interbreed fertilely. That's simple and clear-cut – when you're theorizing at a desk. But out in the field in real life it's not that simple. So now the experts have fallen into two groups: The lumpers gather this group of birds into one species, while the splitters find differences to justify making two separate species.

Consider the song sparrow. Its range extends from the East Coast through Central United States to Alaska out across the Aleutian /islands. The Aleutian bird is 30% larger and much darker than the Atlantic bird. Yet there is a continual intergradation with no interruptions between the two extremes. So they are all one species, even though a stranger would never recognize the two extremes as being the same species. But their voices are all identical!

Traill's flycatcher has been split into two species – willow flycatcher and alder flycatcher – even though they are identical in looks. One says "fitz-bew" and the other "fitz-bee –o" (get it?). Each should nest in the shrub after which it is named. But who is it when it is migrating and silent? It is assumed they do not interbreed. The willow flycatcher breeds in North Dakota, while alders grow in Canada. Birders give up and call the non-breeding bird by its generic name – Empidonax flycatcher.

Baltimore oriole lives in most of North Dakota, Bullock's oriole lives in the Badlands. When some hybrid or intermediate birds were found in the western part

Baltimore oriole. Photograph by Jan Ove Gjershaug

of the state, the two were lumped into the Northern oriole. Then, I presume, it was decided that these intermediates were not fertile. Anyway, now they are split back again to two species – Baltimore and Bullock's. Stay tuned.

Myrtle warbler was an Eastern bird. Audubon's warbler was a Western bird. Myrtle had a white throat, Audubon a yellow throat; both had a yellow rump. Then it was noted each warbler was seen often in the other part of the country. So they are now lumped. Both are now called yellow-rumped warbler.

The abundant house sparrow since being introduced from Europe 150 years ago has spread all over the country, into different environments. In the triple-digit temperature of California's Death Valley the dry climate has caused this sparrow to evolve into a much paler version befitting its bland baked background. I expect in time there will be described a separate species there.

The Western grebe was unequivocally one species until sharp-eyed ornithologists noted that a few of them had the white on the side of the head extending above the eye and the black stripe down the back of the white neck being much narrower. There were no intermediate birds. So splitters created two species, Western grebe and Clark's grebe. The ranges of the two greatly overlap. Then some intermediates were discovered. Were these hybrids, and were they fertile? If fertile that meant the lumpers were right; if sterile the splitters were correct, to conform to the definition of a species. As of this writing, I hear, they are considered to be the same species. Stay tuned.

Bird Names Duck Hunters Use

A ROSE BY ANY OTHER NAME —

Duck hunters have always had their own names for the ducks and other water birds they see in the outdoors. Since they named the ducks before there were any field guides, the ducks were named according to their appearance and actions. So it is that the one group may find it hard to establish rapport with the other, for each group, hunters and birders, speak a different language. Let's see if we can act as an interpreter between the two.

On a map, Northeastern Minnesota is shaped like an arrowhead. This Arrowhead Country had a historic trail, now a paved road, which runs from Lake Superior northerly to lakes near the Canadian border. It is called the Sawbill Trail. Why? Those lakes harbor all three species of the merganser, whose narrow bills have an edge with a row of sharp points resembling the teeth of a saw, ideal for grasping slippery fish. The red-breasted merganser of 23 inch length is the fish duck or sawbill. The common merganser, being 25 inches long, is called the big fish duck or big sawbill. The hooded merganser of 18 inch length is called the little fish duck or little sawbill.

While on the Border Lakes the hunters saw the common loon dive, stay under a long time, then come up again at a spot far from where it went down. So they called it the great northern diver. The Canada jay raided the camps of hunters so deserved a name. Indians called it wiss-ka-tjan, so that translated as whiskey-jack.

Now let's move back to North Dakota, the best duck country. One common duck is distinguished by its green head, so the mallard is the green head. The gadwall's color is predominantly gray, so it is the gray duck. The top of the head of the wigeon reminded hunters of a man who lacks hair on the top of his head, so naturally this duck is the baldpate. Incidentally, wigeon is also the name of a simpleton; does this duck's action justify that name?

The pintail's distinction is the long narrow tail, reminding hunters of a small shoot or twig of a tree, so what better name for this duck than sprig-tail? The most obvious feature of the shoveler is its huge bill, suggestive of a shovel, so what else could a hunter call it than spoon-bill or broad-bill?

Hunters call the wood duck the summer duck. The reason escapes me. They call the redhead the raft duck. This makes sense, since this duck congregates in large flocks, called rafts, especially in sheltered bays of the Gulf of Mexico along the Coastal Bend of Texas. And they have a better name, the ring-billed duck, for field guides' so-called ring-necked duck, for the ring on its bill is obvious, whereas the ring on its neck is well-nigh invisible.

The greater scaup is big blue-bill; the lesser scaup is little blue-bill. Both golden-eyes are the whistler. The American golden-eye is also called whistle-wing. The bufflehead, being stocky with a short neck, is called butterball. Bufflehead is also defined as a foolish blockhead; the logic of calling this duck by this name also escapes me.

The long-tailed duck obviously has a long tail, but used to be called oldsquaw, and still is by hunters because it is noisy and very vocal. I suspect the hunters who called it old wife had been nagged by their wives' scolding!

The white-wing, or white-winged coot, is the white-winged scoter. The sea coot, or surf duck, is the surf scoter. Sea coot could also be black coot, the black scoter. A widgeon-coot, also called spike-tail, is the ruddy duck. What bird guides call the American coot, hunters call mud hen or blue peter.

While out in the marsh looking and listening, the hunter heard an odd ounk-a-lunk sound like that coming from a pump. It was traced to the thunder-pumper, or slough-pumper, or stake-driver, names more descriptive than American bittern. Both this bittern and the green-backed heron have been called shitepoke, maybe because both were shy and dawdled or poked along.

Most of the time the hunter's name for the duck was more descriptive than the birder's name. This is certainly true in this writer's opinion, when the greater white-fronted goose is called speckle-belly. And when the western grebe with its long neck is the swan grebe, the Canada goose is the honker, and the harrier is the marsh hawk.

There are other names duck hunters use which are used locally, but not of general use or interest.

Years ago people called the kestrel the sparrow hawk, the merlin the pigeon hawk, the peregrine falcon the duck hawk, and both the sharp-shinned hawk and the Cooper's hawk the chicken hawk.

How Did That Avian Expression Originate?

How did some of those expressions involving birds ever originate? The answers to this are interesting and informative.

STOOL PIGEON: When passenger pigeons were in flocks of over a million birds, market hunters made a living collecting them for sale as food. One method of catching them was to sew the eyes shut of a few so the birds would stay put, then set them on perches called stools. They would attract pigeons from the passing flock, which were then captured and sold as meat. Hence the term, stool pigeon, meaning a decoy used to entice a victim.

CHICKEN FEED: When everyone had a few chickens in their back yard chicken coop, one could go to the nearby grain and feed store to buy a sack of cracked corn with other seed for only a dime. Chicken feed became synonymous to mean a few small coins for buying something cheap.

GO FOR A LARK: Europeans have relished eating songbirds as a gourmet meal. A net with which to catch them was set out before daybreak and was visited in the morning by young men and maidens. But they soon became distracted from the original purpose of the event, so they had more fun when they went for a lark.

TO PARROT someone: Parrots are renowned for echoing words and phrases spoken to them. So when someone repeats the words spoken by another, he is said to parrot what was not his own thoughts.

THE COCKPIT: When a World War fighter pilot climbed down into the seat of the airplane, he entered the cockpit. It referred to the pit into which a fighting cock or rooster was placed by its handlers for the purpose of engaging in a cockfight.

TO TALK TURKEY meant to early settlers in eastern United States to speak as plainly as the wild turkey's gobble. As plain speak became associated with talk about an unpleasant subject, TO TALK COLD TURKEY came to mean that. Then as stopping smoking or drinking or drugs abruptly was very difficult, to quit COLD TURKEY meant just that.

CRAZY AS A LOON: Imagine a nurse on vacation from an insane asylum where he is employed, now paddling a canoe on a lake in Northern Minnesota. He hears a maniacal laughing echoing across the water, just like one of his patients back in the mental hospital. His guide explains that he is hearing the call of a common loon. "It must be crazy," replies the vacationer.

TO EAT CROW: Being black, the crow is prone to be regarded as sinister or evil, with a hoarse unlovely voice, associated with death and corpses, and eating unappetizing fare. Being not palatable, to eat a crow would stick in one's throat. So, having to admit a wrong or facing the consequences of one's bad judgment, one would have to eat crow.

COCK OF THE ROCK: When I was a boy we had a White Leghorn rooster who was the master of all he surveyed. All other chickens were subservient to him. Any cat or dog or robin that impinged on his territory went fleeing from his barrage of sharp bill, slashing spur on each leg, and stinging blow from the "elbow" of each wing. Such a rooster was a model for a

Rooster. Photograph by Jon Arne Saeter

man who was domineering, bossy, and who forced his will on everyone around him – a true cock of the rock.

BIRD OF PASSAGE is someone who is constantly roaming, named after birds that migrate every spring and fall.

JIM CROW: Discrimination against and segregation of blacks, whose skin color is similar to a crow's plumage.

XII. ADDENDUM

Why Birds Sing

Artists and poets have always rhapsodized about the beauty and uplift that the singing of birds inspires. Their Creator put a song in the birds' hearts, they enthuse, for the song is from "heaven's high and holy muse." It is not my wish to challenge such a sentiment, but any scientist would have a different more mundane interpretation of the sounds made by a songbird.

Any bird makes several utterances, according to the circumstances. We cannot determine all of them, but we list the most obvious and frequent and important.

The primary reason to sing is to attract a mate. Nature's plan is to preserve the species, or as Genesis 1:22 phrases it, "Be fruitful and multiply, and let fowl multiply in the earth." Each species of bird has its own song or utterance that entices the future mate. With one female, the brown thrasher, song is so important that it even chooses the male to be her mate that sings the greatest variety of songs. (See chapter Love Makes Males Do Strange Things.)

Having chosen a small area to be his territory that provides some sustenance and cover, with a good habitat in which to place a nest, the male sings repeatedly to announce his decision, and to defend his territory by warning other males of that species to stay away. He continues to sound his warning until the eggs are hatched and the young are grown enough to be able to fly away.

The nestlings cry for food to satisfy their ravenous appetite, more so when they notice their parents approaching the nest. Some young cry so loud and so incessantly I expect they tax the patience of the harassed and haggard parents. The loudest most incessant I have ever heard was a young crow.

When a chick gets separated from its mother and siblings it utters a long shrill peeep, peeep so the mother hen hears the distress call to reunite the family. (See chapter Barnyard Chickens Have Fifteen Different Voices.) Of course, domestic fowl aren't the only species where this occurs.

To keep in touch with its mate, one bird feels constrained to sound its call note repeatedly. The best example of this that comes to mind is the white-breasted nuthatch, as described in the chapter Our Faithful Winter Friend.

When a flock of birds are migrating they keep in contact with each other and maintain the appropriate distance among them for minimal wind resistance by uttering a call note. The classic example of this is heard from a vee of Canada geese or a single file procession of sandhill cranes up in the sky. This must be more essential when flying at night or in a fog.

I have heard a crow send a coded message to another crow in the distance, then heard the distant crow answer back. That is mentioned in the chapter When A Crow Calls Each Caw Means Something. Another example is hearing the boreal owl, the eight-hooter, call in the woods, then hear its mate hoot eight times from another neck of the woods. So birds call messages to their friends from far off, and listen to hear the answer back.

It appears that every species has an alarm note, used as a warning to all birds, not just fellow members of their own group. This alarm note is higher pitched than the other notes in their vocabulary, and it is always a brief staccato that is recognized as an alarm by all species. So when one bird sends an alarm, all birds within hearing become aware and are alerted, a system of mutual benefit and cooperation. This calls to mind an incident when a Cooper's hawk came in sight every songbird began singing their loudest, confusing the predator as it couldn't choose which bird to attack. So it left without seizing any bird.

In the photograph in the chapter Chat With The Chat the yellow-breasted chat that had just been banded is crying a distress call. It continued this until it was released and flew away silently.

Mob frenzy best describes the notes sounded by the birds participating in the mobbing of an owl they found during the day.

So there are many reasons why birds sing.

They don't have vocal cords like mammals. They have their lower trachea, called a syrinx, modified where it bifurcates with a bronchus going to each lung. Here the membranous tracheal wall vibrates as its muscles adjust the pitch and timbre of the sound created. The adjacent upper part of each bronchus also has the similar muscular membrane, so up to three sounds can emit at once, causing the variations by which we can identify which bird is saying which message. The veery has developed possibilities with this arrangement more than any other bird, as described in the chapter Virtuoso Veery.

Motherly Love

There are many examples of motherly love in some species of birds, where the mother bird will endanger her life to protect her young. The following instances come to mind, to which I can testify as to their veracity.

The mother chukar with her single file of chicks came to the bird feeders to glean seeds scattered to the ground by the careless songbirds. My friend reported this to me promptly, but when I came out to see the young ones they were gone. Instead I saw the mother climb up on top of a boulder to pose for me, instead of scurrying away as always. She was distracting me from her babies, who were hiding in the dense bushes alongside the boulder. That's the closest I ever got to a chukar, close enough to touch her with a wand.

In the chapter Birds Never To Be Forgotten that hen spruce grouse confronted me by spreading her wings, raising her feathers, and blocking my path through the spruce bog. I could have killed her easily as she risked her life to save her chicks. As soon as they finished stumbling over little clods on the bog floor to reach the side of the path, where I could no longer step on them, the hen and her brood vanished into the bog, hidden by their perfect camouflage.

In the chapter Thistle Finch Is Well Named an episode is related where a parent goldfinch purposely risked its life to divert me from possibly harming its young one. It had crashed into a tree trunk and was about to fall to the ground. The old one immediately flew between me and its youngster and hovered there in the air, noisily preventing me from harming her baby. She was ready to sacrifice her life for her baby.

The killdeer is famous for her broken wing act. When a person inadvertently approaches its egg, (that is perfectly camouflaged in the gravel, minus any nesting material), it rushes forward to the intruder, crying noisily. Then, just out of reach, it falls down and goes into contortions. In this series of photos, note how the killdeer tries different contortions and postures to see which will best captivate the intruder. Note

A killdeer, the best avian actor, performing its broken wing display.
Photograph by Aaron Van Ningen

Photograph by Richard Cunningham

Photograph by Richard Cunningham

especially that in every position it assumes it always keeps its eye on the invader.

In the first picture its tail is fanned out and bent, with opened wings on the ground, as a rear view.

In the second picture the killdeer shows itself as a side view, wings on the ground but tail feathers squeezed together.

The third picture has it presenting its fanned tail to the camera again, but pressed on the ground, not tipped vertically, and with one wing pointed up, the other touching the ground.

The killdeer always does three things: it doesn't ever face towards the enemy; it keeps its feet firmly on the ground; and it always keeps its eye on the intruder. So it always is able to outmaneuver any attempt to pounce on it. But it still risks its life as it proves its motherly love.

Some birds that nest in colonies will gang together to attack an intruder. This so-called mobbing is daunting to the animal or to the human that is trespassing. Red-winged blackbirds are an example of this. They even peck a person's head as they swoop down, which puts the bird at great risk of being swatted and disabled or killed, all because they were endangering their lives protecting their offspring.

Someone has compared the mother bird offering her life in place of her young to Jesus. That is wrong. In Christianity, Jesus Christ deliberately behaved so He would lose His life, intending to die, in payment for the believer's sins. The mother bird intends not to die, for to have lost her life would defeat her purpose of protecting her young, since it is essential for her to continue feeding them until they can fend for themselves.

Brood Patch

All birds lay eggs, but after the egg is laid it must be kept warm so the fertilized embryo inside it can grow and develop into a new bird. The parent bird maintains the proper temperature of the egg by holding its abdomen against the egg.

This is accomplished when a patch of skin, the brood patch, loses its feathers, becomes edematous, and enlarges its blood vessels to dispense heat for brooding the eggs. When the parent bird is enjoying a respite from incubating in order to forage for food, the brood patch is protected by being covered by adjacent feathers.

After hatching, the young birds are kept warm and protected by the parent bird cuddling them against her brood patch. As the young ones grow bigger the feathers alongside the brood patch on the parent bird fold over the young to help provide warmth and protection. Then when traveling the gallinaceous mother bird clucks to keep her chicks nearby, and when she rests she provides them sanctuary again under her brood patch and behind the feathers that border her brood patch.

The picture shows the cleft in the mother's breast feathers, which reveals the presence of her hidden brood patch.

The brood patch is but one of a series of sequential phenomena in the life cycle of a bird, all of which seem to have one goal

Chukar with her chicks.
Photograph by Arloene Laskowski

in mind: to preserve the species, and to continue through many generations the adaptation to a gradually changing environment. Frequent mutations often contribute to this evolution. Human logic demands there must be a reason and a purpose in all this. Humans have explained all this by quoting the *Bible*. Genesis 1:22 says, "Be fruitful and multiply and fill the waters in the seas, and let birds multiply on the earth."

Where Are All Those Amazing Incredible Birds?

Use this incomplete list of the amazing incredible birds mentioned in this book, so if you missed any, the page number will show where to locate that bird.

The bird that lays its egg on a roof top: *page* 149.
It picks bugs out of the ears of calves: *page* 179.
The only bird with two toes: *page* 14.
Its nest is people's gourmet food: *page* 322.
Religious bird sings, "Ho-say, Maria:" *page* 361.
It has a magnet on its upper bill: *page* 126.
Seven ways to place a bird in a hypnotic trance: *page* 259.
This bird survives because it has a runny nose: *page* 26.
This one never lands on the ground: *page* 150.
Nomads use its hollowed egg as a canteen: *page* 287.
This one climbs down tree trunks head
  first without falling off: *page* 193.
Forest fires prevent this warbler from
  becoming extinct: *page* 211.
Bird that vomits on its enemies: *page* 35.
This female mates with the male that sings
  the most songs: *page* 358.
One that can fly backwards: *page* 157.
One that likes to fly upside down: *page* 184.
This bird sings with its tail: *page* 330.
Land bird that smells its food from far away: *page* 49.
Water bird that smells its food from far away: *page* 319.
Female that uses its own breast feathers
  to feather its nest: *page* 278.
Bird that shows men where wild bees
  store their honey: *page* 349.
This one feeds its nestlings only once
  every two weeks: *page* 24.
When this bird feeds its young it
  remains behind them: *page* 151.
How birds may lose their ability to migrate: *page* 127.

Synopsis

Being aware of, observing and recording birds is a wonderful way to keep your mind sharp and your body healthy. Whether monitoring a bird feeder outside the window, or hiking through fields and forests, the birder will find every day different and challenging. All the adventures and experiences will be treasured in one's old age.

We hope you will find this book informative and interesting enough to entice you to try birding. It is one of the least expensive hobbies to be enjoyed. A pair of binoculars, a bird book, and perhaps a car for extensive travel will suffice.

Fellowship with other birders will be enriching. Join a bird club, go on their field trips, accompany a birding tour, read a birding magazine. You won't be alone – birding has now included more people than hunters or golfers.

Now to fantasize. In Acts 10:10- 16 and Acts 11:5- 10, when God lowered a large sheet holding beasts and birds for Peter to see, then raised it back up to heaven, we got a preview of what to see in heaven. So when birders arrive there they will be able to help those disadvantaged non-birders by showing them the birds, and so enable them to catch up with birders. And those of you who like to sing can sing along with that greater pewee that sings, "Ho-say Maria!"

Acknowledgements And References

Most of the design, typesetting, and other prepress work for this book was done by Jon Arne Saeter, who was indispensable. My daughter, Xanthe, was invaluable.

Other acknowledgments include:

Adele G. Johnson, my wife, who was always willing to go along with me on my forays, small and large, looking for and at birds; and who critiqued many of these chapters.

All the photographers, whose photographs I am proud to present. Jon Arne Saeter secured many of their pictures for me.

All the elder statesmen of bird lore, whose acquaintance it was my privilege to treasure, such as but not limited to Dr. Thomas S. Roberts, Chandler Robbins, Roger Tory Peterson, and Arnold Small.

My biology professor at Macalester College, Dr. Otto T. Walter, who recognized and nurtured my aptitude in and hunger for natural science.

Judith Ekberg Johnson, who proffered advice and help a number of times.

Many other people, mentioned throughout the book.

Most of the material in this book is from my own personal experiences and observations, but a lot of it is credited to these six references:

Bent, Arthur C.: *Life Histories of North American Birds*, 26 volumes. Dover Publications, N. Y. 1964 (reprint of 1922 U.S. Government Printing Office).

Ehrlich, Paul R.; Dobkin, David S.; and Wheya, Darryl: *The Birder's Handbook*. Simon & Schuster, N. Y. 1988.

Funk & Wagnalls: *New Standard Dictionary of the English Language*. Funk & Wagnalls, N. Y. and London 1914.

Internet Web Sites as indicated.

National Audubon Society editors with David Allen Sibley's illustrations: *The Sibley Guide to Bird Life and Behavior.* Alfred A. Knopf, N. Y. 2001.

Roberts, Thomas S.: *The Birds of Minnesota*, two volumes. Univ. of Minn. Press, Minneapolis 1936.

A Navyman would call this Russian fish factory a rust bucket. See page 264.
Photograph by Kenneth J. Johnson

Autobiographical Note

Kenneth J. Johnson is a retired physician, a Minnesota native who practiced medicine in North Dakota. While in the University of Minnesota he held a teaching assistant position in the Graduate School. Then in Medical School he completed his Master of Science degree in Bacteriology and Immunology before receiving his Doctor of Medicine degree. While practicing medicine in Bismarck his natural history background and M. S. degree aided greatly in his specialty of allergy. Twenty three papers on medical subjects were published in *Annals of Allergy* and other medical journals.

Kenneth J. Johnson and his birding companion wife, Adele G. Johnson

In addition to publications on medical subjects, Dr. Johnson has written about birds in *Senior Lifestyles* and *Birdwatcher's Digest*, and writes a monthly Bird Column for the *Bismarck* (N. D.) *Tribune*. He has done 82 Breeding Bird Surveys for the U.S. and Canadian governments. With his wife Adele and four children they have visited all national parks of both countries. He and Adele have traveled and birded abroad repeatedly.

He attended successive conventions of the American Birding Association, each with its speakers, seminars, and pre- and post-convention field trips. He has gone on various birding tours led by professional guides.

He has birded all his life, during which time he traveled and camped in all fifty states and ten Canadian provinces. During World War II, including combat in Okinawa where he was promoted to captain, he observed birds whenever feasible.

XIII. BIRDS AND HUMANS INDEX